Youth Basketball:

A Complete Handbook

Youth Basketball:

A Complete Handbook

Edited by: Karen Garchow, M.A.
Amy Dickinson, M.S.

Youth Sports Institute
Michigan State University
Vern Seefeldt, Ph.D., Director

COOPER
Publishing
Group

Library of Congress Cataloging in Publication Data:

Garchow, Karen, 1964

Youth Basketball: A Complete Handbook

Cover Design: Garry Schmitt

Publisher: I. L. Cooper

Library of Congress Catalog Card Number: 88-43254

ISBN: 1-884125-44-1

Printed in the United States of America by Cooper Publishing Group LLC, P.O. Box 562, Carmel, IN 46032.

10 9 8 7 6 5 4

The Publisher and Author disclaim responsibility for any adverse effects or consequences from the misapplication or injudicious use of the information contained within this text.

YOUTH COACHING SERIES

The Youth Coaching Series of books were written to provide comprehensive guides for coaches, parents, and players participating in youth soccer, baseball, football, softball, and basketball.

Developed by the Youth Sports Institute of Michigan State University, these books meet the guidelines established for youth coaches by the National Association for Sport and Physical Education.

Books in the Series:

Youth Baseball: A Complete Handbook (ISBN: 01-8)

Youth Basketball: A Complete Handbook (ISBN: 44-1)

Youth Football: A Complete Handbook (ISBN: 45-X)

Youth Soccer: A Complete Handbook (ISBN: 23-9)

Youth Softball: A Complete Handbook (ISBN: 46-8)

For more information or to order books in the Youth Coaching Series:

Call:	1-317-574-9338
Write:	Cooper Publishing Group P. O. Box 562 Carmel, Indiana 46032

Contents

Section VI
Sports Medicine and Training

Introduction

Youth Basketball was written as a comprehensive guide for the beginning level basketball coach. Its 24 chapters contain information that meet the guidelines established for youth coaches, as described in *Guidelines for Coaching Education: Youth Sports*, prepared by the National Association for Sport and Physical Education.

The scope of *Youth Basketball* ranges from a description of the proper role of a youth basketball coach to guidelines for the rehabilitation of basketball-related injuries. The book has been written so that each chapter is self-contained—all pertinent supplements, tables, drills, and references follow the tightly focused and comprehensive text of each chapter. As a result, the book serves as a ready reference for coaches who do not have time to read the book cover-to-cover.

Youth coaches will find that this book provides many answers to the myriad of challenges that pertain to teaching skill techniques. Although Chapters 5 through 13 pertain to the Xs and Os of technical instruction, the remaining chapters address topics such as nutrition and working with parents—topics not typically found in coaching books.

Each chapter was written by a coach, teacher, or former coach. This orientation becomes readily apparent by the practical suggestions that pervade the scientific information. Coaches will find that the suggestions have immediate utility because the authors combined years of scientific study and technical experience in their writing.

The beneficiaries of *Youth Basketball* ultimately are the boys and girls who seek the fun, excitement, and enhanced self-esteem that is associated with good coaching. We hope this book empowers coaches to provide the potential benefits of basketball to all its youthful participants.

Robert M. Malina, Director
Youth Sports Insitute
Michigan State University

Acknowledgments

We wish to thank the following individuals for their assistance in the preparation of this book: Randy Bass of Photographic Emporium, Middleville, Michigan, worked patiently with the performers, reshooting sequences until they represented the actions the authors desired and the high quality that he demanded of his work. His efforts added immeasurably to the final product. Marianne Oren and Eileen Northrup, editorial assistants with the Youth Sports Institute, typed and retyped the manuscript. Their patience and tolerance under the pressure of approaching deadlines is greatly appreciated. Marianne Oren's effort beyond the call of duty to understand the context in which technical sections of the book were written improved our presentation of materials.

Section I
Organizing for the Season

1
Role of the Coach

Paul Vogel, Ph.D.

QUESTIONS TO CONSIDER

- What are the primary roles of a youth basketball coach?
- What benefits does basketball offer participants?
- What potential detriments can occur in the presence of inadequate adult leadership?
- What principal goals should a coach seek to achieve?

INTRODUCTION

For young people participating in a basketball program, the quality and subsequent benefits of their experience is determined largely by their coach. Strong leadership during practices, games, and special events encourages each young person to nurture and develop individual strengths physically, psychologically, and socially. Poor or weak leadership not only inhibits such growth, it actually undermines a youth's existing strengths in these areas.

While it's impossible to provide a totally beneficial experience, as a basketball coach it is your responsibility to ensure that the benefits gained by each youth far outweigh the detriments. To accomplish this, you must know what these benefits and detriments are, and you must set reasonable coaching goals.

Possible Benefits for Participants

The numerous benefits for youth include:

- developing appropriate skills
- developing physical fitness
- learning appropriate conditioning techniques that affect health and performance
- developing a realistic and positive self-image
- developing a lifetime pattern of regular physical activity
- developing a respect for rules as facilitators of safe and fair play
- obtaining enjoyment and recreation
- developing positive personal, social, and psychological skills (e.g., self-worth, self-discipline, team work, goal-setting, self-control)

Many players achieve significant benefits in at least some of these areas depending on the frequency, duration, and intensity of participation and the quality of coaching leadership.

Many significant benefits can be gained in youth basketball.

Possible Detriments for Participants

Players are likely to benefit from a basketball program when the coach sets appropriate objectives in the areas of skill, knowledge, fitness, and personal/social development. If, however, the coach sets inappropriate goals or teaches poorly, detriments may result.

To fully understand the value of a good coach, contrast the benefits listed previously with these possible detriments for the participant:

- developing inappropriate physical skills
- sustaining injury, illness, or loss of physical fitness
- learning incorrect rules and strategies of play
- learning incorrect conditioning techniques
- developing a negative or unrealistic self-image
- avoiding future participation in activity for self and others
- learning to misuse rules to gain unfair or unsafe advantages
- developing a fear of failure
- developing anti-social behaviors
- wasting time that could have been made available for other activities

When incorrect techniques and negative behaviors are learned by young athletes, the next coach must perform the difficult and time-consuming task of extinguishing these behaviors.

To maximize the benefits and minimize the detriments, you must understand your role as a basketball coach and provide quality leadership.

The benefits of participation relate directly to the quality of leadership.

GOALS FOR THE COACH

As a coach, it is important to:

1. effectively teach the individual techniques, rules, and strategies of the game in an orderly and enjoyable environment
2. appropriately challenge the cardiovascular and muscular systems of your players through active practice sessions and games
3. teach and model desirable personal, social, and psychological skills

Winning is also an important goal for the coach and participants but it is one you have little control over because winning is often contingent on outside factors (e.g., the skills of the opposition, calls made by officials). If you concentrate on the three areas mentioned and become an effective leader, winning becomes a natural by-product.

The degree of success you attain in achieving these goals is determined by the extent to which you make appropriate choices and take correct actions in organizing and administering, teaching and leading, and protecting and caring.

Organization and Administration

Effective coaching relies heavily on good organization and administration. Organization involves clearly identifying the goals and objectives that must be attained if you are going to create a beneficial experience (with few detriments) for the participating youths. Steps necessary to organize the season so it can be efficiently administered include:

- identifying your primary purposes as a coach
- identifying goals for the season
- selecting and implementing the activities in practices and games that lead to achievement of the objectives
- evaluating the effects of your actions

Specific information, procedures, criteria, and examples necessary to effectively complete these steps are included in Chapter 3, Chapter 4, and Chapter 19.

Teaching and Leading

Teaching and leading are the core of coaching activity. Principles of effective instruction such as setting appropriate player expectations, using clear instructions, maintaining an orderly environment, maximizing the amount of practice time that is "on task," monitoring progress, and providing specific feedback are included in Chapter 4. This chapter gives you many insights into how you may effectively teach your players. Other important information for teaching and leading young athletes includes motivating your players, communicating effectively, maintaining discipline, and developing good personal and social skills. Coaching guidelines for each of these areas are included in Section 5.

The only real control you have over winning and/or losing is the manner in which you plan and conduct your practices and supervise your games.

Because of the influence you have as "coach," your players will model the behaviors you exhibit. If you respond to competition (successes and failures), fair play, officials' calls, and/or spectators' comments with a positive and constructive attitude, your players are likely to imitate that positive behavior. If, however, you lose your temper, yell at officials, or bend and/or break rules to gain an unfair advantage, your players' actions are likely to become negative. When what you say differs from what you do, your players will be most strongly affected by what you do. Negative behavior by players can occur even if you tell them to "be good sports and to show respect to others" and then ignore this advice by acting in a contrary manner. In essence, "actions speak louder than words" and you must "practice what you preach" if you hope to positively influence your players' behavior.

Protecting and Caring

Although coaches often eliminate the potential for injury from their minds, it is impor- tant for them to (a) plan for injury prevention, (b) effectively deal with injuries when they oc- cur, and (c) meet their legal responsibilities to act prudently. The information on legal liabili- ties in Section 1, and conditioning youth bas- ketball players, nutrition for successful perfor- mance, and prevention, care, and rehabilitation of common basketball injuries in Section 6, pro- vides the basis for prudent and effective action in these areas.

SUMMARY

Your primary purpose as a youth basket- ball coach is to maximize the benefits of partic- ipation in basketball while minimizing the detri- ments. To achieve this, you must organize, teach, model, and evaluate effectively. Your players learn not only from what you teach but from what you consciously or unconsciously do. You're a very significant person in the eyes of your players. They notice when you're or- ganized and fair, are a good instructor, know the rules, are interested in them or in the win/ loss record, know how to control your emo- tions, know how to present yourself, and treat others with respect. The choices you make and the actions you take determine how positive the experience is for them.

2
Legal Liabilities

Bernard Patrick Maloy, J.D., M.S.A.
Vern Seefeldt, Ph.D.

QUESTIONS TO CONSIDER

- In terms of legal liability, what are the coaching duties?
- Against which risks to their players are coaches responsible for taking reasonable precautions?
- Do children who participate in youth sports assume the risk of their own injuries?
- What influence does the age and maturity of the athletes have upon the coach?
- Do coaches' legal responsibilities to their players extend beyond the field of play?
- Are coaches responsible for informing players, parents, and guardians about the risks and hazards inherent in sports?
- What legal responsibilities do coaches have to their players when coaches delegate duties to assistants?

INTRODUCTION

It is inevitable that the role of a coach is expanded beyond that of mere instructor or supervisor when it comes to working with youth sports. Because coaches are the most visible administrators to players, parents, and officials, they are expected to handle anything from correcting player rosters to picking up equipment on the court, from assuaging parents' feelings to arranging transportation for players. While these duties may tax the limits of a coach's patience, they remain very important areas of responsibility.

LEGAL DUTIES

Coaches are subject to certain terms of legal responsibility. However, it would be wrong to assume these legal duties were created by the courts to be imposed on the coaching profession. They are time-honored, recognized obligations inherent in the coaching profession. Thus, they should be termed coaching responsibilities (see Chapter 1). These are responsibilities expected of a coach regardless of pay and regardless of whether the coaching is performed for a school, a religious organization, or a youth sports association.

WHERE DOES COACHING RESPONSIBILITY BEGIN?

The primary responsibility of coaches is to know their players. In that regard it is always important to remember that young athletes are children first, athletes second. The degree of responsibility that coaches owe their teams is measured by the age and maturity of their players. The younger and more immature a player, the more responsibility a coach bears in regard to the instruction, supervision, and safety of that child (see Chapter 22). Additionally, the coach is expected to be aware of any physical or mental handicap that a player may have and must know how to recognize emergency symptoms requiring medical attention (see Chapter 23). A coach in youth sports must always bear in mind that:

- Nine-year-olds participating in organized sport activities for the first time require more instruction and attention than teenagers with playing experience
- A 10-year-old child should not be expected to behave, on or off the playing court, differently than other 10-year-old children
- All children with special needs or handicaps must be identified
- A plan for the emergency treatment of children with special needs and those who sustain injuries should be devised

As will be discussed, coaches do not have to guarantee the safety of their young players. However, they are responsible for taking reasonable precautions against all foreseeable risks that threaten their players. Coaches must realize that those precautions are not measured by what they thought was reasonable, but rather by what was reasonable according to the age and maturity of their players.

Do You Know How to Coach?

The volunteer coach is the backbone of many organized youth activities. Nevertheless, despite good intentions, some degrees of qualifications and certification are necessary for responsible coaching. Therefore, in addition to personal athletic experience and background, coaches should attend programs and seminars on the development of athletic skills, youth motivation, and emergency medical treatment. A coach's responsibility begins with an understanding of current methods of conditioning (Chapter 20), skill development (Section 3), and injury prevention and care (Chapters 22 and 23).

Coaches have certain responsibilities that they may not transfer to assistant coaches, parents, or league officials.

In many cases, a youth sports league or association offers classes, materials, or advice on skill development and injury prevention and care. Generally, those associations require some certification or recommendation regarding coaching background, skills, and experience before an applicant is permitted to coach youth sports. Coaches must avail themselves of instructional programs or other information helpful for coaching youth sports. In other words, coaches are responsible for their own incompetencies. A youth sports coach should create a competency checklist:

- Does the youth sports association certify its coaches?
- Does the association require coaches to attend coaching clinics and emergency medical programs?
- Do you know how to identify the necessary individual athletic skills based on size, weight, and age?
- Do you know of any agencies that help identify those skills?
- What steps should you take to become certified in first aid treatment?

Knowledge of your coaching incompetencies is the first step toward seeking a corrective solution.

Coaches must be able to recognize their limitations. Acknowledging that skills, youth motivation, and medical treatment may be different today than when you played is the first step toward becoming a responsible coach.

Where Do Your Coaching Duties Lie?

As noted, youth sports coaches are many things to their teams, parents and guardians, and supporters. Coaching responsibilities extend to areas beyond the basketball court. These responsibilities require the same effort and devotion as on-the-court duties and may include:

- league or team fund-raising activities
- assisting during registration periods

- talking to interested players and their parents about the league and its athletic and social goals
- providing or planning team transportation to and from practices and games
- attending league or association meetings
- buying, selecting, or maintaining equipment
- maintaining locker rooms and gym areas
- supervising players during pre-practice and post-practice periods

What Misconceptions Do Many Coaches Have?

There are two common misconceptions regarding youth sports. The first is that children participating generally assume the risk of their own injury; the second, that the role of the coach is severely limited by legal liability.

The legal defense of assumption of risk as it applies to sports is very specific. An athlete assumes the risk of injury from dangers inherent to the sport itself. In other words, it is recognized that injuries occur, especially in contact sports such as basketball (e.g., the collision of two players chasing a ball on the court, the injury of a player on the court resulting from a non-intentional foul).

Many risks confronting athletes are not inherent to the sport, however; rather, they're the result of improper instruction, supervision, or equipment (e.g., protective equipment or pads that are defective or have been poorly fit, lack of instruction in athletic skills).

The interpretation of *assumption of risk* is complicated when it is applied to youth sports because young athletes require careful supervision regarding their own welfare. The concept that young athletes must assume the responsibility for their injuries sustained in practices or games must be contrasted with whether or not the coach or other adult supervisors were negligent in their instruction and supervision of the activity. In such a comparison it is unlikely that responsibility for *assumption of risk* will serve as a viable excuse.

When an injury occurs in youth sports, the coach's responsibility is considered a much greater factor than the assumption of risk *by the player.*

Fortunately, most coaches inherently understand the limitations involved in *assumption of risk.* The motivation for many youth coaches is the involvement of their own children in sports. And, like most parents, those coaches accept injury as a natural risk of the sport, but they will not tolerate an injury resulting from lack of proper skill development or poor equipment.

Youth sport coaches should concern themselves less with whether adhering to these responsibilities is good legal protection, and more with the thought that their actions represent the standards expected of youth sport coaches. Actually, the areas of expertise legally required of coaches can serve as measures of qualification and certification. Youth sport leagues and conferences realize that coaches must adhere to legal principles of liability not merely to protect the league and the coach from costly litigation but also to ensure that children continue to participate in athletics. It's very doubtful that parents would continue to support youth sports if it were plagued by poor coaching, lack of supervision, or poor medical treatment procedures. In short, these imposed responsibilities are good business practices for youth sports.

COACHING RESPONSIBILITIES

As a youth basketball coach you have many responsibilities beyond teaching your players to pass, shoot, and dribble a basketball. Your coaching responsibilities are: providing proper instruction, providing reasonable supervision, warning of hazards and risks, providing competent personnel, preventing and caring for injuries, providing safe equipment, and selecting participants. Each of these responsibilities are discussed in subsequent sections.

Providing Proper Instruction

A coach must teach the physical skills and mental discipline or attitude required to play basketball (see Sections 3, 4, and 5). You must enhance the development of those skills while reducing the chance of injury. Specifically, volunteer coaches, who represent that they can teach the sport or activity, must be aware of the rules of safety and know how to teach the proper methods of conditioning. For example, when young players are injured, coaches should be prepared to competently assess whether:

- the conditioning or skill drills are realistic for players of young or immature years
- video, film, or written materials, in addition to on-court instruction, would improve instructional techniques
- the players are taught the correct way to wear equipment
- all the players, starters and substitutes, have been given the same amount of time, instruction, and practice on the correct methods of play, conditioning, and the rules
- conditioning techniques and skill drills are current
- coaching methods are accurately evaluated by the league
- parental comments and concerns have been integrated into the coaching instruction
- provision has been made in coaching instruction for learning-disabled and mentally or emotionally handicapped children who participate
- criticism or comments regarding coaching instruction are met with a positive response

The foregoing list consists of some expectations a parent or guardian has of a coach. While those expectations impact heavily on liability, they more accurately serve as guidelines by which youth sports coaches can evaluate their instruction. Again, a youth sports coach must remember that the age and immaturity of the players are key factors to instructional techniques. The coach must be sensitive to the outside environment in which a young player lives, as well as the sports environment created by the coach. Only then can you ensure a youngster the full benefit of your instruction (see Chapter 1).

Providing Reasonable Supervision

A coach is responsible for the reasonable supervision of the players. There is little question that this responsibility starts on the court of play during all practices and games. Again, the scope of this responsibility depends on the age and maturity of the players. The younger the player, the greater the degree of responsi-bility a coach must take for the player's safe supervision.

In youth sports, a coach's supervisory responsibility may extend to times and places other than the court. In some instances, this may include managing parents or guardians and supporters as well as the players and assistant coaches. A coach's checklist of potential supervisory functions should question:

- Is there a supervisor available for a reasonable time before and after practice?
- Have parents or guardians advised who will pick up their children after practices and games?
- Who is assigned to remain with the players until all have been called for, according to instructions provided by parents or guardians?
- How are parents or guardians notified of practice and game times, dates, and places?
- Who is responsible for player transportation to and from games?
- Are substitute players supervised off the court during games?
- Are players allowed off the court during practice for bathroom or other personal comforts? If so, how are those players supervised?

Many youth sports leagues or associations have a rule that coaches are responsible for the behavior of team parents, guardians, and fans. Such a rule becomes very important in those instances where parents believe their child has been slighted on the court during play, or off the court from lack of play. Coaches should recognize that their conduct can incite parents, guardians, and supporters. A coach must ask:

- Have team and league rules regarding parental involvement, the rules of play, and rules regarding team participation been communicated to parents and guardians?
- Do parents and guardians know my coaching philosophy and team goals?
- Have the team and parents and guardians been notified that only the coach is permitted to discuss a decision with a referee?

The coach's role in supervision of the basketball court can be eased by holding a parents' orientation meeting at the start of the season (see Chapter 14). The parents have a right to know what to expect of the coach. Also, the meeting prepares parents to become actively involved with other parents in stopping any unruly conduct. Again, the supervisory responsibility starts with coaches who conduct themselves in the spirit of good sportsmanship. It also includes a coach's support of game officials in order to defuse angry parents, guardians, supporters, or players.

Warning About Hazards and Risks

A coach is responsible for informing players, parents, and guardians about the risks and hazards inherent to basketball. Obviously, it's not expected that coaches will dissuade parents and guardians from permitting their youngsters to participate. By the same token, a coach's experience and knowledge helps to assure parents and guardians that the greatest care possible will be taken for the well-being of their children.

The age and maturity of the players play a major role in the degree of risk from playing basketball. Older, more experienced children may face a greater risk of injury from basketball simply due to the more sophisticated style of play. However, those children and their parents or guardians already should be fairly well-versed in the risks of basketball. Therefore, they don't need the same information and assurances as parents and guardians whose children are younger and have never participated.

The coach must inform athletes and parents of the potential dangers inherent in playing youth basketball.

The youth league or association may provide information regarding sports hazards, but the responsibility to warn parents and athletes remains a very important coaching duty (see Chapter 22). Therefore, a coach would be well-served to provide parents, guardians, and players with as much information and materials as possible regarding basketball at registration, as well as during the season. The coach must be prepared to instruct or advise:

- how many injuries his or her teams with sim-

ilar age and experience have suffered, and what types of injuries occurred
- what types of equipment, clothing, or shoes are not recommended or permitted for play
- how equipment should properly fit
- what written, video, or audio materials are available that will instruct parents and guardians about the sport and its risks
- what style, conduct, or manner of play is to be avoided due to the likelihood of injury to the player or an opponent
- whether the court and facilities have been inspected for hazards and determined to be safe for play

Hosting a parents' orientation meeting prior to the first game is an excellent way to describe your role in the prevention and care of their children's injuries.

Providing Competent Personnel

We've already examined the coach's responsibility to provide quality instruction. Also, we have examined many of the attendant roles and duties that coaches must provide with that instruction. In many cases, the sheer numbers of players and responsibilities demand that a coach have some assistance. It is not unusual for a coach to delegate some of those coaching or supervisory duties to assistant coaches or parents (see Supplement 14-7). However, the coach must ensure that the people who are assisting are competent. Obviously, having a responsible coach is of little value if the players are subject to the directions of incompetent assistants. Therefore, in a coach's absence, an assistant coach or aide must be able to provide the same responsible instruction and supervision as the players and parents expect from the head coach. It is wise, then, for a coach to learn:

- whether the league or association certifies assistant coaches
- what policies the league or association has regarding the use of parents for supervision, transportation, or instruction
- whether assistant coaches have any hidden past regarding child abuse, or other conduct that constitutes a threat to children
- whether there is any reason to suspect an assistant's or aide's coaching competency

- whether teenagers may be qualified as assistants with coaching and supervisory duties

It is a coach's responsibility to determine whether assistant coaches and team aides are qualified to step into the coach's shoes.

Preventing and Caring for Injuries

There are few areas that demand as much attention as the prevention and care of injuries (see Chapters 22, 23, and 24). It is not uncommon to find youth sports programs conducting basketball practices without qualified medical personnel or knowledgeable athletic trainers readily available. In those instances, the first attendant to an injured player is usually the coach or teammates. The coach's responsibility is to recognize when immediate medical treatment is required and to ensure that assistant coaches and teammates do not attempt to touch, move, or help the injured player. Obviously, the care of injuries can be a very confusing task.

Many problems in the initial care of athletic injuries might be solved if coaches were required to qualify as emergency medical technicians, or to have some type of comparable training in first aid and health care. In the absence of those qualifications, however, coaches must use their best discretion, based on experience. Obviously, those deficiencies are compounded in youth sports where most of the coaches are volunteers.

In addition to recognizing when emergency medical help is needed, a coach must be able to recognize symptoms of ongoing problems. If a player has a disease, diabetes for instance, the coach has the responsibility for checking with the player's parents about medication, learning how to recognize the symptoms of shock or deficiency, and what type of emergency treatment to request.

A coach must also be aware of the effects a conditioning program may have on players (see Chapter 20). For instance, if practices are conducted during hot weather, a coach should provide ample water (see Chapter 21), change the time of practice to early morning or late afternoon, learn the symptoms of heat stroke or exhaustion, and learn how to provide for immediate care (see Chapter 23).

It's impossible to categorize all the areas of concern for injuries that a coach may face. However, there are precautions that you can take to ensure that your responsibilities have been reasonably met:

- Attend league-sponsored programs dealing with athletic injuries
- Check with local health authorities, local hospitals, and coaching associations to learn about the availability of emergency medical care at the gymnasium
- Implement a plan for the immediate notification of parents or guardians in case their child is seriously injured
- Do not attempt unfamiliar care without emergency medical competency or ability
- Identify players with specific medical handicaps before the season and prepare reasonable emergency plans in case of sudden illness
- Do not permit players who have suffered injuries requiring medical attention to play or participate until their return to practice and competition has been approved by a physician
- Notify parents or guardians of any minor injuries occurring to, or complaints by, their children

It is wise to document the circumstances of a serious injury (see Chapter 23). In many cases, a written report shows that coaches have reasonably met their responsibility. Such a report is also helpful to medical personnel in the subsequent treatment of an injury. The documentation should include:

- a record of all facts surrounding the injury including who, when, and where the injury occurred and the injured player's responses
- a list and description of the equipment involved, if any
- a list of those who witnessed the injury
- a record of actions taken in response to the injury prior to the arrival of medical personnel

When completed, provide copies of the injury report to the attending physician, the medical response personnel, and the league or association. Be sure to keep a copy for your own files.

Providing Equipment

A coach must take reasonable care to provide the team with proper and safe equipment (see Supplement 14-6). You should know the various types and brands of equipment, master the proper maintenance procedures, and learn to outfit players properly and safely. Generally, you are not responsible for equipment defects unless you're directly involved in the manufacture of equipment. However, you are expected to know whether or not the proper equipment is being used, or if it is defective, and to ensure that defective equipment is not distributed to players. A coach must take reasonable care to:

- select or recommend the proper equipment for the sport
- select or recommend specific types of equipment for specific uses
- properly fit players
- verify that old equipment has been properly reconditioned or recertified for use
- disallow players who are not properly equipped and dressed to participate in practices or games
- have knowledge of league or association rules regarding proper dress and equipment
- instruct players and parents on the proper maintenance of sports equipment in their possession
- utilize a written inventory for reporting and tracking the repair of damaged equipment
- become aware of manufacturers' recommendations and warnings

Selecting Participants

A basketball coach is obligated to protect the health and safety of players during practices and games. The potential for injuries to occur in basketball is reduced when players are matched according to size, age, and playing experience. Injuries that occur when players are mismatched in terms of body size and playing experience are more likely to be viewed as the result of irresponsible teaching and supervision rather than as an inherent risk of playing basketball.

Coaches should protect players by following these guidelines:

- Never permit an injured athlete to compete in practices and games
- Never allow athletes who are out of condition to participate in drills, scrimmages, or games
- Never place players in drills, scrimmages, or games in which there is the potential for mismatches in physical conditioning, chronological age, and/or skill level.

SUMMARY

A youth sports coach cannot guarantee a child's safety. Legally, a coach is responsible for reasonably foreseeing risks and hazards to the players.

For example, if a youth sports group uses a court that has permanent benches installed near the sidelines, or if the gymnasium is used to store equipment for physical education classes or other activities, a coach should recognize the foreseeable risks to players and supervise, instruct, and/or warn of those dangers.

Some consider this foreseeability factor as a legal precept. However, it is predicated on knowledge and experience of basketball. Therefore, its true application is not in legal theory but in the real world of sports.

The curricular objectives for youth sports coaches are defined in the following reference: *Guidelines for Coaching Education: Youth Sports*, National Association for Sport and Physical Education, 1986. The Guidelines identify the competencies that coaches of young athletes should possess or acquire. The competencies are listed under five categories of content within the general title of "Scientific Bases of Coaching." An outline of the content follows:

Curricular Objectives for Youth Sport Coaches

Scientific Bases of Coaching

A. *Medical-Legal Aspects of Coaching*

Every young athlete should be provided a safe and healthful environment in which to participate. The coach should have basic knowledge and skills in the prevention of athletic injuries, and basic knowledge of first aid.

Every youth sports coach should:

1. Demonstrate knowledge and skill in the prevention and care of injuries generally associated with participation in athletics
2. Be able to plan and coordinate procedures for the emergency care of athletes
3. Be knowledgeable about the legal responsibilities of coaching, including insurance coverage for the coach and athlete
4. Recognize and insist on safe playing conditions and the proper use of protective equipment
5. Be able to provide young athletes with basic information about injury prevention, injury reporting, and sources of medical care

B. Training and Conditioning of Young Athletes

Every youth sport athlete should receive appropriate physical conditioning for sports participation. The coach should use acceptable procedures in their training and conditioning programs.

Every youth sports coach should:

1. Be able to demonstrate the basic knowledges and techniques in the training and conditioning of athletes
2. Recognize the developmental capabilities of young athletes and adjust training and conditioning programs to meet these capabilities
3. Know the effects of the environmental conditions (e.g., heat, cold, humidity, air quality) on young athletes and adjust practice and games accordingly
4. Be able to recognize the various indications of over-training, which may result in injury and/or staleness in athletes, and be able to modify programs to overcome these consequences

C. Psychological Aspects of Coaching

A positive social and emotional environment should be created for young athletes. The coach should recognize and understand the developmental nature of the young athlete's motivation for sport competition and adjust his/her expectations accordingly.

Every youth sports coach should:

1. Subscribe to a philosophy that emphasizes the personal growth of individuals by encouraging and rewarding achievement of personal goals and demonstration of effort, as opposed to overemphasis on winning

2. Demonstrate appropriate behavior of young athletes by maintaining emotional control and demonstrating respect to athletes, officials, and fellow coaches
3. Demonstrate effective communication skills such as those needed to provide appropriate feedback, use a positive approach, motivate athletes, and demonstrate proper listening skills
4. Emphasize and encourage discussion of matters concerning the display of sportsmanship in competitive and noncompetitive situations
5. Be sufficiently familiar with the principles of motivation, including goal setting and reinforcement, in order to apply them in constructive ways
6. Be able to structure practice and competitive situations to reduce undue stress, and/or to teach young athletes how to reduce any undue stress they experience related to performance

D. Growth, Development, and Learning of Youth Athletes

Youth athletes should have positive learning experiences. The coach should have a knowledge of basic learning principles and consider the influence of developmental level on the athlete's performance.

Every youth sports coach should:

1. Recognize the physical and cognitive changes that occur as children develop and how these changes influence their ability to learn sports skills
2. Concentrate on the development of fundamental motor and cognitive skills that lead to improvement of specific sports skills
3. Understand the physical and cognitive differences manifested by early and late maturers

E. Techniques of Coaching Young Athletes

Every young athlete should have the opportunity to participate regularly in a sport of his/her choosing. The coach should provide guidance for successful learning and performance of specific sport techniques, based on the maturity level or proficiency of the athlete.

Every youth sports coach should:

1. Know the key elements of sport principles and technical skills and the various teaching

styles that can be used to introduce and refine them

2. Recognize that young athletes learn at different rates and accommodate these differences by flexibility in teaching styles
3. Be able to organize and conduct practices throughout the season in order to provide maximal learning
4. Be able to select appropriate skills and drills, and analyze errors in performance
5. Be able to provide challenging but safe and successful experiences for young athletes by making appropriate modifications during participation
6. Understand why rules and equipment should be modified for children's sports

Implementation

These guidelines are considered the minimum levels toward which youth sport coaching education programs should strive. To cover the topics of Sections A-D requires at least three hours of clinic time plus additional home study. Another three hours should be devoted to the techniques of coaching session.

Presentations developed for the scientific bases of coaching (Sections A-D) should be as sport specific as possible. The frequent use of audiovisual aids such as videotapes, films, overheads, and slides is helpful. Presentations should be short, with numerous practical examples as well as opportunities for practical exercises and questions. Having materials (e.g., books, pamphlets, self study exams) available for the coaches to study either prior to or following the clinic is essential for adequate coverage of the topics.

For additional information about youth sport coaching education materials and organizations, write the Youth Sports Coalition Steering Committee, 1900 Association Drive, Reston, VA 22091.

REFERENCES

Berry, R., & Wong, G. (1986). *Law and business of the sports industries.* (Vol. II, pp. 227-302, 320-341). Dover, MA: Auburn House.

Clement, A. (1988). *Law in sport and physical activity.* (pp. 27-61). Indianapolis, IN: Benchmark Press.

Maloy, B. (1988). *Law in sports: Liability cases in management and administration.* Indianapolis, IN: Benchmark Press.

National Association for Sport and Physical Education. (1986) *Guidelines for Coaching Education.* Reston, VA: Youth Sports.

Responsibility is also Part of the Game. *Trial,* 13, 22-25, January, 1977.

Schubert, G. et al (1986). *Sports law.* (pp. 220-231). St. Paul, MN: West Publishing Co.

Seefeldt, V. (1985). Legal liability. In P. Vogel & K. Blase (Eds.), *AHAUS associate coaches manual: Fundamentals of coaching youth ice hockey.* (pp. 167-174). East Lansing, MI: Institute for the Study of Youth Sports.

Wong, G. (1988). *Essentials of amateur sports law.* (pp. 336-350). Dover, MA: Auburn House Publishing Co.

3
Planning for the Season

Paul Vogel, Ph.D.

QUESTIONS TO CONSIDER

- Why should planning for the entire season precede day-to-day planning?
- What steps should a coach follow when organizing for the season?
- What skills, knowledge, aspects of fitness, and personal/social skills should be included as objectives for the season?
- How should the season be organized to be most effective from a coaching-learning point of view?

INTRODUCTION

Planning for the season involves two basic tasks. First, coaches must select the content that will be the focus of instruction during the season (objectives that involve physical skills, sport-related knowledge, fitness capacities, and personal/social skills). Second, these desired outcomes should be organized into a plan from which practices, games, and other events can be efficiently managed.

What follows provides reasons why season planning is useful and gives you steps necessary to develop a season's plan as well as examples of season objectives. Materials and examples are also provided at the end of this chapter for completing your season plan.

WHY PLAN?

Coaches agree that teaching the skills, rules, and strategies of basketball are among their primary responsibilities. Most coaches would also agree that improving the physical condition of the players, promoting enjoyment of the game, teaching good sportsmanship, and attempting to avoid physical and psychological injury are also outcomes they wish to achieve. Many coaches fail, however, to recognize the importance of planning to accomplish these goals.

Achievement of goals and objectives requires effective planning.

Organized practices are vital to maximizing the benefits of basketball. Disorganized practices often result in players failing to obtain desired skills, knowledge, fitness, and attitudes and often contribute to injuries and inappropriate skills. Organizing your season and planning your practices prior to going on the court can result in the following benefits:

- efficient use of limited practice time
- inclusion of season objectives that are most essential

- appropriate sequence of season objectives
- directing practice activities to the season's goals and objectives
- reduction of the time required for planning
- enhanced preparation of the team for competition
- improved ability to make day-to-day adjustments in practice objectives
- deterrent to lawsuits involving coaches' liability

DEVELOPING A SEASON PLAN

Use these three steps to develop a season plan:

1. Identify the goals and objectives of the season
2. Sequence the season objectives into the pre, early, mid, and late portions of the season
3. Identify practice objectives

The relationship of these three steps to fulfilling your role as the coach and to evaluating the outcomes you desire for your players is illustrated in Figure 3-1.

Identify Goals and Objectives for the Season

Your primary role as coach is to maximize the benefits for your players while minimizing the potential detrimental effects of participa-

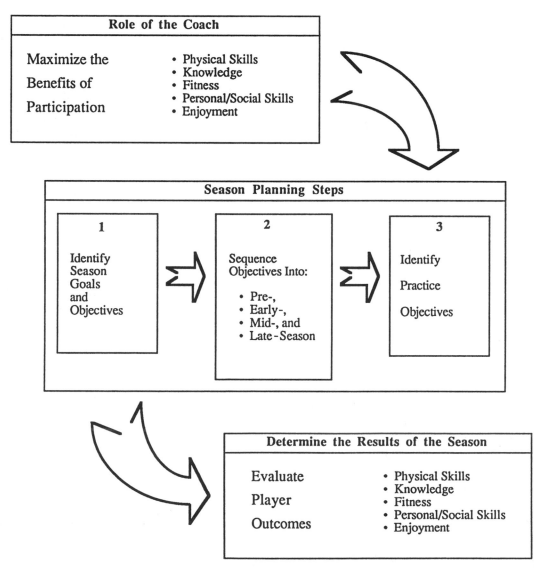

Figure 3-1. A coach's role as it relates to planning the season and evaluating the players.

tion. This alone provides the basis for identifying the specific goals and objectives for your coaching effort. You will affect your players either positively or negatively in each of the following areas:

- physical skills (ball handling, dribbling, footwork, shooting, passing and receiving, rebounding, offensive strategies, defensive strategies)
- knowledge (rules, tactics, training techniques, terminology, nutrition, safety)
- fitness (muscular strength, endurance, flexibility, aerobic fitness)
- personal/social skills (feelings about basketball, motivation, discipline, sportsmanship, other character traits)
- enjoyment (happy to attend practices, likes the coach and teammates)

By thinking of these five broad areas of player outcomes as goals, you are taking the initial step toward fulfilling your major role of "maximizing the benefits" of participation in basketball and "minimizing the potential detrimental effects of participation" by clearly specifying the objectives for the season.

Although the identification of goals is an important first step, it is the selection of specific objectives within each goal area that provides the direction necessary to organize the season and plan effective practices.

Selecting Skill Objectives

Supplement 3-1 provides you with a list of objectives for each physical skill area. By reviewing the individual techniques listed, you can select objectives that are best for your players. To help with this task, appropriate objectives for players at three levels of play (beginning, ages 8-10; intermediate, ages 11-13, and advanced, ages 14 and over) are suggested. A detailed description of each of these individual techniques, including key elements and common errors in their performance, as well as progressions for teaching, can be found in Section 3. The key elements of performance are the bases for assessing players and for focusing your coaching efforts. This information should be reviewed if you do not have a good understanding of these individual techniques.

Selecting Knowledge Objectives

Cognitive outcomes (e.g., knowledge of rules, strategies, and information related to physical conditioning) are important for your players. Rules pertaining to "violations" and "fouls," how to warm up and cool down, what to eat for a pregame meal, and exercises to avoid are all important objectives because they can influence a player's performance. Objectives that include cognitive skills and tactics are listed in Supplement 3-2 and Supplement 3-3, respectively. You may wish to add to, delete from, or alter the objectives on this list as you determine those that are most appropriate for your team. By identifying these objectives, it's more likely they'll be taught at specific times during the season and at an appropriate level of understanding.

Selecting Fitness Objectives

Generally, your primary concern for athletes in the 6-13 age range should be to develop physical skills, knowledge, and appropriate personal/social skills. This is not to suggest that conditioning is unimportant. It is, however, the studied opinion of many coaches and specialists in growth and development that the specific training designed to promote high levels of sport-related fitness should receive a lower priority at this age. For highly skilled basketball players 14 years of age and older, a gradually increasing emphasis should be placed on conditioning the muscular and energy production systems. Part of the reason for this recommendation is that when young athletes train for skilled performance, they also obtain conditioning stimuli that are sufficient to cause the body to adapt to the fitness demands associated with learning and performing basketball skills. As players become highly skilled, conditioning becomes a more important factor for enabling more frequent, more intense, and more enduring application of their abilities. Supplement 3-4 includes an overview of fitness objectives you may wish to include in your season plan for older players who are also highly skilled.

For younger players, fitness should be a by-product of learning the physical skills.

Selecting Personal and Social Skill Objectives

A primary objective in the season plan should be to have all players feel increasingly better about their abilities as the season progresses. This should occur not only in the areas of physical skills, knowledge, and fitness, but should also include qualities such as persistence, self-control, tolerance, respect for authority, encouragement of teammates, concentration on the task, commitment to best efforts, and co-operation. Athletes need guidance (modeling, direction, encouragement, gentle rebuking, etc.) to develop such attributes. When achieved, these personal and social qualities contribute to performance in both athletic and non-athletic situations. Moreover, unlike opponents, officials, and/or the "breaks of the game," these qualities are within the control of individual players. The opportunity for individual control has been strongly linked to motivation, and motivation is strongly linked to performance.

Coaches are responsible for developing socially desirable skills in their players.

As a coach, perhaps your most important and lasting contribution is helping your players improve their feelings of self-worth and socially desirable skills. By focusing on controllable qualities such as "effort" versus uncontrollable "outcomes," which are often dependent on others (e.g., an official's call, a "lucky" bounce, the ability of another team), you have a unique opportunity to make a significant and lasting contribution to the personal character of your athletes.

Contributing to team membership is another worthy objective that coaches should set for every player. Athletes, especially those who engage in team sports such as basketball, must learn to overcome the natural tendency to blame others for a loss or even a bad performance. Players must be taught that their role is to play as well as they can and to think, do, and say those things that can help their teammates do the same. The team will only be as good as its weakest link. Often, an otherwise excellent team performs at a mediocre level due to the dissension created by "putting others down," making excuses, or transferring blame to others.

Coaches should reward effort when they review the accomplishments of the team.

Included in Supplement 3-5 is a listing of several personal and social skill objectives that you may want to incorporate into your season plan. The listing may be modified and made specific to your players.

Sequence Objectives Into Pre, Early, Mid, and Late Portions of the Season

Once you've identified season objectives for your team, they can be listed on the worksheet provided in Supplement 3-6. While the list may need to be revised as the season unfolds, the objectives should become the basis of your planning for the season.

Categorize the listed objectives into goals you want to achieve in the pre-, early-, mid-, and late-season (see Figure 3-2). Some objectives may be emphasized throughout the season, whereas others may be emphasized in only one division of the season. Photocopy Supplement 3-6 and use it to complete this step of your season plan.

Deciding what objectives should be achieved in the pre-, early-, mid-, and late-season is the basis for all subsequent planning.

Pre-season Objectives

If pre-season activity is possible, it can save you valuable practice time. Many of the objectives pertaining to knowledge of the rules and strategies and some of those involving conditioning can be all, or partially, achieved before formal practice even begins.

Objectives appropriate for the pre-season involve skills, knowledge, fitness capacities, or personal/social skills that can be achieved independently (all or in part) by the player in a safe and efficient manner before the initiation of formal practices. This could include learning the basic rules, violations and penalties, and strategies; obtaining appropriate equipment; and developing strength and aerobic fitness.

Early-season Objectives

The early-season should be devoted to determining how well your players have mastered the fundamental and/or prerequisite objectives you have selected and to teaching, reteaching, or practicing those objectives. Objectives appropriate for the early-season should contain abilities that are prerequisite to attaining other identified objectives. For example, players must be able to dribble before they can be expected to dribble and shoot. This attention to the sequence of skills is particularly important for the inexperienced player, who should spend more time on learning skills typically placed in the early-season division. In addition to objectives associated with physical skills, early-season objectives should include logistical and organizational concerns, safety, strategy, discipline, fitness, socialization, rules of play, and team rules. These are all essential in preparing players for early-season games and to provide a foundation for the rest of the season.

SEASON PLAN WORKSHEET

Coach: _____   Season: _____

Goal Areas	Objectives	Season Division			
		Pre	Early	Mid	Late
Physical Skills	Footwork		X	X	
	Dribbling				
	control dribble		X	X	
	speed dribble		X	X	X
	Passing		X	X	X
	Shooting				
	lay-ups		X	X	X
	set/jump shot		X	X	X
	free throw		X	X	X
Knowledge	Rules of the Game				
	starting play	X	X	X	
	scoring	X	X	X	
	violations/fouls	X	X	X	
	Strategies				
	offensive patterns			X	X
	team defense			X	X
	Etc.				
Fitness	Flexibility				
	hip	X	X	X	X
	shoulder	X	X	X	X
	etc.				
	Cardiovascular	X	X	X	X
Personal/Social	Personal				
	best effort		X	X	X
	listening		X	X	X
	Social				
	cooperation		X	X	X
	fair play		X	X	X
	Etc.				

Figure 3-2. An abbreviated example of a season plan for young basketball players.

Mid-season Objectives

Mid-season objectives should continue to focus on teaching individual techniques. However, a large share of practice time should be devoted to refining these techniques within the context of game-like drills and controlled scrimmages. Time should be spent combining individual techniques (e.g., catching the ball, then squaring up for the shot), and integrating these techniques with game strategy. Many of the cognitive, fitness, and personal/social objectives established for the early-season should continue to be emphasized during the mid-season.

Late-season Objectives

Late-season objectives should be focused on the maintenance and refinement of the team's offensive and defensive play. A greater portion of practice time should be spent on small-sided games, game-like drills, and controlled scrimmages. Practices should be organized so fitness levels are maintained and emphasis continues on cognitive and personal and social skills.

Generally, you should focus on single skills in the early-season, skill combinations in the mid-season, and combinations of both within systems of play in the later portion of the season. There are no hard and fast divisions among these three phases of the season (in fact, they should blend or overlap through good transitions). However, you should have them clearly in mind as you view the entire season in terms of what you wish to accomplish and the time in which it must be done.

Identify Practice Objectives

As you place objectives into season divisions and adjust the number of weeks assigned to each division, you will likely find that you have chosen to cover more than your available practice time allows. A good guide in such situations is to devote enough time to the cumulative instruction and practice of each objective so the majority of players are able to make significant improvements on most of the objectives included in the season plan. Merely exposing your team to the individual techniques of the game, without spending sufficient time for them to be learned, results in frustration for you and

the players. Your players must receive sufficient instruction, practice, and feedback to master the objectives at an appropriate level for use in a game situation. Accordingly, select, teach, and practice only the objectives that are essential to the game at your team's level of play. You can always add objectives to your plan as it is implemented, but you cannot recover time wasted on objectives that are not achieved or that are inappropriate for your players' level of development.

Select, teach, and practice the key objectives that are essential to your team.

Generally, the allotment of time to physical skill objectives should be based upon the following instructional sequence and distributed across several practices. You should allow time:

1. to introduce the objective—tell the players what you want them to learn and why it is important
2. for the players to try the individual techniques and for you to determine their levels of performance
3. for you to teach the key elements of the individual techniques and for players to practice these elements
4. for skill refinement and automation such that an individual technique can be used in game situations

The time allotment to fitness, cognitive, and personal/social objectives may not be as structured as the allotment for physical skill objectives. Fitness goals may be achieved along with practice of individual techniques in drills and scrimmages. Similarly, some cognitive, and personal/social objectives may be concomitantly attained during the practice of physical skills. However, some of these objectives may need practice time specifically devoted to them.

Integrating your chosen objectives into a season calendar (see Figure 3-3) will give you a master plan of everything you need to manage your coaching activities. The season calendar converts your plans to practice outlines. The daily entries on the calendar provide a guide from which specific plans can be developed. Supplement 3-7 provides a blank reproducible

SEASON PLANNING CALENDAR

Coach _Goodbody_   Team _Falcons_   Month _____

S	M	T	W	T	F	S
	Coaches' education meeting 7:00-9:00 (High School)		Team rosters distributed, sign-up for practice times/gyms 7:00-8:00 (Rec Office)			
		Parents' orientation meeting 7:00-8:30 (Elementary School Rm. 10)				
		Practice #1		Practice #2		Practice #3
		Practice #4		Practice #5		Practice #6
		Practice #7		Practice #8		

Figure 3-3. An example of a season planning calendar.

Practice #1

05 Overview of practice
10 Team rules and regulations
05 Warm-up

Review and evaluate:

15 Footwork fundamentals
10 Ball handling
20 Dribbling
15 Passing and receiving
05 Cool-down/team talk
05 Handouts: team rules,
    practice and game schedule,
    rules of play

Practice #2

05 Overview of practice
10 Review rules of play
05 Warm-up

Review and evaluate:

10 Ball handling
20 Shooting technique
    (lay-up, set shot)

Practice:

05 Footwork fundamentals
10 Dribbling
10 Passing
05 Cool-down/team talk
05 Handouts: coaching hints
    for individual skills

Practice #3

05 Overview of practice
05 Review rules of play
05 Warm-up

Review and evaluate:

15 Defensive skills
15 Rebounding

Practice:

15 Dribbling, passing,
    lay-ups, and shooting
15 Small group games (1 on 1)
05 Cool-down
10 Chalk talk: offensive
    strategies

Practice #4

05 Overview of practice
05 Warm-up
05 Ball handling drills
20 Practice individual offensive
    moves
15 Review and evaluate: free
    throw shooting technique
10 Practice defensive strategies
    (guarding the player with the
    ball)
15 Small group games and tactics
    (2 on 2)
05 Cool down
10 Chalk talk: two-player offensive
    strategies (give and go, back-
    door cut, pick and roll)

Practice #5

05 Overview of practice
05 Warm-up
10 Full court passing/dribbling/
    lay-up drill
15 Practice partner shooting
    and rebounding drills
30 Practice two player offensive
    patterns (give and go, back-
    door cuts, setting and using
    picks.)
15 Practice 2 on 1, 3 on 2
    half-court drills
05 Cool-down/team talk

Practice #6

05 Overview of practice
05 Warm-up
20 Practice individual skills
    and combination of skills
    (passive pressure)
20 Practice defensive
    strategies (guarding
    the player without the
    ball)
10 Practice 32/21 fast-
    break drill
20 Small group games
    and tactics (3 on 3)
05 Cool-down/handout-
    5 player pattern offense

Practice #7

05 Overview of practice
05 Warm-up
15 Practice individual skills and
    combination of skills
    (moderate pressure)
15 Review and practice five-player
    pattern offense (no defense)
15 Half-court scrimmage (review
    offensive and defensive
    strategies and plays)
10 Free throw shooting
10 Review inbound plays (odd
    and even)

Practice #8

05 Overview of practice
05 Warm-up
10 Review inbound plays
20 Review team strategy and
    positional responsibilities
45 Controlled scrimmage with
    another team
05 Cool-down/team talk

Figure 3-3. (continued)

worksheet that you can use to develop a master plan of practices.

The following list includes examples of entries that can be included on a calender:

- registration dates and deadlines
- date team roster is distributed
- sign-up date for practice time at available courts
- dates and times for coaches' education meetings
- equipment distribution dates and times
- date and time for parents' orientation meeting
- dates and times for league meetings
- sequential numbers designating practices (e.g., #1 designates first practice)
- practice objectives and time allocations
- game days and times
- tournament dates
- dates and times for special events

The most important part of developing a season calendar is the decision you make about what objectives to include and how much practice time you devote to each objective on a practice-by-practice basis. Using your season plan worksheet, select an appropriate number of objectives listed under "early-season" that you wish to include in your first practice and enter them in the space labeled "practice #1" on your season calendar. This process should be repeated for your second, third, and subsequent practices through the early, mid-, and late-season divisions.

The two most important decisions in planning the season are deciding what objectives to teach and how much time you should spend teaching them.

You will spend less total time planning for your season and practice if you use the approach suggested here than if the task is done practice-by-practice throughout the season. This process will also help you verify which skills you believe are most important as you run out of available practice time and are forced to either exclude objectives from your plan or find other ways to achieve them outside of the normal practice time. In addition to the good feeling and confidence that comes with completing a season calendar, you will have developed the base necessary to systematically change your plans as unexpected events develop. More importantly, you will know before the mid- to late-portions of the season whether in your initial plan you assigned too much or too little time to some of your early-season objectives. A completed plan that's been implemented and refined is also an invaluable resource for next year's coaching assignment or as a guide for new coaches coming into the program.

SUMMARY

Your role as a coach can be best filled through the leadership and instruction you provide in practice and game situations. Clearly, those coaches who are most effective in helping their players acquire the necessary physical skills, knowledge, fitness, and personal/social skills are those who have clear objectives and who organize to achieve them. Organization of the season by selecting and then teaching objectives in a proper order, and for an appropriate amount of time, is a major step toward helping players acquire the benefits of basketball.

Skills and Abilities of Basketball

PERFORMANCE AREA	SPECIFIC SKILLS	SUGGESTED EMPHASIS		
		Elem. School Beginner 8-10	Middle School Intermediate 11-13	High School Advanced 14 and up
Footwork Fundamentals	Basketball position	X	X	
	Quick start	X	X	
	Quick stop			
	A. Jump stop	X	X	
	B. Stride stop	X	X	X
	Pivot			
	A. Forward	X	X	
	B. Reverse	X	X	
	Defensive slide	X	X	X
Dribbling	Stationary dribble			
	A. Dominant hand	X		
	B. Non-dominant	X	X	X
	C. Alternating	X	X	
	Control dribble	X	X	X
	Speed dribble	X	X	X
	Crossover dribble	X	X	X
	Change-of-pace	X	X	X
	Reverse		X	X
	Behind the back			X
	Between the legs			X
Shooting	Lay-up			
	A. Stationary			
	Dominant hand	X		
	Non-dominant	X	X	X
	B. Non-stationary			
	Dominant hand	X	X	X
	Non-dominant		X	X
	Set shot	X		
	Jump shot		X	X
	Free throw			
	8-9 ft. rim	X		
	9-10 ft. rim		X	
	10 ft. rim			X

PERFORMANCE AREA	SPECIFIC SKILLS	SUGGESTED EMPHASIS		
		Elem. School Beginner 8-10	Middle School Intermediate 11-13	High School Advanced 14 and up
Receiving	Catching	X		
Passing	Chest pass			
	Stationary target.	X		
	Non-stationary	X	X	X
	Bounce pass			
	Stationary	X		
	Non-stationary	X	X	X
	Overhead pass			
	Stationary	X		
	Non-stationary	X	X	X
Rebounding	Jump.	X	X	
	Box out position		X	X
	Defensive.		X	X
	Offensive.		X	X
Individual Offensive Moves	Direct drive to the basket	X	X	X
	Rocker move	X	X	X
	Jab-step and go	X	X	X
	Crossover step		X	X
	Shot-fake and jump shot	X	X	X
	Post-up position		X	X
	Post square-up and shoot		X	X
	Post drop-step move		X	X
Offensive Movement Without the Ball	Direct cut to ball	X	X	X
	V-cut	X	X	X
	L-cut	X	X	X
	Setting picks	X	X	X
	Using picks	X	X	X
Defensive Stance		X	X	
Defensive Footwork	Slide step	X	X	
	Attack and retreat step	X	X	
	Drop step	X	X	
Guarding the Player with the Ball	Dribbler defense	X	X	X
	Dead ball defense		X	X
	Defending the shot		X	X
Guarding the Player Without the Ball	Deny defense	X	X	X
	Helpside defense		X	X
	Defending the screen		X	X

Knowledge Objectives*

LEVEL OF PLAYER APPROXIMATE AGE	SUGGESTED EMPHASIS		
	Elem. School Beginner 8-10 yrs.	Middle School Intermediate 11-13 yrs.	High School Advanced 14 and up
Rules of the Game			
the playing court	X		
the start of play	X		
method of scoring	X		
substitutions	X	X	
inbounding the ball	X	X	
fouls	X	X	X
violations	X	X	X
jump ball	X	X	
possession rule			X
three-point line			X
Prevention of Injuries			
equipment and apparel	X	X	X
court conditions	X	X	X
structural hazards	X	X	X
environmental hazards	X	X	X
use of appropriate techniques	X	X	X
contraindicated exercises	X	X	X
overuse injuries	X	X	X
Conditioning			
energy production system			X
muscular system			X
principles of training			X
methods of conditioning			X
warm-up/cool-down procedures	X	X	X
Nutrition			
proper diet	X	X	X
vitamins and minerals	X	X	X
water intake	X	X	X
ergogenic aids	X	X	X
steroids	X	X	X
meal patterns	X	X	X
weight control	X	X	X
Basketball Terminology	X	X	X

Other Knowledge Objectives

*Note that these knowledge objectives must be taught. It should not be assumed that young athletes will have learned these just by playing basketball.

Tactics Objectives

PERFORMANCE AREA	SPECIFIC SKILLS	SUGGESTED EMPHASIS		
		Elem. School Beginner 8-10	Middle School Intermediate 11-13	High School Advanced 14 and up
Individual Offensive Tactics				
	Getting open	X	X	X
	Driving to the basket	X	X	X
Two-Player Offensive Patterns				
	Give and go	X	X	X
	Backdoor cut	X	X	X
	Pick and roll	X	X	X
	Pass and pick away	X	X	X
Five-Player Pattern Offense			X	X
Zone Offense			X	X
Fastbreak			X	X
Out-of-Bounds Situations			X	X
Team Player-to-Player Defense			X	X
Zone Defense			X	X
Fastbreak Defense			X	X

Fitness Objectives*

	SUGGESTED EMPHASIS		
	Elem. School	Middle School	High School
LEVEL OF PLAYER	Beginner	Intermediate	Advanced
APPROXIMATE AGE	8-10 yrs.	11-13 yrs.	14 and up

Energy Production

aerobic capacity			X
anaerobic capacity			X
aerobic/anaerobic capacity			X

Muscular Fitness (strength, endurance, and power)

neck			X
shoulder			X
upper arm			X
lower arm			X
wrist			X
abdominal			X
hip/spine			X
low back			X
groin			X
upper leg			X
lower leg			X
ankle			X

Muscular Flexibility

neck			X
shoulder			X
trunk			X
hip			X
ankle			X

Other Fitness Objectives

*Note that progress is made in many of these objectives at the beginning and intermediate levels of play. This development should occur concomitantly through carefully planned practice sessions designed to enhance physical skills. The "Xs" in this chart suggest that coaches should not plan "fitness only" drills for their team until the players have reached approximately 14 years of age and are at the advanced level of play.

Personal and Social Objectives

LEVEL OF PLAYER APPROXIMATE AGE	SUGGESTED EMPHASIS		
	Elem. School Beginner 8-10 yrs.	Middle School Intermediate 11-13 yrs.	High School Advanced 14 and up
Personal			
best effort	X	X	X
initiative	X	X	X
persistence	X	X	X
responsibility	X	X	X
self-discipline	X	X	X
following directions	X	X	X
listening	X	X	X
Social			
respect for authority	X	X	X
leadership	X	X	X
respect for others	X	X	X
fair play	X	X	X
cooperation	X	X	X
appropriate winning behavior	X	X	X
appropriate losing behavior	X	X	X
tact	X	X	X
encouragement of teammates	X	X	X
respect for rules	X	X	X
sport-related etiquette	X	X	X
respect for property	X	X	X

Other Fitness Objectives

		Season Division			
Goal Areas	Objectives	Pre	Early	Mid	Late

SEASON PLAN WORKSHEET

Coach: _____   Season: _____

Supplement 3-7.

SEASON PLANNING CALENDAR						
Coach _____ Team _____ Month _____						
S	**M**	**T**	**W**	**T**	**F**	**S**

4
Planning Effective Instruction

Paul Vogel, Ph.D.
Eugene W. Brown, Ph.D.

QUESTIONS TO CONSIDER

- What four steps can coaches use to systematically instruct their players?
- What guidelines for instruction should be applied to ensure effective instruction?
- What are the features of an effective practice plan?
- What are the characteristics of a good drill?

INTRODUCTION

Effective instruction is the foundation of successful coaching. This is particularly true when you are coaching players in the six- to 16-year-old age range. Successful results in competition are directly related to the quality of instruction that players have received during practices. Effective instruction requires:

- clear communication of "what" is to be learned (objectives which represent skills, rules, strategies, and/or personal/social skills)
- continual evaluation of players' performance status on the objectives selected
- use of a systematic method of instruction
- application of guidelines for effective instruction
- evaluation and alteration of instruction in accordance with the degree to which players obtain the desired objectives

CLEARLY COMMUNICATING THE CONTENT TO BE LEARNED

The results (or outcomes) of effective instruction can be grouped into three areas.

1. Physical—individual techniques and conditioning
2. Mental—rules, strategies, positional responsibilities
3. Social—personal and social skills

Clearly stated objectives are a prerequisite to effective instruction.

To provide effective instruction, you must identify the teaching objectives for each of these three areas. Players do not learn skills merely through exposure and practice. Rather, they must have specific feedback revealing what they are doing correctly and, equally as important, what they are doing incorrectly. Specific feedback cannot be communicated to your players unless the skill to be learned and its key elements of performance are clearly specified and understood by the coach. By using the suggestions and procedures outlined in Chapter 3, you can be confident that the objectives you include are appropriate for your players. Application of the steps explained in Chapter 3 also results in a systematic plan (pre-season to late-season) for covering the objectives you select. This type of season plan provides a solid base from which effective instruction can occur.

CONTINUALLY EVALUATING THE PERFORMANCE OF PLAYERS

As a coach, it's important to evaluate your players' ability based on the objectives you have selected. Their current status on these objectives determines the instructional needs of the team. The evaluation should include physical, mental, and social content because deficiencies in any one of these areas may preclude successful participation in the sport. For example, the highly skilled basketball player who lacks motivation may be a liability rather than an asset to the team because of the poor example set for teammates. Also, knowledgeable players who understand the rules and strategies of offense and defense but who lack the skills and fitness to perform as team members must also be evaluated and taught to improve their deficiencies.

To conduct effective practices, you must continually assess players' needs.

The physical, mental, and attitudinal abilities of players who are new to the program or team are usually unknown. And even when accurate records are available from the previous season, considerable changes normally occur in the abilities of returning players. The result is you know very little about many of your players. Accordingly, you may have to spend more time evaluating players' abilities at the beginning of the season. However, evaluations must also occur, skill by skill, practice by practice, throughout the entire season. As their needs change, so should your instructional emphasis.

Assessment of Physical Needs

Performance Assessment

Assess physical skills by carefully observing your players while they participate in individual and small group drills, scrimmages, and/or games. Descriptions of individual techniques, their key elements, and common errors of performance are found in Section 3. You must have this information to properly evaluate your players.

In addition to knowledge about how individual techniques of basketball are performed, the following visual evaluation guidelines help you make accurate observations and assessments regarding physical performance.

- Select a proper observational distance
- Observe the performance from different angles
- Observe activities in a setting that is not distracting
- Select an observational setting that has a vertical and/or horizontal reference line
- Observe a skilled reference model
- Observe slower moving body parts first
- Observe separate key elements of complicated skills
- Observe the timing of performance components
- Look for unnecessary movements
- Observe the full range of motion

Fitness Assessment

Evaluating the fitness of your players requires two levels of assessment; namely, the aerobic and anaerobic energy systems. Precise physiological abilities are difficult to determine because they often require sophisticated measurement apparatus, take a lot of time, and the results are often confounded by players' skills and experience. Due to these complexities, your assessment of fitness should be at a more practical level. For the most part, you should compare individual players with their teammates on the characteristics of energy and muscular system fitness that are explained in Chapter 20. When skill, size, and maturity levels are judged to be similar between players and one is more (or less) fit than the others on a given attribute, you can assume a differential on that attribute. You can then instruct the underdeveloped player on how to make changes. Similarly, when a player cannot keep up with teammates on a series of drills that require either maximum effort or longer, sustained effort, it is prudent to assume that one or both of the energy systems is inadequately trained.

Assessment of Cognitive Needs

Knowledge of strategy, rules, positional responsibilities, and set plays can be evaluated during drills, scrimmages, and games by noting the response of your players to situations that require a decision prior to action. By clearly communicating what you want the players to know in certain circumstances, and then asking questions and observing how they react, you can learn what they know and what skills and knowledge they can appropriately apply.

Assessment of Personal/Social Needs

An assessment of social needs, though subjective, is not difficult. Informally converse with your players and observe their interactions with other team members during practices, games, and informal gatherings to determine what needs exist. Strengthening the personal/social weaknesses of your players, however, may be more difficult than enhancing their performance of individual physical techniques and their knowledge about the game.

As skilled performance is contingent on learning the key elements of each skill, the modification of a negative or interfering attitude requires you to correctly analyze the underlying problem. Ask yourself, the parents, or the player why the behavior in question is occurring. This may require some probing. Often the problem is not related to basketball. The fact that you care enough about the individual player to invest some time and energy may be all that is needed to reverse or eliminate a negative quality that could become a burden for the individual and the team. Based upon the information obtained, generate a specific strategy for modifying the behavior. The information in Chapters 15 through 18 will help you identify strategies for dealing with important personal/social skills.

Evaluating the status of players in the physical, mental, and attitudinal areas of performance is necessary in order to obtain insight about how to conduct practices that match your players' needs. Whether your players are performing at low, moderate, or high levels, they can all improve with good instruction.

USING A SYSTEMATIC MODEL FOR INSTRUCTION

Although there are many ways to instruct young basketball players, the following approach has proven both easy to use and effective in teaching and/or refining skills.

1. Get the attention of the players by establishing credibility
2. Communicate precisely what needs to be learned
3. Provide for practice and feedback
4. Evaluate results and take appropriate action

Step 1: Establish Credibility

Players must direct their attention to the coach before instruction can occur. To encourage this, arrange the players so that each one can clearly see your actions and hear your instructions. Choose where you stand in relation to the players so that you avoid competing with other distractions. Often it's a good strategy to have the players seated or kneeling in front of you as you begin.

Immediately establish the precedent that when you speak, important information is being communicated. Point out that the team cannot maximize its practice opportunity when several people are talking at once.

Establish and maintain the precedent that when you speak, important information is being communicated.

As you begin your instruction, establish the need for competence on a particular physical skill or ability by relating it to some phase of successful team and/or individual play. An excellent way to gain your players' attention and motivate them to want to learn individual techniques is to mention how a local, regional, or national level player or team has mastered the skill and has used it to great advantage. The objective of your introductory comments is to establish the idea that mastery of this skill is very important to individual and team play and that the key elements of its execution are achievable.

The next, and perhaps even more important, task is to clearly establish in the minds of the players that they need to improve their abilities on this skill. This can be accomplished with the following steps:

1. Briefly describe the new skill and then let them try it several times in a quick paced drill
2. Carefully observe their performance and identify their strengths and weaknesses (use the key elements of the skill as a basis for your observations)
3. Call them back together and report your observations

This approach allows you to point out weaknesses in performance on one or more key elements that are common to many, if not all, of the players. Using this approach enhances your credibility and motivates the players to listen to and follow your instructions. Also, your subsequent teaching can be specifically matched to the needs (weaknesses) you observed. Of course, if in observing you determine that your players have already achieved the desired skill level, then you should shift your focus to another skill. This might mean moving on to the next phase of your practice plan.

Step 2: Communicate Precisely What Needs To Be Learned

When you and your players know their status (strengths and weaknesses of their performance) on a particular skill, you have created an environment for teaching and learning. Because individuals learn most efficiently when they focus on one aspect of a skill at a time, it's important to precisely communicate the one key element you want an individual, pair, group, or team to concentrate on. Demonstrate the key element, and explain it, so that all players know exactly what they're trying to achieve.

Individuals learn most effectively by focusing their practice efforts on one clearly understood element of skilled performance.

When your players are at two or three different levels of ability, you may want to establish two or three instructional groups. This can be accomplished using the following three divisions:

1. Early Learning—focus on learning the key elements of the skill in a controlled situation
2. Intermediate Learning—focus on coordination of all key elements in common situations
3. Later Learning—automatic use of the skill in game-like conditions

Step 3: Provide for Practice and Feedback

Organize your practice time and activities to provide players with:

1. as many repetitions (trials) as possible within the allotted time (minimize standing in lines)
2. specific, immediate, and positive feedback on what they did correctly and then on what they can do to improve. Follow this instruction with some form of encouragement to continue the learning effort.

Repetitions and feedback are essential to players' achievement and are therefore fundamental to effective coaching. You can expect a direct relationship between the gains in players' performances and the degree to which you find ways to maximize these two dimensions of instruction. John Wooden, UCLA basketball coach of fame, was found to provide over 2,000 acts of teaching during 30 total hours of practice, of which 75 percent pertained directly to skill instruction. This converts to more than one incidence of feedback for every minute of coaching activity!

Repeated trials and specific feedback on what was right, followed by what can be improved and an encouraging "try again," produces results.

Feedback can be dramatically increased by using volunteers and/or the players themselves as instructional aids. When instruction is focused on one key element of performance and the important aspects of performing the skill have been effectively communicated to the players, they are often as good, and sometimes better, at seeing discrepancies in a partner's performance as some adults. Thus, working in pairs or small groups can be very effective in increasing both the number of trials and the amount of feedback that individuals get within a given amount of practice time. Also, by providing feedback, players are improving their mental understanding of how the skill should be performed.

Step 4: Evaluate Results and Take Appropriate Action

Evaluation of players' performances must occur on a continuing basis during practices and games. This is the only valid means to answer the question, "Are the players achieving the skills?" If they are, you have two appropriate actions to take:

1. Enjoy it. You're making an important contribution to your players.
2. Consider how you can be even more efficient. How can you get the same results in less time or how can more be achieved within the same time allotment?

If the players are not achieving the instructional objectives, it's important to ask why. Although it is possible that you have players who are very inept at learning, this is seldom the case. First assume that you are using inappropriate instructional techniques or that you simply did not provide enough instructional time. Go through the instructional factors related to effective planning, motivating, communicating, and discipline in this section, and conditioning in Section 6, to determine which of the guidelines or steps were missed and/or inappropriately implemented. Then alter your subsequent practices accordingly. Steps for how to complete this type of evaluation are described in more detail in Chapter 19. Continuous trial, error, and revisions usually result in improved coaching effectiveness, which then translates into increased achievement by the players. In those instances where you cannot determine what to alter, seek help from a fellow coach whose teams are consistently strong in the physical skills that are causing difficulty for your players. This is an excellent way to obtain some good ideas for altering your approach.

APPLYING GUIDELINES FOR EFFECTIVE INSTRUCTION

As you provide for practice and feedback to your players (Step 3), you may wish to use some of the guidelines for instruction that have been found by recent research to be effective in improving student learning. Nine guidelines for effective instruction are named below and described in more detail in Supplement 4-1.

1. Set realistic expectations
2. Structure instruction
3. Establish an orderly environment
4. Group your players according to ability
5. Maximize on-task time
6. Maximize the success rate
7. Monitor progress
8. Ask questions
9. Promote a sense of control

PLANNING EFFECTIVE PRACTICES

If practices are to be effective, they must be directed at helping players meet the objectives defined in the season plan. Objectives are best achieved by using appropriate instructional methods. Instruction is both formal (planned) and informal (not planned) and can occur during practices, games, and special events. Virtually any time players are in your presence, there is potential for teaching and learning.

All coaches, even those who are highly knowledgeable and experienced, are more effective teachers when they organize and plan their instruction. This does not mean that unplanned instruction should not be used to assist your players in learning more about basketball. In fact, unplanned events that occur often present ideal opportunities to teach important skills. By capitalizing on temporary but intense player interest and motivation, a skilled coach can turn an unplanned event into an excellent learning opportunity. For example, an opponent's offense may prove so effective during a game that your defensive players become highly motivated to learn the tactics necessary to stop such an attack. Often these "teachable moments" are unused by all but the most perceptive coaches.

Features of an Effective Practice

Scheduled practice sessions usually constitute the largest portion of contact between you and your players. Each practice session requires you select both the content of instruction and its method of presentation. To do this effectively and efficiently, each of your practice plans should:

- be based upon previous planning and seasonal organization (see Chapter 3)
- list the objectives that will be the focus of instruction for that practice
- show the amount of time allotted to each objective during the practice
- identify the activities (instructional, drill, or scrimmage) that will be used to teach or practice the objectives
- identify equipment and/or special organizational needs
- apply the guidelines for effective instruction (included in Supplement 4-1)

An effective practice combines the seasonal plan, assessment of your players' abilities, instruction, and an evaluation of practice results. The evaluation portion should be retained even if it means changing future practices to meet the needs of players that may have been unanticipated. The features of an effective practice plan are outlined in Table 4-1. Not all of the features are appropriate for every practice you conduct. There should be a good reason, however, before you decide not to include each feature.

Format and Inclusions in a Practice Plan

Several ingredients that should be included in a practice plan are: the date and/or practice number; the objectives and key points, drills and/or activities; amount of practice time devoted to each objective; equipment needs; and a place for evaluation. The date and/or practice number are helpful to maintain organizational efficiency. The objectives are the reason for conducting the practice and, therefore, must be clearly in mind prior to selecting the activities, drills, games, or scrimmage situations you believe will develop player competence. The key points of each objective you desire to have your

Table 4-1. Features of an effective practice.

Features	Coaching Activity
Practice overview	Inform the team about the contents and objectives of the practices (e.g. important new skills, positional play, new drills) to motivate and mentally prepare them for the upcoming activity.
Warm-up	Physically prepare the team for each practice by having them engage in light to moderate aerobic activity sufficient to produce slight sweating. Follow this by specific stretching activities.
Individual skills and drills	Review and practice objectives previously covered.
Small group skills and drills	Introduce and teach new objectives.
Team skills and drills	Incorporate the individual and small group drills into drills involving the entire team.
Cool-down	At the end of each practice, use activities of moderate to light intensity followed by stretching to reduce potential soreness and maintain flexibility.
Team talk	Review key points of the practice, listen to player communications, make announcements, and distribute handouts.

players achieve must be clearly in mind. It also helps to have the key points written prominently on your plan or notes. Supplement 4-2 provides an example plan written to cover the objectives of Practice 5 listed on the season calendar in Chapter 3. In order to communicate the essential features of a practice plan to many readers, this example contains far more narrative than is necessary for most coaches. You need to record only information that will be needed at some later date. Accordingly, phrases, symbols, key words, and other personalized communications will substitute for the more extensive narrative included in the example. A full-sized copy of the practice plan form that you may reproduce is included in Supplement 4-3.

Practice Time

Allotting time for each objective during practices is a difficult but important task for the coach. Sufficient practice time results in the majority of your players making significant improvement on each objective. Although these changes may not be noticeable in a single session, they must occur over the season. Assigning too little time may result in players' exposure to individual techniques but often in little change in performance. Keep in mind, however, that practice time must be distributed across several objectives (and/or drills or activities within the practice of a single objective) to keep players' interests high. This is particularly true for younger players who tend to have short attention spans and thus need frequent changes in drills or activities.

Instructional Activities

The selection and implementation of instructional activities, drills, or games should constitute most of each practice session. Players' achievements are directly related to your choices and actions in these important areas. Instructional activities should be conducted in accordance with the guidelines presented in Supplement 4-1. Because most practices are composed largely of drills, you should follow the same guidelines in Supplement 4-1 and develop your drills to include these important features:

- have a meaningful name
- require a relatively short explanation
- provide an excellent context for mastering an objective
- match skill, knowledge, or fitness requirements of basketball
- keep the players' "on-task time" high
- are easily modified to accommodate skilled and unskilled players
- provide opportunity for skill analysis and feedback to players

Drills should be written on file cards or paper. It's also helpful to organize drills according to objective, group size (individual, small group, team), possession (offensive and defensive), and position (guard, forward, or center). When you find a good drill, classify it and add it to your collection. A format for collecting drill

information is provided in reproducible form in Supplement 4-4.

Equipment Needs

The equipment needed to conduct a drill or activity should be recorded on the practice plan. It's frustrating and ineffective to discover after you've explained and set up an activity or drill that the necessary equipment is missing. Therefore, after you've planned all the activities for your practice, review them and list the essential equipment needed.

Evaluation

The evaluation/comment portion of the practice plan can be used to highlight ways to alter the practice to accommodate players at unexpected skill levels, or to note changes to be made to improve the plan. It also provides a place for announcements or other information that needs to be communicated to your players.

SUMMARY

Effective instruction is the foundation of successful coaching. It requires practices that include clear communication of what is to be learned, a continuous evaluation of players' performance on the objectives of the practices, a systematic method of instruction, and the use of guidelines for instruction that have been associated with player achievement.

Systematic instruction includes: (a) establishing credibility; (b) providing precise communication of what needs to be learned; (c) providing many practice trials and specific, immediate, and positive feedback; and (d) evaluating the achievement of your players. Use of the guidelines for effective instruction (realistic expectations, structured instruction, order, grouping, maximizing time, success, monitoring, and providing a sense of control) in combination with systematic instruction maximizes the results of your coaching effort.

Guidelines for Effective Instruction

QUESTIONS TO CONSIDER

- What are the nine guidelines for effective instruction?
- How can setting realistic expectations for your players influence their achievement?
- How can you coach players of different ability levels on the same team?
- When players are attempting to learn new things, what success rate motivates them to want to continue to achieve?

Introduction

This supplement provides an overview of nine guidelines for effective instruction. As you plan your practices, this list should be reviewed to help maximize your coaching effectiveness. The nine guidelines are:

1. Set realistic expectations
2. Structure instruction
3. Establish an orderly environment
4. Group your players according to ability
5. Maximize on-task time
6. Maximize the success rate
7. Monitor progress
8. Ask questions
9. Promote a sense of self-control

1. Set Realistic Expectations

The expectations coaches communicate to their players can create a climate for learning that will positively influence player achievement (Rutter et al. 1979). Clear, but attainable, objectives for performance and expenditure of effort for all players on your team will facilitate achievement. As stated in a recent review (Fisher et al. 1980), the reasons associated with this occurrence may be related to the following ideas.

In comparison to athletes for whom coaches hold high expectations for performance, the athletes perceived to be low performers are:

- more often positioned farther away from the coach
- treated as groups, not individuals
- smiled at less
- receive less eye contact from the coach

- called on less to answer questions
- have their answers responded to less frequently
- praised more often for marginal and inadequate responses
- praised less frequently for successful responses
- interrupted more often

Players tend to achieve in accordance with the coaches' expectations.

Coaches and former athletes will be able to understand how even a few of the above responses could reduce motivation and achievement. It is saddening that many capable children are inappropriately labeled as non-achievers on the basis of delayed maturity, poor prior experience, inadequate body size, body composition, and/or many other factors which mask their true ability. Yet, if expectations are low, achievement is likely to be low.

There are at least two important messages in this guideline:

- Expect that, as the coach, you're going to significantly improve the skills, fitness, knowledge of rules and strategies, and attitude of every one of your players during the course of the season.
- Set realistic goals for your players. Make a commitment to help each player achieve those individual goals, and expect improvement.

2. Structure Instruction

Your players' achievements are strongly linked to clear communication of the intended outcomes of instruction (objectives), why the goals and objectives are important (essential or prerequisite skills), and what to do to achieve outcomes (instructional directions) (Bruner 1981 and Fisher et al. 1980). Effective instruction is based upon the systematic organization of the content to be taught. The critical steps to take are as follows:

- Select the essential skills, fitness capacities, knowledge of rules and strategies, and personal/social skills from the many options available
- Clearly identify the elements of acceptable performance for each objective that you include in your plans
- Organize and conduct your practices to maximize the opportunity your players have to acquire the objectives by using the effective teaching practices contained in this chapter

3. Establish an Orderly Environment

High achievement is related to the following elements (Fisher 1978):

- an orderly, safe, business-like environment with clear expectations
- player accountability for effort and achievement
- rewards for achievement of expectations

Where such conditions are missing, achievement is low.

The following coaching actions will lessen behavioral problems that interfere with learning and, at the same time, promote pride and responsibility in team membership.

- Maintain orderly and disciplined practices
- Maintain clear and reasonable rules that are fairly and consistently enforced

Caution: strong, over-controlling actions can backfire. Over-control causes frustration and anxiety while under-control leads to lack of achievement. The best of circumstances is a relaxed, enjoyable but business-like environment. The ability to balance these two opposing forces to maximize achievement and enjoyment by keeping both in perspective may be one of your most difficult tasks.

4. Group Your Players

Decisions about the size and composition of groups for various learning tasks are complex, but nonetheless related to achievement (Webb 1980). Typically, in groups of mixed ability, the player with average ability suffers a loss in achievement, while the player with low ability does slightly better. The critical condition for grouping to be effective is to have players practicing at the skill levels needed to advance their playing ability. Typically, this involves groups of similar ability being appropriately challenged. Although this can be difficult to achieve, most effective coaches design practices that maximize a type of individualized instruction.

Your team will have individuals at many levels of ability. While this situation presents a seemingly impossible grouping task, there are some good solutions to this problem:

- When a skill, rule, or strategy is being taught that all your athletes need to know, use a single group for instruction
- As you identify differences in your players' abilities, divide the team and place players of similar ability in small groups when working on these tasks
- When a skill, rule, or strategy is being practiced where individual athletes are at several levels of ability (initial, intermediate, or later learning levels), establish learning stations that focus on specific outcomes to meet each groups' needs

The placement of players into smaller learning groups must be independently decided for each skill, rule, or strategy. A player who is placed at a high level group for practicing individual techniques for dribbling and passing the ball should not necessarily be placed in a high level group for shooting or defensive techniques. It is important that the following occur at each learning station:

- order is established and maintained (an assistant may be necessary)
- tasks that are to be mastered at each station must be clearly understood
- many opportunities must be provided at each station

- a means for giving immediate, specific, and positive feedback must be established.

5. *Maximize On-Task Time*

Research on the amount of time that athletes are active in the learning process, rather than standing in lines or watching others perform, reveals that actual "engaged" learning time during practices is regularly less than 50 percent of the total practice time, and often falls to five or 10 percent for individual athletes. There are several actions you can take to maximize the use of available time.

- Reduce the number of athletes who are waiting in line by using more subgroups in your drills
- Secure sufficient supplies and equipment so that players do not have lengthy waits for their turn
- Reduce the transition time between drills by preplanning practices to minimize reformulation of groups and equipment set-up time
- Use instructional grouping practices that have players practicing skills at their appropriate performance level
- Clearly outline and/or diagram each portion of practice and communicate as much of that information as possible before going on the court
- Complete as many pre and post warm-up/cool-down activities as possible outside of the time scheduled on the court
- Recruit assistants (parents or older players) to help you with instructional stations under your supervision

Remember: Saving ten minutes a day across 14 weeks of two practices per week equals 280 minutes of instructional time for each player. Time gained by effective organization is available for practicing other skills of the game.

6. *Maximize the Success Rate*

The relationship among successful experiences, achievement, and motivation to learn is very strong (Fisher 1978 and Rosenshine 1983.) The basic message in this research is to ask players to attempt new learning that yields 70% to 90% successful experiences. This level of success motivates them to want to continue to

achieve. There are two major implications of the finding:

- Reduce each technique, rule, or strategy into achievable sub-skills and focus instruction on those sub-skills
- Provide feedback to the players such that, on most occasions, something that they did is rewarded, followed by specific instructions about what needs more work, and ending with an encouraging "Try again!"

7. *Monitor Progress*

If you organize your practice to allow athletes to work at several stations in accordance with their current abilities and needs, it follows that players often will work independently or in small groups. When players are left to work on their own, they typically spend less time engaged in the activities for which they are responsible. When coaches are actively moving about, monitoring progress, and providing individual and small group instructional feedback, players make greater gains (Fisher 1978). Within this context, you can provide much corrective feedback, contingent praise, and emotionally neutral criticism (not personal attacks or sarcasm) for inappropriate behavior. These actions have a positive influence on both achievement and attitude.

8. *Ask Questions*

Asking questions also relates to player achievement (Brophy 1976). Questions must, however, promote participation or establish, reinforce, and reveal factual data associated with physical skills, rules, or strategies. Use of this teaching technique seems to work best when there is a pause of three or more seconds before you ask for a response, at which time the players are cued to think about the answer (Rowe 1974).

9. *Promote a Sense of Control*

Your players should feel that they have some control over their own destiny if they are to reach their potential as basketball players. This sense of control can be developed by:

- organizing your instruction to result in many

successful experiences (i.e., opportunities to provide positive feedback)

- teaching your players that everyone learns at different rates and to use effort and their own continuous progress as their primary guides (avoid comparing their skill levels with those of other players)
- encouraging individual players to put forth their best effort (reward best efforts with positive comments, pats on the back, thumbs up signs, or encouraging signals)

In these ways, players quickly learn that the harder they work and the more they try, the more skillful they will become. At the same time, you'll be eliminating the natural feeling of inferiority or inability that grows in the presence of feedback which is limited to pointing out errors. Although some players develop in almost any practice situation, many potentially excellent players will not continue in an environment where they feel there is no possibility of gaining the coach's approval.

Summary

The information in this supplement provides a base from which effective practices can be developed and implemented. Not all coaches can claim that they use all of these guidelines throughout all of their practice sessions. All coaches should, however, seek to use more of these techniques more frequently as they plan and implement their practices.

REFERENCES

Brophy, J.E., & Evertson, C. (1976). *Learning from teaching: A developmental perspective.* Boston, MA: Allyn and Bacon.

Bruner, J. (1981, August). On instructability. Paper presented at the meeting of the American Psychological Association, Los Angeles, CA.

Fisher, C.W. et al. (1978). Teaching behaviors, academic learning time and student achievement. Final report of Phase III-B, *Beginning teacher evaluation study, technical report.* San Francisco, CA: Far West Laboratory for Educational Research and Development.

Fisher, C.W. et al. (1980). Teaching behaviors, academic learning time and student achievement: An overview. In C. Denham and A. Lieberman (Eds.), *Time to learn.* Washington, D.C.: U.S. Department of Education, National Institute of Education.

Rosenshine, B.V. (1983). Teaching functions in instructional programs. *The Elementary School Journal, 83,* 335-352.

Rowe, M.B. (1974). Wait time and rewards as instructional variables: Their influence on language, logic, and fate control. Part one, Wait time. *Journal of Research in Science Teaching, 11,* 81-94.

Rutter, M. et al. (1979). *Fifteen thousand hours.* Cambridge, MA: Harvard University Press.

Webb, N.M. (1980). A process-outcome analysis of learning in group and individual settings. *Educational Psychologist, 15,* 69-83.

Supplement 4-2.

Sample Practice Plan

Eugene W. Brown

QUESTIONS TO CONSIDER

- How should coaches determine the amount of detail to be included in their practice plans?
- How is a practice plan related to a season planning calendar?
- What are the features of an effective practice?
- How can practice plans help a coach to achieve objectives previously listed for the team?

Introduction

This supplement contains a sample practice plan and an overview of the organization and content of the plan. This plan is presented as an example of what might be included in a well-organized practice of intermediate level youth players (10 to 13 years of age) conducted by a highly organized coach. This plan illustrates the fifth of eight practices before the first game. Its outline is derived from the procedures outline in the season planning calendar presented in Chapter 3.

Organization and Content of the Sample Practice Plan

Note that a considerable amount of detail is included in the sample plan. This is provided to make it easier to understand the nature of the activities included in the practice. When you prepare a plan for your own use, the level of detail can be substantially reduced. If you're a seasoned coach, you may only need the names of the drills, key coaching points, and a few diagrams. However, most inexperienced coaches will need more detail.

Note that this sample practice plan contains all of the features of an effective practice that are presented in Table 4-1 of this chapter. These features have also been checked at the bottom of the first page of the sample practice plan.

Objectives

The objectives of the sample practice plan should be taken directly from the objectives previously listed by the coach in a season planning calendar in Chapter 3. These objectives may need to be modified slightly because of what the coach was able to cover in previous practices and what the coach has learned from assessing the abilities of the players in previous practices.

Overview of Practice Activities

The overview of practice activities should last only a minute or less. The coach only needs to simply state what is planned for the practice. This helps to mentally prepare and organize the players for the practice. The overview gets the players to "think basketball" again. Therefore, a good time to respond to players' questions is immediately after the overview.

Warm-up & Stretching

The basketball-specific warm-ups included in this sample practice plan consist of two light aerobic activities. These activities are used to increase the breathing rate, heart rate, and muscle temperature to exercise levels. They also help to reacquaint the athletes to their practice environments and prepare the muscles and joints for stretching activities which follow.

The six stretching activities were selected to maintain flexibility in several muscle groups and joints of the body. On average, approximately 45 seconds can be spent on each of the eight activities included in this phase of the practice. Thus, it is assumed that the players are familiar with each of the eight activities and can quickly change from one to the next. If any of these stretches needs to be taught to the players, more time will be needed for the warm-up session or some activities will need to be excluded.

Review & Practice Set Plays

The coach must be ambitious and highly organized to cover four activities in the 75 minutes allotted. The only way this could be achieved is for the players to have received handouts on these set plays at a previous practice and to have been encouraged to read and study these set plays before the current practice. Key points of each of the set plays is briefly reviewed on a portable chalkboard before having the players practice them.

Note that practice for setting a pick on the ball is positioned together at the end of this phase of the sample practice plan. This is organized in this manner because this activity requires players to work in groups of threes. This same grouping is used for all practice activities in the next phase of the practice. This organizational arrangement saves the time necessary for players to change from one group size to another.

Individual Skill Techniques

The drills selected and the manner in which they are conducted should challenge the players to achieve higher levels of performance of individual skills. Selection and conduct should be based upon what the coach has learned from observing the players in previous practices and an understanding of the direction players must proceed to achieve future goals.

In this sample practice plan, 25 minutes is

provided for four drills. Players should be required to use both hands during this phase of their practice. While the players are engaged in the practice of individual techniques, the coach should be active in observing performances, providing individual and immediate feedback to the players, and developing ideas about what to include in future practices to improve their level of performance.

Note that in addition to passing and receiving the ball, players should be alerted to other aspects of play that are integral parts of these drills. These aspects include offensive and defensive techniques, making lead passes, and communicating. Also, if the drills run at a brisk pace, the players may concomitantly enhance their fitness level. The potential for simultaneous enhancement of individual techniques, tactical knowledge, and fitness of players within the same practice activities is an example of economical training.

Small Group Games

Twenty minutes has been allotted for two small group (2 on 1 and 3 on 2) drills in this practice plan. From the players' perspectives, competitive games are often the highlight of the practice. Alerting your players at the beginning of the practice (Overview of Practice Activities) that you have scheduled some competitive game for the end of practice encourages them to participate in other phases of the practice in an efficient manner. It should be noted, however, that small group games and controlled scrimmages are not just a reward for a team that pays attention during the practice. These competitive and dynamic activities are lead-up games to full-scale competition. A knowledgeable coach can use 3 on 3 drills and controlled scrimmages to teach players offensive and defensive tactics as well as the transition of individual techniques into the skills of play.

The two group drills selected for this sample practice plan build upon less complicated games (1 v 2 and 2 v 2) included in previous practices and lead up to a controlled scrimmage.

Cool-Down

In this sample practice plan the same activities are used in the cool-down as were planned for the warm-up and stretching for the beginning of the practice. The cool-down activities could differ from the warm-up activities. The important aspect of the cool-down activities, however, is that they involve the body parts exercised during the practice. This helps clear out waste products built up in the muscle, reduce the pooling of blood in the extremities, reduce the potential for soreness in the muscles, and prevent the loss of flexibility that may accompany intense muscular exercise.

Note that, in an attempt to save time, simple information can be given to the players while they're engaged in their cool-down activities.

Equipment

After coaches plan their practice, they should review each activity to determine what equipment will be needed to carry out the practice. A written list, included on the practice plan, is helpful when coaches are in a hurry to get to practice on time.

Evaluation

The evaluation of the practice should be completed after the practice and before planning the next practice. This evaluation should address (a) the appropriateness of the organization and content of the practice, (b) the success of the coaching methods used, and (c) the degree to which planned objectives (physical skills, tactics, personal and social skills, and fitness) were achieved. This type of evaluation is helpful in improving your coaching methods and in directing future practices to meet the needs of your players.

Summary

The sample practice plan and overview of its organization and content are presented in this supplement to provide guidance and insight to coaches for planning their own practice plans. It is not presented to be directly used by coaches because each team is unique in its needs at any point in time during the season. Therefore, coaches should plan each practice session to meet the specific needs of their players.

PRACTICE PLAN

OBJECTIVES: *Review & practice two player offensive patterns (give and go, backdoor cuts); practice shooting and rebounding techniques; practice 2 on 1, 3 on 2 player strategies; review passing, dribbling and footwork fundamentals.*

DATE: *March 27*

#: *5*

TIME	COACHING ACTIVITIES (name, description, diagram, key points)
5 min.	*Overview of Practice Activities:* *(1) two player offensive patterns: give and go and backdoor cuts;* *(2) individual shooting and rebounding techniques;* *(3) improve passing, dribbling and footwork fundamentals.* *(Key point: respond to any questions from the players)*
5 min.	*Warm-up:* *(1) Ballhandling drills* *(2) Jog 2 times around the basketball court*
10 min.	*Stretching:* *(1) calf-stretch* *(2) seated straddle* *(3) kneeling quad stretch* *(4) trunk and hip stretch* *(5) arm circles* *(6) jumping jacks*

EQUIPMENT: *One basketball per player, portable chalkboard, chalk, eraser, whistle and clipboard.*

NOTE: Features of an effective practice include: √ practice overview; √ warm-up; √ individual skills and drills; √ small group skills and drills; √ team skills and drills; √ cool-down; √ team talk. (Check the features included in this practice plan.)

EVALUATION: _____

(additional space on back)

PRACTICE PLAN CONTINUED

TIME	COACHING ACTIVITIES (name, description, diagram, key points)
10 min.	**3 Minute Full-court Lay-up Drill** a) Record the number of lay-ups made by the team in 3 minutes b) Have players set team goals to strive for each week. (Key points: dribble with eyes up and under control, lead teammate with the pass.) **Practice shooting and rebounding techniques:** (divide team into groups of 2 at each basket)
5 min.	(1) Pressure Power Drill
5 min.	(2) Pick up and Shoot Drill
5 min.	(3) Partner Shooting Drill (from the elbow and block areas)

(Key Points: rebound the ball aggressively with two hands and power the ball back up using the backboard).

PRACTICE PLAN CONTINUED

TIME	COACHING ACTIVITIES (name, description, diagram, key points)
	Practice two player offensive patterns: give and go, backdoor cuts, setting a pick on the ball (Keep groups of 2 from previous drill.)
10 min.	(1) *Give and go from the pointguard to the wing.* (Key points: *receiver*-execute v-cut on the wing, stress target hands, lead *passer* – take 2 steps away from pass and then cut back to the basket to receive the return pass for a lay-up).
10 min.	(2) *Backdoor cut* (Key points: *receiver*-v-cut and pop out high on wing, reverse the direction of the cut by planting the outside foot and exploding back to basket; *passer*-signal the backdoor by faking a pass at the wing, lead teammate with a bounce pass for the lay-up.)
10 min.	(3) *Setting a pick on the ball* (groups of 3) a) Rotate positions (guard, wing, defense). b) Run drill on both sides of floor. (Key points: establish stationary position at least one step away from the defender, plant both feet perpendicular to the path of oncoming defender, knees flexed, arms close to body in a protective position, stay low and hold the pick for three seconds or until the pick has been used.)

PRACTICE PLAN CONTINUED

TIME	COACHING ACTIVITIES (name, description, diagram, key points)
	Practice 2 on 1 and 3 on 2 Strategies
	(1) <u>2 on 1 – half-court drill</u>
10 min.	(Key Points: a) <u>offense</u>-dribble down one side of court until stopped by defender, if defense covers the ball, pass off. b) <u>defense</u> – stop ball, hedge, and box out.)
10 min.	(2) <u>3 on 2 – half-court drill</u> (Key Points: a) <u>offense</u>-dribble down middle of the court, fill lanes wide, pass and cut quickly. b) <u>defense</u> – tandem defense, stop ball, call first pass, and box out.
	Cool-down (same stretching exercises performed at beginning of practice). During cool-down activities, remind players to: 1) review handouts on offensive-defensive strategies and individual skills. 2) practice shooting and rebounding techniques at home. 3) bring a basketball for every practice. 4) prepare for 3 on 3 tournament on Saturday!

PRACTICE PLAN

OBJECTIVES: _____ **DATE:** _____
_____ **#:** _____
_____
_____
_____

TIME	COACHING ACTIVITIES (name, description, diagram, key points)

EQUIPMENT: _____
_____

NOTE: Features of an effective practice include: ___ practice overview; ___ warm-up; ___ individual skills and drills; ___ small group skills and drills; ___ team skills and drills; ___ cool-down; ___ team talk. (Check the features included in this practice plan.)

EVALUATION: _____
_____

(additional space on back)

PRACTICE PLAN CONTINUED

TIME	COACHING ACTIVITIES (name, description, diagram, key points)

Supplement 4-4.

DRILL NAME: _____ CLASSIFICATION(S): _____

SOURCE: _____ _____

OBJECTIVES: _____

FACILITIES AND EQUIPMENT: _____ _____

DIAGRAM: DIRECTIONS:

COMMENTS: _____
_____
_____

Section II
Rules of Play

5
Basic Basketball Rules with Modifications for Youth Players

Karen Garchow, M.A.

QUESTIONS TO CONSIDER

- What modifications could be made to the rules of basketball to meet the developmental needs of youth players?
- How should the rules of basketball be applied in order to promote safety, enjoyment, and fairness?

INTRODUCTION

Statements and interpretations of the official basketball rules as well as suggested modifications for youth play are contained herein. The contents are systematically organized to help those associated with youth basketball (players, parents, coaches, and officials) gain a practical understanding of the rules of the game.

Practical Considerations

Throughout this chapter, practical considerations for the applications of the rules of the game are suggested to promote safety, enjoyment, and fairness.

Modifications for Youth Play

Throughout this chapter, modifications to the rules for youth play are suggested. These modifications are presented with the intent of

maintaining the principles and rules of the game while meeting the educational and developmental needs of youth players. Modifications are not stated with the intent of ultimately changing the rules of the game, but are presented as a progression to:

- assist coaches in developing a systematic approach to teaching the game of basketball to their athletes
- assist youth players in developing their understanding and skills of basketball in order to ultimately play under the official rules of the game

RULE I-THE PROPER BALL

A spherical ball made of leather or molded fabric, with a 28.5 to 30 in. circumference and a weight of 18 to 22 ounces, is to be used for play. When inflated properly, it should bounce to a height of not less than 49 in. nor more than 54 in. after it has been dropped from a height of 6 ft. (measured to bottom of ball).

Practical Considerations

- Balls must be safe for play.

Modifications for Youth Play

Use of smaller and lighter-weight balls permits younger players to dribble, pass, and shoot with greater accuracy.

A lightweight vinyl coated foam ball may be more appropriate for youth play (ages seven and below). Younger players can successfully learn skills without the fear of being hurt. Downsized balls allow for better manageability and a greater chance of student success.

Basketballs are presently being manufactured in many different sizes and materials. Sizes range from mini, junior, intermediate, official women's and men's regulation size balls (see Figure 5-1). Different materials used in the construction of the ball include: foam, rubber, synthetic leather, and leather. Ball sizes commonly used for different age groups with their corresponding dimensions are presented in Table 5-1.

- Balls used for youth play should be compatible with the physical characteristics of young athletes.
- Balls that are too large, heavy, or hard may discourage or hurt younger players.

RULE II-THE PLAYING COURT

The playing court must be rectangular, the surface free from obstructions and with dimen-

Figure 5-1. Various sizes of basketballs.

sions not greater than 94 ft. in length by 50 ft. in width. Each line, mark, circle, or fixture designating the basketball court has a specific purpose (see Figure 5-2). These purposes include:

- determining if a goal is scored
- determining if the ball is in or out of bounds
- identifying important areas of the court
- aiding in the start and restart of play

Practical Considerations

- The court must be safe for play and free from obstructions.
- A regulation court permits use of crosswise (bold) courts for practice and youth games.

Modification for Youth Play

- Coaches should use proper terminology when referring to the boundary lines of the basketball court so that players become familiar with their name and function (i.e., baseline, sideline, half- court line, free-throw line).

Table 5-1. Ball Sizes Commonly Used for Play.

AGE GROUP Years	Material	Size	DIMENSIONS Circumference (inches)	Weight (ounces)
7 and below	Foam/Rubber	Mini.	22.5	8
8-11	Rubber	Junior	27.25-27.75	14
12-14	Indoor-Leather	Intermediate	27.75-28.5	18
15-17	Indoor-Leather*	Women's	28.5-29	18-20
	Outdoor-Rubber* Indoor-Outdoor* Synthetic Rubber	Men's Regulation	29.5-30	20-22
Advanced Play & Conditioning	Rubber	Heavy Trainer	Men's and Women's Regulation Size	40

*Available in Women's, Men's, and Regulation Size.

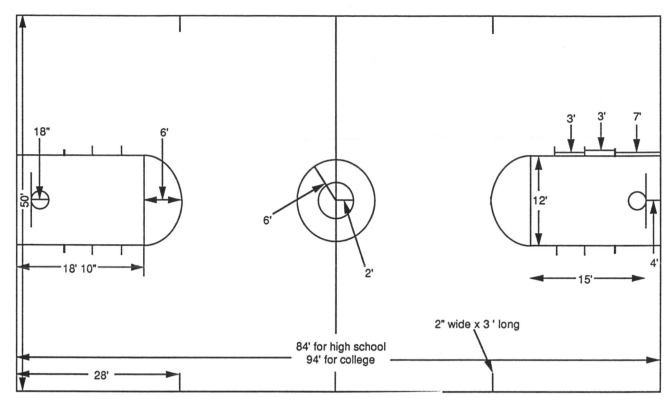

Figure 5-2. Regulation basketball court.

- Court sizes for younger players (ages 8-11) should be smaller than the regulation court (see Table 5-2).
- Half court 3-on-3 basketball is recommended for all ages (see Table 5-3 and Figure 5-3).

Table 5-2. Recommended Court Dimensions for 5-a-Side Play.

AGE GROUP		DIMENSIONS	
Years	School	Width (Feet)	Length (Feet)
8-11*	Elementary	35-40	54-60
12-14	Middle	50	84
15-17	High	50	84
17 and above	College	50	94

*Note that 5-a-side games are not recommended for youth players below the age of 11 years. However, if a league tradition of full-sided games is difficult to alter, the above dimensions are recommended.

Table 5-3. Recommended Half-Court Dimensions for 3-Players-Per-Side Play.

AGE GROUP	DIMENSIONS	
Years	Width	Length
all ages	42 ft.	28 ft.

RULE III-THE PROPER BASKET HEIGHT

Regulation backboards are constructed of plate glass, fiberglass, steel, aluminum, wood, or any other material which is permanently flat and rigid. All backboards shall be white and unmarked except where transparent material is used, in which case a rectangle shall be centered around the basket. The backboard shall be either rectangular or fan-shaped (see Figure 5-4a).

A *regulation* goal consists of a net of white cord or other material suspended from a metal ring of 18 in. inside diameter. The ring is a bright orange color. The ring shall be parallel to the floor, rigidly attached to the backboards *10 ft.* above the floor.

Adjustable goals are presently being manufactured for use in youth play. Portable and stationary standards are available. They are designed for use in schools, recreational facilities, and home driveways. They adjust as desired from 6 ft. to 10 ft., power driven or manual. The ability to raise and lower the basket allows any age athlete to make use of the goal. Mini-goal adapter units provide an inexpensive way

Figure 5-3. Half-court 3-on-3 play.

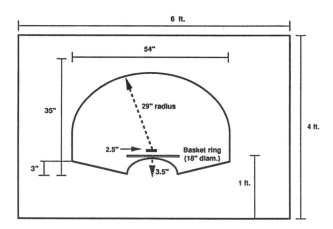

Figure 5-4a. The rectangular and the fan-shaped backboard.

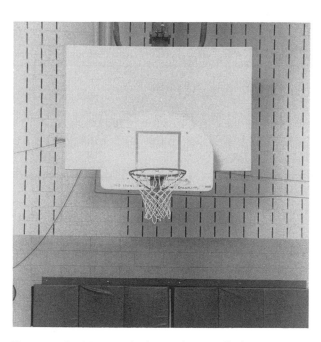

Figure 5-4b. Mini-goal adapter for youth play.

to convert an existing indoor basketball facility to a court suitable for young players (see Figure 5-4b). It attaches to any regulation size rim, converts rim height to 8-1/2 ft. and projects the rim 2 ft. closer to the foul line. Recommended basketball standards used for different age groups, with their corresponding basket heights, are presented in Table 5-4.

Practical Considerations

- Basketball goals (indoor and outdoor) must be safe for play.
- The rectangle on the backboard should be used to identify a point of aim for lay-ups and bank shots.

Table 5-4. Recommended Basket Heights for Youth Play.

AGE GROUP (Years)	BASKET HEIGHT (Feet)
below 6	6 or lower
6-8	8
7-12*	8½*
8-10	9
11 and above	10

*A mini-goal adapter unit attaches to any regulation size rim. It converts rim height to 8½ feet and projects the rim 2 feet closer to the foul line.

Modifications for Youth Play

- Basketball goals for younger players (ages six-11) should be lower than the regulation goal.
- Basketball goals used for youth play should be compatible with the physical characteristics of young athletes.
- Basketball goals that are too high may discourage younger players.
- Adjustable goals allow for experimentation and a higher rate of success by younger players.
- Shooting at a lower goal enables youth players to shoot with more confidence while using correct shooting form.

RULE IV-NUMBER OF PLAYERS/SUBSTITUTIONS

Regulation (full-sized) games are played by two teams of five players.

Teams

A team must have at least five players to start the game. If at any time, so many players are disqualified that the team has less than three players available, the game is defaulted to the opponents.

At least 10 minutes before the game is scheduled to start, the coach shall be responsible for supplying the scorers with the names and numbers of all players, in numerical order, and must designate the starting lineup. Any change in this lineup shall result in a technical foul except when the change is necessitated by obvious injury.

Substitutions

Substitutions may be made in accordance with the rules of competition under which the game is being played. During regulation play, if entry is at any time other than between quarters and halves, the timer shall sound a horn when the ball is dead. When the clock is stopped the substitute must give the scorer his/her number and the number of the player she is replacing. The substitute shall remain outside the court until he/she is beckoned by an official, whereupon he/she shall enter immediately and play shall resume promptly. Failure to do so shall result in a technical foul.

During intermissions the substitutions must be reported to the scorer but are not required to be recognized by an official. Unless a player has been disqualified, he/she may reenter any number of times.

In youth games, substitution is commonly permitted, for either team, at the start of any quarter, after a predetermined number of minutes are played, after a basket is scored, after a time-out, or before the ball is inbounded.

Practical Considerations

- The number of players on a team should allow the coach to give every player equal attention in practice and game situations. Avoid having a permanent "first" and "second" team.
- A substitution may be made only during certain stoppages of play in accordance with the rules of competition under which the game is being played.
- Making numerous substitutions helps youth players learn the skills and develop a thorough understanding of the game.
- A substitute may not enter the court until permitted by the official.
- Dividing youth games into four six minute quarters provides an additional stoppage of play to assist coaches in making substitutions.

Modifications for Youth Play

Small-sided games are recommended for players below the age of 11 years (see Table 5-5).

- Small-sided games provide a greater opportunity for involvement by each player.
- Small-sided games are not as complicated as full-sided games.
- It is easier to coach a team with a smaller number of players.
- Frequent substitutions are recommended for all youth players. This helps to ensure an equal amount of playing time for all participants, regardless of ability level.

RULE V-LENGTH OF THE GAME

The length of the basketball game varies among age groups.

For college and independent teams the game is divided into two 20-minute halves. A

Table 5-5. Recommended Number of Players Per Side and Court Dimensions.

AGE GROUP (Years)	NUMBER OF PLAYERS (per side)	——DIMENSIONS*——
Below 8	3	Elementary Gym
8-10	3-5	Elementary Gym
11 and above	5	Middle/High School Gym

*Determined by the local facilities which are available.

15-minute intermission between halves shall be provided.

For high-school-age teams the game is divided into four eight-minute quarters. A 10-minute intermission between halves shall be provided.

For teams younger than high school age or when the experience of the players is a factor or by state high school association adoption, *playing time may be reduced to four quarters of less than eight minutes each.* Each period ends when time expires, but a shot in flight when time expires, if successful, counts as a score even if made after the period ends. Both men and women in college basketball use a shot clock to avoid excessive stalling tactics. College men use a 45-second clock, while college women use a 30-second clock. A few state high school associations require their girls' teams to use the 30-second clock.

Tie Game

If the score is tied at the expiration of playing time, the game shall be continued for one or more extra periods. As many extra periods as necessary to break the tie game shall be played. Teams change baskets at the beginning of the first extra period but do not change again regardless of the number of extra periods which must be played. The game is terminated if either team is ahead at the end of any extra period.

In games played in halves, the length of each extra period shall be five minutes. In games played in quarters, the length of each extra period shall be three minutes.

Time Out

The following rules apply:

a. A player on the court may request a team time-out from an official when his/her team is in possession of the ball or when the ball is dead. This includes throw-ins and free throws.

b. The coach may request a team time-out from an official when his/her team has the ball or when the ball is dead.

c. A time-out cannot be called during a loose ball situation.

d. Players must remain on the court during an official's time-out.

e. Time-out shall be taken for:

- all fouls
- violations
- held ball situations
- team time-outs—not more than one minute at the request of any team—four time-outs without penalty for each team during regular playing time; one additional time-out for each extra period of a tie game.

Practical Considerations:

- In youth games ending in a tie, the overtime period may be eliminated. This allows both teams to experience the feeling of success and a game well-played.
- Team time-outs may be extended longer than one minute to allow for additional instruction.

Modifications for Youth Play

- The time period for a game should be modified for youth play (see Table 5-6).
- Youth players should be instructed of the rules which govern time-out procedures so that they gain necessary knowledge and application.
- Youth coaches should be permitted four *or more* time-outs throughout game play. This provides coaches with additional opportunities to make substitutions and provide instruction to players.

RULE VI-SCORING

A three point field goal scores 3 points, a field goal 2 points, and a free throw 1 point. The official scorer shall keep the record in the official score book. The running score kept in the score book shall constitute the official score of the game.

Table 5-6. Recommended Length of a Game.

AGE GROUP (Years)	DURATION (Total Minutes)	DIVISIONS	O.T. PERIOD (Minutes)
8-10	20-24	4 quarters/5-6 min. each	—
11-12	24	4 quarters/6 min. each	2 min.
13-14	32	4 quarters/8 min. each	3 min.
14-high school	32	4 quarters/8 min. each	3 min.
college level	40	2 halves/20 min. each	5 min.

Practical Considerations

- Coaches may want to consider eliminating the three point play for youth play.
- An official score need *not* be kept for youth games involving participants below the age of 11.
- In youth play, emphasis should be placed on enjoyment and learning the *skills* of the game, not on win-loss records.

The Free Throw

A free throw is an unguarded shot taken from a position behind the free throw line. A successful free throw counts one point.

Subsequent to a personal foul for which a free throw is awarded, the teams are entitled to line up at the free throw lanes within alternate lane spaces. The defensive team is entitled to both lane positions nearest the basket. A maximum of four players may line up on each side. They must have both feet within the lane space.

After the ball is placed at the disposal of the player at the free throw line, the following are considered violations:

1. failure to attempt the free throw within 10 seconds after the ball has been awarded at the free throw line
2. stepping on the free throw line
3. failure to cause the ball to touch the ring
4. entering a restricted area before the ball leaves the shooter's hand
5. any player entering or leaving a marked lane space after the ball is given to the shooter
6. any opponent disconcerting the player taking a free throw
7. intentionally faking a free throw to draw players into a restricted area

They result in a *PENALTY* if the violation is committed:

1. by an offensive player—the goal, if made, shall not count and whether made or missed, the ball shall be awarded to the opponents for a throw-in at the out-of-bounds spot nearest the violation
2. by a defensive player—the goal, if made, shall count, and the violation is disregarded. If the goal is missed, the free throw shall be repeated under the previous conditions
3. by players of both teams—the goal, if made, shall not count and the play shall be resumed by the team entitled to the alternating possession arrow at the out of bounds spot nearest to where the double violation occurred

The offended player is awarded free throws as follows:

1. *No free throws* for:

   a. a non-shooting personal foul before the bonus rule is in effect (except fouls which are flagrant or intentional)
   b. any offensive player control foul
   c. a double personal foul

2. *One free throw* for:

   a. a player fouled in the act of shooting whose try is successful

3. *Two free throws* for:

   a. each personal foul (except offensive) when in the bonus
   b. a player fouled in the act of shooting whose try is unsuccessful
   c. each intentional foul or flagrant personal foul and ball possession at the out-of-

bounds spot nearest the foul. If flagrant, the offender is disqualified.

   d. each technical foul on the coach or on the bench and ball possession

4. *Bonus free throw* for:

   a. each common foul (except player control) beginning with a team's fifth personal foul during the half, provided the first attempt is successful.

Modifications for Youth Play

- It is strongly advised to allow youth players to shoot from a line *closer* than the regulation 15 ft. free throw line, especially when a 10 ft. goal is being used for play. Modified free throw lines can be taped on the floor for easy identification or the bottom of the restraining circle may be used as the restraining line. The official rules apply for administering and attempting the modified free throw.
- Moving the free throw line closer to the goal or using a lower basket height greatly increases a youth player's success and understanding of the rules which govern play. Modified free throw lines commonly used for youth players are presented in Table 5-7.

Table 5-7. Free Throw Line Modifications.

AGE GROUP (Years)	FREE THROW LINE (Feet from Rim)	BASKET HEIGHT (Feet from Floor)
Below 7	9	6
8-9	11	8
10-11	13	9
12 and above	15	10

RULE VII-STARTING PLAY

The game shall be started with a jump ball in the center circle, between two opposing players. After the ball is put in play, play continues and the clock runs until a violation occurs, the ball goes out of bounds, a personal foul occurs, or a time-out is called. Whenever a field goal is scored, the ball is put into play by an opponent out of bounds at any point behind the endline where the goal was scored. The teams shall exchange goals to begin the second half. To start

the second, third, and fourth quarters, the ball is put in play by a throw-in under the alternating possession rule.

Possession Rule

In all jump ball situations, other than the start of the game and each extra period, the teams will alternate taking the ball out-of-bounds for a throw-in. To start the second, third, and fourth quarters, the ball is inbounded at the division line opposite the table.

The team that controls the jump ball at the beginning of the game, starts the alternating possession procedure. The possession arrow (located at the scorer's table) is set toward the opponent's basket. The direction of the possession arrow is reversed immediately after an alternating possession throw-in ends.

An alternating possession throw-in results when: a held ball occurs; a double free throw violation occurs; a live ball lodges on a basket support; the ball becomes dead when neither team is in control; a double personal or double technical foul occurs.

Practical Considerations

- Instruct players that during a jump ball situation, they must remain motionless while the referee steps into the center circle.
- Clearly explain the possession rule prior to game play.

RULE VIII-THE OFFICIALS

The officials have full responsibility for the game. They decide whether the ball is in play or dead. They blow the whistle when any of the following occurs: held ball, violation, foul, time-out or suspension of play for any reason. They have the power to order time-out or time-in and give players permission to leave or enter the court (see Figure 5-5).

Practical Considerations

- The official shall conduct the game in accordance with the rules.
- The official must be neutral.
- The official must be concerned for the safety of the players. The official shall not permit any player to wear jewelry.

Permission was granted from the National Federation of State High School Associations to reprint this information.

Figure 5-5. Official basketball signals.

- Fair play must be promoted so players, coaches, and spectators enjoy the game as much as possible.
- Communication with the official during play should be politely carried out by the team captains.
- Young players should be encouraged to acknowledge an official's call with "respect" by raising their hand after committing a foul.
- The coach is the key influence in the conduct of players and spectators toward officials. Any questioning of calls by officials should be done in an orderly manner or during a time-out.
- Good sportsmanship should be displayed by coaches, players, and spectators on and off the basketball court.

Modifications for Youth Play

In youth play, the official should avoid stopping play by repeatedly calling trivial fouls. Whenever possible, the official should inform youth players about the nature of the calls that are made. This is extremely helpful in teaching beginning players the rules of the game.

- Officials of youth play must know the rules of the game in order to project the knowledge to young or inexperienced basketball players.

RULE IX-FOULS

Although basketball is theoretically a non-contact sport, it is obvious that personal contact cannot be entirely avoided when players are moving rapidly over a limited space. Personal contact which does not hinder the opponent from participating in normal offensive or defensive movement should be considered incidental and not a foul. Contact in which pressure is applied shall be considered inhibiting and a foul should be called.

A *foul* is an infraction of the rules which is charged and penalized. *Types* of fouls include: personal, double, flagrant, intentional, multiple, offensive (player-control), and technical. These fouls are defined as follows:

- A *personal* foul results when contact is made with an opponent while the ball is alive.
- A *double* foul is a situation in which two op-

ponents commit personal fouls against each other at approximately the same time.
- A *multiple* foul is a situation in which teammates commit a personal foul against the same opponent at approximately the same time.
- A *flagrant* foul involves an act of violent nature, or excessive unethical behavior. A flagrant foul is always a disqualifying foul. It may or may not be intentional.
- A *technical* foul is a non-contact foul committed by a player, coach, non-player, or a contact foul committed by a player while the ball is dead. A technical foul is awarded for situations such as delaying the game, unsportsmanlike conduct, making illegal substitutions, and using excessive time-outs.
- An *intentional* foul is a personal or technical foul which, in the judgment of the official, appears to be designed or premeditated. Judgment is not based on the severity of the act.
- A *player control* foul is a common foul committed by a player while he or she is in control of the ball, or by an airborne shooter.

Youth players need to understand what actions constitute a *personal foul*. Coaches need to explain that a personal foul is charged to the player who causes bodily contact whether on offense or defense.

A *personal foul* is called if:

1. a player *holds, blocks, pushes, charges, hacks,* or *trips* an opponent
2. a player screens and is not stationary and does not take a position at least a normal step away from an opponent (see Figure 5-6).

Coaches can help inexperienced players learn the rules of basketball by explaining the nature of the calls made during practice, scrimmages, and game play. Youth coaches should demonstrate the six personal fouls and encourage their players to avoid committing them carelessly.

Players also need to understand the *penalty* for committing a personal foul. One or more free throws are awarded depending upon whether the player was shooting when the foul was committed and how many fouls the player's team has committed in the half.

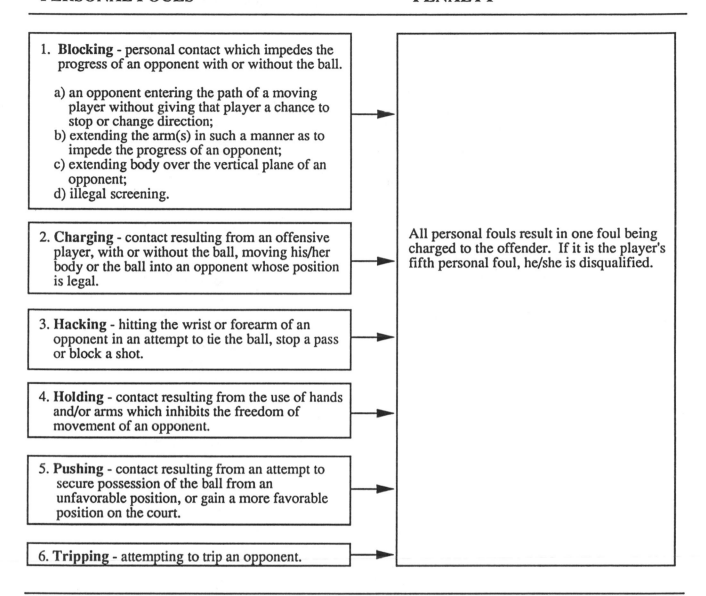

PERSONAL FOULS	PENALTY
1. **Blocking** - personal contact which impedes the progress of an opponent with or without the ball. a) an opponent entering the path of a moving player without giving that player a chance to stop or change direction; b) extending the arm(s) in such a manner as to impede the progress of an opponent; c) extending body over the vertical plane of an opponent; d) illegal screening.	All personal fouls result in one foul being charged to the offender. If it is the player's fifth personal foul, he/she is disqualified.
2. **Charging** - contact resulting from an offensive player, with or without the ball, moving his/her body or the ball into an opponent whose position is legal.	
3. **Hacking** - hitting the wrist or forearm of an opponent in an attempt to tie the ball, stop a pass or block a shot.	
4. **Holding** - contact resulting from the use of hands and/or arms which inhibits the freedom of movement of an opponent.	
5. **Pushing** - contact resulting from an attempt to secure possession of the ball from an unfavorable position, or gain a more favorable position on the court.	
6. **Tripping** - attempting to trip an opponent.	

Figure 5-6. Flow chart of personal fouls.

If a player was fouled in the act of shooting, *two* free throws are awarded unless the try was successful, in which case only *one* free throw is awarded. If a player is fouled while *not* in the act of shooting, no free throws are awarded except under the following circumstances:

- In junior and senior high games—the foul is the opponent's *fifth team foul* during the half, in which case the player is awarded one shot plus a *bonus* if the first shot is successful

- A player is disqualified after committing five personal fouls in a high school game

Practical Considerations

- The rule on fouls is designed to prevent roughness in the game and to encourage good, open playing.
- Basketball is a game that should be won through the use of skill. Rules provide a framework for penalizing unacceptable ac-

tions and behaviors that detract from the skill of playing the game.

- For more serious fouls, such as flagrant and technical, there should be more severe penalties.

Modifications for Youth Play

- Personal fouls, committed by young players, are often the result of not knowing the rules of play, carelessness or lack of appropriate skill.
- Coaches and officials of youth play can help beginners learn the rules of basketball by explaining the nature of the calls made during practices, scrimmages, and game play.

RULE X-RULES OF PLAY

Youth players should be taught the rules governing the sport as they relate to the *skills* of basketball and *modified* game play. Most often, the game of basketball played in youth leagues is similar to the official game played in junior and senior high schools. These rules should be modified to meet the needs of younger children. The following basic rules apply to the game for children ages 10 and older.

Introduce basic basketball rules (i.e. double dribble, traveling) as an early instructional focus and *apply* these rules later during a player's development. Rules should be taught concurrently as skills and strategies are learned. Players can become familiar with traveling violations as they are learning to start, stop, change direction, and receive passes. Once the key elements of the skill are learned, both form and function are developed as rules of play are applied and reinforced.

For example, dribbling violations are introduced to beginning players as they practice execution of the non-stationary dribble. Lecture, discussion, and demonstration of rules demand immediate application. This is best achieved in a controlled "drill" or lead-up game.

Caution should be used, however, not to combine "form and function" until the player has mastered *all* the key elements of form correctly. A common error is to permit beginning basketball players to play full-court basketball before they have demonstrated the proper

knowledge and skills necessary to successfully participate (see Table 5-5).

Prior to game play, coaches must introduce and demonstrate the following violations as they relate to the skills of basketball (see Figure 5-7).

Many young players do not fully understand the *three-second rule*. Extra instructional time should be allotted to instruct players about this rule during preseason practice. Explain that if an offensive player receives the ball within 3 seconds, he/she has three *additional* seconds to shoot or get out of the lane, because the ball in the air on a try for a goal is no longer in possession of his/her team. However, stepping off the court to avoid a three-second violation is illegal. Also, point out that the three-second count is in effect regardless of the position of the ball on the court. The three-second count terminates at the end of the third second. Encourage youth players to move in and out of the lane and avoid "camping" in the lane. Help your players gain an understanding of the three-second violation to avoid further confusion of this rule.

Practical Considerations

- Introduce basic rules as an early instructional focus; apply these rules later on during a player's development.
- Discussion and demonstration of rules demand immediate application, prior to game play.

Modifications for Youth Play

- Youth players should be taught the rules of basketball as they relate to skills and modified game play.
- Coaches of youth players must know the violations and penalties of the game in order to project this knowledge to their players.

TEACHING BEGINNERS THE GAME OF BASKETBALL

Teaching beginners the game of basketball is a challenging, demanding, yet rewarding task. Basketball is difficult to teach (and learn) because the ball moves almost constantly, and the players must adjust not only to the moves of their teammates, but also to those of their op-

VIOLATION	PENALTY

1. **Double Dribble** - occurs when a player continues dribbling after grasping the ball with both hands.

2. **Traveling** - (also referred to as steps or walking) occurs when an offensive player takes more than one step with the ball without passing, dribbling, or shooting.

3. **Palming** the ball - permitting the ball to come to rest in one hand while dribbling.

4. **Kicking** the ball - intentionally with foot or lower leg.

5. **Stepping out of bounds** - touching the 2" boundary line with any part of the body while in possession of the ball.

6. **Causing the ball to go out-of-bounds**

The ball is awarded to the opponent out-of-bounds at the nearest spot where the violation occurred.

7. Violating provisions governing the **throw-in**. The thrower shall not:
   a) Leave the designated throw-in spot;
   b) Fail to pass the ball directly into the court so it touches or is touched by another player (inbounds or out-of-bounds) on the court before going out-of-bounds;
   c) Consume 5 seconds from the time the throw-in starts until the ball is released on a pass directly into the court;
   d) Carry the ball onto the court;
   e) Throw the ball so that it enters the basket before it touches, or is touched by, another player.
   f) Replace the thrower or be out-of-bounds after a designated spot throw-in begins.
   g) Be out-of-bounds when he or she touches, or is touched by, another player.
   h) The opponent(s) of the thrower shall not have any part of his or her person over the inside plane of the boundary line until the ball has been released on a throw-in pass.

The ball is awarded to the opponent for a throw-in at the out-of-bounds spot nearest the violation.

8. Violating any provision of the jump ball.

If both teams simultaneously commit violations during the jump ball, or if the official makes a bad toss, the toss shall be repeated.

Figure 5-7. Flow chart of violations.

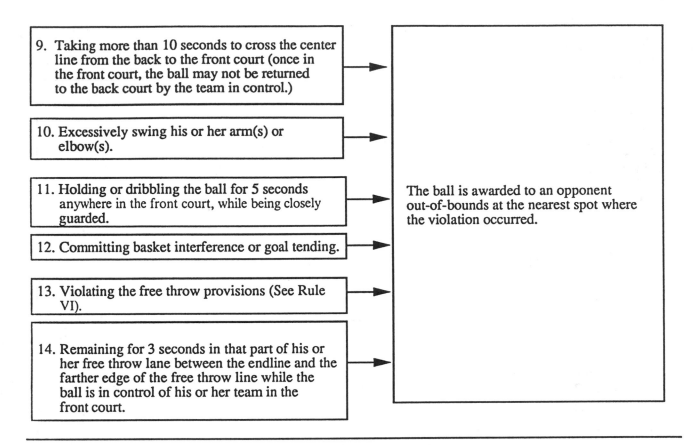

9. Taking more than 10 seconds to cross the center line from the back to the front court (once in the front court, the ball may not be returned to the back court by the team in control.)

10. Excessively swing his or her arm(s) or elbow(s).

11. Holding or dribbling the ball for 5 seconds anywhere in the front court, while being closely guarded.

12. Committing basket interference or goal tending.

13. Violating the free throw provisions (See Rule VI).

14. Remaining for 3 seconds in that part of his or her free throw lane between the endline and the farther edge of the free throw line while the ball is in control of his or her team in the front court.

The ball is awarded to an opponent out-of-bounds at the nearest spot where the violation occurred.

Figure 5-7. (continued)

ponents. This means that players must make continual adjustments from offense to defense and defense to offense. Players must acquire an *understanding* of the ways in which individual skills are performed and how to *execute* them properly. All of this takes time, practice, and patience!

Problems of Beginners

Beginning players who are in the early stages of learning the game of basketball exhibit certain incompetencies regardless of their ages or grade levels.

1. *No organization for play.* Players are grouped near the ball or under the basket. When the opponents obtain possession of the ball, a long pass down court usually results in a goal.

2. *Players on offense stand* (because they do not know where to move or when to move), often very close together, which cuts off the passing lanes. Standing, rather than moving without the ball, creates a lack of floor balance and allows the defense to overplay the ball and their player.

3. *Ineffective dribbling or frequent dribbling,* often while standing still without improving their offensive position. Beginners often bounce the ball without a purpose each time it is received. "Dead dribbling" is the most difficult habit to overcome later on and one that should never be developed.

4. *Frequent traveling or double dribbling* violations as the speed of the dribble is increased.

5. *Poor passing and shooting,* usually the result of not pivoting and "squaring up" to the basket into a *triple threat position.* Predetermined passes may be made automatically regardless of whether the teammate is closely guarded. Passes are made to players standing still, with a resultant interception by an alert defensive player.

6. *Players have little confidence* in their ability to score. Often, they lack the proper footwork

or cutting techniques to free themselves from an overplaying defensive player.

7. *Frequently off balance* upon receiving a pass from a teammate, or they have not provided a necessary target as a receiver. The resultant shot is inaccurate because the ball is released from a very low height (waist level).

8. *Defensive players maintain poor position.* Their weight is too high or too far forward. They generally fail to see both "ball and man" and concern themselves primarily with their offensive player. Therefore, when "one" offensive player beats his/her defensive player, he/she is usually free to dribble toward the basket.

9. *Defensive players often guard too closely* and make every effort to "steal" the ball. This generally brings their weight on their toes which results in a foul or leaves the opponent free to drive or cut toward the basket.

10. *One or two more skilled or knowledgeable players dominate game play.* The other players on the "team" seldom come in contact with the ball or have an opportunity to experience success.

The ten problems listed above are common to beginning basketball players. These errors must be curtailed, if not eliminated, as rapidly as possible. This requires careful planning and critical analysis of individual skills throughout the learning process. The coach must understand and recognize correct performance (key elements) so that he/she may lead each player through a natural progression. Considerable attention should be devoted to drills of a game-like nature in order that skills and elementary tactics are *overlearned* and may be applied in modified play.

Coaching Hints

Various aids and techniques may be used for beginning players to help them acquire skill more quickly, or to help them with their understanding of basketball.

1. Use smaller balls for youth players (see Rule I).

2. Decrease the size of the playing court (see Rule II).

3. Modify free throw line distances and/or basket heights for youth players (Rule III).

4. Decrease the number of players involved in small-sided play. Half-court 3 on 3 basketball is recommended for all ages (see Rule IV).

5. Decrease the length of the youth basketball game. Dividing games into four six-minute quarters provides an additional stoppage of play to assist coaches in making substitutions (see Rule V).

6. Introduce basic rules (violations) as an early instructional focus. Apply these rules later when the player's development is compatible with the requirements of the rules (see Rule VI).

7. Teach youth players the rules of basketball as they relate to skills and modified play (see Rule X).

8. During practices and scrimmages, inform youth players about the nature of the calls that are made. This is extremely helpful in teaching beginners the rules of the game. Limit the number of fouls and violations that are called (see Rules VIII and IX).

9. Teach a very basic offensive pattern to create floor balance. The pattern gives players specific directions and responsibilities. It helps them to know where and when to cut so that all players do not end up in the same place at the same time. A pattern also encourages the use of all players in the ball movement.

10. Introduce team tactics in small groups. Practice with two offensive players against two defensive players; progress slowly to the regulation five player team.

11. Practice offensive patterns *without* a ball first, then progress to passive and active defense.

12. Teach player-to-player defense prior to zone defense. The basis for all guarding must be player-to-player defense. Beginners should be given the opportunity to become proficient in its use so they may also become skillful zone defenders.

13. Do not allow the defensive team to apply a full or half-court press until the players

have developed adequate dribbling and passing skills. As soon as the ball changes hands, youth players are instructed to sprint back to their opponent's basket.

14. Instruct your guards to avoid picking up their dribble at half-court or using a "dead dribble."

15. Place markings on the backboard to identify a point of aim for lay-ups and other bank shots if glass backboards are not available.

16. Place tape on the floor to show the angle of a cut from a specific position or a designated pattern.

17. Targets on the wall can be utilized to help players develop accuracy in shooting and passing techniques.

18. If players tend to be very slow in offensive passing, instruct them to "pass on the whistle" or imagine the basketball is "hot."

19. Use of films and instructional videos can be valuable in demonstrating various skills or offensive and defensive strategies. Video tape is an excellent tool for reviewing skills or game action so that players can become aware of their strengths and weaknesses. Observing high school, college, and professional games can also be a learning experience, particularly if they demonstrate the skill techniques that your team must acquire or perfect.

Goals

When practicing individual skills, it's desirable to establish *goals* toward which your players may work. For example, in shooting lay-ups, the goal for beginning players might be three successful stationary shots out of 10; for intermediate players, five out of 10 non-stationary shots; and for advanced players, seven out of 10 lay-ups preceded by a dribble. These goals may be adjusted upward or downward, depending upon the players' abilities, so that their skill development continues to be motivating.

Players should recognize the progress they have made throughout the season. This may be done by means of progression charts, station task cards, or recording of statistics (see Figure 5-8; Figure 5-9a-b; and Chapter 20, Supplement 20-3, Tables 20-12s and 20-13s). Players should also be aware of areas in which they have weaknesses so they may be motivated to improve them. Attainment of goals for youth players can become as important a reward as winning when coaches stress the positive aspects of both.

SKILL EVALUATION CHART

(+ = good; √ = satisfactory; 0 = needs much work)

NAMES

SKILLS OBSERVED	John	Michelle								
example: Dribbling - right hand	+	√								

Figure 5-8. Skill progression chart.

Shooting Statistics Chart

12 - missed
⑫ - made

_____   _____
OPPONENT   (DATE)

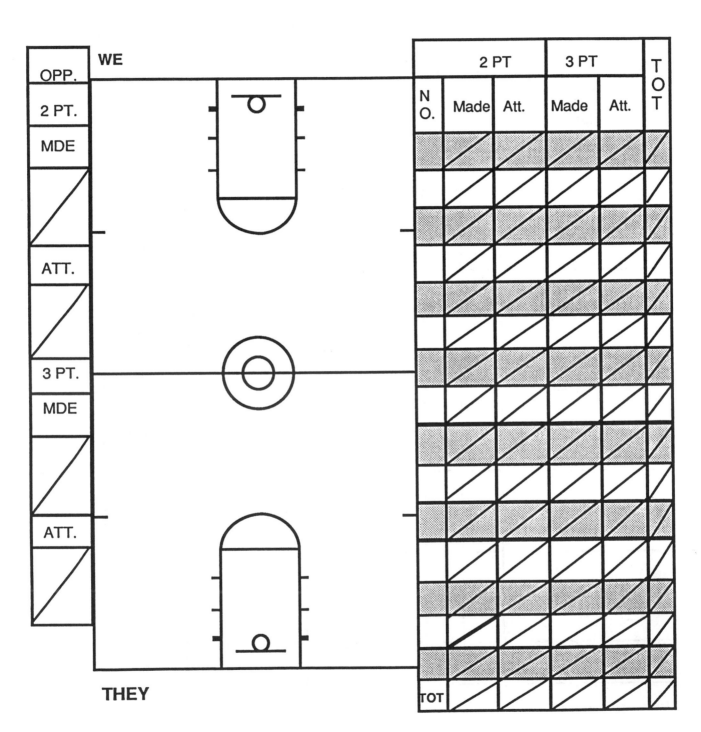

Figure 5-9a. Shooting statistics chart.

Rebounding Statistics Form

Name	First Half		Second Half		Totals
	1st	2nd	3rd	4th	
Lyndsey					
Lauren					
Etc.					
Totals					
	1st	2nd	3rd	4th	Totals
Opponent					

Figure 5-9b. Rebounding statistics form.

6
Glossary of Basketball Terms

Amy L. Dickinson, M.S.

INTRODUCTION

This glossary contains a listing of terms and definitions that are common to the game of basketball. It is intended to familiarize coaches, players, and parents with the vocabulary that is used in relation to youth basketball so that they may gain a greater understanding of the game and may communicate better with others about basketball. The terms are listed alphabetically and are often accompanied by common variations of the defined term when appropriate.

Airball   A shot attempt that does not make contact with the basket or backboard.

Assist   A pass that immediately precedes and sets up a scored basket.

Backboard   A rectangular (6 ft. wide x 4 ft. high) or fan-shaped (54 in. wide x 35 in. high) board behind the basket that can be used to bank shots into the goal.

Backcourt   The half of the court (divided by the center line) that is opposite a team's offensive basket; the court a team is attempting to defend.

Backdoor cut   A cut made behind the defender and to the basket when the defense is overplaying.

Ball side   The side of the court in which a player has possession of the ball.

Bank shot   A shot in which the backboard is used for a target so that the ball strikes the backboard before continuing its flight to the basket.

Baseball pass   A pass that is thrown using an overhand throwing motion similar to that used in throwing a baseball or softball.

Baseline   The boundary line located behind each basket that marks the end of the court.

Block   Usually called "the block"; the area just outside of the key and around the first position line (many times a 1 ft. "block") on each side of the key (see Figure 6-1). This term is often used in positioning post play-

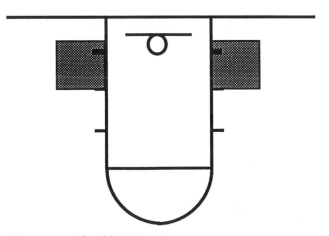

Figure 6-1. The "block" areas.

74

ers and to indicate specific areas in offenses and defenses.

Blocked shot A deflection of a shot by an opponent as the ball is on an upward trajectory. Contact of the ball on its downward trajectory is illegal (see "Goal tending").

Blocking out See "Boxing out."

Bonus free throw See "One-and-one."

Bounce pass A pass that strikes the floor before it reaches the receiver.

Box-and-one A combination defense in which four players play a zone defense in a "box" formation and one player plays a man-to-man, usually on the opponent's top player.

Boxing out Also called "blocking out" or "screening out"; a technique used to gain position between the basket and an opponent in order to rebound the ball.

Carrying the ball Also called "palming"; a violation committed by a dribbler that involves placing the dribbling hand under the ball and momentarily holding or carrying it while dribbling.

Center Also called the "pivot player"; an offensive position typically played by a tall player on a team who will play primarily in the key areas (at the post). Players at this position need to be strong and able to jump well, as well as possessing sound skills in rebounding, inside shooting, and receiving the ball.

Change-of-pace An offensive technique in which speed is reduced and then quickly increased in order to evade or leave a defender. It may be used while dribbling or on a cut.

Charging A personal foul committed when an offensive player illegally contacts a defensive player who has established position or is stationary.

Chest pass A two-handed pass thrown from the passer's chest in a straight line to the chest area of the receiver.

Controlling the boards Securing a majority of the rebounds.

Conversion A made basket or free throw.

Crashing the boards Going aggressively for the rebounds.

Crossover dribble A dribble in which the ball is moved from one hand to the other while the dribbler changes directions (see Chapter 8).

Cut A quick movement by an offensive player to elude an opponent or to receive the ball.

"D" Shortened term for "defense."

Dead ball Occurs whenever the whistle blows to stop play and after a field goal, but before the opponent gains possession of the ball.

Defense The team that is not in possession of the ball whose objective is to keep the opponent from scoring; also, a specific pattern of play used by a defending team.

Defensive rebound A rebound of a shot attempted by the opponent.

Deny defense A player-to-player defensive technique in which a defender plays close to the offense and keeps an arm and leg in the passing lane in order to keep the player from receiving the ball.

Double dribble A dribbling violation that occurs when a player dribbles the ball with two hands simultaneously or stops a dribble and then dribbles again.

Double team A defensive tactic in which two defenders temporarily guard the player with the ball.

Dribble Process by which a player bounces the ball off the floor so that it returns to his/her possession. It is the only legal means by which a player in possession of the ball may progress across any distance of the playing court.

Drive A quick dribble directly to the basket in an effort to score.

Dunk shot Also, "dunking" or "slam dunk"; a shot in which the hand is above the rim and forcefully drives the ball straight down through the basket.

Elbow Also called the "junction"; a term often used to indicate the area of the court where the free throw line and side of the key meet (see Figure 6-2).

Fake A movement used to draw a defender out of position.

Fastbreak An offensive situation or strategy in which a team attempts to move the ball upcourt and into scoring position as quickly as possible so that the defense is outnumbered and does not have time to set up.

Field goal A basket scored on any shot other than a free throw, worth two or three points depending on the distance of the

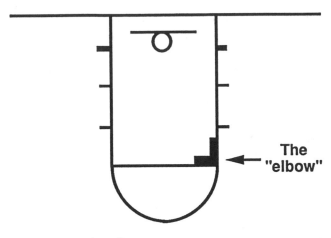

Figure 6-2. The "elbow."

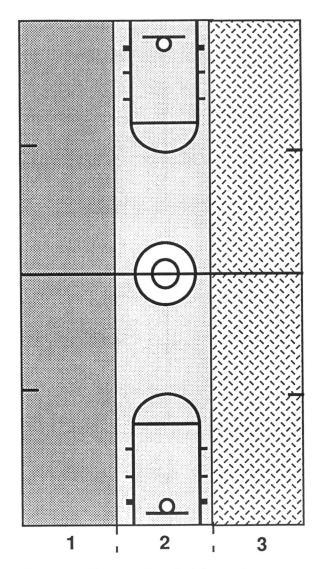

attempt from the basket (see "Three-point field goal" for qualification).

Filling-the-lanes   A segment of the fastbreak in which the offensive players cut into the three hypothetical lanes of the court: right, center, and left (see Figure 6-3).

Flagrant foul   A foul of a violent nature or of excessive unethical behavior. It may or may not be intentional, but is always a disqualifying foul.

Floor balance   Positioning of offensive players so that the key areas of the court are occupied and there is a balance of players on the right, left, and middle area of the court.

Forward   An offensive position played to the sides of the basket near the key area and out toward the sideline along the baseline. Players at this position play both on the perimeter (like a guard) and inside (like a center) and therefore need to have sound ball handling, shooting, and rebounding skills.

Foul   A violation resulting from illegal contact with an opposing player.

Foul line   See "Free throw line."

Free throw   An unguarded shot taken from behind the free throw line which is awarded following a foul committed by an opponent and, if successful, counts for one point.

Free throw lane   Also called the "key" or "lane"; the area extending from the baseline to the free throw line and is 12 ft. wide. Players are excluded from this area during a free throw attempt.

Figure 6-3. The three "lanes" of the court.

Free throw line   A line of 12 ft. in length that is parallel to and 15 feet from the backboard.

Front court   The half of the court (divided by the center line) that contains the offensive team's basket; the offensive half of the court.

Fronting the post   A defensive technique where the defender gets position between a post player and the opponent with the ball in an effort to prevent a pass to the post player.

Full-court press   A defensive tactic in which a team guards the opponents closely over the full length of the court. It may utilize both player-to-player and zone principles.

Give and go   An offensive play in which a player

passes to a teammate and immediately cuts to the basket for a return pass.

Goal tending The act of touching the ball or the basket while the ball is within, on, or above the basket or on the downward trajectory to the basket. The shot is counted if this violation occurs.

Guard An offensive position played primarily at the perimeter, or away from the basket. Players at this position need to possess sound dribbling, passing, shooting, and play-making skills. Guards typically are the primary ball handlers on a team.

Held ball Often called a "jump ball" prior to the addition of the Possession Rule; a situation in which two players of opposite teams are in joint control of the ball and neither can gain sole possession, or when a blocked shot results in temporary suspension of the ball between the hands of the shooter and opponent.

Helpside defense A situation in which a defensive player who is away from the ball assists a teammate who has been out-maneuvered in guarding the opponent.

High post An offensive position near the free throw line.

Intentional foul A personal foul which the official judges to have been premeditated.

In the paint In the "key" area, so named because this area of the floor is painted.

Jab-step A type of fake that is performed by moving the non-pivot foot with a quick "jabbing" motion six to eight inches ahead.

Jump ball The procedure for starting play at the beginning of a game or an overtime period. The official tosses the ball into the air between the two opponents positioned at the center-court circle; the two players attempt to jump up and tap the ball to a teammate.

Jump shot A shot that is released after the shooter has jumped into the air.

Jump stop A technique used to stop quickly and on balance by landing with both feet on the floor at the same time and assuming the triple-threat position.

Key Also called the "free throw lane" or "lane"; the area measuring 12 ft. in width and extending from the free throw line to the endline.

Lay-up shot A shot taken close to the basket that is usually banked off the backboard.

Lead pass A pass thrown ahead of an intended receiver who is moving.

Low post An offensive position played in the "block" area near the basket (see Figure 6-1).

Man-to-man defense See "Player-to-player defense."

Offense The team that has possession of the basketball. Also, a structured pattern of play that a team uses in the attempt to score.

Offensive rebound A rebound of a shot attempted by oneself or a teammate.

One-and-one The "bonus" free throw situation which is awarded for non-shooting fouls after the opposing team exceeds a certain number of team fouls in a half. The shooter is awarded one free throw, and if it is successful a second is awarded.

Outlet pass The first pass made following a defensive rebound. This pass typically will start the fast break.

Over-and-back violation A violation that occurs when the offensive team returns the ball into the backcourt once its position has been established in the front court.

Overhead pass A two-handed pass thrown from above the forehead.

Overtime An extra period that is played in order to break a tie score at the end of a regulation game.

Palming See "Carrying the ball."

Pass Intentionally throwing the ball to a teammate.

Passing lane The imaginary path that a ball will travel which lies in a direct line from the passer to the receiver.

Peripheral vision The ability to see to the sides (the wide angle) while looking ahead.

Pick An offensive technique whereby a player legally blocks the path of a defender in order to "free" a teammate.

Pick and roll An offensive maneuver in which a player sets a screen for a teammate with the ball and then pivots or "rolls" to receive a pass.

Pivot Footwork technique where a player keeps one foot in contact with a "spot" on the floor while moving the other foot in order to adjust the position of the body or to evade a defensive player.

Player-to-player defense Also, "man-to man defense"; a team defense in which each player is assigned to guard a particular opponent.

Player control foul A common foul committed by a player who is in control of the ball, or a foul made by an airborne shooter.

Point guard An offensive position played by a guard whose responsibility it is to initiate the offense and usually to bring the ball up the court; the "quarterback" of the team.

Possession arrow A device located at the scorer's table which is used to indicate the direction of a team's basket for the alternating possession rule.

Post An offensive position played close to the basket along the key.

Posting up An offensive maneuver whereby a player establishes position in the "block" area in order to receive a pass.

Press An aggressive defense which attempts to force the opponents to make errors by guarding the opponents closely from either half-court, three-quarter court, or full-court. The "press" use player-to-player and/or zone defensive tactics.

Power lay-up A lay-up which is taken from a two-foot take-off using a strong upward movement to the basket.

Rebound The act of gaining possession of the ball following a missed shot.

Screen See "Pick."

Screen and roll See "Pick and roll."

Scrimmage An unofficial game between two teams, or five-on-five play between team members in a practice situation.

Second shot A shot attempt which follows an offensive rebound.

Set shot A shot taken from a stationary position with both feet maintaining contact with the floor.

Skip pass An overhead pass thrown to a player who is two or more players away, often across the key.

Speed dribble A high dribble in which the ball is pushed out in front of the running dribbler in order to advance the ball down the court quickly.

Squaring-up Positioning the body so that the feet and shoulders are facing the basket (or other target).

Stall A strategy in which the offense attempts to maintain possession of the ball but makes little effort to score.

Strongside The side of the court on which the majority of offensive players are positioned.

Technical foul A foul that does not involve contact with an opponent; involves unsportsmanlike conduct by a player, coach, or nonplayer; or a contact foul committed by a player while the ball is dead.

Telegraphing a pass Letting the defense know of the intention to pass to a particular player/area by looking directly at the target.

Ten-second line The mid-court line over which the offensive team must advance the ball from the backcourt within ten seconds to avoid a violation.

Ten-second violation A violation that occurs when the offensive team uses more than 10 seconds to cross the half-court line from backcourt to front court.

Three-point field goal A made basket from a distance greater than 19 ft. 9 in. during a high school or college game.

Three on two A common fastbreak situation in which three offensive players attempt to score on two defenders.

Three seconds A violation in which an offensive player remains within the key (free throw lane) for more than three seconds at a time.

Trailer An offensive player who follows the initial fastbreak down court and takes a position near the "elbow" to receive a pass.

Transition The movement of players from offense to defense and defense to offense.

Trap A defensive tactic in which two defenders double-team an opponent who has the ball but cannot dribble, usually near the sideline or half-court line.

Traveling A violation occurring when a player with the ball takes a step without dribbling (moving the established pivot foot).

Triple-threat position Possessing the ball in a balanced, ready position so that one can shoot, pass, or dribble (drive).

Turnover A loss of possession of the ball by means of an error or violation.

Violation   An infringement of the rules that is not a foul. The penalty for a violation is the awarding of the ball to the opponent.

Warm-up   A series of stretches and drills done prior to a contest or practice in order to physically prepare the players for the activity.

Weakside   The side of the court away from the ball or on which a minority of offensive players are positioned.

Wing area   The area of the court outside of the key to the sideline; and below the free throw line and high of the block.

Zone defense   A team defense in which each player is responsible for defending an area of the court and the opponents within that area.

Zone offense   An offensive pattern of play designed to attack (score against) a particular zone defense.

Section III
Individual Basketball Techniques

7
Footwork Fundamentals

Karen Garchow, M.A.

QUESTIONS TO CONSIDER

- What footwork fundamentals are essential in basketball?
- What are the key elements and common errors of each skill?
- What progression is recommended for teaching footwork skills to youth players?
- What drills are effective in teaching footwork skills?

INTRODUCTION

Basketball is a game characterized by movement. Mobility is the essence of the game and team success is dependent upon the ability of the players to move effectively and rapidly.

To execute the fundamental motor skills involved in basketball, a player must begin with good foot positioning. How and where the feet are positioned has a great effect on how the rest of the body moves, and, therefore, on the quality of performance.

The footwork skills presented herein include: the *basketball position*, the *quick start*, the *jump stop*, the *stride stop*, the *forward and reverse pivot*, and the *defensive slide*.

For a summary of the footwork skills and drills that are appropriate for each level of play (beginning, intermediate, and advanced), see Supplements 7-1 and 7-2.

BASKETBALL POSITION

The basketball position is one of the most important fundamentals of the game. It refers to the "stance" that a player's body must maintain while on offense and defense. In this position, the body is low, the knees are flexed, the feet are shoulder-width apart, the hands are raised at chest level and close to the body, and the arms are slightly bent and at the sides.

The key to proper body position is *balance*. If players have established good basketball position, they are ready to receive the ball on offense or make a quick transition to defense.

Head Position

Coaches must stress the importance of proper head position. To be properly balanced, have your players imagine that a straight line runs through the middle of their head and body to a spot on the floor exactly between their feet. Their head must be in a position in the middle of this invisible line at all times. The chin is up so that players can see the whole court.

Arm Position

The arms should be slightly flexed and held close to the sides. The wrists and elbows are flexed and the fingers spread. The hands should be open with the palms facing forward.

Leg Position

The legs should always be flexed at the knees in a semi-crouched position. This helps a player's muscles to be "loaded" and ready to react to any situation.

Foot Placement

The feet should be kept at a shoulder-width distance. The non-pivot foot should be slightly in front of the other, and the toes of the pivot foot in line with the heel of the lead foot. Body weight is evenly distributed on both feet with most of the weight on the balls of the feet.

Key Elements: (see Figure 7-1)

1. Maintain a staggered stance with feet shoulder width apart and in a heel to toe relationship from front to back.
2. Distribute body weight evenly on both feet with most of the weight on the balls of the feet.
3. Carry head in the middle of the base of support.
4. Hold arms slightly bent at the sides of the body.
5. Raise hands at chest level with fingers spread.

Common Errors:

1. Positioning feet closer than or wider than shoulder width apart, side by side, flat on the floor with weight on the heels.
2. Distributing body weight over the hips with the upper body leaning forward.
3. Carrying head off to one side.
4. Keeping knees fully extended.
5. Positioning hands on hips or down at sides.
6. Extending arms in front of or at the sides of the body.

QUICK STARTS

Quickness is an important physical attribute used in the game of basketball and can be developed through practice. Young players can

Figure 7-1. Basketball position.

improve their quickness by maintaining their basketball position and by diligently working on their starts and stops.

Throughout the game, players must keep their legs flexed, arms in, hands at chest level, and body weight on the balls of their feet. Most importantly, they must be alert, ready to react, and to move quickly.

When making a movement to the right, players should start by turning their hips, trunk, and head in that direction while at the same time shifting their weight over the right foot. As they move, make sure that the forward foot is pointing in the direction of movement. If, instead, the foot points sideways, they will not be able to generate enough power to push off explosively in the new direction.

It is extremely important for a player making a quick move to stay low and pump the arms to develop a powerful drive. Initial steps should be kept short and fast. Contrary to the belief of many young players, quickness is not enhanced by taking long steps. Coaches should stress that moving the feet rapidly is much more important than how much distance they can cover with each stride. As a player learns to start quickly, the feet should strike the floor with enough lateral spread to maintain adequate body balance for possible changes in direction. (See Sprint-Jog-Sprint and Diagonal Run Drill.)

Key elements: (see Figure 7-2a-c)

1. Maintain the basketball position.
2. Turn the head, trunk, hips, and forward foot in the direction of travel.
3. Push off with the planted (rear) foot.
4. Pump arms forward and back in opposition to leg action.
5. Make the first steps short and fast.

Common errors:

1. Keeping knees extended.
2. Opposing direction of travel with hips, trunk, or head.
3. Keeping upper arms motionless.

4. Steps pointing in a direction other than forward.
5. Prolonging the first step.

STOPS

In basketball, a player's ability to come to a quick stop and still be in good basketball position is as important as getting a quick start. Players must be ready to play offense or defense at all times.

There are many instances in the course of a game when a player receives the ball on the run or speed dribbles up the court on a fast-break. Being able to stop immediately in these situations, pivot, take a shot, or make a cut while maintaining good balance, makes a player an effective offensive threat.

A frequent error of beginners is to stop in an off-balanced position. This may result in a traveling violation or may force the player to take the time to set up again, allowing the defensive player to regain the advantage.

Have your players practice jump stops (see description in the next section) *without* a ball so they learn proper body balance and position. Begin with a walking approach, then progress to moderate and full speed stops. Once body

| (a) | (b) | (c) |

Figure 7-2. Quick start.

control is properly executed, add the dribble, gradually increasing the ballhandler's speed while performing stops at ¼ court, ½ court, ¾ court and full court distances. Stress holding each stop for at least a count of three seconds before continuing the dribble.

Beginning players should be taught the jump stop and the stride stop prior to other instruction involving footwork. These stops must be practiced often and should become instinctive and part of each player's basketball repertoire (see "Footwork Drills").

Jump Stop

The quick stop, or *jump stop,* is made off a run by landing with both feet on the floor at the same time.

The jump or quick stop is normally associated with a dribble and is started by modifying the final running stride to a close-to-the-floor hop in which both feet touch down simultaneously (see Figure 7-3a-d). Although some players jump into a foot planting stop, a sliding technique is more effective in controlling balance and is a much more difficult action for a defensive player to anticipate.

The quick stop is properly executed as a sliding motion on the balls of both feet at the conclusion of the close-to-the-floor hop. Prior to the feet touching the floor in a parallel stance, the body weight is lowered by shifting the hips and trunk slightly backward. The head is held in the middle of the body, with the ball held firmly under the chin in an offensive stance (see Figure 7-3d).

A common error among youth players is to fall forward after the stop is executed. Stress to your players that the greater the running speed at the time the stop is initiated, the greater the weight shift needed to counteract the forward motion of the runner. A good visual example is to have your players imagine that they are going to *sit down in a chair* at mid-stride. This encourages proper knee flexion in preparation for landing.

Beginners should understand that by landing simultaneously on both feet they may establish *either* foot as a pivot foot. Instruction in pivoting should follow shortly after the jump stop and stride stops have been mastered.

Knowledge of the traveling violation should also be presented at this time (see Chapter 5).

Key elements: (see Figure 7-3a-d)
1. Jump slightly (or close-to-the-floor hop) off of one foot.
2. Flex knees upon landing.
3. Move center of gravity backward with slight trunk extension.
4. Hit floor simultaneously with balls of both feet.
5. Land in a parallel stance.
6. Use either foot as a pivot foot.

Common errors:
1. Leaning forward due to excessive height on jump during take-off phase.
2. Leaning forward or sideways with upper body.
3. Keeping knees and legs extended upon landing.
4. Landing with flat feet in a staggered stance.
5. Landing with the heel of one foot ahead of the other.

Stride Stop

The stride stop is used when a player is moving forward and needs to change or reverse directions, or when a dribbler stops to pull up for a jump shot.

Because most players favor one foot in front of the other in the basketball position, this foot placement is the most commonly used in stopping. This skill is usually referred to as a stride stop or staggered stance, distinguishing it from the jump stop in which the feet are placed parallel to each other.

When performing the stride stop, a player should land on the ball of the rear foot first (this then becomes the pivot foot) and then the front foot.

In preparation for the stop, the knees are flexed and the trunk is tilted slightly backward to slow down forward momentum. As the counter action of the stop takes effect, the hips move forward, causing a shift in the center of gravity back over the feet as the player assumes the basketball position again (see Two-Step Stride Stop Drill).

(a)

(b)

(c)

(d)

Figure 7-3. The jump stop.

Key elements: (see Figure 7-4a-d)

1. Land on rear foot first.
2. Extend trunk slightly to move center of gravity posteriorly.
3. Land on front foot shortly after rear foot.
4. Use rear foot (first one down) as pivot foot.

Common errors:

1. Loss of balance caused by a forward lean during stride stop.
2. First foot to touch the floor is not used as the pivot foot, resulting in a traveling violation.

(a)

(b)

(c)

(d)

Figure 7-4. The stride stop.

PIVOT

A pivot is a turn made on the ball of one foot for the purpose of moving away from a defensive opponent, or to maneuver into a more favorable shooting or passing position.

A player may pivot with or without the ball and may execute a turn with either the right or left foot. Generally, right-handed players will lead with their right foot and pivot on their left. This allows them to remain in a triple-threat position at all times. The same is true for a left-handed player who leads with the left and pivots on the right foot.

There are two ways to turn: to the front or to the rear. These skills can also be referred to as *forward* and *reverse* pivots. Both pivots are classified as either a right or left pivot depending upon the direction of the body turn.

Forward pivots are used primarily in the front court as a means of moving away from a defensive player, for a shot or for a more favorable passing situation. When making a *front pivot* to the left, the player pushes off in a forward direction with the right foot, and turns to the left on the ball of the left foot. As the turn is made, the weight is transferred to the pivot foot (left) and the left arm and elbow swing in the same direction to help the body move more quickly (see Figure 7-5a-d).

A pivot can be executed in whatever degree

(a)

(b)

(c)

(d)

Figure 7-5. Front pivot to the left.

of turn is most effective for the offensive player. A player can make a full 360-degree pivot, or a half (180-degree), or even a quarter (90-degree) pivot. The key is to keep the body low, with feet spread at shoulder width or wider throughout the execution of the pivot.

A *reverse* pivot is a turn in which the non-pivot foot is toward the rear. This skill is usually used by an offensive player in an attempt to place his/her body between the ball and the defensive player.

In making a reverse pivot to the left from the basketball position, the player pushes off to the rear with the right foot and pivots to the left on the ball of the left foot. As the turn is made, the left shoulder is lowered, the ball is moved with both hands to the right side of the body providing it with maximum protective coverage. The right foot is placed a full stride's length away from its original location in a direction away from the defensive player (see Figure 7-6a-c).

Begin by teaching stationary pivots *without* a ball, making certain your players can execute both the forward and reverse turns effectively. Then have them practice the jump stop and

pivot without a ball as they gradually increase from walking to sprinting speed. Progress to having players jump stop and pivot with a ball, and finally, add defensive pressure in a drill situation (see Pivot Drill, Triple Threat Position Pivot Drill and Four Corner Pivot and Pass Drill.)

Key elements: (see Figure 7-6a-c)

1. Begin in the basketball position.
2. Keep feet shoulder width apart or wider.
3. Push off with the ball of the outside foot (forward or reverse turn).
4. Transfer weight to the ball of the pivot foot.
5. Rotate the outside foot and leg (180 degrees) around the stationary pivot foot.
6. Swing the arm in the new direction of travel.
7. Hold the ball under the chin with elbows out to the side.
8. Complete all the key elements of form in a smooth pivoting action.

Common errors:

1. Lifting or dragging the pivot foot, resulting in a traveling violation.

(a) (b) (c)

Figure 7-6. Reverse pivot to the left.

2. Standing straight up before executing the full pivot and turn.
3. Leaning with the head during the turn and losing balance.
4. Attempting to pivot on the heel.

DEFENSIVE SLIDE

Defensive footwork depends upon teaching youth players the fundamentals of the *slide step*. The movement of the feet is one of the most important aspects of good defensive play.

Begin by teaching proper defensive position, starting with the feet and moving upward. Instruct your athletes to keep their feet spread at approximately shoulder width in a slightly staggered stance. Stress that the weight must be maintained on the balls of the feet in order to achieve proper balance. The body is in a semi-crouch position with the knees flexed, back straight, head up and arms outstretched (see Figure 7-7).

Once your players have learned proper defensive position, progress to teaching the slide step in a lateral direction. Begin by having your players point their lead foot in the direction of the desired movement. For example, if sliding

to the right, the first movement is with the right foot, sliding it approximately 12 in. to the right. The next move involves dragging the left foot (trail foot) to a spot near the previous position of the right foot (lead foot). A period of non-support should be maintained while moving the trail foot forward. The reverse would be true for a slide step to the left.

Instruct your athletes to guard against crossing their feet, because this causes a loss of balance and may allow their opponent to drive past them. To help players visualize proper sliding technique, tell them to imagine that a *"ruler"* is placed between their feet and that their feet should never come any closer together than this distance.

Encourage your athletes to concentrate on taking short, quick steps, while keeping their weight and buttocks low. The knees should remain flexed at *all* times. Defensive drills (i.e., Lane Defensive Slide Drill, Lane Defensive Attack and Retreat) that call for constant shifting of the feet must be used frequently in order to develop proper footwork techniques. For further drills and information, see Chapter 13 for specific defensive situations.

Key Elements: (see Figure 7-7)
1. Keep feet at shoulder width in a slightly staggered stance.
2. Maintain most of the weight on the balls of the feet.
3. Keep knees flexed and the body in a semi-crouched position.
4. Keep the head level and arms out.
5. Point the lead foot in the direction of desired movement.
6. Step with the lead foot followed by a drag step of the trail foot to a spot near the previous position of the lead foot.
7. Maintain a short period of non-support while moving the trail foot forward.
8. Take short, quick steps.
9. Complete all key elements of form in a smooth sliding motion.

Common Errors:
1. Keeping feet closer than or wider than shoulder width.
2. Crossing the feet.
3. Taking long, slow steps.

Figure 7-7. The feet should never come any closer together than the distance of a ruler in the defensive slide.

4. Sliding feet with no period of non-support.
5. Contacting floor with flat feet (so that the heels are in contact with the floor).
6. Standing up straight.

FOOTWORK DRILLS

1. Ladders Drill (see Figure 7-8)

Purpose: To improve conditioning and to develop proper running form; to develop proper techniques for changing direction.

Procedure:
a. Players line up along the endline in groups of two or three.

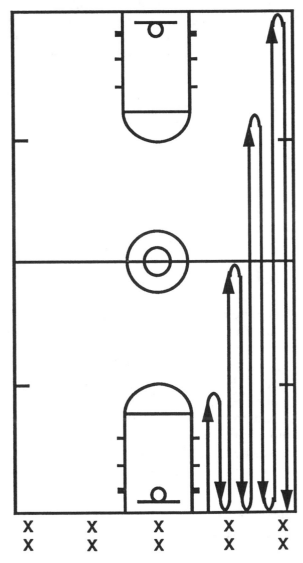

Figure 7-8. Ladders drill.

b. On a signal from the coach (whistle), the players who are first in line sprint forward to the nearest free throw line and back again to the baseline.
c. After touching the endline, the players sprint to the half-court line and back again, sprint to the far free throw line and back again, and sprint to the opposite endline and back to their original starting position.
d. The next players in line begin on the coach's whistle.

Variations:
Have the players sprint forward to each line and run backwards to the starting point, or require players to complete five sit-ups or push-ups at each line (i.e., ¼ court, ½ court, ¾ court) before returning to the endline. Players may be timed on this drill and encouraged to set goals for improving the time each day. This drill may also be done using the defensive slide technique.

2. Agility Jumps

Purpose: To develop coordination and foot quickness and to improve conditioning.

Procedure:
a. Each player is positioned with both feet on one side of a line on the court.
b. The players jump rapidly and continuously from one side of the line to the other.
c. A partner may count the number of jumps completed in 30 seconds if the drill is timed.

Variation:
Square Jumps - with the feet together, the players jump in a square pattern by jumping forwards, sideways, backwards, and then sideways again. This pattern should be repeated quickly for 30 seconds.

3. Sprint-Jog-Sprint (see Figure 7-9)

Purpose: To develop a quick start and the ability to change speeds while running.

Procedure:
a. Players line up along the endline.
b. On a signal from the coach (whistle), the players jog to the near free throw line, sprint to the half-court line, slow down and jog to the far free throw line, then sprint to the half-court line.

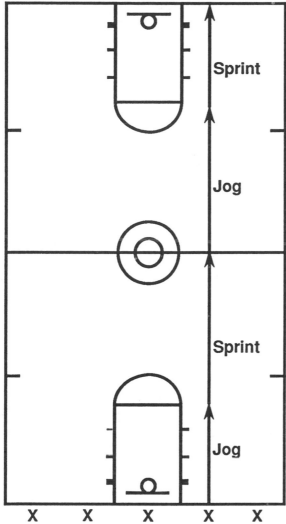

Figure 7-9. Sprint-jog-sprint.

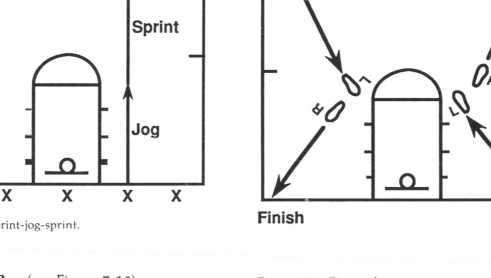

Figure 7-10. Diagonal run.

4. Diagonal Run (see Figure 7-10)

Purpose: To improve the ability to change directions quickly when running.

Procedure:

a. Players form a single file behind the endline in a corner of the court.

b. The first player in line sprints diagonally to the free throw line (elbow) and makes a sharp cut to the right, pushing off the left pivot foot.

c. The player then sprints diagonally to the junction of the half-court line and the sideline and makes a sharp cut to the left, pushing off the right pivot foot.

d. This pattern continues, as the player continues to the elbow, the corner of the court, across the endline, and then returns up the opposite side of the court.

e. After a player makes the first cut at the elbow, the next player begins the drill (so that several players are on the court at one time).

f. Emphasis should be placed on maintaining good basketball position while cutting.

5. Jump Stop Drill (see Figure 7-11)

Purpose: To develop body control and proper technique when coming to a jump stop.

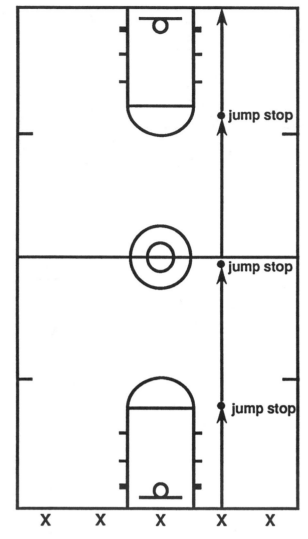

Figure 7-11. Jump stop drill.

Procedure:

a. Players line up along the endline.

b. On a signal from the coach (whistle), the players run to the near free throw line and execute a jump stop. The jump stop should be held (in the triple threat position) for two seconds, and then the players move on to do jump stops at the ½ court and far free throw line.

Variations:

The jump stop can take place on the whistle (instead of at set lines) and a speed "dribble-jump stop-pivot" sequence can be added for intermediate and advanced players.

6. Footwork Line Drill (see Figure 7-12)

Purpose: To improve the skills of coming to a jump stop and changing directions.

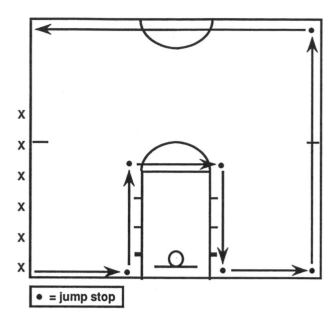

Figure 7-12. Footwork line drill.

Procedure:

a. Players form a single file at the corner of the court (along the sideline).

b. The first player in line jogs forward, then runs around the key, up the sideline, across the half-court line, and returns down the opposite sideline. A jump-stop is performed at each corner.

c. When changing directions, push off with the leg that is opposite the new direction

d. Repeat the drill twice from each side of the court.

Variation:

The drill may be done without a jump stop, or with the addition of a dribbling pattern.

7. Two-Step Stride Stop

Purpose: To develop a controlled two-step stop from a run.

Procedure:

a. Players spread out along the sideline, facing the opposite sideline.

b. The players run diagonally (to the right) five steps and execute a stride stop.

c. The stop should be done with a one-two step (left-right or right-left) with the feet hitting the floor in a quick succession.

d. Pivoting on the foot that hits first, players then run diagonally five steps in the opposite direction.

e. A stride step is made again, and this pattern is repeated.

Variation:
A whistle may be used as a signal to start and stop. For intermediate and advanced players the same drill may also be done using a jump stop or while dribbling.

8. Pivot Drill (see Figure 7-13a-b)

Purpose: To develop proper technique in performing front and reverse pivots.

Procedure:
a. Players spread out across the court area, each with a ball (or in pairs).
b. The ball is held in triple-threat position as the players perform a right-front pivot (180-degree), stop, and then do another (returning them to the starting position).
c. Repeat the drill performing a left-front pivot, and both the left-reverse and right-reverse pivots.

9. Triple-Threat Position-Pivot Drill
(see Figure 7-14a-b)

Purpose: To develop pivoting techniques (from the triple threat position) to be used when squaring up to the basket.

Procedure:
a. Players spread out in pairs around the perimeter of the key— one ball per pair.
b. The player with the ball, who is facing the half-court line, tosses the ball in the air and catches it.

c. Next, the player performs a pivot by planting the foot closest to the basket, squaring up into the triple-threat position.
d. Each player repeats this process five times and then alternates with his/her partner.
e. When each partner has done the drill twice, the pairs should move to the opposite side of the key and perform the same drill.

10. Four-Corner Pivot and Pass
(see Figure 7-15)

Purpose: To develop the skills of jump stopping, pivoting, and passing.

Procedure:
a. Divide players into four lines positioned in the four corners of a half-court. Players at the front of two of the lines in opposite corners have a basketball.
b. On the whistle, the players with the basketballs dribble to the center of half-court (near the free throw line).
c. Players execute a jump stop, and reverse pivot to square-up to the line in the next corner (counter-clockwise).
d. The balls are passed to the first person in each line, and the passer follows his/her pass to the end of the line.
e. The receiver now begins the same sequence, starting by dribbling to the middle.
f. Make sure the players all use the same pivot foot for the *reverse.*
g. Once the initial pattern has been learned,

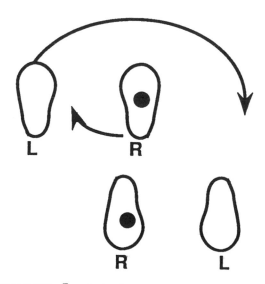

Figure 7-13a. Front pivot.

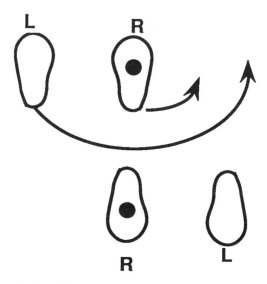

Figure 7-13b. Reverse pivot.

(a)

(b)

Figure 7-14. Squaring up into a triple-threat position.

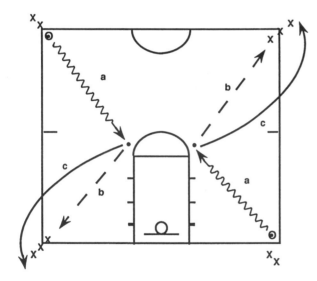

Figure 7-15. Four-corner pivot and pass.

the drill may be done with four balls, one in each corner.

Variations:
The drill can be modified by changing the type of passes or pivots used.

11. Lane Defensive Slide Drill

Purpose: To develop lateral, defensive quickness and improve a player's ability to change direction when moving side to side.

Procedure:
a. The player begins in the key facing the free throw line with the left foot on the lane line.
b. The body is in a semi-crouched position with the knees flexed. The feet are positioned shoulder-width apart with the weight on the balls of the feet. The arms are outstretched to the sides of the body and the head is up.
c. Using quick slide steps, the player moves across the key to touch the opposite lane line with the right foot. The first step should be made with the right foot (the lead foot), pointing the toe in the direction of movement, followed by a drag step of the trail foot.
d. Be sure players maintain a low, balanced position, and do not cross the feet (have athletes focus on not placing feet closer than shoulder-width apart).
e. The drill should be done for 30 seconds, with the players moving back and forth across the key as quickly as possible. Players count the total number of lines touched.

12. Hands Drill

Purpose: To develop the skills of jump stopping, pivoting, and passing.

Procedure:
a. Divide players into four lines positioned in the four corners of a half-court. Players at

the front of two of the lines in opposite corners have a basketball.

b. On the whistle, the players with the basketballs dribble to the center of half-court (near the free throw line).

c. The player must stay down in a low defensive position, move the feet quickly, and catch each ball and toss it back to the manager standing beside the coach.

d. Continue the drill for 30 seconds or until 10 balls have been retrieved. The player then moves to the end of the line and the next player in line begins the drill.

Variation:

For intermediate and advanced players, throw "bad passes" with a basketball and have the player catch them and return the ball to the passer using a chest pass.

13. Lane Defensive Attack and Retreat
(see Figure 7-16)

Purpose: To develop defensive quickness in forward and backward directions with either foot leading; to improve ability to change from attack to retreat and retreat to attack; to improve ability to make a quick drop step with either foot.

Procedure:

a. Players begin facing the foul line with the left foot on the left block and the right foot forward and in the lane. Position the feet shoulder width apart and distribute weight evenly on the balls of the feet. Knees should be bent to keep the body low.

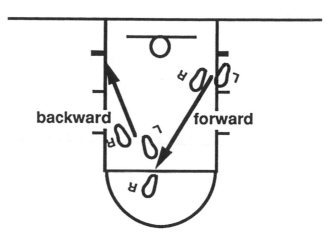

Figure 7-16. Lane defensive attack and retreat.

b. Using short, quick attack steps with the right foot as the lead foot, players move in a forward direction and touch the middle of the foul line with the lead (right) foot. Execute a quick drop step of the trail foot (left) while pivoting on the front foot (right).

c. Players now move in a backward direction toward the right block using short, quick retreat steps, touching the right block with the right foot. The players then change directions immediately and use attack steps with the left foot leading to approach the free throw line.

d. Players repeat the pattern of attacking and retreating for 30 seconds.

e. Emphasize that players should remain in a balanced, low defensive position. Keep the arms outstretched and hands up while making quick changes of direction.

Footwork Fundamental Skills

PERFORMANCE AREA	SPECIFIC SKILLS	SUGGESTED EMPHASIS		
		Elem. School Beginner 8-10	Middle School Intermediate 11-13	High School Advanced 14 and up
Footwork Fundamentals	Basketball position	X	X	
	Quick starts	X	X	
	Quick stops			
	A. Jump stop	X	X	
	B. Stride stop	X	X	X
	Pivot			
	A. Forward	X	X	
	B. Reverse	X	X	
	Defensive slide	X	X	X

Footwork Drill Matrix

Drill	SKILL LEVEL		
	Beginning	Intermediate	Advanced
Ladders drill	X	X	X
Agility jumps	X	X	X
Sprint - jog - sprint	X	X	X
Diagonal drill	X	X	X
Jump stop drill	X	X	
Footwork line drill	X	X	X
Two-step stride stop	X	X	X
Pivot drill	X		
Triple-threat position pivot	X	X	
Four corner pivot and pass		X	X
Lane defensive slide drill	X	X	X
Hands drill		X	X
Lane defensive attack and retreat		X	X

8
Ball Handling and Dribbling

Karen Garchow, M.A.

> ### QUESTIONS TO CONSIDER
>
> - What are the ball handling and dribbling skills used in basketball?
> - What are the key elements and common errors of ball handling? Of dribbling?
> - What progression is recommended for teaching youth players how to dribble and handle a basketball?
> - What factors influence the level of difficulty players experience when dribbling a basketball?
> - What drills or activities are effective in teaching dribbling?

COACHING HINTS FOR IMPROVING BALL HANDLING AND DRIBBLING SKILLS

A sound method for teaching basketball techniques to your players is to begin with skills that are relatively easy for them to learn and perform. After being successful, they will be eager to try more difficult techniques.

While players are in the early stages of learning ball handling skills, coaches should stress the importance of *practice*, not outcome. Reinforcement of practice encourages children to continue to practice. Eventually, with practice of correct techniques, children (beginners) achieve the desired outcome.

When teaching ball handling and dribbling skills, it's helpful to provide a visual demonstration first, followed by clear and concise verbal instructions. If the skill involves complex movements of both the arms and legs (e.g., between-the-leg dribble), *simplify* the drill by practicing

the movement for each part of the body before putting it together. It is sometimes necessary to point out the common errors and provide corrective feedback to the entire team. However, beginners will benefit from specific correction of repeated errors and may require hands-on guidance (tactile assistance) in order to get a feel for performing the skill correctly. Repeated trials and specific feedback on what was done well, followed by what can be improved and an encouraging "try again," produces results.

Keep in mind that some players have small hands and have not yet developed adequate hand strength. A ball *smaller* than a basketball is recommended for some children when teaching ball handling drills (see Chapter 5).

In teaching more difficult techniques, you should be aware that several factors can increase or decrease the difficulty players experience in handling or dribbling a ball. When selecting drills and instructing players, consideration should be given to the number of movements involved, the weight and size of the ball, the speed and strength requirements, and the pressure created by the addition of defense.

For a summary of dribbling skills and ball handling and dribbling drills that are appropriate for each level of play (beginning, intermediate, and advanced), see Supplements 8-1 and 8-2.

BALL HANDLING DRILLS

The drills in this chapter are designed to develop an individual's dribbling skills, specifically: eye-hand coordination, peripheral vision, hand and finger strength, speed and rhythm with both dominant and non-dominant hands, and improved ball handling for *all* players.

In all of the drills listed, it is recommended that youth players begin slowly and that they be encouraged not to fear making mistakes. Encourage players to continue to work on ball control using the proper techniques. Emphasize the importance of gaining a *"feel for the ball"* and keeping the head up.

A portion of daily practice should be devoted to ball handling and dribbling skills at the beginning of the season *and* throughout the year. Players will find a tremendous positive re-

lationship between how much they practice and how successful they become. Players must be encouraged to practice aspects of the skill that are weak, e.g., dribbling with the non-preferred hand. Naturally, as players develop specific skills, they gain self-confidence and a sense of accomplishment. Mastery of basic skills greatly increases the probability of continued participation in youth sports, making involvement both challenging and enjoyable.

Ball Handling Series

Select a subset of drills from the following series. Execute each drill for 30 seconds. If needed, vary total time of series by age and ability of players, e.g., for eight- and nine-year-olds select five drills; for 10- and 11-year-olds select eight to 10 drills.

1. Ball slapping

Hold ball near shoulder in one hand and "pound" it firmly into the other with a forceful overhand throwing motion, then pound it back to the hand you started with.

2. Fingertip control (see Figure 8-1a-c)
a. Extend arms above the head, resting the ball on the fingertips of both hands.

| (a) | (b) | (c) |

Figure 8-1. Fingertip control drill.

b. By using the fingertips as a guide, move the ball quickly from the right hand to the left hand and back, continuously.

c. Keep the arms extended throughout this back and forth movement from one hand to the other.

d. Without looking at the ball continue this movement while lowering the ball down to eye level, chest level, waist level, and knee level.

e. Reverse the process by bringing the ball from the knees to the head.

3. Stationary dribble with dominant hand (see Figure 8-2)

4. Stationary dribble with non-dominant hand (see Figure 8-3)

5. Stationary dribble with alternating hands

6. Stationary dribble chest high and hard— keeping hand on top of ball (dominant/non-dominant/alternating)

7. Stationary dribble as low as possible — near knee (dominant/non-dominant/alternating)

Figure 8-3. Stationary dribble with the non-dominant hand.

8. Around the world drill (see Figure 8-4a-f)

a. Position the feet side by side in a parallel stance.

b. Move the ball from one hand to the other while circling the waist, knees, and then neck.

c. Handle the ball with the fingertips, do not allow the palms to touch the ball.

Variation:

Instruct beginners to roll the ball on the floor or against their body in order to learn the pattern and to help support and control the ball.

9. Circle around both legs without a dribble.

a. Keep body in a low-crouched position.

b. Circle the ankles by carrying the ball around the left side with the left hand, and right side with the right hand.

c. Start with the ball around the ankles, then move it up around the knees, then straighten the body to an erect position and circle the ball around the waist.

d. Continue to circle around the body moving the ball back down to the ankles

e. See variations, Drill 8.

Figure 8-2. Stationary dribble with the dominant hand.

(a)   (b)   (c)

(d)   (e)   (f)

Figure 8-4. Around the world drill.

10. Single leg circle—without a dribble
(see Figure 8-5)

a. Begin with feet shoulder-width apart and knees bent.

b. Pass the ball from one hand to the other, circling just the right leg. Change legs.

c. See variations, Drill 8.

11. Figure "8" (between-the-legs) without a dribble (see Figure 8-6a-e)

a. Spread your legs shoulder-width apart and bend your knees slightly.

b. Take the ball and move it around one leg and then the other, transferring it from hand to hand to do so.

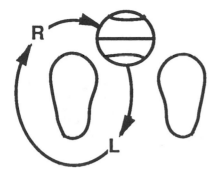

Figure 8-5. Single leg circle drill.

(a)

(b)

Figure 8-6. Figure "8" without a dribble drill.

(c)

(d)

(e)

c. Move the ball quickly around either leg in a figure 8 pattern as shown in the diagram.
d. Start the ball from in front, and move it through the legs. Continue for 30 seconds, then switch and start the ball in back and bring it through to the front for 30 seconds.
e. Keep your movements fluid and continuous, and never let the ball touch your palms or the floor.
f. See variations, Drill 8 (also see Figure 8-7a-e).

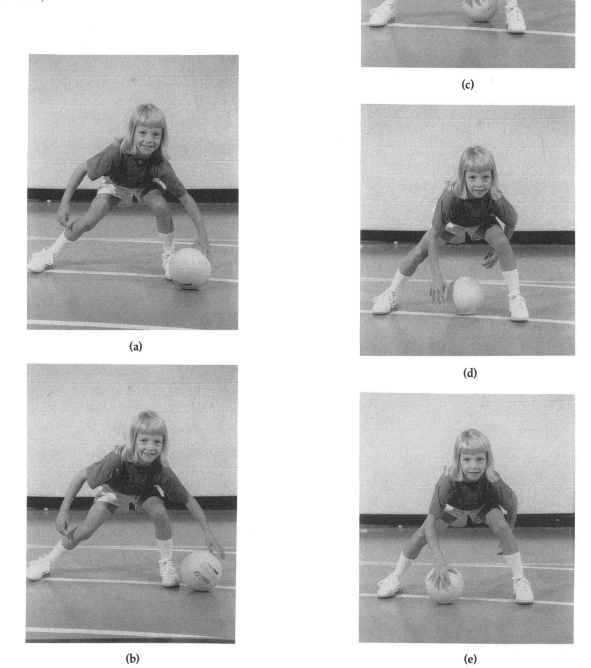

(a)

(b)

(c)

(d)

(e)

Figure 8-7. Variation of figure "8" without a dribble drill. Beginners roll the ball on the floor in a figure "8" pattern.

12. Figure "8" dribble (stationary)
(see Figure 8-8)

a. Assume the correct stance for dribbling; knees bent, back lowered, head up.

b. Use the fingertips to dribble the ball back and forth in front of the body, transferring it from the right to the left hand.

c. Circle the ball in front of the right leg, and behind the left leg. Circle the left leg and complete the figure "8" by passing behind the right leg.

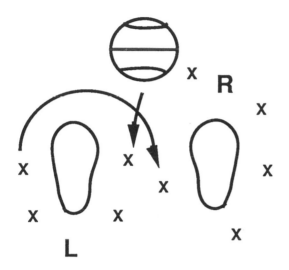

Figure 8-8. Figure "8" dribble drill (stationary).

d. Complete the drill by dribbling around the legs in a figure "8" pattern (as shown) once you can dribble around each leg separately.

13. 4 tap dribble or machine gun or butterfly
(see Figure 8-9a-c)

a. Bounce the ball in front of the body once with left hand, once with right hand.

b. Bring the left hand behind the body, through the legs and bounce the ball once; then bring the right hand behind the body and through the legs and bounce the ball once.

c. Move the hands back in front again and bounce one-two (left-right); then back behind, bounce three-four (left-right).

d. Keep repeating until this becomes a smooth motion. It helps to count 1, 2, 3, 4 while performing this drill.

14. Cradles (see Figure 8-10a-b)

a. Ball is held between legs, right hand on the ball in front of the legs, left hand on the ball behind the legs.

b. Releasing the ball, quickly reverse the arm position to grab the ball with the right hand behind and left hand in front.

c. Repeat above pattern.

d. Beginners may allow the ball to bounce once on the floor before catching it.

| (a) | (b) | (c) |

Figure 8-9. 4 tap dribble drill.

(a)

(b)

Figure 8-10. Cradles drill.

e. As players become more proficient, eliminate the bounce and catch the ball before it hits the floor.

15. Sitting dribble (see Figure 8-11)

a. Sit on the floor with legs outstretched.
b. With dominant hand bounce the ball near the side of the body.
c. With non-dominant hand bounce the ball near the side of the body;
d. under the legs;
e. behind the back, changing hands;
f. while doing sit-ups, dominant and non-dominant hand;
g. with two balls (see Figure 8-11);

Figure 8-11. Sitting dribble with two balls.

h. with two balls bouncing together, then alternating bounces one high, one low.

16. Reaction dribble drills

A. Hike drill

a. Hold the ball with two hands in front of the body spreading the feet slightly further than shoulder-width apart.
b. Bounce the ball between the legs near the heels and catch it with two hands behind the body as it bounces up toward the hips.
c. Bounce the ball back between the legs and catch it in front.
d. The bounce should be hard and quick.
e. Repeat the drill 10 to 15 times as quickly as possible.

B. Clap and catch

a. Toss the ball into the air and clap as many times as possible before catching it.
b. Bounce the ball and clap hands in front and back before catching.
c. Start with the ball in front, throw it up and over the head using a controlled toss and catch it behind the back.
d. Start with the ball held behind the back, throw it up and over the head, and catch it in front.
e. Hold the ball with two hands behind the knees, release the ball and clap hands in front of knees, then catch the ball behind before it touches the floor. A beginner may allow the ball to bounce once behind them, catching it off the bounce (see Figure 8-12a-c).

| (a) | (b) | (c) |

Figure 8-12. Clap and catch drill.

C. Skip dribble (see Figure 8-13a-d)

a. Move legs in scissors-like fashion, toes pointing straight ahead. Keep back straight, not bent over.
b. Dribble ball through legs from side to side from one hand to the other.
c. Complete 25 - 50 bounces.

D. Flip drill (see Figure 8-14a-c)

a. Bend over with feet shoulder width apart.
b. Hold ball with both hands behind legs.
c. Flip the ball forward through legs, reach forward, and catch ball in front of legs with arms extended.

| (a) | (b) | (c) | (d) |

Figure 8-13. Skip dribble drill.

(a)

(b)

(c)

Figure 8-14. Flip drill.

d. Hike the ball back through legs, reach backward, and catch the ball behind legs.
e. Alternate from front to back, back to front.

E. Crab run

a. Begin in a crouched position with an exaggerated long stride.
b. Step forward with the right leg, pass the ball under the right thigh with a left hand to right hand movement.
c. Then, as the left leg steps forward, use a right hand to left hand movement to pass the ball under the left thigh.
d. Continue on down the court moving the ball in the same motion used in Stationary Figure 8 Drill (see Figure 8-15a-b).

PROGRESSIONS FOR TEACHING DRIBBLING

1. As an obvious first step in learning to dribble, beginners must learn to bounce the ball. Initially, younger players will have to watch the ball, keep it well away from their body, and maintain a relatively erect position in order to control its action. It is helpful to have players "feel the rhythm" of the hand and arm motion *without* a ball before they attempt the stationary dribble.

2. From the earliest stages in this learning process, attention must be concentrated on the development of the stroking motion of the dribbling hand. Beginners should think of "petting"

(a)

(b)

Figure 8-15. Crab run drill.

the ball rather than hitting it. (Let the ball rebound into the hand.) Stress the importance of not pounding the ball, but pushing it away firmly and quickly with the wrist and pads of the fingers. The base of the fingers and palm of the hand should not contact the ball during this action.

3. While developing the dribbling technique, beginners should practice bouncing the ball in a *stationary position* with both the *right and left* hands. The ability to use either hand in the execution of basic fundamental skills is a mark of a good basketball player. It is possible to become almost as proficient with the non-dominant-hand dribble as with the dominant-hand dribble and it can prove very valuable for every position. Therefore, the development of skills with both hands at a young age must not be neglected.

4. As bouncing skill increases, the coach should add the element of having the players dribble *without looking* at the ball. Begin with drills in which the ball is bounced in place while the players move their heads from side to side, focusing their visual attention on a spot 10 feet ahead. Players should try to keep the bounce of the ball within sight without looking directly at it. The range of one's *peripheral vision* can be extended through practice. Coaches must stress to youth players that they need to acquire the ability to control the dribble and still keep their heads up. This helps develop a basic requisite of the game—maintaining visual concentration on the developing game situation at all times.

5. As soon as players begin to acquire some degree of skill in bouncing the ball with a relaxed hand and without staring at it, *locomotion* should be added to the drills. Start with a walking dribble and increase the speed of movement as rapidly as the player can learn to control the ball. Often times coaches place inexperienced players in "speed relay teams" before the players have developed the proper mechanics needed for the task, thus producing negative attitudes from an unsuccessful experience in dribbling.

6. Because ball position is a most important aspect of effective dribbling, the player must learn to dribble low for maximum ball protection (control) and somewhat higher for maximum speed of movement (speed dribble). The ball must be protected by using the body

as a screen in crowded areas of the court; therefore it is necessary for players to learn to dribble the ball under control on either side of the body. Drills which call for constant shifts of the ball relative to body position—from right side to left side—are invaluable learning aids (see Dribbling Drills).

Development of a Mature Dribbling Pattern

The following task variables can be adjusted to either increase or decrease the level of difficulty experienced by the dribbler:

1. Stationary/non-stationary dribble
2. Dominant/alternating/non-dominant hand
3. Eyes on task/eyes up
4. Walking/jogging/running speeds
5. Straight/curved/zig-zag pathways
6. Distance of travel
7. Active/passive defensive player
8. Size/weight/material of ball

Types of Dribbles

There are many different ways to dribble a basketball but any accomplished player at the elementary, junior or senior high school level must be able to use one of seven ways to advance the ball or elude an opponent. The dribbling skills included in this chapter are presented in an order arranged from simple to complex. Not all types apply to all levels. Select those appropriate for the players' ability. These skills include the *control* dribble, *speed* dribble, *crossover* dribble, *change-of-pace* dribble, *reverse* dribble, *behind-the-back* dribble, and the *between-the-legs* dribble.

Basketball players must be able to perform these seven dribbles with either hand. Learning to dribble with either hand demands long hours of practice and a great deal of discipline. Players who master the skill of dribbling with either hand open up their offensive game and prevent the defense from attacking their weak side.

Selecting the Dribble

Selection of the most effective dribble should be determined by:

- the position and movement of the defensive players

- intended activity after dribbling
- the ability of the players

When and When Not to Dribble

Mastering the art of dribbling is vital to a player's development as an offensive weapon. Before teaching the specifics of *how* to dribble, a player must learn correct body position. This begins with a good *triple-threat position* (see Figure 8-16). Players who assume this position are considered a triple threat because they are now ready to shoot, pass, or dribble. Far too many players and coaches pay little attention to this aspect of the game, and performances suffer for it.

Dribbling is probably the most misused element in the game. Players who dribble the ball at the wrong times handicap themselves and their team. Many times players receive a pass and begin dribbling right away. Some players, particularly beginners, dribble out of nervousness. A common error with all levels of players is dribbling without a purpose or dribbling once or twice and then picking up the ball and holding it, which results in a *dead dribble*. Dribbling should be used only when a pass is not possible.

Coaches need to help youth players understand that giving up the dribble reduces their options and allows the defense to apply pressure. Players should always be able to conclude a dribble with a good, quick pass, shot, or jump stop and pivot. Players should get rid of the ball quickly—as soon as they have completed their dribble. Appropriate feedback from a coach to a player to help correct this problem would be "square up, look first, dribble last, pass ahead whenever you can."

Players will take a giant step toward offensive improvement if they work at not wasting their dribble. The key is to help youth players understand when and when not to use the dribble.

The dribble should be used to:

- drive to the basket when an opening presents itself
- advance the ball on a fastbreak when the defense is already downcourt and when teammates are covered
- make a quick getaway with an intercepted pass
- move away from a tight area, such as a corner of the court
- beat defensive pressure, particularly player-to-player pressure
- get the ball away from the defensive board and out of congested areas
- "pick off" your defensive player using a screen
- kill time and control the ball in your "stall game"
- improve your passing angle to teammates, or move closer to them so you can make a shorter, and thus safer, pass
- balance the court when too many players are on one side

The dribble *should not* be used:

- at the moment the ball comes into your hands without first squaring up to the basket into a triple-threat position
- if a teammate is closer to the basket and standing in an open passing lane
- as a primary strategy against a zone defense, unless to penetrate the seams in the zone or exploit a defensive weakness
- if you are not a designated outlet player and you have the ball a long way from the basket. In that case, give the ball up to a guard, and fill the lane wide to create a fastbreak opportunity.

Figure 8-16. Triple-threat position.

- indiscriminately, at any time. If you don't have a plan in mind as an offensive weapon, don't dribble.

The dangers of overdribbling:

- Dribbling is a much slower way to move the ball than passing
- The more the ball is dribbled, the greater the chance the ball will be stolen or mishandled
- Dribbling often makes the players without the ball stand around. As a result, the offense loses its flow allowing the defense to concern itself only with stopping the player with the ball.

Fundamentals of Dribbling

The motor-appropriate components of each type of dribble are listed beneath the heading entitled "Key Elements." Inappropriate motor patterns often observed are listed beneath the heading entitled "Common Errors."

Individuals learn most effectively when they focus on one aspect of a skill at a time. It is important to communicate precisely the *one key element* of the skill on which you want the team to concentrate. Demonstrate the key element visually (and explain it verbally) so that all players know exactly what they are trying to achieve.

Basic Dribble Position

In each of the individual dribbling techniques, a proper *ready position* is fundamental to execution. In the ready position the head is up, knees are flexed, eyes are focused down the floor, and the body is in a semi-crouched position (basketball position). The degree of body crouch varies according to the speed of the dribble and the conditions under which the dribbler performs. The fingertips and pads of the fingers contact the ball. The hand is on top of the ball toward the back half of the top surface.

Basic dribble position:

- Head up: Eyes focused ahead
- Knees Flexed: Body in semi-crouched position
- Ball contacted with fingertips and pads of fingers
- Free arm is held out for balance and ball protection

Stationary Dribble

Once a player has learned the basic dribble position, begin with the stationary dribble. Begin instruction with the dominant hand, the non-dominant hand, and then alternating hands. Do not begin teaching the non-stationary dribble until your players have mastered these skills and can coordinate the elements of form in a smooth dribbling action. In the stationary dribble, the fingers are spread loosely over the ball. The ball is projected slightly forward using fingertip control. The lower arm, from the elbow to fingertips, moves in a pumping action. The ball is pushed to the floor with a flexing motion of the wrist. Players should avoid dribbling with the palm because it reduces control and tends to create a slapping motion at the ball.

The elbow of the dribbling hand is kept close in at the side, with the forearm roughly parallel to the floor. Not much force is necessary to maintain the dribble; therefore, youth players should be instructed to avoid pushing the ball too hard.

The knees are flexed and the body is low to gain better balance and control. The feet are shoulder-width apart with the ball-side foot placed slightly behind the lead foot. The ball is dribbled knee to waist high with short, close bounces, so as to reduce the time the ball is not in contact with the hand (see Figure 8-17a-e).

Control Dribble

The control dribble is used when the player is closely guarded and wants to keep the ball well-protected and under complete control. The forearm of the non-dribbling hand is used to shield the ball from the defender. The basketball is protected with both the arm and leg nearest the defender. Offensive players should be careful, however, not to thrust the arm so far out that it appears the ball handler is warding off defenders with it. This could result in an offensive foul. Also, caution players *not* to begin the habit of backing into the defender, or dribbling backwards.

The control dribbler moves his/her feet with a sliding motion as if in a defensive stance. The head is turned away from the ball to look down the court in order for the dribbler to see offensive options.

(a)   (b)   (c)

(d)   (e)

Figure 8-17. Stationary dribble.

The ball is dribbled on the side of the body away from the defender. Keep the ball on the right side when dribbling with the right hand, and the left side when dribbling with the left hand.

Key Elements: (see Figure 8-18a-c)

1. Assume a ready position with ball-side foot back.
2. Project ball slightly forward using fingertip control and lower arm pumping action.

3. Keep ball low (below waist) and protected by body.
4. Protect ball with forearm and leg nearest the defender.
5. Use sliding motion of feet.
6. Keep head up and eyes focused downcourt.

Common Errors:

1. Positioning feet in a parallel stance (see Figure 8-19).

(a)

(b)

(c)

Figure 8-18. Key elements of the control dribble.

Figure 8-19. Common error of the control dribble: positioning the feet in a parallel stance (instead of keeping the ball-side foot back).

2. Contacting the ball with the palm of the hand (slapping motion).
3. Pushing the ball too forcefully to the floor, resulting in a high dribble.
4. Standing erect while dribbling the ball thus causing a high dribble and an inability to move with the ball.
5. Keeping shoulders square to defensive players allowing for the ball to be unprotected by the body.
6. Keeping forearm opposite the ball at the side of the body.
7. Seeing only the ball (looking downward) instead of forward and ahead.

Speed Dribble

The speed dribble is used by a player on a fastbreak to get from one spot to another as quickly as possible or when dribbling downcourt ahead of the defense while not being closely guarded.

Certain adjustments need to be made from the basic dribble position to execute a speed dribble effectively. The hand is not directly over the ball as in the control dribble (see Figure 8-20a). The fingers are spread *behind* the ball at nearly a 45-degree angle to the floor (see Figure 8-20b).

In the speed dribble, the ball is pushed out in front of the body at waist level, as opposed to the control dribble where the ball moves almost straight up and down. In the speed dribble, the bounce should be higher and longer to cover a lot of ground (see Figure 8-21).

For maximum speed, the body must lean slightly forward and into the dribble. The ball is pushed out and away with the arm completely extended, then "caught up to" and pushed out again. Coaches need to inform players of this

Figure 8-20a. Control dribble.

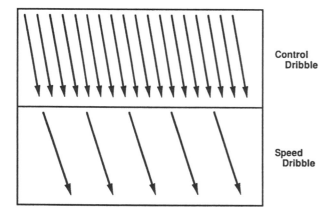

Figure 8-20b. Speed dribble.

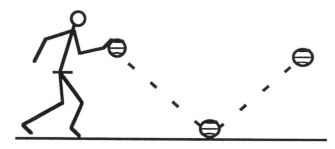

Figure 8-21. The proper angles of bounce for the control and speed dribbles.

simple fact: the faster they run, the farther out in front the ball must be pushed.

The ball can be dribbled higher (above waist) as speed increases with a full running stride. As the player runs and dribbles at the same time, it is important to stress the need to keep the head up so players can see the entire court, their teammates, and the defenders that may be in front of them. A helpful hint for coaches is to simply remind players to keep their shoulders square to the direction of travel.

A common error among youth players occurs when the ball is allowed to get too high above the waist. The higher the bounce, the less control they have. If the ball is sufficiently pushed out in front, the advanced player should not have to use more than a few dribbles to move from one half of the court to the other.

Often times on a speed dribble, the ball will be overrun on a wide-open lay-up either because the ball is not kept out and away from the player's body, or because the sprint is attempted faster than necessary. Players who cannot control the speed dribble also have difficulty executing a jump stop under control. Emphasize ball control and inform players that it is better to risk being overtaken and having to set up the offense than to lose the ball by kicking it away or over-running it.

Key Elements: (see Figure 8-22a-d)

1. Lean the body slightly forward from the basic dribble position.
2. Spread fingertips behind the ball at nearly a 45-degree angle to the floor.
3. Push the ball out in front of the body with the dribbling arm completely extended.
4. Control the ball between the waist and chest level.
5. Use a full running stride.
6. Keep shoulders square to the direction of travel.
7. Move only at a speed where the dribble can still be controlled.

Common Errors: (see Figure 8-23)

1. Spreading the fingers on the top half of the ball.
2. Bouncing the ball straight downward.
3. Pushing the ball too close to the side of the body.
4. Dribbling the ball too high so the player loses control.
5. Running in an erect body position.
6. Sprinting too fast and overrunning the ball.

Crossover Dribble

The crossover dribble is used by a player to move the ball quickly from one hand to the other. It is the fastest way to change directions and lose the opponent.

(a)

(b)

(c)

(d)

Figure 8-22. Key elements of the speed dribble.

Figure 8-23. Common error of the speed dribble: dribbling the ball too high.

The crossover dribble begins from a control dribble. Certain adjustments need to be made from the basic dribble position to execute a crossover dribble effectively. The hand is moved a few inches to the outside of the ball as the crossover move is executed rather than staying directly over the ball as in the control dribble. The key is to use a lower, quicker bounce just before switching hands.

For example, if a player is using a right-hand control dribble, the crossover to the left begins by shifting the right hand a few inches to the right side of the ball. The ball is angled toward the left hand using the fingertips and the wrist.

As the ball crosses over to the left hand, the player must also execute a crossover step in that direction. Body weight is shifted to the left as the change of direction is executed. The player must drive off the right foot (or trail leg), and cross the right leg just in front of the defender. The ball is protected with the free arm (in this case, the right arm) and leg (right) nearest the defender.

Youth players should not be encouraged to attempt the crossover dribble in front of the body. This allows the ball to be unprotected and more easily stolen by the defender. To avoid this, teach youth players to keep their shoulders low and turned toward the direction of travel.

Coaches should also stress the importance of the change of direction being executed sharply and quickly with knees kept flexed throughout the cut. A quick acceleration should be executed after the crossover.

Key Elements: (see Figure 8-24a-d)

1. Begin crossover dribble from a control drible. Bounce the ball lower and quicker just before switching hands.
2. Shift the dribbling hand a few inches to the outside of the ball.
3. Maintain a slight side orientation by turning shoulders toward the direction of travel.
4. Drive off the trail leg.
5. Shift body weight quickly with change of direction move.
6. Protect ball with arm and leg nearest the defender.

Common Errors:

1. Executing the transition dribble slowly in front of the defender.
2. Dribbling the ball too high on the crossover dribble.
3. Keeping shoulders square to defender on the crossover step.

(a)

(b)

(c)

(d)

Figure 8-24. Key elements of the crossover dribble.

4. Following the crossover move, the dribbler does not accelerate beyond defender.

5. Not using the arm and leg nearest the defender to protect the ball.

6. Crossing over to the right hand and moving to the left, or crossing over to the left hand and moving to the right.

Change-of-Pace Dribble

The change-of-pace dribble is a combination of the speed dribble and the control dribble. It involves an abrupt change in the speed of the dribble from fast to slow or slow to fast.

The change-of-pace is one of the greatest aids to successfully executing offensive maneuvers. Players use this dribble to make the defense think they're slowing down or are about to pick up their dribble. They then explode past the defender. Successful execution of this move involves changing both the height of the ball's bounce and the speed and direction of the player's foot movement.

The change-of-pace dribble is an excellent way to elude the defense or catch them off guard. For example, the ball handler is dribbling to the basket with the right hand while being closely guarded by the defender. The dribbler slows down abruptly and pulls the head and shoulders back, as though to stop the drive. As the defender begins to relax and stand up, the dribbler moves at top speed with a quick first step—pushing off hard with the left foot and protecting the ball with the free hand. The dribbling hand slides from the top to the back of the ball, to create nearly a 45-degree angle to the floor. This allows the ball handler to push the ball outward while moving around the defender.

When teaching the change-of-pace dribble, it is best to have youth players first practice controlling the height of the ball's bounce. Begin practice of this move using a control dribble. Have players bounce the ball at waist level, then suddenly lower the hand and dribble the ball only as high as the knee. Point out to your players how the dribble speeds up, thus changing its pace.

Once players develop the feel for how to make the ball bounce faster or slower, start combining the dribble with different walking or running movements. Begin by having them walk and dribble the ball at normal height, then surge to a run, simultaneously speeding up the dribble. Instruct the players to slow to a trot, dribbling the ball at an appropriate pace; then sprint. These foot-speed/dribbling height combinations should be practiced often in different directions (see the "Stop-and-Go Dribble Drill").

Key Elements: (see Figure 8-25a-e)

1. Slow down the dribble when executing the head and shoulder fake.

2. Time the change-of-pace correctly (as the defense begins to stand up and relax).

3. Explode into full speed again, driving hard off the trail leg and taking a big step forward with the leg positioned on the ball side.

4. Push the ball out hard and long as the dribbling hand slides behind the ball to nearly a 45-degree angle to the floor.

5. Protect the ball with the arm and leg nearest the defender.

6. Alternate the change-of-pace with distinct differences in speed.

Common Errors:

1. Increasing speed of the dribble as the head and shoulder fake is executed.

2. Picking up the dribble before the change-of-pace is completed.

3. Driving too soon before the defender has reacted to the head and shoulder fake.

4. Executing the change-of-pace dribble without a recognizable difference in speed.

Reverse Dribble

The reverse dribble allows a player to change directions quickly. The dribbler's body is momentarily placed between the defense and the ball, while advancing the ball to the basket.

The reverse dribble begins from the control dribble. The key to learning this offensive move is executing a reverse pivot (see Chapter 7). The reverse pivot begins by stopping temporarily on the foot opposite the dribbling hand. The legs are flexed at the knees with body weight slightly forward on the extended foot. The dribbler turns away from the defender, using a reverse pivot as the ball is moved to the other hand. In reversing the ball from side to side, the ball is protected with the arm and leg nearest the defender.

For example, a right-handed dribbler fac-

(a)

(b)

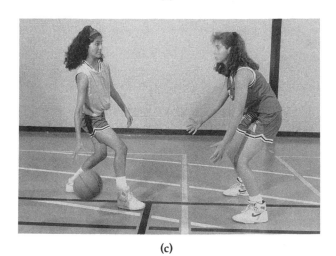

(c)

(d)

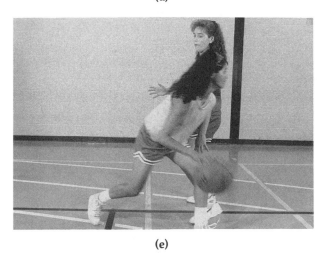

(e)

Figure 8-25. Key elements of the change-of-pace dribble.

ing the defender plants the left leg and reverse pivots, bringing the right leg around behind, following the lead of the right shoulder while still dribbling with the right hand, the ball is pulled back toward the right hip. The ball must be quickly shifted to the left as the player ex-

plodes past the defender with the left-hand dribble. Emphasize to the dribbler the importance of planting the foot close to the defender's foot, so they almost brush shoulders.

Although the crossover dribble also accomplishes the task of changing directions, the reverse dribble is used when the ball handler is closely guarded. In this case, it is a safer and more efficient maneuver to perform.

The reverse dribble is a useful dribble when the crossover dribble cannot be used because the defender is too close to risk crossing the ball over in front. It should be executed quickly, however, as it is a disadvantage to turn away from the play. Be careful not to allow the ball to be stolen by another defensive player coming up on the blind side.

When teaching youth players the reverse dribble, begin by establishing the pivot foot and footwork first. Practice the movement without a ball from various angles. Then practice the move at ¼, ½, and full speed with a ball. When learning the move, encourage beginners to take two or three dribbles if needed, but do not allow players to develop the bad habit of carrying the ball. Next, add defensive pressure, and attempt to make the pivot as sharp as possible. This drill allows the ball handler to "pin the defense" and get past before he/she can react.

Coaches must stress that the reverse pivot is a continuous motion. Through practice the player will be able to make the move more fluid. An advanced player should be able to execute the spin with one dribble.

Key Elements: (see Figure 8-26a-e)

1. Begin the reverse pivot from the control dribble.
2. Stop on the foot opposite the dribbling hand.
3. Pivot on the front foot.

4. Keep the ball low while transferring ball to opposite hand.
5. Complete pivot on opposite foot.
6. Protect ball with arm and leg nearest the defender.
7. Dribble hard at the defender before beginning the spin, and make the pivot as sharp as possible.

Common Errors:

1. Pivoting on the wrong foot—pivoting forward towards the defender.
2. Changing the ball from one hand to the other *before or after* the reverse pivot has been executed.
3. Palming or carrying the ball.

See the "Twelve Cones Drill." This is an excellent drill to practice the reverse pivot dribble from various angles with or without defensive pressure.

(a)

(b)

(c)

(d)

(e)

Figure 8-26. Key elements of the reverse dribble.

Behind-the-Back Dribble

The behind-the-back dribble allows players to change directions and hands, placing the body between the ball and the defender, while still facing the play.

The behind-the-back dribble is a bit more difficult to execute, but can be more useful than a reverse dribble. In this dribble, the ball must be directed behind the back with one hand and recovered with the other hand using a fluid motion.

Players dribbling with the left hand must take the last dribble near the side of their left heel. They must draw the ball *back* so that the palm of the dribbling hand is facing the floor and the elbow is pointing toward the ceiling (see Figure 8-27).

Once the ball is "behind the back" the palm must slide over to the outside of the ball, swinging it across the lower back, to push the ball to the right hand. The movement ends with the left arm as close as possible to the right hip. Once the player has control of the ball and has switched hands successfully, the tempo should be increased as the first dribble is made.

When teaching the behind-the-back dribble to youth players, begin *without a ball* and check for proper arm position. This is a *two-step motion* requiring that: (1) the ball be brought back sufficiently behind the body, and (2) the ball be pushed across to the other hand. Many times, beginners try to execute the behind-the-back dribble in one motion rather than two.

Once the arm motion is correct, practice the mechanics with a ball. Beginners should be allowed to stand in one spot and attempt this move. Once the key elements of the skill are learned, focus on coordinating all of the elements while dribbling up court. Encourage advanced players to avoid turning the head and shoulders to see the ball coming around the back.

It is also important to check that the last dribble on the ball side is placed close to the heel and not in front of the foot. Once the ball is drawn back, watch closely the angle of the player's arm motion and check that the lower body is in somewhat of a sitting position. Do not allow players to push their hips forward to avoid being hit in the back with the ball.

Extreme caution should be used when teaching these skills to avoid introducing them too soon or before other fundamental skills are well-established. Young players with small hands may have difficulty executing this advanced skill.

Long arms are advantageous in the behind-the-back dribble for placing the ball in the most efficient spot. As with all dribbles, the behind-the-back dribble should be used when necessary and when the player has confidence in using it.

Key Elements: (see Figure 8-27a-e-Beginner; Figure 8-28a-e-Advanced)

1. Draw the ball behind the back on the bounce.
2. Place the last bounce near the back of the heel.
3. Suspend the ball behind the back with the palm facing the floor and the elbow facing the ceiling (see photo).
4. Slide the palm over toward the outside of the ball.
5. Push the ball at an angle so that it bounces toward the receiving hand.
6. Lower the body into a sitting position as the ball switches hands.
7. Increase the tempo as the first dribble is made with the other hand.

Common Errors:

1. Bouncing the ball at the side of the body rather than behind the back.
2. Turning the head and shoulders to see the ball coming around the back.
3. Pushing the hips forward to avoid being hit in the back with the ball.
4. Traveling with the ball.

Between-the-Legs Dribble

The between-the-legs dribble is a quick way to move the ball from one hand to the other when being closely guarded or overplayed.

Begin teaching the between-the-legs dribble to youth players by having them straddle a line on the floor with their right foot on one side and their left foot on the other (see Figure 8-29).

Players stand with the left foot placed one stride in front of the right, and begin by holding the ball on the right side of the body. With the right hand on the outside of the ball, the

(a)

(b)

(c)

(d)

(e)

Figure 8-27. Key elements of the behind the back dribble (beginner).

ball is pushed downward toward the floor so that it bounces directly *on* the line.

The left hand must be close to the left leg to receive the ball with fingers spread and pointed down to the floor. Beginners may watch the ball come into the other hand and look at the line on the floor between their legs where the ball should hit. Once the players can successfully bounce the ball between their legs from the right hand to the left, encourage them to try this *without* looking at the ball.

Next, have players begin with a stationary dribble on the right side of the body. On the last dribble before the crossover, the right hand must shift to the outside of the ball as before when the ball is received by the left hand. The dribble then continues with the left hand. Once a player can successfully transfer the ball from the right to the left hand without an error, begin between-the legs practice from the left hand to the right in the same manner.

As a player learns to dribble between-the legs with either hand, begin practice on the "Skip Drill" (see ball handling Drill 16C) which

(a) (b) (c)

(d) (e)

Figure 8-28. Behind-the-back dribble while moving up the court (advanced).

Figure 8-29. Between-the-legs dribble in a stationary position.

involves switching the ball back and forth from the right to the left and the left to the right. Stress quickness, keeping the dribble low, and shoulders facing the direction of travel.

Advanced players may wish to *walk* and dribble the ball between-the-legs the length of the court. This can be attempted by walking both in a forward and backward direction.

Key Elements: (see Figure 8-30a-d)

1. Keep the dribble low between the legs.
2. Shift the hand on the outside of the ball before the changeover dribble.
3. Push the ball hard to the floor to a spot halfway between both legs.
4. Place the receiving hand close to the leg under which the ball is crossing.
5. Spread and point the fingers of the receiving hand toward the floor.

(a)　(b)

(c)　(d)

Figure 8-30. Between-the-legs dribble while moving up the court.

Common Errors:

1. Dribbling the ball too high (near waist).
2. Pushing the ball too hard or too softly to a spot not located one-half of the way between-the-legs.
3. Keeping the receiving hand close to the hip.
4. Turning shoulders, hips, and feet sideways rather than straight ahead.

DRIBBLING DRILLS

Drills are divided into two categories: *dribbling and team games.* Lead-up games are arranged by skill emphasis, skill level, formation, procedure, and variations.

- Select and organize your practice to provide players with as many repetitions (trials) as possible within the allotted time for instruction.

Maximize participation and minimize standing in lines.

- Provide specific, immediate, and *positive* feedback on what they did correctly and then on what they can do to improve. Follow this with some encouragement to continue the effort.
- Use a "Skill Evaluation Chart" (as shown in Supplement 8-3) to aid in monitoring players' progress in performance of the skills and

drills. This chart may also be used to record the number of trials performed or the results of a timed performance for advanced players.

Dribbling Drills

Purpose of Dribbling Drills: The objectives of the following dribbling drills are to develop the proper techniques for performing the various type of dribbles with both the dominant and non-dominant hands, and to provide practice of dribbling skills against defensive pressure.

1. Blind Stationary Dribble

Procedure:

a. The player stands in one spot and dribbles the ball first with the dominant hand, then with the non-dominant hand.

b. The eyes should be kept closed to help develop a "feel" for the ball. Wear a pair of blinders for this drill, as well as the rest of the drills, if available (see Figure 8-31).

2. Zig-Zag Dribble

Procedure:

a. Players line up at the end of the court with a ball.

b. They dribble to the right, protecting the ball with the left forearm; then dribble to the left, protecting the ball with the right forearm. The path defines a "Z."

c. Players dribble the length of the court and back, changing hands each time a change-of-direction is made.

d. Passive or active defense may be added to this drill, causing the ball handler to utilize the crossover dribble.

3. Stop-and-Go Dribble

Procedure:

a. Players begin at the endline with a basketball.

b. On the whistle, players start dribbling while running at a fast pace, slow down, then speed up again.

c. A change of direction may be made while doing this, making sure that the dribbling hand is changed each time.

d. Encourage players to stay low and to protect the ball with the body and forearm.

4. Dribbling the Lines (see Figure 8-32)

Procedure:

a. The dribbler begins in the left corner of the court and dribbles along the lines, following the pattern in the diagram.

b. At each left or right turn, the player must switch dribbling hands.

c. Encourage players to stay low and to keep the head up to look downcourt.

d. Players should make their cuts at the corners and around the keys sharp and precise while maintaining as much speed and ball control as possible.

Figure 8-31. Stationary dribble with blinders.

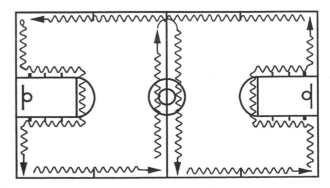

Figure 8-32. Dribbling the lines drill.

5. Obstacle Dribble

Procedure:

a. Set cones 10-15 feet apart along the length of the court and begin players at the endline with a ball.

b. The player dribbles in and out of the cones for 30 seconds - 1 minute, working both on speed and ball control.

c. The dribbler must alternate hands and keep the ball in the hand furthest from the cone around which he/she is dribbling.

d. All types of dribbles may be utilized in this drill.

6. Dribble Against the Wall Drill
(see Figure 8-33)

Procedure:

a. The player stands approximately three feet from a solid, flat wall and dribbles a ball against it.

b. The ball is held above the head and dribbled off the wall 25 times with the right hand, then 25 times with the left. Complete the drill by dribbling the ball 25 times with both hands (or the drill may be timed- max. two minutes).

c. The fingertips should be used to control the ball. Have players close their eyes to help develop a "feel" for the ball.

Variation:

Alter this drill for younger players by using a lighter ball, moving players closer to the wall (one-two feet); or decreasing the duration (one minute)/ number of repetitions (15) of the drill.

7. Zig-Zag Dribble Between the Legs
(see Figure 8-34)

Procedure:

a. The player begins dribbling to the right, then dribbles the ball under the right leg (on the forward step) with a low sharp bounce, crossing over into the left hand.

Figure 8-33. Dribbling against the wall drill.

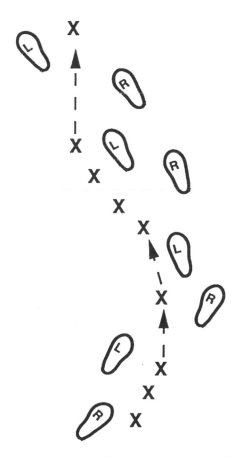

Figure 8-34. Zig-zag dribble between the legs drill.

b. The dribbler immediately changes the direction of body movement to the left and executes the same crossover bounce under the left leg on the third dribble in that direction.

c. Have players do this drill slowly at first, and then increase speed as technique is improved.

8. Combination Dribble

Procedure:

a. The player begins dribbling forward with the right hand, then performs the following sequence while going down the court: (1) switch to the left hand using a crossover dribble; (2) do a reverse dribble going from left to right then right to left; and (3) do a behind-the-back dribble going both directions.

b. The skills should be performed smoothly and as fast as possible while still maintaining ball control.

c. Emphasize keeping the head up and maintaining good body position.

9. Reverse-Dribble-Square Drill
(see Figure 8-35)

Procedure:

a. Players start at the corner of the court using the right hand only.

b. They dribble along the sideline to a point free throw line extended, reverse dribble

making a ¼ turn, and dribble to the free throw line.

c. Players then reverse dribble and drive to the baseline where they reverse dribble and dribble to the starting line.

10. Full-Court Speed Dribble
(see Figure 8-36)

Procedure:

a. Divide team into partners of *equal ability* levels.

b. Player 1 stands with the ball behind the baseline near the right corner of the sideline.

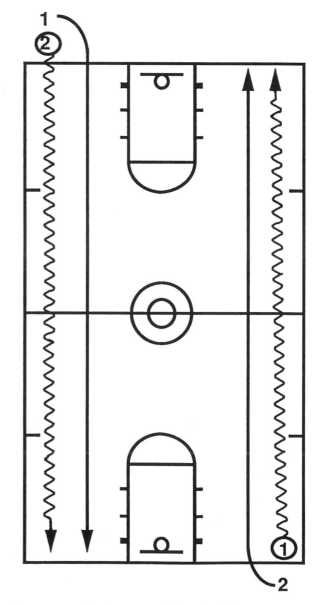

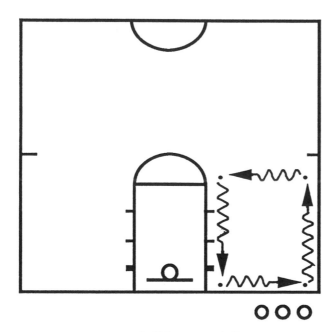

Figure 8-35. Reverse-dribble-square drill.

Figure 8-36. Full-court speed dribble drill.

Player 2 stands behind his/her partner without a ball.

c. Player 1 speed dribbles to the other end of the court performing under the passive defense of player 2 who may begin chasing as soon as the dribbler moves off the baseline.

d. When they reach the other end of the court, players 1 and 2 come back along the left sideline. Positions are switched, with player 2 speed dribbling and player 1 applying defensive pressure.

e. The next group of partners begin the drill when the players in front of them reach the half-court line.

Variations:

a. Player 1 may dribble in for a lay-up at the other end of the court.

b. This is an excellent drill to teach defensive positioning to get *in front* of the dribbler. Do not allow players to run to the side of the dribbler. If the defense is unable to catch the ball handler, teach them to come from behind the dribbler on the ball side and deflect it away.

11. Crossover Dribble Drill
(see Figure 8-37)

Procedure:

a. A cone is placed at the free throw line to the right side of the key.

b. Using the right hand, the player dribbles to

the cone, crossover dribbles to the left hand and drives in for a lay-up.

c. Switch the cone to the opposite side to work the other hand.

Variations:

a. Have players take a six-to-eight foot shot off the dribble instead of a lay-up.

b. Move the cone to the wing or baseline.

12. Count Fingers Dribble Drill
(see Figure 8-38)

Procedure:

a. Place cones in a line down the length of the court. Players line up at both endlines with a ball at one end.

b. Player 1 dribbles in and out of the cones,

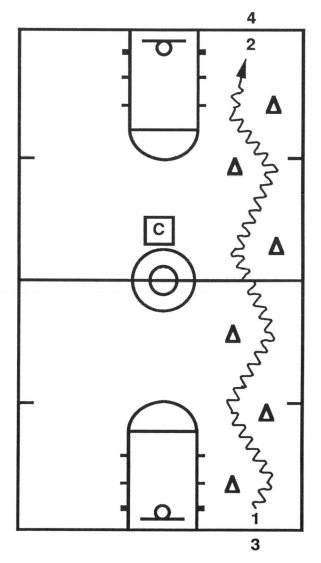

Figure 8-38. Count fingers dribble drill.

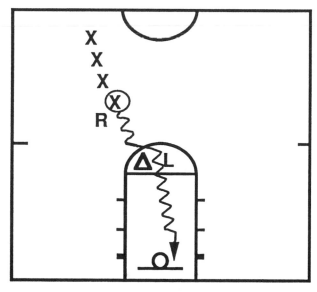

Figure 8-37. Crossover dribble drill.

keeping his/her body between the ball and the cone.

c. Player 2 waiting at the opposite endline, holds up one hand showing a certain number of fingers. Player 1 calls each number out loud (1-5) as they pass each cone.

d. When player 1 reaches player 2, player 2 dribbles in the opposite direction as player 3, holds up fingers and so on.

e. The spin, between-the-legs, and behind the back dribbles can also be practiced in this formation.

13. The Seven Cones Drill
(see Figure 8-39)

Procedure:

a. Place seven cones three or four feet apart in a straight line up the middle of the court.

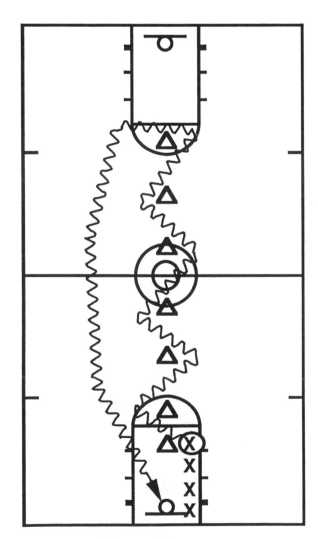

Figure 8-39. Seven cones drill.

b. Players start at the baseline, and dribble the ball in a zigzag pattern around each cone.

c. To control the ball, the dribbler must keep the body low and change hands between cones using a crossover dribble.

d. After reaching the last cone, the player dribbles back up the court using a speed dribble and shoots a lay-up.

e. Switch directions by starting from the other side of the key.

Variation:

This drill can be used to work on shooting by using a jump shot or by adding a defender for the lay-up.

14. The Twelve Cones Drill
(see Figure 8-40)

Procedure:

Place 12 cones on the basketball court as follows: three on the sideline, one near the free throw lane on the baseline, one at the top of Figure 8-40 the key, and one at the free throw line, and the other six in the same arrangement at the other end of the court.

a. A player begins on a sideline with three cones in front of him/her and dribbles toward them, using a change-of-pace dribble at the midcourt line until reaching the first cone. A fake is made to the inside, planting the inside foot and pushing off in the opposite direction, the player then dribbles around the outside of the cone. The dribbler continues on in a similar fashion to the second and third cones. Then, heading toward the fourth cone, which is near the baseline, the player makes a reverse dribble and shoots a regular lay-up. After shooting, the player rebounds the ball and dribbles up the middle of the court.

b. After reaching the cone at the top of the opposite key, the dribbler fakes, plants the pivot foot, changes direction by pushing off and dribbles around the cone. A cone is encountered immediately at the free throw line. Using a crossover dribbler to continue to the basket, the player moves around the cone and pulls up for a jump shot.

c. After taking the shot, the player now dribbles the length of the court as fast as possi-

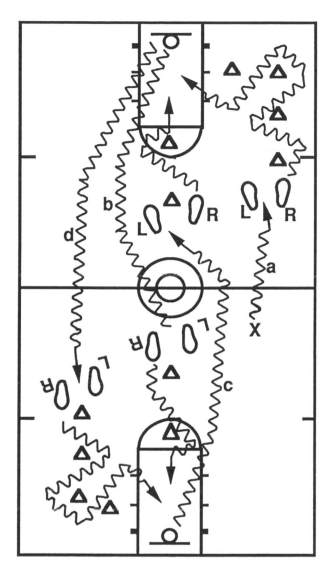

Figure 8-40. Twelve cones drill.

ble and makes the same maneuvers as in step B.

d. After taking the second shot, the player drives the length of the court, dribbles up the far side of the floor, and repeats the maneuvers performed in step A.

e. The Twelve Cone Drill can be performed by one player or with a teammate (or teammates) simply by alternating who takes the shot.

Variation:

Start the drill on the opposite side of the court to work the opposite hand. Shots may be varied to include lay-ups, bank shots, and perimeter shots from various areas.

Team Games Drill

1. Dribble Tag (see Figure 8-41)

Emphasis: Change of pace, control, and speed dribbles.

Formation: One half of the court is used, baseline and sidelines serve as boundaries.

Skill Level: Beginner, intermediate.

Procedure: Each player has a ball and all are dribbling simultaneously. One person is chosen as "it" and tries to tag another player while dribbling the ball.

Rules: If a ball is lost out of bounds as player attempts to dribble away from "it," or is tagged by "it," that player is out and should take his/her ball to the sideline to practice the stationary dribble. (Or instead of one player being "it," have both players be it until all players are tagged.)

Note: Stress head up and importance of using both hands when dribbling.

Variation: As fewer players remain in the game, a smaller area may be used.

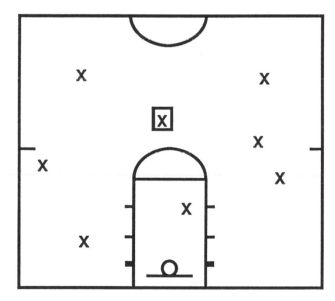

Figure 8-41. Dribble tag.

2. Circle Dribble Relay (see Figure 8-42)

Emphasis: Change of direction, crossover, and control dribbles.

Formation: Divide group into two equal teams. Arrange in a circle formation, with players standing about six feet apart.

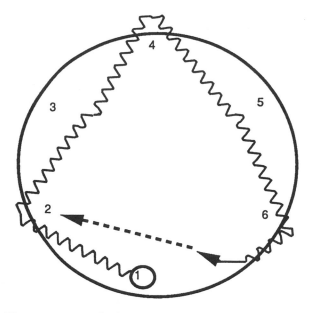

Figure 8-42. Circle dribble relay.

Skill Level: Intermediate diagram

Procedure: Player 1 starts dribbling with the right hand and dribbles to the outside of player 2, to the inside of player 3, and the outside of player 4, etc., until they reach their starting place. The ball is passed to player 2 who repeats the process. The winning team is determined by the last dribbler (6) who reaches their starting place first.

Note: Instruct players to dribble with the "away" hand when going around stationary players

3. **Shuttle Dribbling** (see Figure 8-43)

   Emphasis: Control dribble
   Skill Level: Beginner, intermediate
   Formation: Shuttle dribbling begins at the

head of a line. Form two equal teams with four players in each line. diagram

Procedure: The head player dribbles across to another line, and hands the ball off to the player at the head of the second line. The head player then takes a place at the end of that line. The player receiving the ball dribbles back to the first line.

Variation: A number of shuttles can be arranged for dribbling across a basketball court.

4. **Dribble Catch-up** (see Figure 8-44)

   Emphasis: Speed dribble
   Skill Level: Intermediate
   Formation: Two teams are arranged in parallel lines standing 15 feet apart facing each other.

   Procedure: A ball is given to the players at the right end of each line. On command, the players dribble to their left, around the rectangle formed by the two squads. When they reach their starting point, they hand the ball to the nearest player, who then dribbles around the rectangle. If a dribbler succeeds in overtaking the dribbler of the opposite team, his/her group is the winner.

   Variation: Continue the drill and give points when a player is passed rather than end the drill and award a winner.

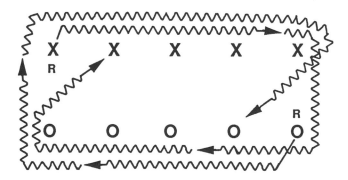

Figure 8-44. Dribble catch-up.

5. **Basketball Relay** (see Figure 8-45)

   Emphasis: Passing, catching, and shooting
   Skill Level: Beginner, intermediate
   Formation: Seven-to-10 on a team; two basketballs and goals.

   Procedure: The object is for the player whose number is called to pass the ball to each one of

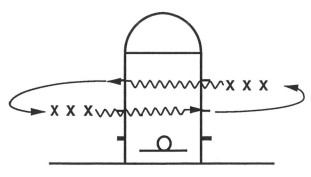

Figure 8-43. Shuttle dribbling.

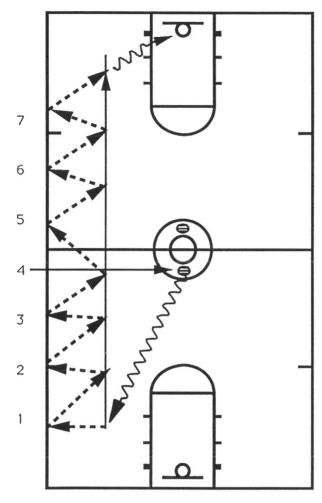

Figure 8-45. Basketball relay.

his/her teammates, try for a basket, and return the ball to the starting position before his/her opponent.

a. Divide the group into two equal teams. Each team is lined up and numbered off along opposite sidelines.
b. Number players 1-7 for Team A and 1-7 for Team B.
c. Place two basketballs on the floor in the middle of the court.
d. When a number is called, the player runs to get one ball and dribbles to a spot approximately 5 feet in front of player 1 of their team.
e. The player passes to player 1, receives the pass back, passes to player 2, receives the pass back, and so on all the way down the line.

f. When the player has thrown to each teammate, he/she dribbles to his/her basket and takes one shot.
g. The player then rebounds the shot and dribbles to the center of the court where he/she places the ball down.

Scoring: Two points are scored for the player finishing first, and two more are scored if a basket is made.

Variations:
1. Specify the kind of pass to be used (chest, bounce, overhead) or shot to be made (lay-up, free throw, jump shot).
2. Have the player shoot until a basket is made.

6. **Sideline Basketball** (see Figure 8-46)

Emphasis: The fundamental skills of basketball

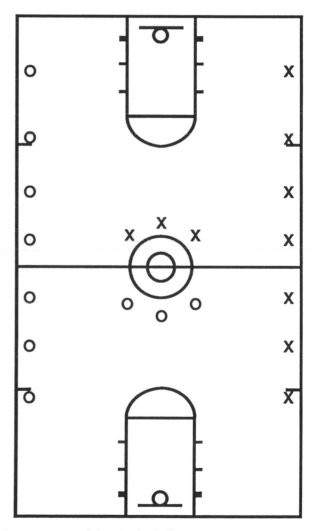

Figure 8-46. Sideline basketball.

Skill Level: Intermediate

Formation: Divide the group into two equal teams, each lined up along one side of the court, facing the other.

Procedure:

a. The game is played by three-to-five active players from each team. The remainder of the players who stand on the sideline can diagram catch and pass the ball to the active players. Sideline players should be spaced an arms length away from each other.

b. The active players play regulation basketball, except that they may pass and receive the ball from sideline players. The game begins with the active players occupying their own half of the court. The ball is taken out-of-bounds under the basket, and by the team that was scored on. Defensive pressure can be dictated by the coach (zone, player to player).

c. Play continues until one team scores or until a period of two minutes elapses. The active players then take places on the left side of their line and three-to-five new active players come out from the right. All other players move down in the line.

Rules:

1. Sideline players may not shoot, nor may they enter the playing floor. They must keep one foot completely out-of-bounds at all times.

2. No official out-of-bounds on the sides is called. Players on that side of the floor simply recover the ball and pass it back into play to an active player.

3. Out-of-bounds on the ends (baseline) is the same as in regular basketball.

4. If any of the sideline players enters the court and touches the ball, it is a violation, and the ball is awarded out-of-bounds on the other side to a sideline player of the other team.

5. When a player is fouled, a one-and-one opportunity is awarded. If fouled on the shot, a two-shot free throw is awarded.

6. Sideline players may not pass to each other, but must pass back to an active player.

Variations:

1. A team must pass the ball to their sideline players at least five times before attempting a shot.

2. No dribbling allowed. This encourages team passing and proper pivoting.

7. Russian Basketball

Emphasis: Passing, catching, cutting, starting, stopping, pivoting, and player-to-player defense.

Skill Level: Beginner, intermediate, advanced

Formation: Five-to-six players on a team, regulation basketball court, one basketball

Procedure:

a. Divide team into two groups.

b. Official rules of play apply, *except no dribbling is allowed.*

c. Game begins with a jump ball at the center circle.

d. Each player guards an opponent.

e. The object of the game is to move the ball into scoring territory using a variety of passes and fakes.

f. Optional rule: May not pass back to a teammate in succession.

Variation: The coach may also introduce the skill of setting *off-the-ball screens* in order to free the offensive player.

Dribbling Skills

PERFORMANCE AREA	SPECIFIC SKILLS	SUGGESTED EMPHASIS		
		Elem. School Beginner 8-10	Middle School Intermediate 11-13	High School Advanced 14 and up
Dribbling	Stationary dribble			
	A. Dominant hand	X		
	B. Non-dominant	X	X	X
	C. Alternating	X	X	
	Control dribble	X	X	X
	Speed dribble	X	X	X
	Crossover dribble	X	X	X
	Change-of-pace	X	X	X
	Reverse		X	X
	Behind the back			X
	Between the legs			X

Ball Handling and Dribbling Drill Matrix

Drill	SKILL LEVEL		
	Beginning	Intermediate	Advanced
Ball Handling Series:			
Ball slapping		X	X
Fingertip control		X	X
Stationary dribble (dom. hand)	X		
Stationary dribble (non-dom.)	X	X	
Stationary dribble - Alt.	X	X	
Stationary dribble - High	X	X	
Stationary dribble - Low	X	X	
Around the world	X	X	X
Circle around both legs without dribble	X	X	X
Single leg circle without dribble	X	X	X
Figure 8 without dribble	X	X	X
Figure 8 with a dribble		X	X
4 tap dribble		X	X
Cradles		X	X

	SKILL LEVEL		
	Beginning	**Intermediate**	**Advanced**
Sitting dribble			
a) Dominant hand	X	X	X
b) Non-dominant hand	X	X	X
c) Under legs			X
d) Behind back			X
e) Sit-ups			X
f) Two balls			X
g) High-low			X
Hike drill		X	X
Clap and catch			
a) Toss	X		
b) Bounce	X		
c) Overhead	X	X	
d) Behind the back	X	X	
e) Ball behind - clap in front		X	X
Skip dribble			X
Flip drill			X
Crab run		X	X

Dribbling Drills:

	Beginning	Intermediate	Advanced
Blind stationary dribble	X		
with blinders		X	
Zig-zag dribble	X	X	
with defense		X	X
Stop-and-go dribble	X	X	
Dribbling the lines	X	X	
with defense		X	X
Obstacle dribble	X	X	
Dribble against the wall		X	X
Zig-zag dribble between the legs			X
Combination dribble			X
Reverse dribble square drill		X	X
Full court speed dribble	X	X	X
Crossover dribble	X	X	X
Count fingers	X	X	X
Seven cones		X	X
Twelve cones		X	X

Team Games:

	Beginning	Intermediate	Advanced
Dribble tag	X	X	
Circle dribble relay		X	X
Shuttle dribbling	X	X	
Dribble catch-up	X	X	
Basketball relay	X	X	
Sideline basketball	X	X	
Russian basketball	X	X	X

Skill Evaluation Chart

(+ = good; √ = satisfactory; 0 = needs much work)

NAMES

SKILLS OBSERVED	John	Michelle									
example: Dribbling - right hand	+	√									

9
Shooting Techniques

Karen Garchow, M.A.

QUESTIONS TO CONSIDER

- What are the shooting skills used in basketball?
- What sequence is recommended for introducing these skills to young players?
- What are the key elements and common errors of each skill?
- What drills and activities are effective in teaching shooting?

INTRODUCTION

Shooting is one of the most important fundamentals in the game of basketball. It is extremely important to learn correct shooting fundamentals at an early age. This is accomplished through the use of modified equipment (i.e., smaller basketballs, lower basket heights) and sound shooting fundamentals taught by knowledgeable coaches. The vast majority of good shooters are "developed" through numerous hours of correct practice. The coach must guide the player into proper shooting form, provide sufficient feedback, and supervise shooting drills in practice so that the proper technique becomes habitual.

For a summary of the shooting skills and drills that are appropriate for each level of play (beginning, intermediate, and advanced), see Supplements 9-1 and 9-2.

TYPES OF SHOTS

There are four basic shots that all players should learn:

1. the lay-up shot
2. the set shot
3. the jump shot
4. free throw or foul shot

Lay-Up Shot

The lay-up is the most basic shot in basketball. It is the shot used when a player is close to the basket or to culminate a fastbreak. It is a shot that skilled players cannot afford to miss and one with which beginning players can achieve reasonable success.

The key element of the lay-up shot is *footwork*. The take-off is from the foot opposite the shooting hand. This allows for greatest upward extension of the body, thus decreasing the distance between the ball as it leaves the hand and the basket. Lay-ups from the right-hand side are off an upward jump from the left, or inside foot, and on the left-hand side the shot goes off the right foot, shooting with the left hand.

When teaching the lay-up, it's best to have players begin practicing without a running step (see Figure 9-1). Have players stand to the side

Figure 9-1. A youth player practicing a stationary lay-up at an 8-ft. basket.

"A string is tied from the right knee to the right elbow. When the right arm moves up to shoot, it pulls the right knee up too." On the left side of the basket, it's the right foot that is planted and the left hand and knee that are brought up.

Stress to ALL players at an early age, whether they're left- or right-handed, that they must learn to shoot the lay-up with EITHER hand. Once a player feels comfortable taking the shot from a stationary position, back them up a few feet and add a dribble and *one step*. Do not worry about speed when first teaching the lay-up; instead, have players work on coordinating the knee and shooting motion.

Coaches should emphasize these important points:

1. Aim high on the board (see Figure 9-2). The lay-up should hit the backboard at least a

of the basket at a 45-degree angle, about two feet from the basket. For beginners, lines can be placed on the floor at a 45-degree angle to the basket so that they approach the basket from the proper angle. Youth players have a tendency to increase or decrease this angle, which makes the shot more difficult.

On the right side of the basket, the left foot should be planted and the right knee brought up as the player jumps straight up toward the basket. Make sure the jump is vertical. Jumping forward will cause the shooter to get too far underneath the rim. If beginners have difficulty with the approach to the basket, practice this leg movement repeatedly, without the use of a ball or basket. A good verbal cue is,

Figure 9-2. Using the backboard on a lay-up shot.

foot over the rim at a spot in the top corner of the square.

2. Do not get too far under the hoop before the shot. A common problem for beginners is taking an extra dribble and getting almost directly under the basket (see Figure 9-3). Plant the opposite foot and go up for the lay-up while still a few feet away from the basket.

3. Until ready to shoot, the ball should be kept low and just outside the hip that is away from the basket. This position protects the ball from the defenders and makes it easier to get the ball up into shooting position.

4. Concentrate on the target—not the ball. Pick out the spot on the backboard and keep the eyes fixed on it throughout the shooting motion.

Figure 9-3. Common errors of the lay-up: taking off from the same foot as the shooting hand and getting too far under the basket.

5. The take-off should be nearly vertical. The most common error among inexperienced lay-up shooters is attempting the shot with a flying forward leap, resulting in out-of-control shots. Get into the habit of driving hard to the basket, but then pulling up and going up straight toward the basket with maximal upward momentum and minimal forward momentum. Experienced players will be able to add distance to their take-off.

6. Keep the non-shooting hand on the side of the ball until the moment the shot is released. Taking it off too soon makes it difficult to control the ball.

Key Elements: (see Figure 9-4a-c, 9-5a-b)

1. Approach the basket from a 45-degree angle whenever possible.
2. Jump off the foot opposite the shooting hand.
3. Maximize upward momentum and minimize forward momentum.
4. Bring knee up high on jump and straighten just before peak of jump.
5. Carry the ball overhead just prior to release.
6. Aim slightly higher than and to the side of the backboard square.
7. Lay ball gently against the backboard.
8. Follow through toward the target and release ball off the fingertips.

Common Errors:

1. Pushing the ball to the basket with the palm of the shooting hand.
2. Approaching the backboard at a poor angle—either too acute or too near the baseline (see Figure 9-6)
3. Releasing the ball before or after the maximum height of the jump.
4. Dribbling in too fast and losing control of the ball.
5. Jumping with too much forward momentum with little arc on the shot.
6. Laying the ball too hard against the backboard.
7. Taking off from the same foot as the shooting hand.
8. Shooting a lay-up from the left side with the right hand (or shooting a lay-up from the right side with the left hand).
9. Committing a traveling violation.

(a) (b) (c)

Figure 9-4. Key elements of the right-hand lay-up.

(a)

(b)

Figure 9-5. Key elements of the left-hand lay-up.

Figure 9-6. Approaching the backboard at a poor angle.

Power Lay-up

The power lay-up is a shot taken close to the basket when a defender is near and may block a regular lay-up attempt. The body and feet are squared-up to the backboard and the take-off is from both feet. The shooter explodes straight up on the jump and carries the ball upward with *both* hands to the shooting position, then extends the shooting arm and follows through by flexing the wrist. (The non-shooting arm is used to protect the shot.) The backboard should always be used on the shot, and players should be instructed to expect contact (a foul) by the defender.

A power lay-up may be performed off the dribble, off a pass, or following an offensive rebound. The key is to *power* the ball up, take off from both feet, and square up to the backboard. The use of a shot-fake prior to shooting the power lay-up can make the shot even more effective!

Set Shot

The set shot is most commonly used at the free throw line and may be shot effectively around the perimeter by beginning and intermediate players.

The set shot serves as a basis for instruction in shooting mechanics at all levels of play. Beginners should learn the fundamentals of the set shot and develop proper shooting technique *before* learning other types of shots.

Triple-Threat Position

The single most important point to stress to beginners is to *square up*. This means to pivot so that the shoulders are directly facing the basket. When a player receives the ball in scoring position in the front court, the ball normally should be held close to the hip on the side of the shooting hand. This enables the player to shoot, drive, or pass and is commonly termed the *triple-threat position* (see Chapter 7). The feet should be staggered and shoulder width apart with the foot corresponding to the shooting hand placed slightly forward. Also, it should be stressed that the knees be kept in a bent position. *Bent knees* greatly improve beginners' balance, body control, and supply a great deal of the power required to get the ball up to the basket. The eyes should sight the target and remain focused on the basket throughout the shot.

Hand Placement

Ball control and *hand placement* are also important elements of good shooting. The ball is controlled with the pads of the fingers. The fingers should be slightly cupped so the ball is *not* resting on the palm. There should be a small space between the palm and the ball when it is held properly. The shooting hand should be behind and slightly under the middle of the ball. To check for the proper position, find the valve on the ball and place the shooting hand so the valve is directly between the "V" formed by the index and middle fingers (see Figure 9-7). The off-hand is directly on the side of the ball to provide balance and control (see Figure 9-8). A good way to encourage proper hand placement is to have youth players set the ball on the "shooting platter" (see Figure 9-9). Have beginners start with their hand under the ball, then rotate so the wrist is cocked and the elbow is bent at a 90-degree angle. To reinforce proper hand placement, use this technique with the beginning shooting drills described at the end of this chapter.

Figure 9-9. The shooting platter.

Figure 9-7. Proper shooting hand placement on the ball.

Elbow Position

Another key ingredient of good shooting involves *elbow position*. The elbow should be directly under the ball and in line with the basket and bent in an "L" position. The elbow is in a straight line with the foot, knee, hip, and shooting hand (see Figure 9-10). A common mistake among beginners is to let the elbow drift out and away from the body. If the elbow is out to the right (for a right-hander), the ball will go to the left of the rim. Be sure that the elbow is aligned properly and is acting as a hinge when shooting. Long and short shots which are straight (i.e., in line with the basket) are a good indication that the technique is correct, but that the force applied is not exact.

Shooting Motion

To begin the shooting motion, the ankles, knees, and hips are flexed and the ball is held in a triple-threat position. As the legs extend to provide an upward force, the ball is raised so that the shooting arm forms a 90-degree angle

Figure 9-8. Proper placement of the non-shooting hand.

Figure 9-10. Proper positioning of the elbow so that it is directly under the ball.

Figure 9-11. Proper follow-through—the "gooseneck."

or an "L position." The ball is released by extending the arm and snapping the wrist (called the "follow-through"). The set shot should be performed in a *continuous* motion beginning with the legs and ending with the release.

Follow-through

The ball should roll off the fingertips with a smooth, even backspin. The follow-through is high and toward the target. Instruct players to hold the follow-through after the shot so the hand is *"in the basket."* A visual picture of the appropriate follow-through resembles a "gooseneck" (see Figure 9-11).

Players should be encouraged to develop a smooth, consistent rhythm throughout each phase of the shot. When teaching beginners the set-shot, emphasis should be placed on proper form. As players learn the fundamentals, timing and accuracy should be stressed.

Key Elements: (see Figure 9-11)

1. Basketball position—stand with the foot, corresponding to the shooting hand, slightly forward with knees slightly flexed.
2. Hand Placement
   a. Shooting hand—spread pads of fingers comfortably behind and under the middle of the ball.
   b. Guide hand—place on the side of the ball.
3. Flex wrist backward to support the ball.
4. Position the elbow in line with foot, knee, shooting hand, and target.
5. Focus eyes on the target throughout the shot.
6. Extend knees and shooting arm, flex the wrist to release the ball.
7. Roll ball off the fingertips to produce backspin.

8. Follow through directly in line with the target with fingertips pointing toward floor.
9. Complete all key elements in a smooth shooting motion.

Common Errors:

1. Placing feet wider than shoulder width apart.
2. Turning shoulders to either side of the basket.
3. Placing the palm of the shooting hand on the ball.
4. Placing the guide hand in front of the ball.
5. Positioning the elbow outside or inside of the shooting hand (instead of directly below).
6. Squatting too far down in preparation to shoot.
7. Lacking flexion in the joints resulting in lack of power.
8. Following through improperly—fingers pointing to either side of the target.
9. Pushing the ball from chest level straight at the basket (elbow in a "V" position instead of "L").
10. Watching the ball in flight.
11. Shooting with the body off balance, upper body leaning too far forward, backward, or to the sides.

Figure 9-12. Appropriate jump shot technique.

Jump Shot

The jump shot is the most common shot in the game of basketball today. A player can execute this type of shot more quickly and with more power than most other shots. It is also a more difficult shot for the defense to block than the set shot. The key to getting the jump shot off is a combination of how high the player jumps, and how fast he/she releases the ball. Therefore, positioning and timing is of the utmost importance (see Figure 9-12).

When teaching the jump shot, remind players to work on proper form *before* attempting to "hang" at the apex of their jump. A *quick release* is more critical than the height of the jump. This is best achieved through repetition of drills that have players receive the ball in the triple-threat position and immediately shoot the jump shot in a continuous motion.

Balance is very important to the success of

the shot. Many beginners fall forward, sideways, or backwards when attempting a jump shot, which decreases accuracy and allows bad habits to form. Coaches must suggest changes in shooting technique and supervise each player's shooting practice carefully so that the player can develop proper shooting form.

Once players have learned the key elements of the jump shot, encourage as much shooting practice as possible. The jump shot should be practiced from three specific situations: from a stationary position, after a dribble, and after cutting to receive a pass. Increased range and jumping strength will improve with physical maturation, concentration, and practice.

Key Elements: (see Figure 9-12)

1. *All set shot techniques apply.*
2. Initiate power through legs with a slight jump upward.

3. Release ball just prior to reaching peak of the jump.
4. Jump straight up and land in the same spot.
5. Complete all key elements of form in a continuous motion.

Common Errors:

1. *All set shot errors may apply.*
2. Lack of timing between the jump and shooting motion.
3. Releasing the ball after maximum height has been reached.
4. Jumping forward or to the side.
5. Shooting with the body off balance, upper body leaning too far forward, backward, or to the sides.

The Free Throw

The importance of free throw shooting should not be underestimated. It is one of the most vital scoring opportunities in any game. A team's ability to make free throws is often the decisive factor in close contests.

The key elements of successful free throw shooting are *concentration* and *relaxation*. Players need to learn to relax at the free throw line. This will help relieve any anxiety and tension that they might experience. Dribbling the ball a set number of times and taking a deep breath are some of the methods used to help with relaxation.

Players need to develop a routine at the line to help them relax and be confident. Be certain to line the ball up with the basket and not the head. Also be sure there is sufficient time to align the seams of the ball, and to line the shooting finger or fingers up with the valve or other marks at the midpoint of the ball.

Players should be encouraged to use the same type of shot for free throws that they use for other shots at a distance of 15 feet. Most players use the one-handed set shot. The *five basic mechanical principles of shooting* should be checked:

1. balance
2. hand position
3. elbow-in alignment
4. eyes on basket
5. follow-through

Players should be instructed to not copy fads or repeatedly change their routines for shooting free throws. Instead they should develop a sound style and stay with it, learn to shoot the proper way and then practice daily to make the routine and mechanics automatic.

Stress concentration. It is important to eliminate all distractions from the mind and to focus concentration on the rim. A free throw should never be shot without concentrating, either in practice or in a game.

As a player practices to develop free throw shooting ability, success may be slow at first due to tension and inconsistencies in rhythm. Individuals need to develop a feel for shooting correctly, and should also learn to analyze the reaction of the ball on the rim or in the net. This will reinforce what they have done correctly, or help to determine what has been done wrong so that the necessary adjustments can be made.

Free throw practice should be incorporated into every practice session. For best results, practice should be held at various times in the daily schedule throughout the season. Shooting early in the practice session when players are fresh is suggested during the preseason when shooting form is being perfected or while beginners are learning proper technique. After the shot is learned, practice should occur when players are somewhat fatigued, under more game-like conditions. At this stage, players should take no more than two shots at a time to simulate game conditions. Shooting ten in a row is of little value beyond the early learning stage.

Practice builds confidence and is the difference between being an average or a great free throw shooter. (The mechanical principles of free throw shooting are also a part of field goal shooting. Improving the free throw contributes to improving shots from the floor.) Never underestimate the value of practicing free throws. Keep working to build mastery of this vital part of the game.

Key Elements: (see Figure 9-13a-c)

1. Once in the free throw area, the player should check the positioning of teammates and opponents.

(a)

(b)

(c)

Figure 9-13. Key elements of the free throw.

2. Approach the free throw line, accept the ball from the official, place feet in a comfortable shooting stance behind the line. (When players are learning, pay particular attention to their foot position to ensure that they do not touch or go over the line during the shot or on the follow-through).

3. Bounce the ball a few times to get the feel of the ball and also to relax shoulders, arms, and fingers. The idea is to get comfortable at the line. Remind players there is no need to rush; they have a full 10 seconds after the official hands them the ball before they must shoot.

4. Place hands on the ball and check for proper alignment of the foot, knee, hip, elbow, shoulder, and head.

5. Sight the target—concentrate on the eyelet at the center of the front edge of the rim and look just past it.

6. Visualize the ball swishing through the net, prior to shooting. The body tends to actualize what the mind suggests.

7. Take a deep breath for further relaxation and then shoot with a high arch on the ball.

8. Follow through by putting the shooting hand "in the basket," as on the jump shot.

9. Follow the shot for a rebound, but not until the ball reaches the rim.

10. Use the legs! It makes it much easier to get the ball to the hoop with a smooth, flowing, shooting-motion accompanied by more flexion of the knees.

Common Errors: (see set shot common errors)

1. Improper foot, hand, and elbow position.
2. Rushing the shot at the free throw line.
3. Stepping on or over the free throw line.
4. Remaining at the free throw line after a missed shot.
5. Lack of relaxation, concentration, and confidence.

Free Throw Practice

Purpose: To develop confidence, concentration, relaxation, routine, and rhythm in free throw shooting. To improve the five basic mechanical principles of shooting:

1. balance
2. hand position
3. elbow in alignment
4. eyes on basket
5. follow-through

Procedure:

a. Players should shoot at least 50-100 free throws every day. Practice free throws after other strenuous drills. Perform five or more drills and then shoot 10 free throws. Because players will seldom shoot more than two free throws in a row during a game, *never have them shoot more than two free throws in a row without moving off the line.*

b. Practice under pressure. Try using the following methods to create "game-like" situations:

   1. Have players imagine there is no time left on the clock and they are shooting the free throw that will win the game.
   2. Set a definite number of free throws to be made in a row.
   3. After a physically demanding drill, record the number of free throws made out of 10 (shooting two at a time). Encourage your players to constantly challenge their own records.
   4. Continue to shoot 10 free throws after each physically demanding drill until the players have recorded the total number of free throws made out of 50-100 attempts.
   5. As a mid-season pick-me-up for advanced players, stop practice before the assigned time. If a player chosen by the coach can make a successful free throw (given one attempt), everyone is released early.
   6. Position players (advanced) along the baseline. Call one player at a time to shoot a free throw. If made, no one runs; if missed, the entire team runs one wind-sprint down-and-back. Record the *team's* free throw percentage each day.

Coaching Points: Free Throw Shooting

1. Be confident and imagine the ball going through the net before the shot.
2. Relax by taking a deep breath and dribbling the ball a set number of times.
3. Use a routine that includes lining the ball up with the basket. Check one or more of the basic mechanical principles of shooting. Do not repeatedly change routine of shooting free throws. Adopt a sound style and stay with it.
4. Eliminate all distractions, and concentrate on the basket.
5. Try for a smooth, flowing, consistent shooting motion.
6. After the shot, analyze the ball reaction on the rim or in the net and make adjustments, if necessary.
7. Never shoot more than two free throws in a row without moving off the line.
8. Shoot at least 50-100 free throws everyday.
9. Practice under pressure conditions.

TEN HELPFUL HINTS FOR BETTER SHOOTING

1. Start close to the basket and work on proper shooting form. Begin practicing with 3-6 ft. shots. Shoot for "touch" first and worry about range later. Get comfortable taking shots from all spots on the court, then gradually work your way out, being conscious of maintaining the same proper form.

2. Strive for consistency of form. After proper shooting technique is learned, every shot should begin to feel the same. The more you practice, the more natural your shot will feel. Keep at it so you are able to feel when you have done something incorrectly, such as not following-through properly, not using enough leg power, or letting the elbow stray from your body. Keep your elbow directly under the ball, in line with the basket and bent in an "L" position. Imagine the ball is a pizza that you are carrying on your shooting platter. Cock your wrist way back and spread your fingers beneath the ball.

3. Stay relaxed. Tension can destroy the soft touch needed to shoot well. The body, from feet to fingertips, should feel loose and fluid throughout the shooting motion. Bend your knees in preparation to shoot and use your leg strength to power the ball to the basket. Imagine your body as a hose transporting water that begins at your feet and runs smoothly up to your fingertips.

4. Build your confidence. To be a successful shooter you must believe that every attempt

will result in a score. Believe in yourself and in your ability to make a shot. Go up with confidence. Think positively. Visualize and tell yourself, "I'm going to put this ball in the hoop." Practice the *Four Cs of a Good Shooter:*

1. Concentration
2. Control
3. Consistency
4. Confidence

5. Don't waste practice time. Practice the shots you'll most likely be taking in a game. Develop a repertoire of offensive moves and fakes you're confident in, and put extra practice time in on your weaker skills. Repeat basic drills often to practice your shooting form.

6. Be patient. Even the best shooters have trouble making over 50 percent of their shots. Don't worry if you miss your first few shots; keep shooting and concentrate on proper technique. The more attempts your team takes in a game, the better chance they have of scoring. Keep setting new individual and team goals, and strive for improvement everyday.

7. Square up to the basket every time you touch the ball in the offensive end of the court. Being in a *triple threat position* (see Chapter 8) gives you three options: to shoot, pass, or dribble. Keep feet shoulder-width apart and balance your weight evenly. You should be "comfortable" and in control before you attempt a shot.

8. Keep your eyes on the basket at all times—from the moment you're preparing to shoot, to the end of the follow-through. Don't watch the flight of the ball or the defender's hand.

9. You have more margin for error when you shoot the ball high than when you shoot it as a low line drive. Try to arch your shots so they go well over the basket, whether you're shooting for the backboard or straight for the basket. As the ball descends, it has more rim within which to land. A high-arching shot is also much softer, so you'll increase the chances that your shot, if not perfect, will roll off the rim and still drop through. When in the shaded areas, you should generally shoot for the backboard instead of the rim (see Figure 9-14).

10. Hold your follow-through after every shot. Keep your shooting hand up, your arm

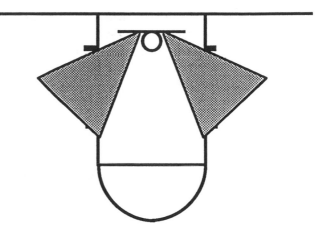

Figure 9-14. Players should shoot for the backboard when in the shaded areas.

fully extended, and pretend you're looping the index and middle fingers just over the front edge of the rim. Your wrist should be loose and flexed forward for a nice, fluid finish to your shot. A good follow-through also lets you check your shooting technique. If the shooting hand is turned inward or outward, you know you've released the ball with a twist—extra motion that you don't want. Get into the habit of holding your follow-through after every shot is released.

SHOOTING DRILLS
Introduction

When youth players are learning a particular shot, they should practice without opposition and from a relatively close range—that is, jump shots within a 3-6 ft. range. Once they learn the proper technique of the shot and become somewhat proficient in its use, more game-like conditions should be added in a progressive sequence. It is strongly suggested that an adjustable or hook-on basketball rim be used, which will decrease the basket height to 8 ft. for players ages 6-8, and 9 ft. for players ages 9-10. (See rule modifications in Chapter 5.)

Depending upon the type of shot, the next progression would permit the shooter to dribble or receive a pass prior to the shot. Because the player will have control of the ball, the addition of the dribble is easiest. This can be done while teaching the lay-up, jump, and hook shots.

Following the dribbling sequence, the player should receive a pass and execute the shot directly; later, a dribble and drive can follow the reception of the pass if court position permits. It is better *not* to precede set shots with a dribble. The player should shoot immediately after receiving a pass.

After your players have perfected the previous sequence of skills prior to shooting, an opponent should be added. At first, the defender should remain stationary, putting a hand up to distract the shooter. Next, the defender should be permitted to move one foot, and finally he/she is free to try to oppose the shooter under game-like conditions. The shooter should then practice adding a fake to the sequence to gain an advantage over the defender.

Throughout this progression of drills, the coach can ensure the shooter that he/she is able to get his/her shot off by designating where the defender may take position. For example, if set shots are being attempted, the defense should be instructed to guard loosely. If driving shots are being practiced, the defender should move closer to the shooter. As the shooter gains confidence in both situations, the defense should be permitted to defend in any manner, so that the shooter can learn to adjust to the defenders position—that is, to drive if the defense is too close and to shoot if he/she is too loose.

1. No Basket-Shooting Drill

Purpose: To develop and practice proper shooting form, emphasizing the follow-through.

Procedure:
a. Place a piece of tape on the floor between two players positioned about 10 ft. away from each other.
b. Using a regular, high-arching shooting motion, players practice "shooting" the ball back and forth trying to make the ball land on the tape.
c. Emphasize proper back spin and follow-through
d. Players keep practicing proper shooting technique until each partner has hit the tape 5-10 times.

Variation:
Wall Shooting (see Figure 9-15)
Place tape on wall; player stands close to wall (4-5 ft.) and shoots to hit target on the downward flight of the ball.

Figure 9-15. Shooting against the wall helps to develop good shooting form.

2. 3-Ft. Wrist Drill (see Figure 9-16)

Purpose: To develop proper arm positioning and follow-through technique in shooting; to create a "soft touch" on the shot; and to improve arm and wrist strength.

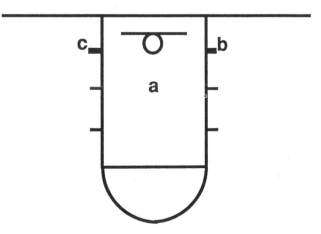

Figure 9-16. Shooting spots for the 3-ft. wrist drill.

Procedure:

a. Players stand in front of the basket, 3 ft. from the hoop at spot A.

b. Stress getting a soft feel for the ball. Players must bend the knees and release the shot with a snap of the wrist, extend the arm, and follow through. As the ball rolls off the fingertips, check for the desired backspin.

c. Emphasize follow-through by holding the hand up until the ball drops through the net and hits the floor.

d. A partner or coach may stand behind the shooter to assess the position of the elbow.

e. Players take 10 shots from each of the three shooting positions shown (shots B and C should be bank shots), maintaining sound form.

f. Advanced players may want to attempt to make three shots in a row at each spot, before they are allowed to take one step back.

Variation:
Chair Shooting

Position chairs at spots A-C. Sit on the edge of a chair with ball in "shooting pocket." Player stands up and shoots in one motion, using legs to propel ball up and over the rim softly. Rotate to a new spot after making three consecutive shots.

3. Shooting from a Chair (see Figure 9-17 a-c)

Purpose: To help develop consistency in lifting the ball to the basket and extending the elbow on the follow through. This is an excellent drill for players who have a tendency to throw the ball rather than lift the ball when shooting.

Procedure:

a. Place a chair about 6-8 ft. in front of the basket. From a sitting position, have players check their hand position and elbow in alignment.

b. Emphasize complete extension of the elbow and flexion of the wrist and fingers on the shot. With a soft touch and backspin the ball should go in the basket and bounce back to the shooter.

Variation:

To help younger players develop force from their legs, complete this drill using a "SIT-STAND AND SHOOT" motion. The power is generated from the toes to the fingertips like a hose running water upward. The flight of the ball follows a "rainbow arc."

(a)

(b)

(c)

Figure 9-17. Shooting from a chair emphasizes the "sit-stand and shoot" motion.

4. On-Your-Back Drill (see Figure 9-18)

Purpose: To develop shooting form and strength with both the dominant and non-dominant hand.

Procedure:

a. The shooter lies flat on the floor (on his/her back) with a spotter standing above him/her to retrieve the ball.

b. The ball is held in proper shooting position: elbow in, ball on the pads of the fingers, off hand on the side of the ball; and the ball above the shoulder, aligned with the foot, knee, and hip.

c. The ball is shot directly upward, snapping the wrists and rolling it off the fingertips so it will fall right back into the hands.

d. Repeat exercise until the ball has come back to the shooter 10 times with both the dominant and non-dominant hand.

e. Change positions—spotter becomes the shooter.

Figure 9-18. On-your-back drill.

5. One-handed Shooting (see Figure 9-19a-d)

Purpose: To concentrate on keeping the forearm at a right angle with the floor, forming an "L" with the upper arm, and to check for proper elbow-in alignment.

Procedure:

a. Players begin 6-8 ft. in front of the basket in a balanced shooting stance. Only the shoot-ing hand is used in this drill. The non-shooting hand is kept behind the back.

b. Have players position the ball on the "shoot-ing platter" with the wrist flexed back at a 45-degree angle. Be sure that the forearm is at a right angle with the floor, forming an "L" with the upper arm. Check for elbow-in alignment, with the ball kept in front and above the ear and shoulder. Do not allow the elbow to go out or in because this will cause shot to drift to either side of the rim.

c. The shooter must focus the eyes on the rim, and follow through toward the target.

6. 21-Set Shot

Purpose: To practice perimeter shooting and lay-ups in a competitive situation.

Procedure:

a. Place two players at each basket with one ball.

b. Each player, in turn, takes a long shot from behind a designated spot (or a free throw) and follows the shot with a lay-up.

c. If made, the long shot counts 2 points; the lay-up counts 1 point.

d. If both shots are made, the player has an-other turn.

e. The first player to reach 21 points wins.

Variation:

Team 21 Drill (see Figure 9-20)

a. Form two equal teams under the basket with one ball per team.

b. First player for each team dribbles out to the elbow or junction, pivots, and shoots at that basket (shot 1).

c. Players rebound their ball and turn to speed dribble to the other end of the court for a lay-up (shot 2).

d. Players rebound, turn and dribble back to the other end for a 4-5 ft. bank shot from the block (shot 3).

e. Players rebound and pass to a teammate who is positioned on the elbow awaiting a first shot.

f. Each player takes three shots for the team; jump- shot from the elbow, lay-up at the other end, and bank shot.

g. Each basket that is made counts 1 point for the team.

h. First team to 21 points wins.

(a)

(b)

(c)

(d)

Figure 9-19. One-handed shooting can be used to check for proper elbow-in alignment and backspin on the set shot.

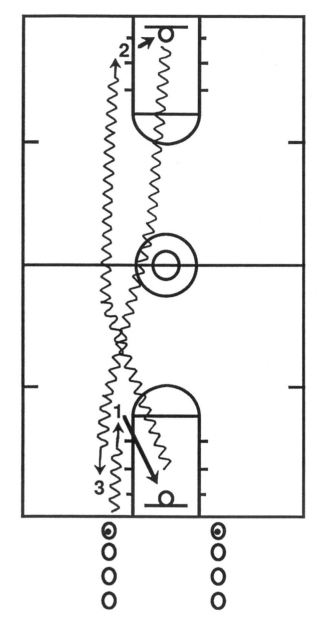

Figure 9-20. Team 21 drill.

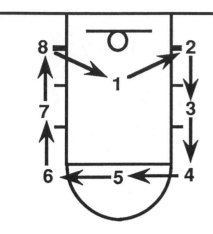

Figure 9-21. Around the world drill.

c. After a miss, the player has two choices: stay at that spot and let the other player begin, or take the "risk" (meaning they take another shot from the spot of the missed shot.)

d. If the player makes it, he/she continues on to the next spot.

e. If the player misses it, he/she must go all the way back to spot 1.

f. Beginning players enjoy this game. It is also a good drill for them to practice shooting at home with friends.

Variation:

Two-player version—spots remain the same, but the object is to be the first player to go around the world and back home again.

8. Lay-up Drills

Procedure:

a. *Stationary*

1. Assign four players at each basket with two balls.

2. Two players shoot a stationary lay-up, positioned at 45-degree angles to the right and left sides of the basket.

3. Stress "right hand-right knee" motion on the right side and "left hand-left knee" on the left side.

4. Progress to one-two-three step approach as proficiency in skill increases.

5. Rebound shot and switch lines.

6. Add criterion of three consecutive lay-ups before player is allowed to progress to step and dribble approach.

7. Around the World (see Figure 9-21)

Purpose: To practice undefended perimeter shooting.

Procedure:

a. Set-up six to eight spots around the lane take 10 shots from each spot and keep track of baskets made.

b. Players begin shooting at spot 1; if a player makes a shot, he/she moves to the next spot and continues until he/she misses.

b. *Non-Stationary* (see Figure 9-22)
1. Form two equal lines, one on each side of the basket at a 45-degree angle; the right line has a ball.
2. First player in each line stands at the edge of the free throw line. More advanced players should start from the top of the restraining circle.
3. Right line is the shooting line and the left is the rebounding line.
4. First player in the shooting line dribbles in, shoots a lay-up and then goes to the outside and end of the rebounding line on the left.
5. First player from the line on the left runs in, rebounds, pivots to face the next shooter, passes, and then runs to the inside and end of the right-hand line.
6. Encourage rebounders to jump for the rebound and do not permit any ball to hit the floor following a lay-up.
7. Continue drill. Shoot lay-ups from the left side and down the center.

c. *Power*
1. Same as drill (b) above, only the shooter executes a 2-ft. jump stop prior to the shot.
2. Shoulders remain square to the backboard as the player explodes off both feet and powers the ball straight upward with both hands to a point above and in front of the head.
3. The body and shooting arm should be fully extended in a vertical plane.

d. *Pick up and Shoot Variation*
1. Place a basketball on each block (low post area).
2. One player is a rebounder. The second player is a shooter.
3. The shooter starts by picking up one ball and scoring with a power move to the basket. Stress shooting without a dribble.
4. The shooter then moves quickly to the opposite block, picks up the other ball, and shoots a power lay-up with the non-dominant hand.
5. The rebounder replaces the ball on the blocks after the shot.
6. Continue the drill for 30 seconds or for a certain number of shots, then rotate positions.

e. *Pressure Power* (see Figure 9-23)
1. Two players at each basket with one ball positioned on the blocks.
2. Player 1 is the shooter, player 2 is the tosser.
3. Player 2 tosses the ball up high and over the rim to the other side.
4. Player 1 rebounds the ball above the head and powers the ball right back up for a shot.
5. Player 1 moves to the left block and player 2 to the right block.

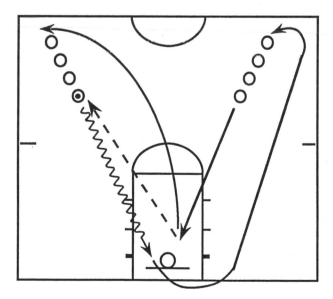

Figure 9-22. Non-stationary lay-up drill.

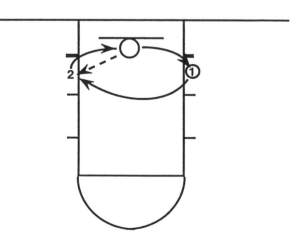

Figure 9-23. Pressure power lay-up drill.

6. Player 2 tosses the ball again against the backboard so that it will rebound without hitting the rim; player 1 rebounds and shoots a power lay-up.

7. Continue for 30 seconds, then switch positions.

Variation:

After player 2 tosses the ball up for player 1, player 2 moves over to apply defensive pressure on player 1 making the power lay-up more difficult. It is important to stress the need for the offensive player to execute a head and shoulder fake prior to the shot to draw the defensive player up in the air.

f. *Give and Go Intensity Lay-up Drill* (see Figure 9-24)

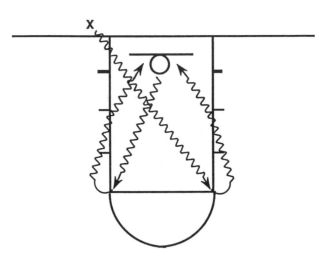

Figure 9-25. X-out lay-in drill.

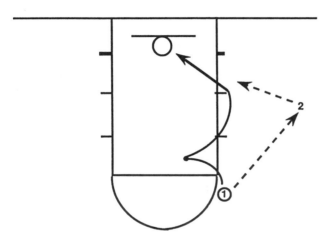

Figure 9-24. Give and go intensity lay-up drill.

1. The shooter (1) starts with the ball near the foul line. Player 1 sends a crisp chest pass to player 2 positioned on the wing.

2. Player 1 fakes away from the ball (two steps) then cuts sharply to the basket.

3. Player 2 returns the pass at the point shown, roughly six feet out.

4. Player 1 goes in for a lay-up, dribbling as little as needed depending on where the ball is received.

5. Player 1 rebounds the shot, dribbles back to the foul line and repeats the drill for 30 seconds.

6. Repeat the drill on the other side of the lane.

g. *X-out Lay-in Drill* (see Figure 9-25)

1. Begin with a player positioned under the left side of the backboard with a basketball in hand.

2. The player dribbles out with the right hand to the right elbow, pivots to the outside, and dribbles in for a right-hand lay-up.

3. The player then rebounds and dribbles out with the left hand to the left elbow, pivots to the outside, and dribbles in for a left-hand lay-up.

4. The shooter travels in an "X" pattern across the key, alternating right-hand and left-hand lay-ups. Continue the drill for 30 seconds, counting the number of lay-ups made.

5. Encourage advanced players to use only one dribble and a long first step for the lay-up.

h. *Three Person Weave Drill*—see Chapter 10, "Passing Drills" no. 6

9. Cone Shooting Drill (see Figure 9-26)

Purpose: To develop a player's ability to dribble and to shoot a jump shot while going up and down in one spot.

Procedure:

a. Divide team into three lines. The first two players in each line have a basketball.

b. Place three large cones inside the key—one on each block and one in the middle of the key.

c. The first player in each line dribbles slowly

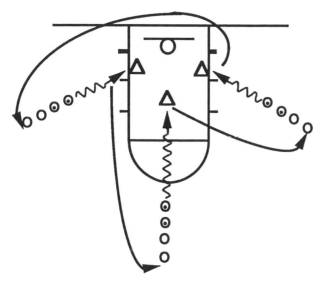

Figure 9-26. Cone shooting drill.

toward the cone, stride stops in front of the cone, and shoots a jump shot.

d. Make sure the shooters are landing in the same spot and not drifting forward, backward, or sideways.

e. Shooter rebounds shot and rotates to new line.

f. Encourage bank-shots at the wings.

10. Basketball Golf

Purpose: To develop shooting technique and accuracy while participating in a competitive game.

Procedure:

a. Mark nine spots on the court. These are the "tees" from which the shots are taken.

b. Assign four players to a team (a "foursome") at each basket. Begin at the first tee (1) and progress through the nine holes.

c. Players must make the basket at each tee before moving on to the next hole. Each shot counts as one "stroke" and the player with the fewest shots following all nine holes is declared the winner.

d. The coach can dictate which type of shot is taken at each tee (set-shot, jumper, fake-drive-jumper, etc.)

11. Beat the Professional

Purpose: To improve shooting confidence and concentration on each shot; to improve game-condition shooting off individual offensive moves.

Procedure:

a. Each player has a basketball. Position two players at each basket.

b. Players use their imagination and pick a professional basketball star to shoot against (e.g., Michael Jordan, Lynnette Woodard, etc.).

c. For every shot the player makes, he/she gets one point.

d. For every shot the player misses, the pro gets two points. Twenty-one points wins the shooting game.

e. Players take game condition shots off individual offensive moves.

f. Players are not allowed to shoot from the same spot twice in a row.

g. Encourage players to concentrate on each shot and use judgment in shot selection.

h. Instruct players to be confident and to learn to not worry about missed shots or the score.

12. Jump Shot Warm-up

Purpose: To practice the key elements of the jump shot from a relatively close distance to the basket, to practice shooting at the top of the jump, to practice jumping and landing in the same spot.

Procedure:

a. The player starts in a balanced stance about eight feet in front of basket. The ball should be higher than on the one-hand shooting drill. The forearm is at a right angle to the floor, but the upper arm should be parallel with the floor or higher.

b. When performing the jump shot, be sure players jump and then shoot the ball. They must jump straight up off both feet, fully extending the ankles, knees and hips. Check that they do not float forward, backward, or to the side. Players should land in balance in the same spot as the takeoff.

c. Have the shooters strive for a balanced jump which enables them to shoot without straining. Gaining maximum height on the jump should not be over emphasized. Balance and control are more important.

13. Jumpers (see Figure 9-27)

Purpose: To strengthen jump shooting form against a passive defensive player.

Procedure:

a. Divide team into four lines. Position lines at the wings and baseline.

b. The four defenders begin under the basket with a basketball facing their respective lines.

c. Play begins with the defense passing the ball out to the first offensive player in line.

d. The defense waves a hand in the face of the shooter but does not block the jump shot.

e. After attempting the shot, the shooter goes on defense, and the defender goes to the end of another line.

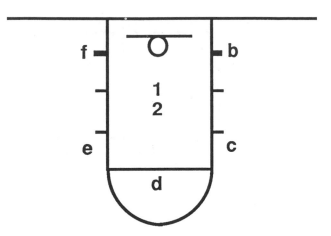

Figure 9-28. Competitive shooting drill (five-point panic).

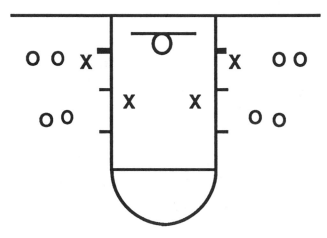

Figure 9-27. Jumpers drill.

14. Competitive Shooting/Five Point Panic
(see Figure 9-28)

Purpose: To improve confidence while shooting under pressure; to develop a quick release on the shot upon receiving a pass from a teammate and following the shot for the rebound.

Procedure:

a. Form a line of two players at each designated spot with one ball at each basket.

b. Begin with each team at spot A in front of the basket with the ball in front of the line.

c. Player 1 shoots from the spot, recovers the rebound, and quickly chest passes to player 2 who catches the ball in the ready position and is the next shooter.

d. Each shot that is made is counted out loud, and the group that reaches five baskets first wins a point.

e. Move to spots A-F positioned around the key, stressing proper form on each attempted shot.

15. Rapid Fire (see Figure 9-29)

Purpose: To improve concentration in shooting while moving.

Procedure:

a. Three players begin at each basket with two balls.

b. Player 1 shoots from spot 1 and moves up and down outside the lane, looking for the next ball.

c. The shooter receives the second ball for another shot (from player 2).

d. Player 1 must be in a ready position to catch the ball, shoot, move, and receive another ball.

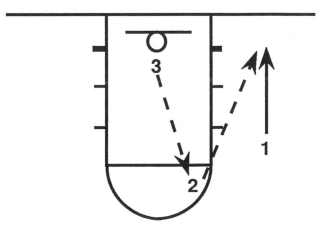

Figure 9-29. Rapid fire drill.

e. Player 3 is the rebounder who feeds player 2, who passes to the shooter, player 1.

f. Continue switching until all players shoot from the three spots daily and for 30 seconds at each spot.

g. Stress getting behind the ball, elbows in, squaring up, and pivoting on the inside foot.

16. Full-court Lay-up Drill (see Figure 9-30)

Purpose: To practice lay-ups and driving to the basket when fatigued and with defensive pressure; to improve general conditioning.

Procedure:

a. Divide team into two lines.

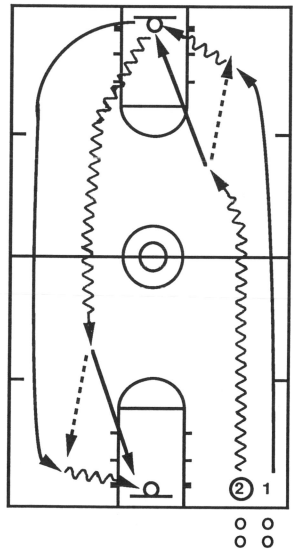

Figure 9-30. Full-court lay-up drill.

b. Beginning near the baseline, player 1 sprints hard down the sideline as player 2 dribbles toward midcourt.

c. Player 2 passes to 1 who shoots a driving lay-up and continues on down the opposite sideline.

d. Player 2 rebounds the ball and again dribbles hard to midcourt for another pass to 1.

e. Two balls should be used so that another pair of players may start downcourt as player 1 and 2 come back up the opposite sideline.

f. Beginners should be instructed to jump stop at the junction (player 2) and then lead their teammate (player 1) with a bounce pass.

17. Three-Minute Full-court Lay-up Drill (see Figure 9-31)

Purpose: To improve the skills of passing, driving, and shooting a lay-up at full speed; and to improve conditioning.

Procedure:

a. Divide team into two lines at opposite ends of the court. The first player in each line has a basketball.

b. On the coach's signal, the first player in each line dribbles downcourt and shoots a driving lay-up, rebounds the ball, and passes upcourt to the second player (2) in the line.

c. Player 2 then dribbles downcourt and shoots a driving lay-up.

d. Continue drill for three minutes. Record the number of lay-ups made by the team in three minutes, and have players set team goals to strive for each week.

18. Circuit Drill (see Figure 9-32)

Purpose: To improve shooting technique and accuracy.

Procedure:

a. Players work as partners at a basket, each player has a basketball.

b. One partner begins at spot 1, while the other begins shooting from spot 9.

c. Each player shoots ten shots (or more), one from each of the numbered areas. Shots 2 and 10 are lay-ups.

d. Each player must rebound his/her own shot.

e. Players record their shooting percentage and make efforts to improve each trial.

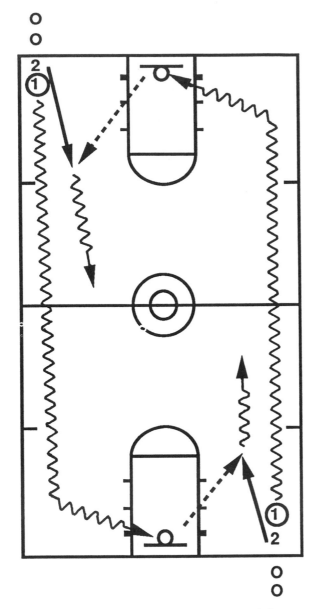

Figure 9-31. Three-minute full-court lay-up drill.

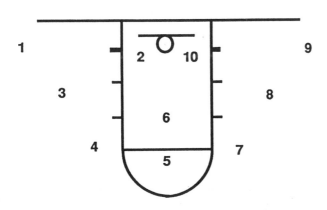

Figure 9-32. Circuit drill.

19. Daily Dozen Shooting Drills
(see Figure 9-33)

Purpose: To improve lay-up technique and accuracy, emphasizing the approach to the basket from various angles; to develop both the dominant and non-dominant hands.

Procedure:

a. Divide team equally into a shooting and rebounding line.

b. Each player performs six skills and movements from the right side of the court.

c. Each player performs six skills and movements from the left side of the court.

d. **Drill 1** - Driving lay-up

e. **Drill 2** - Power lay-up

f. **Drill 3** - Spin dribble at elbow and lay-up

g. **Drill 4** - Crossover dribble and reverse lay-up

h. **Drill 5** - Spin dribble at baseline with reverse lay-up

i. **Drill 6** - Rocker-step jump shot at elbow, wing, or baseline

j. Drills can be performed with partners. One player is shooting while the other is applying passive defensive pressure.

20. Partner Shooting Drills

Purpose: To improve concentration in shooting while guarded closely by a defender, and to develop the individual offensive moves of faking and driving.

Procedure:

a. Pairs stand informally at each basket. The shooter is guarded closely. He/she fakes in one direction, drives to another, and does a jump shot. If the guard is able to remain with him/her, the shooter fakes before shooting the jump shot. Exchange places after five shots.

b. The shooter is guarded closely. He/she fakes a shot and drives around the opponent for a jump shot. Rebound and exchange places (jump shot may be replaced with a power lay-up). Encourage as few dribbles as necessary.

c. The shooter is guarded closely. He/she uses a rocker step to fake the defense out of position and executes a jump shot. Also practice faking a drive, faking a shot, and then driving.

d. The shooter starts on the left side of the

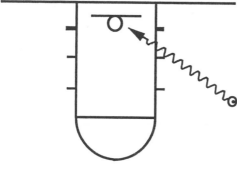

Drill 1: Driving lay-up.

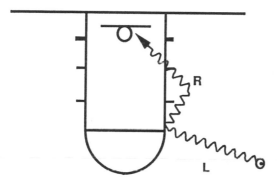

Drill 2: Power lay-up.

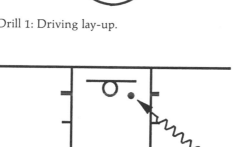

Drill 3: Spin dribble and lay-up.

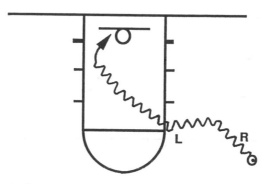

Drill 4: Crossover dribble and reverse lay-up.

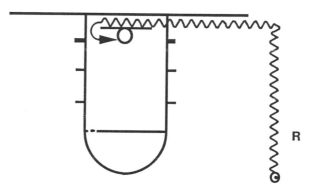

Drill 5: Spin dribble and reverse lay-up.

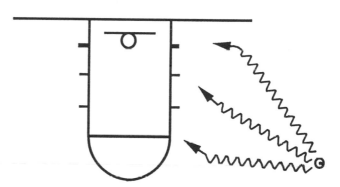

Drill 6: Rocker-step jump shot.

Figure 9-33. Daily dozen shooting drills:

basket, drives across the lane, jump stops, fakes a shot drawing the defense in the air, steps to the left with his/her right foot and executes a jump shot or power lay-up. Exchange places after five times, then begin the drill from the right side.

21. Triple-Threat Position Pivot Drill

Purpose: To develop pivoting techniques (from the Triple-Threat position) to be used when squaring up to the basket.

Procedure:
a. Players spread out in pairs around the perimeter of the key—one ball per pair.
b. The player with the ball, who is facing the half-court line, tosses the ball in the air and catches it.
c. Next, the player performs a pivot by planting the foot closest to the basket, squaring up into the triple-threat position.
d. Each player repeats this process five times and then alternates with his/her partner.

e. When each partner has done the drill twice, the pairs should move to the opposite side of the key and perform the same drill.

22. 3-2-1 Shooting Game (see Figure 9-34)

Purpose: To have the shooter perform three and two point field goals when fatigued and to provide practice in following each shot.

Procedure:

a. Divide the team into groups of two. Each player has a basketball.

b. Players start together on the whistle with the first shot taken from outside the three point line at the top of the key (worth three points).

c. The second shot is taken at the wing 15 feet from the basket on either side (two points).

d. The third shot is taken as close as desired (one point).

e. The shots must be performed in the a, b, c point order.

f. Game ends when a player reaches 21 points.

g. The coach can decide which type of shot must be taken at each spot (jumper, bankshot, power lay-up.)

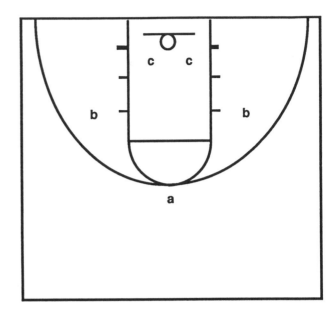

Figure 9-34. 3-2-1 shooting game.

Supplement 9-1.

Shooting Skills

PERFORMANCE AREA	SPECIFIC SKILLS	SUGGESTED EMPHASIS		
		Elem. School Beginner 8-10	Middle School Intermediate 11-13	High School Advanced 14 and up
Shooting	Lay-up A. <u>Stationary</u> 　Dominant hand	X		
	Non-dominant	X	X	X
	B. <u>Non-stationary</u> 　Dominant hand	X	X	X
	Non-dominant.		X	X
	Set shot	X		
	Jump shot		X	X
	Free throw 　8-9 ft. rim	X		
	9-10 ft. rim		X	
	10 ft. rim			X

Shooting Drill Matrix

Drill	SKILL LEVEL Beginning	Intermediate	Advanced
No basket shooting	X		
3-ft. wrist	X	X	X
Shooting from a chair	X	X	
On-your-back drill	X	X	
One-handed shooting	X	X	X
21-set shot	X	X	
Team 21		X	X
Around the world	X	X	
Lay-up drills			
Stationary	X		
Non-stationary	X	X	X
Power		X	X
Pick-up and shoot		X	X
Pressure power		X	X
Give and go drill		X	X
X-out lay-in drill		X	X
Three person weave		X	X
Cone shooting drill	X	X	X
Basketball golf	X	X	
Beat the professional	X	X	X
Jump shot warm-up	X	X	X
Jumpers	X	X	
Competitive shooting or 5-point panic		X	X
Rapid fire		X	X
Full court lay-up		X	X
Three-minute full court lay-up drill		X	X
Circuit drill		X	X
Daily dozen		X	X
Partner shooting			X
Triple-threat position pivot drill		X	X
3-2-1 shooting game			X

10
Passing and Receiving

Karen Garchow, M.A.

QUESTIONS TO CONSIDER

- What are the passing and receiving skills used in basketball?
- What sequence is recommended for introducing passing skills to young players?
- What are the key elements of each skill?
- What are the common errors young basketball players make when executing the skills of passing?
- What drills or activities are effective in teaching passing and receiving?
- What are some of the general passing rules coaches can share with their players?

INTRODUCTION

A primary ingredient to winning basketball games is to score points and to score more of them than the opponent. Basic to the development of scoring opportunities is the ability to perform fundamental skills in order to get the ball into a position where shooting percentages are highest (more open and closer to the basket). In order for any team offense to be effective, there must be a combination of accurate and crisp passes that can be received easily. Youth coaches must constantly stress the basics of "good passing" to their players because it's the fastest way to move the ball around the court, it challenges the defense and creates scoring opportunities, and it's an enjoyable way to play because everyone feels they are an integral part of the team.

For a summary of the passing skills and drills that are appropriate for each level of play

(beginning, intermediate, and advanced), see Supplements 10-1 and 10-2.

GENERAL PASSING RULES

Passes should be snappy, crisp, and thrown to the side furthest from the defender. Potential receivers who are closely guarded should extend an arm away from the defender for a target. Passes to loosely guarded teammates may be made directly to them. Passes should be received between waist and shoulder level, with the exception of bounce passes, which should be received at waist level. Although generally the pass should be crisp, the speed and type should be adjusted according to the defensive situation.

Passing in a skilled game should be fast and continuous. A deliberate type of passing attack gives the defense time to adjust their positions. Players should learn to catch and pass in one continuous motion and in the same plane. Before releasing the ball however, the passer must exercise judgment in determining whether the receiver is free. Automatic passing to a predetermined receiver can be extremely dangerous. The responsibility for a successful pass must rest with the passer.

RECEIVING A PASS

Seven Rules for Receiving Passes

Rule #1—A pass is good only if it is caught.

Passing accuracy will improve if a player starts in a balanced position with his/her center of gravity over his/her base of support. Beginners should always step in the direction of the pass to gain more power and get the body's force behind the pass. Remind your players to pass the ball so the receiver can catch it.

Another key is gaining a sense of where and when a player is a likely target for a passer. This depends on two factors—the position of the ball and the position of the defender. Players must be alert to both. A teammate may see a passing opportunity that another player does not. That's why it is important to see the ball and to assume the *basketball position* (see Chapter 7) whenever possible. In this position, the body is low, the knees are flexed, feet shoulder-width apart, and the hands are raised at chest level and close to the body. Not knowing where the ball is or not being ready to catch is all it takes for a perfectly good pass to become a turnover.

Rule #2—The receiver must always give his/her teammate a target.

Stress that your players should ask for the ball where they want to receive it. *"Target hands"* should be used whether they are standing still or cutting across the lane at top speed. As the ball is passed, extend the arms from the body and hold the hands with fingertips up. Thumbs should be pointing toward each other, with the fingers spread comfortably so they will touch as much of the ball as possible.

Rule #3—The receiver should go to meet each pass.

A coach's verbal cue might be "come to the ball." This may be done by cutting toward the

ball against a pressing defense or by taking a step and reaching for the ball against a sagging defense. By slightly shortening the distance the ball has to travel, this small effort is often the difference between a completed pass and an intercepted one. It is also a good way to draw a foul on the defender. If the receiver meets the pass and the defense tries to steal it, chances are good that the defender may get a piece of the body instead of the ball and a foul will be called.

Rule #4—Give with the ball.

Bend the elbows and give with the ball as it arrives by bringing both hands toward the body. A coach's verbal cues might include: "Soft hands," "give with the ball," "fingers and thumbs are relaxed." If a pass is not made immediately, the ball should be held at chest level so that the player is a threat to pass, dribble or shoot. Feet are comfortably spread in a side-stride position, with trunk and elbows slightly flexed to protect the ball.

Rule #5—Look the ball into your hands.

Most missed passes are fumbled not because of defensive pressure, but because the receiver takes his/her eye off the ball. Concentrate and follow the ball into the hands. A helpful coach's cue is to have the player read the brand name of the basketball as they receive it.

Rule #6—Do one thing at a time.

Too many fumbles occur when a player concentrates on his/her next move before he/she actually has caught the ball. Get firm possession of the ball before trying to execute the next skill.

Rule #7—Get behind the pass.

Whenever possible, position the body so it is directly behind the ball. Move so that the body is squarely in line with the ball. Getting behind the pass gives the player added insurance against losing possession.

Key Elements: Receiving (Catching)
(see Figure 10-1a-e)

1. Begin in the "basketball position" with hands providing a target. Point thumbs toward each other with fingertips pointing up.
2. Extend arms to meet the ball.

(a)   (b)

(c)   (d)   (e)

Figure 10-1. Key elements of receiving the ball.

3. Bend elbows and "give" with the ball by bringing both hands toward body.
4. Step forward to meet the pass.
5. Eyes focused on the ball throughout the catch.

Common Errors:

1. Holding arms and hands near sides of body, while not providing a target.
2. Attempting to catch the ball with stiff hands (palms) and arms.
3. Taking the eyes off the ball just prior to receiving the pass.
4. Concentrating on the next move before the player has actually caught the ball.
5. Standing in an erect, stationary position upon receiving the pass, which allows the defensive player to step in front and intercept.

FINDING AN OPEN PASSING LANE

A passer should be aware that the defender may take any of three defensive positions (or modifications of these) while guarding him/her— normal, sagging, or pressing. He/she should recognize that problems in passing differ according to whether the defender is guarding closely or loosely. When an opponent is pressing or when he/she moves closer following the pick-up of a dribble, the passer should find the passing lanes open. It becomes a matter of faking his/her opponent out of position *before* releasing the pass, so that his/her defender cannot deflect the pass or force him/her to make a badly thrown pass.

If an opponent guards loosely or sags after a dribbler picks up the ball, the ball handler finds it easy to pass well, but finds that the passing lanes are not open. By dropping back, the defender places him/herself in a passing lane 6-8 ft. from the passer, which allows more time to react and intercept the pass. Against a sagging defender it is important for a player to pass immediately after he/she stops the dribble. This does not allow the defender time to drop back and intercept. On the other hand, if the defender plays loosely most of the time, the ball handler may dribble toward and then more easily pass around the defensive player. The ball handler should use some means of deception in order to ensure that the passing lane is open (see Figure 10-2a-c). He/she may fake one kind of pass and alter the plane and/or type of pass before releasing the ball. A player with good peripheral vision can also look in one direction and pass accurately in another. Whatever technique is used, the offensive player must not telegraph the pass.

BASIC TYPES OF PASSES

Chest Pass

The chest pass is one of the most commonly used passes in the game of basketball. Thus, it is recommended that it be the first type of pass taught to beginners. Good technique in performing a chest pass will serve as a basis for learning the other passes. The hands are positioned on the sides of the ball, fingers well spread and thumbs pointed toward each other (see Figure 10-3). Elbows are flexed, bringing

Figure 10-3. A "W" is formed when the hands are correctly positioned on the ball.

the ball close the the chest. Step toward the target to initiate the pass, shifting weight from the back foot to the front foot to apply force. Thrust the arms outward from the chest, and release the ball with both hands with a quick snap of the wrists. Finish the chest pass with a good follow-through: arms fully extended and thumbs pointing down (see Figure 10-4). This will provide extra power, backspin, and accuracy to the pass.

Beginners often have difficulty in keeping the elbows in and applying wrist snap. They derive most of their force from elbow extension only. Coaches must stress the position of

(a)

(b)

(c)

Figure 10-2. Faking high before making a bounce pass will open up the passing lane.

Figure 10-4. Proper follow-through for a chest pass.

the back of the hands facing one another on the follow-through to ensure proper wrist snap.

Beginners also often start with the ball 10-12 inches or more from the chest. This means that they have relatively little distance over which to apply force. If the ball is brought close to the chest in preparation to pass, there is greater distance over which force can be applied.

A good verbal cue for a coach is to instruct players to "aim for the numbers of a teammate's jersey." Thrown anyplace else, a snappy chest pass can be difficult to handle. Work on making the chest pass "crisp," as they must be in a game. "Lazy passes" give the defense more time to react and greatly increase the chance of an interception.

Key Elements: (see Figure 10-5a-d)

1. Begin with ball at chest level, close to the body. Keep elbows in.
2. Spread fingers on the sides of the ball with the thumbs behind the ball and pointing toward each other.
3. Step toward the target to initiate the pass. Shift weight from the back foot to the front foot.
4. Accelerate extension of the arms from the chest toward the target.
5. Pronate wrists inward with thumbs pointing down and palms facing out.

Common Errors:

1. Initiating the pass with ball at waist or shoulder level and 10-12 inches from the body with the elbows out (see Figure 10-6a).

2. Gripping the ball with the palms of both hands.
3. Standing with feet parallel with no shift of weight forward upon release.
4. Directing the arms above, below, or off to the sides of intended target upon release(see Figure 10-6b).
5. Pointing thumbs up and palms facing in with little or no follow-through.

Bounce Pass

The bounce pass is a valuable offensive weapon in several specific situations. It is an effective pass when attacking a zone defense, feeding a post player, and leading a teammate on a fast break. Defenders seem instinctively to prevent the ball from going over their head. While an opponent has his/her arms up, the ball may be bounced under them. But players must recognize that the bounce pass is one of the slowest of all passes because it must travel a long path to cover a given distance.

The bounce pass is executed similarly to the chest pass, except that the force is exerted downward and forward rather than just forward. The passer steps toward the target, knees flexed, and snaps off the pass with an outward thrust of the wrists, following through by extending the arms with thumbs pointing down toward the floor. The ball should strike the floor about *two-thirds* of the way to the receiver so that he/she may catch it at waist level. The angle of a bounce pass is extremely important; coaches must stress to beginners that bouncing the ball halfway between the passer and intended receiver results in a higher pass which allows time for an opposing player to steal the pass. On the other hand, if the ball is bounced too close to the target (three-fourths) it will reach the receiver at about knee level and will be difficult to handle.

The most common error in bounce-passing is starting with the ball too high. Beginners attempt to start the pass from near the shoulder, resulting in a high bounce. The pass then has little speed and even less accuracy. Encourage youth players to push the ball off from waist or hip level in order to place the force of the whole body behind the pass.

Often, the bounce pass must be preceded

(a)

(b)

(c)

(d)

Figure 10-5. Key elements of the chest pass.

Figure 10-6a. *Incorrect* starting position for a chest pass.

Figure 10-6b. Poor follow-through on a chest pass.

by a high pass or an "up-fake" to raise the arms of the opponent. When a bounce pass is used for a "lead" pass, it may be desirable to use backspin to cause the ball to bounce higher and slower on the rebound. If the defense is playing "tight" and there is little opening through which the ball may be passed, top spin can be used to cause the ball to rebound lower and faster. Backspin can be applied by rolling the thumbs sharply downward under the ball at release, and topspin is applied by rolling the thumbs over the top of the ball at release. Bounce passes with top spin should bounce further from the receiver than normal and those with backspin closer to the receiver. Use of spins should be delayed for advanced play.

(a)

Key Elements: (see Figure 10-7a-c)

1. Spread fingers on the side of the ball with the thumbs behind the ball. Hold ball between waist and chest level.
2. Extend arms forward and downward toward the spot on the floor where the ball will land (approximately ⅔ of the distance toward receiver).
3. Step forward toward the target, shift weight from back foot to front foot.
4. Follow through with thumbs pointing down toward the floor.
5. Pass ball to be received at about waist level.

Common Errors:

1. Initiating the pass with the ball held at or above the shoulder level.
2. Extending arms straight down toward a spot too close to the passer (¼) or too close to the receiver (¾).
3. Standing in a parallel stance with no shift of weight forward upon release.
4. Pointing thumbs up with little or no follow-through.
5. Passing the ball to be received at knee or shoulder level.

(b)

Overhead Pass

The overhead pass is used when the opponent is in a deep crouch position, when throwing an outlet pass to begin a fast break, when making a skip pass against a zone, or when getting the ball to a taller post player inside.

(c)

Figure 10-7. Key elements of the bounce pass.

The ball is held with both hands just above the top of the forehead, with elbows bent, and thumbs close together near the bottom of the ball. Step toward the target and shift body weight from back to front foot and release the ball with a snapping movement of the elbows and wrists, following through with the arms extended as with a chest pass, only higher. The ball should be aimed so that the receiver can catch it between chest and shoulder level. If the overhead pass is received below the chest level, its downward arc from an overhead position can make it extremely difficult to catch.

The degree of snap depends on how the pass is being used. To lob it into a post player, pass the ball more softly and arch it over the defense. When attempting a sharper pass, such as to a teammate 10 yards away, the forward snap should continue until the hands are almost parallel to the floor.

A common error among beginners is to bring the ball behind the head to gain more force before throwing. This incorrect pattern should be discouraged because it allows other defensive players to steal the ball from behind very easily. Helpful verbal cues for coaches include: *"step and snap," "throw your hands toward the target,"* and *"ball above the head, not behind."*

Key Elements: (see Figure 10-8a-d)

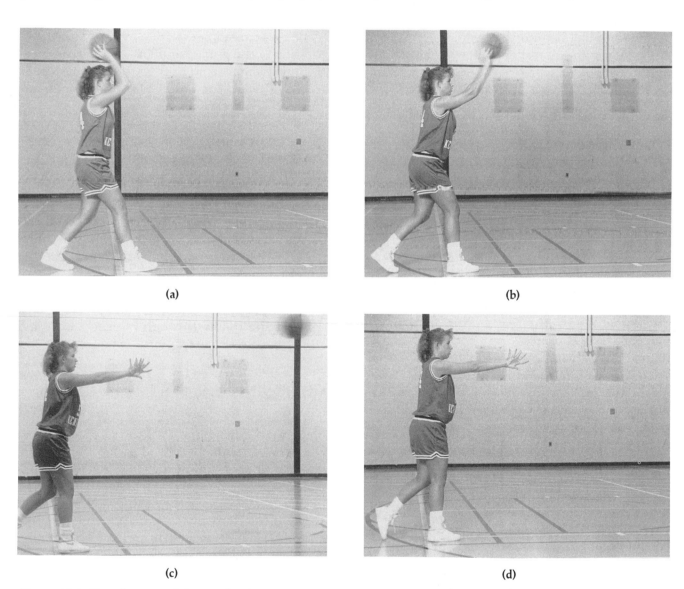

(a)

(b)

(c)

(d)

Figure 10-8. Key elements of the overhead pass.

1. Grasp ball firmly with both hands and fingers spread, thumbs close together near the bottom of the ball.
2. Hold the ball just above the top of the forehead, wrists flexed.
3. Step toward target, shift weight from back foot to front foot.
4. Release ball with snapping movement of elbows and wrists.
5. Follow through with arms extended and thumbs forward.
6. Aim between chest and shoulder level of receiver.

Common Errors:

1. Positioning thumbs far apart and near top of the ball.
2. Holding ball behind the head.
3. Standing in a parallel stance without shifting weight forward.
4. Releasing ball with little or no forward wrist snap.

Baseball Pass

The baseball pass is used when the receiver is a wide-open player much farther upcourt. It is not effective in heavy traffic because it takes more time to release than other passes. The baseball pass is best used with advanced players when both speed and distance are desirable, on a fast break, or on any half- or full-court throw.

The baseball pass is thrown in the same manner as an overhead throw used in softball or baseball. From the ready position, draw the ball back over the throwing shoulder with both hands. Place the throwing hand behind the ball, with the off hand slightly lower and in front. Draw the ball back a little more, release the guide hand from the ball, transfer weight from back foot to forward foot and release ball at full arm extension. Follow through toward the target by bringing the throwing arm down in front of the body. Fingertip control and wrist snap are essential elements for an effective pass.

Controlling the baseball pass is difficult, particularly for beginners because of their relatively small hands. Frequently during the release, the ball is rotated slightly so that the fingers are to the side of the ball, thus applying force off-center and resulting in sidespin as the ball is released. Over a long distance this side-spin is magnified and the ball may curve out of the range of the receiver. Some backspin is desirable when using the baseball pass to prevent the ball from drifting, and this can be achieved by stressing correct execution and follow through. To achieve this, coaches can teach the skill using smaller balls (see Chapter 5) as well as using corrective feedback such as *"crack the whip"* or *"step and throw"* to help encourage proper form. It's also helpful for the passer to place arc on the ball so it will carry farther and will be easier for the receiver to catch it.

Key elements: (see Figure 10-9a-d)

1. Draw ball back with both hands over throwing shoulder.
2. Place the throwing hand behind the ball with fingers spread.
3. Release the guide hand low and in front.
4. Shift weight from back foot to front foot.
5. Step toward the target with non-dominant foot.
6. Release the ball by bringing the throwing arm down in front of the body with wrist snap and full arm extension.

Common Errors:

1. Drawing ball back only to ear.
2. Placing the palm of the throwing hand on the sides of the ball.
3. Releasing the guide hand too soon in preparation to throw.
4. Stepping forward on same foot (dominant) as the throwing arm.
5. Stopping follow-through too soon with little or no wrist snap.

CHOOSING THE BEST TYPE OF PASS

One of the most difficult tasks for youth players to understand is *when* to execute the chest, bounce, and overhead passes. As players gain confidence and proficiency in skill during isolated drills, they can then progress to game-like situations where they can practice passing without the element of competition. There is a suitable pass for every situation. This is the reason for learning a variety of passes. Some general rules to follow are:

1. Overhead passes should be used if the passer is much taller than the opponent. If a

(a)

(b)

(c)

(d)

Figure 10-9. Key elements of the baseball pass.

passer is confronted by a taller opponent, he/she should not try to pass over him/her; similarly, a passer should not use bounce passes against a shorter stationary player.

2. If the opponent guards with a wide stride stance, passes can be made between the defender's legs.

3. If the opponent has a forward-backward stride with one arm up and one arm out, the pass should be made under the high arm or over the shoulder ear on the side of the lower arm.

4. If both of the opponent's arms are low and to the side, the pass should be made over either shoulder or above the head.

5. Two-hand passes should be used for relatively short distances and one-hand passes should be used for long passes; i.e., distances greater than 20 ft.

6. Passes intended for a cutter should lead the player so that he/she does not have to slow down to make the reception. Pass in front of the moving target.

7. Encourage the use of bounce passes for entry passes to players in the low-post position.

8. Encourage the use of the dribble only in an attempt to increase the passing angle or to improve the passing lane.

9. Attempt to use basic passes rather than fancy, more risky passes; e.g., behind the back.

10. The cross-court lob pass in both the back court and the front court is easy to intercept and should be used with caution.

TEN HELPFUL HINTS FOR BETTER PASSING

These simple passing rules can greatly improve a team's passing game. Youth coaches should choose *1 or 2* rules to stress during each practice and review the importance that each has in game-like situations.

1. *Don't telegraph your passes.* This refers to letting the defense know your intent by looking directly at the target. The simplest way to avoid this is by looking away at another teammate, at the basket, or in the opposite direction.

2. *Fake before every pass.* This action causes the defense to second guess the direction either you or the ball will take. Practice faking a pass to a teammate, then quickly pivoting and passing to another. An excellent rule is to fake low (bounce pass) and then pass high (overhead pass), or just the opposite— fake high and pass low.

3. *Vary the types of passes.* Do this to avoid interceptions and to keep the defense off balance (bounce, chest, overhead, baseball).

4. *Pass away from the defense.* Direct your passes to the side (outside arm) of your teammate and away from the defender.

5. *Pass crisply.* Lazy passes are the number one cause of interceptions. Be very careful when attempting to pass cross-court (lob or overhead skip-pass). The chances of successfully passing the ball over and through so many defenders are low. Only when a teammate is wide open, or when you have a clear opening, should players think about passing cross-court.

6. *Fingertip touch.* Keep palms off the ball whenever possible. The ball should rest on the pads of the fingers to ensure top accuracy and backspin.

7. *Always pass to a teammate who is in a better position to score.* This rule is called "hitting the open player," and if your players can do it consistently, they will become better basketball players.

8. *Acknowledge a good pass.* If you see players make a good pass, tell them so by nodding your head, pointing at them or giving them a high-five. Get in the habit of praising the pass that leads to the basket, as much as the basket itself. Your scorer could not have gotten the points without the assist. Encourage unselfish play at all times. It will greatly improve your teamwork.

9. *Do not make "automatic" passes.* Teach your players to size up the situation before making a pass. Check the defense and the positions of teammates. Quickly scan the court for passing opportunities. Who's open? Can you safely get the ball to them? Is anyone cutting to the basket? Don't force the ball to a teammate just because a planned play calls for the ball to go to them. Starting a

play over or going to the next option is a lot better than causing a turnover.

10. *Don't dribble before every pass.* It slows the team's flow and ball movement, making it easier for the defense to stop you, and may also cause you to miss an open teammate.

PASSING DRILLS

1. Timed Partner Passing

Purpose: To improve passing and receiving techniques, hand-eye coordination, and build strength in the hands, wrists, and forearms.

Procedure:

a. Using proper passing and catching form, see how many times you and a partner can pass back and forth, without missing, in a certain time period.

b. Continue in 1 minute intervals using the bounce, chest, and overhead pass.

c. Vary the distance between partners, depending upon age and strength of player.

2. Long and Short Drill (see Figure 10-10)

Purpose: To develop passing and receiving techniques while utilizing a moving target.

Procedure:

a. Divide team into two lines. Drill begins at baseline.

b. Two players move (slide-step, run) the length of the floor, chest passing the ball back and forth without traveling or letting the ball hit the floor.

c. When they reach the other end of the floor, they start back on the outside, making longer overhead passes.

d. As each pair gets past half-court, the next pair starts. Passes must be accurate so that the pairs of passers do not interrupt each other in the drill.

e. Concentration is required to stay clear of other pairs, particularly when passing over inside pairs from outside to outside.

f. Stress the importance of "target hands" when receiving the ball and passing "in front of" the moving target.

3. Chest Passes—Wall Drill (see Figure 10-11)

Purpose: To improve passing and receiving tech-

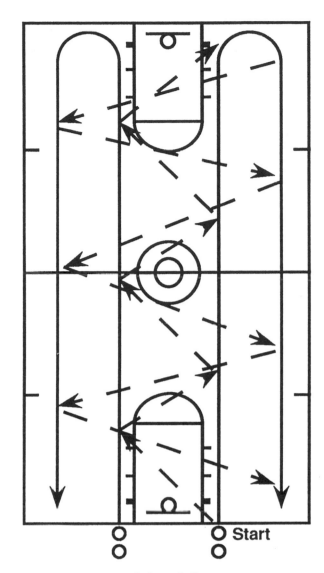

Figure 10-10. Long and short drill.

Figure 10-11. Practicing chest passes against the wall.

niques, hand-eye coordination, and to build strength in the wrists and forearms.

Procedure:

One ball per player.

a. Stand approximately 6-8 ft. from a smooth-surfaced wall.
b. Aim for a 3-ft. target.
c. Pass and catch the ball at chest level.
d. Step in the direction of the pass.
e. Count how many times the ball hits inside the target in a 30 second interval.
f. Keep a daily record.
g. Increase distance from the wall as strength and accuracy improves.

4. Bounce-Pass Wall Drill

a. Try bounce passes from many angles and distances, hitting the floor in several different places, so players can learn how the angle of the pass affects the angle at which they receive it.
b. Learn to aim for the spot that gets the ball to you in the most direct line possible.
c. Practice until you can hit that spot two or three times successfully.

5. Six Player Split Vision Passing Drill
(see Figure 10-12)

Purpose: To improve hand-eye coordination and peripheral vision. It is a great way of instilling a sense of teamwork among players.

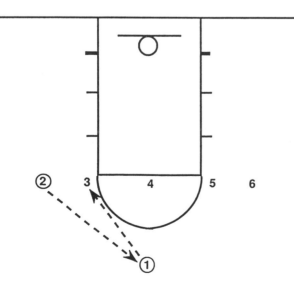

Figure 10-12. Six player split vision drill.

Procedure:

a. Five players line up along the free throw line and one player faces them at the top of the key.
b. Two balls are used. Player 1 and 2 begin the drill.
c. Player 1 (at the head of the circle) makes a two-handed chest pass to player 3.
d. As the ball leaves player 1's hands, player 2 passes to 1.
e. Player 1 passes to player 4 as 3 in return passes to 1 and so on down the line.
f. Each player has a turn as player 1, and everyone takes a forward step as they receive the pass, then moves back to the original position after they have passed it.

6. Shuttle Passing Drill (see Figure 10-13)

Purpose: To develop passing and receiving techniques.

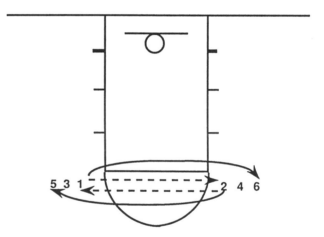

Figure 10-13. Shuttle passing drill.

Procedure:

a. Divide team into two lines with three players in each. Lines are facing each other.
b. Player 1 passes to 2 and goes to the end of that line.
c. Player 2 passes to 3 and goes to the end of the line and so on.
d. All players keep moving and should use chest, bounce and overhead passes.

7. Triangle Passing

Purpose: To improve passing accuracy, quickness, and concentration.

Procedure:

a. Form groups of three into triangles.
b. Two players with a ball pass alternately to the player without the ball.
c. Pass quickly. Increase the pace. Change positions.

8. Defender in the Middle

Purpose: To improve passing and faking against defensive pressure.

Procedure:

a. Two offensive players stand about 10 feet apart, with a defender in the middle.
b. Passers use whatever pass is necessary to get the ball directly past the defense.
c. Defender remains in the middle until he/she touches a pass (doesn't have to gain possession) and is replaced by the player who passed it.
d. Rules: No high lob passes over the head of the defensive player. Encourage fakes, pivots, and crossover steps before every pass. Do not allow offensive players to hold the ball for more than five seconds.

9. Keep-Away (see Figure 10-14)

Purpose: To improve passing and faking techniques, and to develop decision making skills in hitting the open player.

Procedure:

a. Offensive players form a circle. One player is designated as the defensive player and stands in the center of the circle.

b. Offensive players on the outside of the circle attempt to pass to teammates without allowing the defensive player in the middle to touch the ball.
c. Offensive players may not pass to the player directly to the left or right of them.
d. The offensive player replaces the defensive player inside the circle if the ball is touched or a bad pass is thrown.

10. Three-Person Weave Drill
(see Figure 10-15)

Purpose: To develop accuracy in passing to a moving target in a fastbreak situation (half or full court); to develop proper lay-up shooting technique.

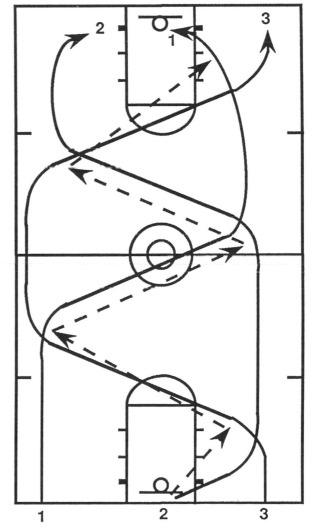

Figure 10-15. Three-person weave drill.

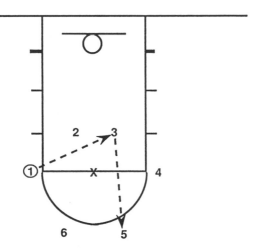

Figure 10-14. Keep-away drill.

Procedure:
a. Divide team into three equal groups.
b. Start the drill with the first player in the middle passing the ball to either wing.
c. After making the pass, the player goes behind the player to whom they just passed.
d. The receiving wing meets the pass, and in turn passes to the other wing, and follows behind that receiver.
e. The outlet receiver returns the ball to the next middle player and the drill continues with the next three players.

Variations:
Encourage drill to be run with the lines widely spread; this then becomes a great tool for learning the fastbreak. Use a heavyweight ball. Include a lay-up to be shot by a player at the opposite end of the court.

11. Circle Passing Drills

Purpose: To improve passing accuracy and reaction time.

Procedure:
a. Circle of six players with a leader in the center. The leader passes the ball to each player who immediately returns it to the leader.
b. Same as above, except a second ball is added. The leader, A, and a player in the outside circle, B, have a ball.
c. A and B pass at the same time—A to C and B to A.
d. Passing continues twice around the circle; then someone replaces A.
e. Simple rule: Players in the circle always return the pass to A, and A always passes to the next player in the circle.

12. Dukes Passing Drill (see Figure 10-16)

Purpose: To develop accuracy in passing to a moving player and stepping to meet the pass; to improve peripheral vision.

Procedure:
a. A circle is formed at the free throw circle with 10 to 12 players. The players stand stationary and hand the ball around the circle, always giving it to the same player as in Figure 10-16a. Player 1 gives it to player 2 and 2 to 3, etc.
b. When the coach whistles, the players break the circle and run anywhere on half the floor as in Figure 10-16b. Now each player must

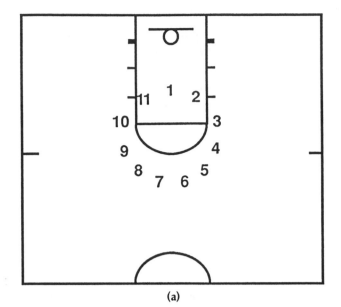

(a)

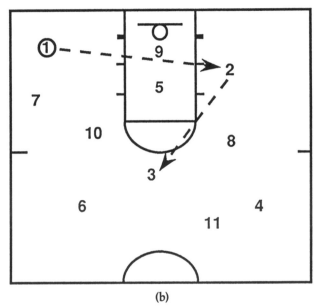

(b)

Figure 10-16. Dukes passing drill.

find the person to whom he/she handed the ball and pass the ball to that player without taking a step or a dribble.
c. The player who is to receive the pass must move to meet the pass and call for it so the passer can find him/her. Because the passer is initially a receiver, he/she must be alert to receive the pass and very quickly find who he/she is to pass to and deliver a crisp accurate pass.
d. The entire drill is conducted with the players in constant motion. This causes a variety of passes to be thrown as well as passes that

must avoid hitting another player who crosses the passing lane as he/she moves about the court.

13. Post Passing Drill (see Figure 10-17)

Purpose: To improve passing, receiving and pivoting to and from the post position.

Procedure:

a. Five players and two balls are used.
b. Player 2 passes to 1 who pivots and passes to 4.
c. Player 3 then passes to 1 who pivots and passes to 5.
d. Each ball is kept moving in its respective triangle.
e. Player 1 should use pivot footwork to slide back and forth to meet the passes coming from the guards.

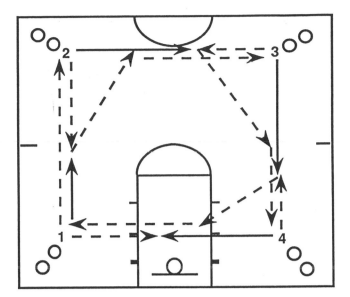

Figure 10-18. Corner passing drill.

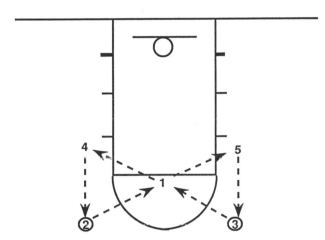

Figure 10-17. Post passing drill.

14. Corner Passing Drill (see Figure 10-18)

Purpose: To develop passing, receiving, and cutting techniques for a player in motion.

Procedure:

a. Players form lines in the corners of the half-court area.
b. Player 1 passes to the line to the left and follows the pass.
c. The receiver (2) passes back to 1 and 2 cuts toward the next line to the left.
d. Player 1 passes to player 2 and goes to the end of that line.
e. Player 2 now follows the same procedure with player 3, and the drill continues in this fashion.

Variation:

After the drill is going well, two balls may be used. Start them at opposite corners. A variety of passes may be used (chest pass, bounce pass, etc.).

15. Two-Ball Crisscross (see Figure 10-19)

Purpose: To develop passing skills and concentration.

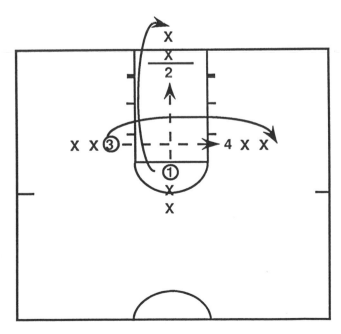

Figure 10-19. Two-ball crisscross drill.

Procedure:

a. Players set up in four lines around the key area facing another line.

b. Players 1 and 3 begin with the balls.

c. Player 1 passes to 2 and follows the pass to the end of the opposite line.

d. As Player 1 crosses, player 3 passes to 4 and follows the pass to the end of the opposite line.

e. This pattern continues and players in opposite lines continually rotate, with the first person in line passing and following to the opposite line.

Variation:

Vary the distance of the passes by moving the lines further out. Use a bounce or over-head pass, or a combination of passes.

16. Two-Ball Pass Drill

Purpose: To improve hand-eye coordination and reaction time while passing and receiving with a partner.

Procedure:

a. Partner drill—positioned 8 ft. apart, and using two balls, partners pass back and forth using different passes each time.

b. Pass simultaneously—one throws a bounce pass, the other throws a chest pass. Concentrate on getting the passes in and out of your hands as quickly as possible.

c. Make 50 passes each, then switch roles— the bounce passer becomes the chest passer, and vice versa.

d. Advanced variation—throw the baseball pass back and forth alternating hands.

e. Throw at the same time—one throws with the left hand, the other with the right, and vice versa.

17. Five-Star Passing (see Figure 10-20)

Purpose: To develop quickness, accuracy, and concentration in passing. This drill looks great in warm-up.

Procedure:

a. Player 1 begins with the ball at the baseline and passes to the far corner to player 2 and follows his/her pass to the end of that player's line.

b. The receiver passes to the opposite corner and player 3 follows his/her pass.

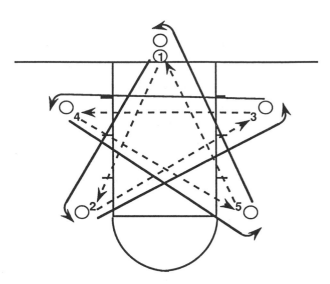

Figure 10-20. Five-star passing drill.

c. That receiver passes across the lane to player 4 and follows his/her pass.

d. Player 5 passes to 1 and follows his/her pass.

e. Repeat pattern as the ball starts around again.

18. Full-Court Passing, Receiving, and Lay-Up Conditioning Drill (see Figure 10-21)

Purpose: To improve non-stationary passing skills, lay-up techniques, and level of conditioning.

Procedure:

a. Player 1, 2, 3, and 4 are stationary outlets.

b. Player 5 passes to 1, receives a return pass; then passes to 2, receives a return pass and shoots a right-handed lay-up.

c. Player 5 quickly rebounds the ball out of the net and passes to 3, receives a return pass; then passes to 4, receives a return pass and shoots a right-hand lay-up at the other end.

d. The next player, 6, begins as soon as player 5 gets to midcourt.

e. Players continue this drill for several minutes at full speed.

f. Rotate all players to the outlet and shooting positions.

g. Players change directions and repeat the drill shooting left-handed lay-ups.

19. Crossfire Passing Drill (see Figure 10-22)

Purpose: To develop skills in passing to a cutting

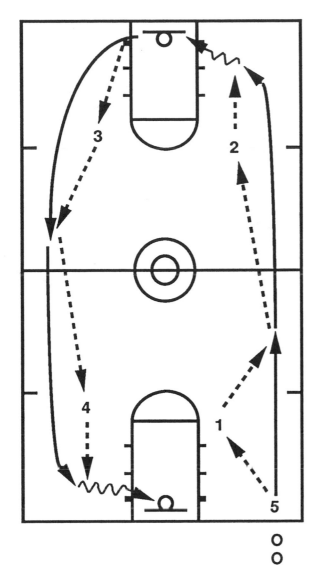

Figure 10-21. Full-court passing drill.

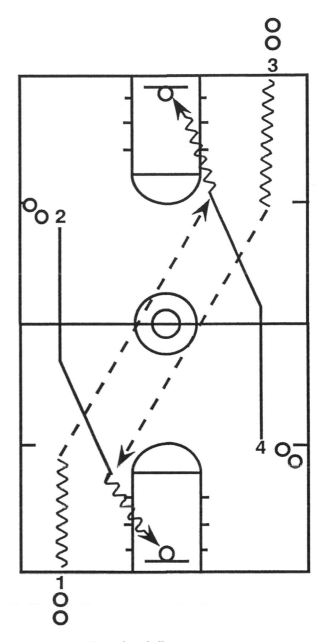

Figure 10-22. Crossfire drill.

player; to improve skills in driving to the basket and shooting the lay-up.

Procedure:

a. Players line up at the endline and hash-marks on each side of the court. The first player (1 and 3) at each endline has a ball.

b. Player 1 dribbles out and passes downcourt to player 2 who is cutting to the basket from the opposite sideline. Player 3 dribbles and passes to player 4 in similar fashion.

c. Players 2 and 4 should receive the ball near the top of the key and then drive in for a lay-up.

d. Players need to *concentrate* to avoid passing to the other receiver and should avoid unnecessary dribbling.

Variation:

Players may shoot a jump shot rather than a lay-up, or defense may be added on the shot. Drill may be done from the opposite direction to work on lay-ups with the opposite hand.

Supplement 10-1.

Passing Skills

PERFORMANCE AREA	SPECIFIC SKILLS	SUGGESTED EMPHASIS		
		Elem. School Beginner 8-10	Middle School Intermediate 11-13	High School Advanced 14 and up
Receiving	Catching	X		
Passing	**Chest pass**			
	Stationary target	X		
	Non-stationary	X	X	X
	Bounce pass			
	Stationary target	X		
	Non-stationary	X	X	X
	Overhead pass			
	Stationary target	X		
	Non-stationary	X	X	X
	Baseball pass			
	Stationary target	X		
	Non-stationary		X	X

Supplement 10-2.

Passing Drill Matrix

Drill	SKILL LEVEL		
	Beginning	Intermediate	Advanced
Timed partner passing	X		
Long and short drill	X	X	
Wall drill—chest and bounce	X	X	
Six player split vision		X	X
Shuttle passing	X	X	
Triangle passing	X	X	
Defender in the middle	X	X	
Keep away	X	X	
Three person weave		X	X
Circle passing		X	X
Dukes passing		X	X
Post passing		X	X
Corner passing		X	X
Two-ball crisscross		X	X
Two-ball passing			X
Five star passing		X	X
Full court passing		X	X
Crossfire			X

11
Rebounding

Karen Garchow, M.A.

QUESTIONS TO CONSIDER

- What are the rebounding skills used in basketball?
- What are the key elements and common errors of each skill?
- What sequence should be used in introducing these skills?
- What drills and activities are effective in teaching rebounding?

DEFENSIVE REBOUNDING

There are two kinds of rebounds—*offensive and defensive.* (For a summary of the rebounding skills and drills that are appropriate for each level of play—beginning, intermediate, and advanced—see Supplements 11-1 and 11-2.) Defensive rebounds result when the opponents miss a shot—offensive rebounds occur when your own team misses. Important facts to remember are: (1) most shots in a basketball game are missed, and (2) the team that controls the boards usually wins. The better your team does at defensive rebounding, the fewer shots the opponents get and the fewer their opportunities to score.

The key to defensive rebounding is *boxing out.* Also called screening out, this action involves turning the back to and putting the body between the opponent and the basket after every shot. Players must keep their opponents behind them so that the all-important inside position for the rebound is always available.

Once the shot is taken, the first thing a defensive player must do is to yell "shot." This alerts the team to start boxing out. The box out begins with a pivot into the opponent, turning the back to the opponent, and making physical contact with his/her body. The player must keep a wide base, both to improve balance and to obstruct the opponent's path to the basket. Because the rebounder has only one or two seconds before having to find the ball, it is important to quickly establish a position to enable "feel" of the opponent with the body.

For the best rebounding position, the feet should be spread slightly wider than shoulder width, and the elbows kept well away from the body with the hands up, ready to gain possession. The buttocks should be down (almost sitting on the opponent's thighs) and the knees should be well-flexed in preparation to jump. The head is erect and the eyes are focused on the ball (see Figure 11-1).

If the opponent is cutting to the left, a forward pivot should be made: leading with the chest, the left foot is used as a pivot and the right foot is brought around so it lies squarely

Figure 11-1. Proper defensive box out position.

in the opponents path. The defensive player should now be facing the basket with the offensive player positioned behind him/her (see Figure 11-2a-b). If the opponent is cutting to the right, a right forward pivot should be used.

If the opponent is a determined offensive rebounder, the defensive player may have to "feel" for him/her with the upper arms and backside, shuffling with short, choppy steps to cut off the opponent. Stress to your players that they should never be caught flat-footed, and to keep their box out position when the opponent tries to slip past them.

As the rebound comes off the boards, the defensive player jumps into the air with elbows wide and body in a slight jack-knife position commonly called the *eagle spread.* The jack-knife movement of the body throws the rear of the defensive rebounder backward. This encourages youth players to become as big an obstacle as possible to the offensive player.

(a)

(b)

Figure 11-2. To establish proper defense box out position, a forward pivot is made into the opponent.

The defensive rebounder should grasp the ball firmly with both hands. On returning to the floor, the feet should be spread, the elbows out, and the ball protected under the chin. Beginners will often bring the ball down to waist level following a defensive rebound. Stress the importance of keeping the ball moving to prevent the opponent from gaining possession. Like every other skill, boxing out and rebounding must be practiced until they become *automatic*.

Key Elements (see Figure 11-3a–c)

1. Pivot into opponent using a forward or reverse turn.
2. Make contact with the opponent's body.
3. Move the feet slightly wider than shoulder width.
4. Keep the elbows and arms out and away from the body.
5. Point hands and fingers up.
6. Keep buttocks down and out.
7. Flex knees in preparation to jump.
8. Shuffle feet with short, choppy steps to keep the body between the opponent and the basket.
9. Focus eyes on ball.
10. Jump strongly for the ball and grasp it with two hands.

Common Errors:

1. Going in for the rebound without boxing out.
2. Having stiff knees and an erect body position.
3. Holding arms near sides of body.
4. Reaching back with the hands and trying to hold the opponent.
5. Taking the eyes off the ball by looking back at the opponent.
6. Standing flat-footed in the box out position.
7. Releasing contact with opponent before the ball is secured.
8. Getting too far under the basket.

OFFENSIVE REBOUNDING

The offensive rebounder faces the defensive player's efforts to box him/her off the boards. Realizing that the defensive player will turn into his/her path, the offensive player must attempt to counteract this defensive objective by using quick fakes.

Clever fakes and changes of direction are essential ingredients of successful offensive rebounding. The offensive player fakes left-goes right, or fakes right-goes left, in an effort to avoid a defensive blockout. However, fakes

(a)	(b)	(c)

Figure 11-3. Key elements of the defensive rebound.

must be done quickly, because only seconds exist between the shot attempt and the rebound. The offensive rebounder who hustles toward the boards using clever fakes is difficult to block out.

Because the defensive player must "feel" the offensive player in order to have continuous success at boxing out, the offensive player must prevent this by changing direction. If the offensive player senses the slightest contact with the opponent's back or elbows, he or she steps *backward*, then fakes and cuts around the block out. Faking in one direction and then cutting in another is a very difficult move to defend.

If the offensive player succeeds in getting by the block out, he/she crouches with knees bent, enabling a quick spring into the air for the rebound. The ball should be caught with two hands above the head with arms extended. Because most offensive rebounds are obtained near the basket (inside the free throw lane) in a high-percentage shooting area and at a time when it is difficult for the defense to adjust, the rebounder should return to the floor and immediately go back up for a shot attempt. However, the rebounder should expect contact from a defender on the shot and therefore must *power* the ball to the basket in such a manner as to be able to score despite the contact.

Beginning players often attempt to dribble the ball from the basket after securing the offensive rebound. Point out to your players that the ball is in a key scoring area near the basket. Why take it out of this area or pass to another player who is further from the basket? Encourage the rebounder to thrust upward for the second shot and a possible three-point play (see Figure 11-4a-e)

Key Elements:

1. Anticipate a shot by a teammate and move into rebounding position before the defender attempts to block out.
2. Use quick fakes, changes of direction, and spin moves to get around a defensive block out.
3. Be aggressive. Hustle to the boards on every shot.
4. Rebound the ball with two hands above the head. If the rebound is taken in the area in-

side the free throw lane, go back up immediately for a second shot attempt.
5. Power the ball back up "strong" under the boards. Use "fakes" with the head, shoulders, and ball to get the defense into the air.

Common Errors:

1. Standing motionless behind the defensive blockout.
2. Jumping "over the back" of the defense, resulting in a potential foul.
3. Watching the ball in flight and not following the shot.
4. Dribbling the ball after an offensive rebound.
5. Dribbling or passing the ball back out of a key scoring area.
6. Falling away from the second shot in an attempt to avoid contact.

REBOUNDING: TEN HELPFUL HINTS

Share these ten helpful hints with your players, and watch how your team's offensive and defensive rebounding improves!

1. Assume that every shot attempted is a miss. Anticipate the angle of the rebound and move into prime rebounding position.
2. On defensive rebounds, make sure the three prime areas around the basket are properly covered. Communicate with teammates to box out within the rebounding triangle (see Figure 11-5). Remember not to get too far underneath the basket. Optimum position is about three to four feet away from the basket.
3. Cover the boards on the weak side at all times. The ball rebounds to the opposite side of the basket more than 75 percent of the time. Therefore, if a shot is taken to the left of the lane, chances are very good that the ball will rebound to the right.
4. Defensive rebounding is a *team* responsibility. Five players must work hard after every shot to box out properly.
5. Keep your hands up and elbows out. Take up as much space as possible under the boards. Extend fully as you go after the ball with two hands.
6. Jump and explode powerfully into the air. Be ready to spring toward the ball with a powerful upward thrust.

Figure 11-4. "Powering" the ball back up for the shot following the offensive rebound.

7. Be aggressive. Go after the ball with both hands and grasp it with authority. Body contact is a part of the game under the boards. Many players want the ball and if it's going to be yours, you'll have to go after it harder than anybody else.

8. Avoid over-the-back fouls. Get position first, then go straight up for the ball.

9. If you've secured a defensive rebound and don't have a ready outlet pass, hold the ball firmly and keep it moving close to the body. The best way to stop the opposition from tying you up is by keeping the ball moving and protecting it under the chin.

10. When you get an offensive rebound under the boards, go right back up without drib-

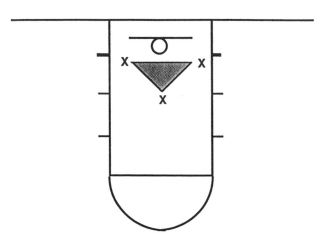

Figure 11-5. The rebounding triangle.

bling and "power" it up strongly. If you're too closely guarded to get off a good shot, give a quick upward fake with your head and shoulders. If the defenders go for the fake and leave their feet, wait for them to begin coming down—then go up for your power lay-up. You stand a great chance of drawing a foul and possibly a three-point play.

REBOUNDING DRILLS

1. Mass Drill (see Figure 11-6)

Purpose: To establish a proper player-to-player box out position, to develop quickness, and to develop the ability to maintain balance during contact.

Procedure:

a. Divide team into partners. Player A is offense, Player B is defense. Pairs are spaced throughout half-court with the offensive player (A) facing the coach, and the defensive player (B) facing player A at an arms length away.

b. The coach points to the right or left, player A shoots a jump shot *without* a ball and moves a few steps diagonally forward in the signaled direction.

c. Player B must yell "shot" and quickly reverse pivot to box out player A for a three-second count. This causes the defensive player to work on foot- work and to maintain contact with the offensive player. The defensive player's feet are shoulder width apart, the knees are bent, the buttocks are out, and the hands are up. Encourage player B to keep the feet moving on the box out while maintaining a wide stance.

d. Continue this drill for two minutes, then have players A and B switch positions.

2. Circle Box Out Drill (see Figure 11-7)

Purpose: To strengthen proper defensive box out position and to encourage the offensive player to execute quick fakes, cuts, and spin moves.

Procedure:

a. Position four offensive and defensive players around the center circle facing one another.

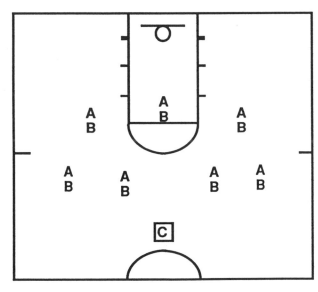

Figure 11-6. Mass rebounding triangle.

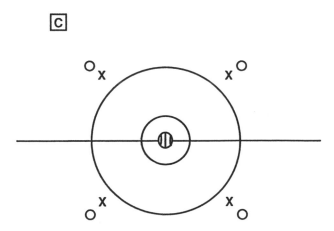

Figure 11-7. Circle box out drill.

b. Place one ball on the floor in the middle of the circle.
c. The coach yells "shot" to begin the drill, and the team on defense must keep the offense from the ball by boxing out the player opposite them.
d. Drill ends after an offensive player touches the ball or after the coach blows the whistle.
e. Record how many seconds a team of four players can keep the other team away from the ball.
f. Change positions after five possessions.
g. Encourage offensive players to spin off the box out, or to fake a step in one direction and then cut aggressively to the ball in the other direction.

3. Rip Rebound Drill

Purpose: To develop an aggressive attitude in rebounding and going after the basketball with strength.

Procedure:
a. Players pair off on each side of the basket. Every player has a ball.
b. Each player tosses the ball off the backboard and jumps strongly for his/her own rebound with exaggerated body movements.
c. Encourage players to time their jump so they reach the ball at their peak.
d. The ball is grasped firmly overhead with both hands and the elbows out.
e. Players should position themselves with the legs spread to take up space under the boards.
f. Players turn to the outside as if to seal off an opponent.
g. Repeat drill for 30 seconds on each side of the basket.

4. One-On-One Rebounding (see Figure 11-8)

Purpose: To develop the block out technique required when defending the shooter and to develop rebounding skills necessary in the open floor.

Procedure:
a. Divide team into groups of four players.
b. The first offensive player (O_1) is stationed at the free throw line.
c. The first defensive player (X_1) is stationed under the basket with a ball.
d. X_1 walks out and passes the ball to O_1.

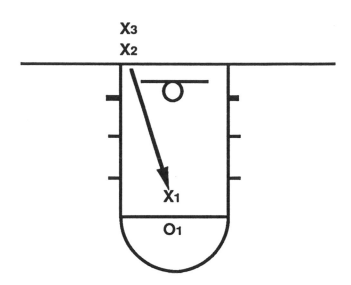

Figure 11-8. One-on-one rebounding drill.

e. O_1 shoots the ball and X_1 contests the shot, executing a front pivot with hands up. X_1 must anticipate the direction of the rebound, make contact with the shooter and then go after the basketball.
f. Both players battle for the rebound.
g. After the rebound, X_1 moves to become the offensive player and X_2 becomes the defense.

Variation:
Move the offensive line to practice shooting from different areas on the floor (i.e., wing, baseline). Drill continues in same manner.

5. Two-Line Rebound and Outlet Drill
   (see Figure 11-9)

Purpose: To improve aggressive rebounding technique; to improve jumping ability and timing; to learn outletting technique.

Procedure:
a. Form two lines with one line on each side of the basket. One ball for each line.
b. First player in each line establishes a strong rebounding position in preparation to jump.
c. A second player (2) in each line tosses the ball high off the backboard and calls "ball."
d. The rebounder (1) jumps and "rips" the ball off the board with arms extended overhead.
e. On returning to the floor, check for feet spread in a balanced stance, elbows out, and ball protected under chin.
f. Player 1 then pivots to the outside and makes

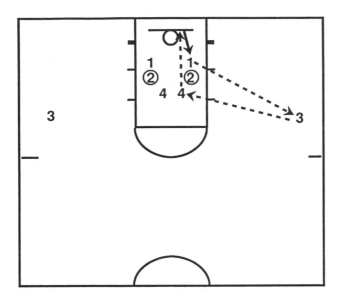

Figure 11-9. Two-line rebound and outlet drill.

a pass to the outlet (3) located at the wide wing position. Stress player 3 calling "outlet" on each pass.

g. For intermediate and advanced play, progress to rebounding and turning in the air, and adding a pivot and outlet pass (to the sideline nearest the rebound.)

h. Rotate tosser to rebounder, rebounder to outlet (3), outlet (3) to the end of the (2) line. The next person in line (4) becomes the next tosser (2).

i. Switch lines.

Variations:
The tosser may apply defensive pressure on the rebounder making the outlet pass, or a defensive player may guard the outlet.

6. Tipping Drill

Purpose: To increase wrist and arm strength; to improve muscular endurance for rebounding, vertical jumping ability, and the ability to time the jump when rebounding.

Procedure:
a. The player stands with a ball in front of the right side of the backboard in a balanced stance.

b. The ball is balanced in the right hand with the wrist flexed back at a 45-degree angle, elbow in, and the ball in front and above the right shoulder. Both the tipping hand and non-tipping hand must be kept above shoul-

der level when tipping and when on the floor preparing to jump.

c. The ball should be shot high and soft on the right side of the backboard. The player jumps and tips the ball back to the backboard with the right hand only. It is important to time the jump so that the tip takes place at the top of the jump. Emphasize that the ball should be controlled with the pads of the fingers. The ball is lifted by extending the elbow and flexing the wrists and fingers.

d. The player lands on the balls of the feet with the legs spread shoulder width apart and knees flexed in preparation for the next vertical jump.

e. Using the right hand, the player tips the ball high on the board five times, changes to the left side of the backboard, and uses the same procedure with the left hand.

f. Tipping is an advanced skill; therefore, lead-up drills for tipping are particularly helpful for beginning players.
   1. Practice tipping the ball up into the air or against a wall *without* jumping.
   2. Substitute a wall for the backboard, especially when players are having trouble tipping with the non-dominant hand.

Variation: Team Tipping Drill
Drill may be used as a *team* tipping drill, with one line positioned on each side of the basket. Each line tries to keep the ball in the air, with each successive player catching it in the air as it comes off the back-board and tipping it back up, then getting out of the way and moving to the end of the line so the next player can catch and tip it.

7. Sandwich Drill (see Figure 11-10)

Purpose: To develop concentration when getting the offensive rebound and powering the ball back up for a shot (and a possible three-point play).

Procedure:
a. Three players are lined up beside each other in front of the basket.

b. The middle player is on offense (O) and is in the "sandwich" between the two defensive players (X).

c. The middle player tosses the ball off the backboard so that it comes right back to

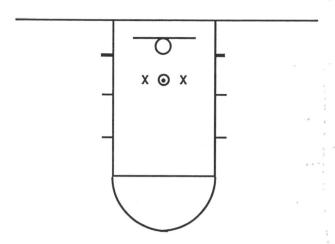

Figure 11-10. Sandwich drill.

him/her. He/she goes right back up and attempts to score.

d. The two players on each side of him/her defend the shot with arms extended, but are not allowed to block the shot or foul.

e. Each player performs five offensive rebounds, then the players rotate so that a new player is "sandwiched."

8. Superman/Superwoman Drill
(see Figure 11-11)

Purpose: To develop aggressiveness in going for *all* rebounds; to improve muscular endurance for rebounding; and to develop the rebounding skills of catching the ball with two hands, protecting the ball at the chin with the elbows *out*, and landing in a balanced position.

Procedure:

a. Start one player with a ball at each basket in a balanced stance outside the lane and above the middle hash mark.

b. A strong two-handed chest pass is made, aiming for a spot high on the opposite corner of the backboard.

c. The ball should be passed so that it rebounds to the opposite side of the lane and is high enough to be rebounded above the head.

d. The player runs across the lane, rebounds the ball with two hands, lands in balance on the soles of the feet with feet spread shoulder width, and knees flexed.

e. The ball is then passed to the opposite corner of the backboard, and the player runs across the lane and rebounds the ball to a protective position below the chin with the elbows out. Stress keeping the ball high so that it cannot be stolen.

f. Continue the drill for thirty seconds or the required numbers of rebounds (10 for advanced players).

g. Rebounding outside the lane may be too difficult for beginning level players. Lead up to the goal by attempting to rebound and land touching or straddling the lane line above the box.

9. Reaction Rebounding (see Figure 11-12)

Purpose: To teach players to position themselves

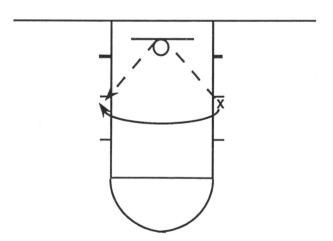

Figure 11-11. Superman/superwoman drill.

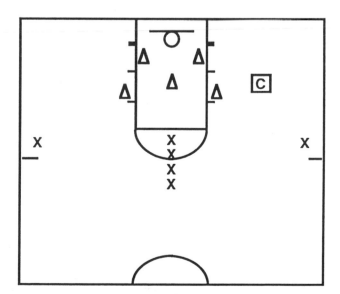

Figure 11-12. Reaction rebounding drill.

properly for rebounds and to encourage a quick reaction when going after the ball.

Procedure:

a. Place cones at random in and around the key.
b. Position players in a single line behind the free throw line and at the outlet positions.
c. The coach/manager shoots the ball from different spots on the court.
d. The first player in line must react around the cones and get to the area where the shot will come off the backboard.
e. The ball must be rebounded before it hits the floor, and the player pivots and passes the ball to the proper sideline.

10. Three-on-Three Box Out Drill
(see Figure 11-13)

Purpose: To strengthen defensive rebounding position, to improve ability to anticipate the angle of the rebound, to teach the proper rebounding triangle position around the basket (see Figure 11-5).

Procedure:

a. Position three offensive and three defensive players around the rebounding triangle.
b. The coach shoots the ball off the backboard as the defensive players (X) pivot and begin boxing out the opposing player (O) behind them as they rebound the shot.
c. Change positions after five defensive rebounds or rotate players as follows: offense to defense—defense goes out and three new players come in on offense.

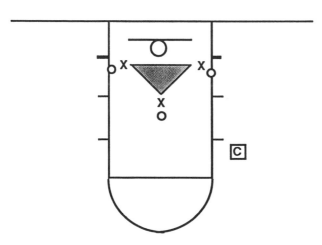

Figure 11-13. Three-on-three box out drill.

Variation:
Continue the drill until the offense scores or a defensive rebound is secured.

11. Rotation Rebounding Drill
(see Figure 11-14)

Purpose: To provide realistic situations for the offense and defense to practice all rebounding skills.

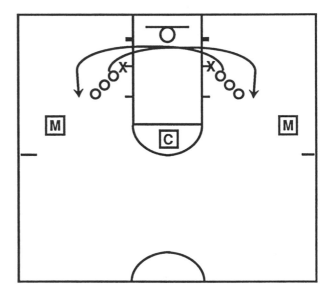

Figure 11-14. Rotation rebounding drill.

Procedure:

a. Form two lines outside the lane, one line on each side of the basket.
b. The defensive players box out the first player in each line as the coach (C) shoots the ball.
c. The two offensive players crash the board while the defense must box out away from the basket, rebound the missed shot, and throw the outlet pass to a manager (M) in the outlet area.
d. The two offensive players then go to the end of the line and are replaced by two new offensive players.
e. The two defensive players stay and box out against each player in the line, and then two new defensive players take over.
f. Move the lines to practice rebounding from different areas on the floor.
g. Keep score and give the pair of defensive players getting the most rebounds a reward.

12. Weakside Rebounding Drill
(see Figure 11-15)

Purpose: To develop the block out technique and the rebounding responsibilities of the helpside defenders.

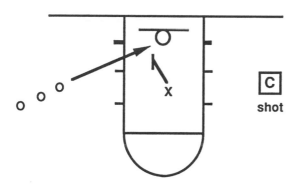

Figure 11-15. Weakside rebounding drill.

Procedure:
a. Coach or manager (C) shoots the ball from the wing position.
b. The defensive player (X) sets up in the middle of the key and attempts to block out the offensive player (O) coming from the weakside.
c. The offensive player (O) crashes the boards, although beginners may be instructed to hold position.
d. The defensive player (X) must block out properly and go after the ball aggressively.
e. Players rotate from offense to defense, and from defense to the end of the line.
f. Change sides, coach shoots ball from the other wing position.

13. Five-on-Five Rebounding Drill
(see Figure 11-16)

Purpose: To develop offensive and defensive rebounding skills in a game-like half-court situation.

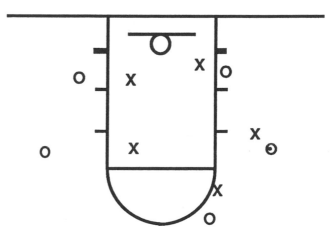

Figure 11-16. Five-on-five rebounding drill.

Procedure:
a. Five offensive players (O) and five defensive players (X) position themselves around the key.
b. Offensive players pass the ball around while defensive players maintain position until a shot is taken by one of the offensive players.
c. The defensive players then attempt to gain block out position and secure the rebound, allowing the offensive team only one shot. If the offense gets the rebound, they attempt to score again.
d. To begin play, the offensive team is given *five* possession points. If they score, no points are deducted. If the defensive team gains possession after a shot, one point is deducted from the offensive team.
e. Play continues until the offensive team has lost five possession points.
f. Rotate the offensive team to defense, and the defensive team to offense, then repeat the procedure.

Variation:
Coach requires five passes on offense before a shot is attempted.

Supplement 11-1.

Rebounding Skills

PERFORMANCE AREA	SPECIFIC SKILLS	SUGGESTED EMPHASIS		
		Elem. School Beginner 8-10	Middle School Intermediate 11-13	High School Advanced 14 and up
Rebounding	Jump	X	X	
	Box out position		X	X
	Defensive		X	X
	Offensive		X	X

Supplement 11-2.

Rebounding Drill Matrix

Drill	SKILL LEVEL		
	Beginning	Intermediate	Advanced
Mass drill	X	X	
Circle box out drill	X	X	
Rip rebound drill	X	X	
One-on-one rebounding	X	X	
Two-line rebound and outlet	X	X	X
Tipping drill		X	X
Team tipping drill		X	X
Sandwich drill		X	X
Superman drill			X
Reaction rebounding		X	X
Three-on-three box out		X	X
Rotation rebounding		X	X
Weakside rebounding			X
Five-on-five			X

Section IV
Basic Strategies of Basketball

12
Offensive Strategies

Amy Dickinson, M.S.
Karen Garchow, M.A.

QUESTIONS TO CONSIDER

- What are the individual and team offensive techniques used in the game of basketball?
- What sequence should be used when introducing offensive skills?
- What are the key elements and common errors of each skill?
- What drills and activities are effective in teaching offensive strategies?

INTRODUCTION

This chapter contains individual-player offense and team offense strategies for youth play. The skills are systematically arranged from individual live ball and dead ball offensive moves to individual offense away from the ball. Also included are coaching hints for coordinating individuals offensive techniques into two and three player patterns. For more advanced play, five player offenses and fastbreak techniques are also presented.

The drill portion of this chapter contains activities that are appropriate for developing both *offensive and defensive* strategies. The execution of the drill may vary dependent upon the coach's intended emphasis and purpose.

For a summary of the offensive strategies and drills that are appropriate for each level of play (beginning, intermediate, and advanced), see Supplements 12-1 and 12-2.

INDIVIDUAL OFFENSIVE MOVES

Although basketball is a team game, the foundation for team offense is *one-on-one* play. Each player needs to possess individual offensive skills that allow him/her to be a scoring threat and to contribute to the scoring efforts of teammates. As a coach, it is important that you teach your players how to get open, how to get free for a good shot, and how to free-up teammates to pass or shoot. This can be done most effectively by first teaching offense in the context of one-on-one situations.

Triple-Threat Offensive Moves

When a player receives the basketball in the front court, the player should immediately square up to the basket in the triple-threat position. From this position, the player can see the court, his/her teammates, and the defense,

195

and may then make the decision to shoot, pass, or drive. If guarded closely by an opponent, the player must make a move to get open to shoot or pass.

The following series of individual offensive moves should be taught to all youth players, once they have developed sound fundamental footwork, dribbling, and shooting techniques. They are presented in the order in which they should be taught, though a player does not necessarily need to master one move before you teach him/her the other moves.

1. Direct Drive to the Basket

This move is used when the defense is playing tight on the ball and the offensive player can take advantage by making a strong, quick move past him/her to the basket.

Beginning from the triple-threat position, the player uses the non-pivot foot and quickly steps past the opponent. Coaches can instruct players to "explode" by the defender to encourage them to make a strong, quick step. The ball should be pulled close to the body and away from the defense. The step must be made so that the foot is past the opponent but planted next to the outside of his/her foot. The offensive player should pass the defender as closely as possible and in a direct line to the basket. It is important to emphasize that the ball must be dribbled *before* the pivot foot (trail foot) leaves the floor, otherwise a traveling violation will occur. Once past the defender, he/she drives strongly to the basket for a lay-up or if stopped, may pull up for a jump shot or to pass.

Key Elements:

a. Begin in the triple-threat position.
b. Step with the non-pivot foot directly past the defender.
c. Stay low and on balance, planting the weight on the ball of the foot.
d. Pull the ball in close to the body and away from the defender.
e. Begin the dribble before the pivot foot leaves the floor.
f. Drive directly to the basket with the head up.

Common Errors:

a. Standing up out of triple-threat position before making the move.

b. Stepping with the pivot foot (traveling).
c. Stepping out to the side (away from) the defender.
d. Taking too long of a step and getting off balance.
e. Swinging the ball out away from the body.
f. Failing to dribble before the pivot foot leaves the floor.

2. Rocker Moves

The "rocker move" utilizes a jab-step to back up a defender so that the player has room to shoot. From triple-threat position, the non-pivot foot is "jabbed" directly at the defender. The step should be no more than 6-8 in. in length and should be aimed at the center of the defender's body. It is important that the ball of the foot be planted on the jab step and the knees remain flexed so that balance is maintained.

Since the object of the rocker is to make the defender believe that the player is driving, the body must also move forward on the jab step. A good defender will watch the *midsection*, not the feet, when guarding a player with the ball. Therefore, as the jab is made, the body must also shift forward. A good coaching technique is to tell players to "keep their nose over their toes" when they perform a jab-step.

As the jab step is made, the eyes should be focused on the basket, and the ball pulled into the hip and away from the defense. Stepping directly at the defender will cause him/her to drop back to protect against the drive. The offensive player then "rocks" back to triple-threat position immediately brings the ball up to the position, and shoots. If the defender lunges forward to stop the shot, the offensive player should then drive directly to the basket.

Key Elements: (see Figure 12-1)

a. Begin in triple-threat position.
b. Make a 6-8 in. jab step directly at the defender with the non-pivot foot.
c. Land on the ball of the foot.
d. Keep the "nose over the toes."
e. Pull the ball back to the hip, away from the defender.
f. As the defense backs away, return to a low triple-threat position and prepare to shoot.
g. If the defender lunges to block the shot, explode by and drive to the basket.

Common Errors:

a. Standing up prior to making the move.
b. Taking too long of a jab step (more than 6-8 in.).
c. Jabbing to the side of the defender.
d. Jabbing with only the foot and leg.
e. Keeping the ball out in front of the body.
f. Standing up when returning from the rocker step.

3. Jab-Step-and-Go

The *jab-step-and-go* move is used when the defender fails to drop back on the initial jab-step. From the triple-threat position, the offensive player makes a 6-8 in. jab-step at the defender, pulling the ball away from the opponent. As with the rocker move, it is important to stay on balance and to move the body as well as the foot/leg. If the defender does not react and back away, a second step is made with the *same* foot. This step should be an *explosive* step past the outside foot of the defender. The ball must be dribbled before the pivot foot (trail foot) leaves the floor, and the player then continues to drive to the basket.

When learning this move, beginners may have the tendency to want to make the second step with the pivot foot (a traveling violation). Encourage your players to go through the steps slowly and to listen for the "bang-bang" sound made by the foot hitting the floor. (As a teaching technique, you may want to have beginners say "bang-bang" as they perform the steps or have them over-exaggerate the stomping.)

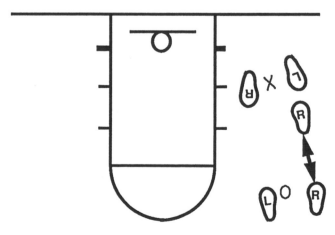

Figure 12-1 The rocker move.

Key Elements:

a. Begin in the triple-threat position.
b. Using the non-pivot foot make a 6-8 in. jab step directly at the defender.
c. Keep the "nose over the toes."
d. Pull the ball back to the hip, away from the defender.
e. If the defense does not react, make an explosive step by the defender, using the *same* foot that was used for the first jab-step.
f. Drive directly to the basket.

Common Errors:

a. Standing up prior to making the move.
b. Taking a long first jab-step (more than 6-8 in.).
c. Jabbing to the side of the defender.
d. Jabbing with only the foot and leg.
e. Keeping the ball out in front of the body.
f. Pulling the foot back before taking the second step.
g. Taking the second step with the pivot (trail) foot—traveling.
h. Failing to dribble before lifting the pivot foot.

4. Crossover Step

The crossover step is a modified version of the "jab-step-and-go." From the triple-threat position, a 6-8 in. jab step is made directly at the opponent. If the defender fails to react or drops back to cover the drive to the strong (jab-foot) side, a *crossover* step is made with the *same* foot. The crossover step should land past and to the outside of the defender's foot that is opposite the pivot foot. Once again it is important that the move be done in a balanced position and that the steps occur in the "bang-bang" pattern.

As the crossover step is made, the ball must be moved from the outside hip, across the body, and to the opposite hand for the drive. To keep the defender from grabbing the ball as it is switched, the player must hold the ball securely with two hands, and swing it across low and close to the body. Once the ball is in the opposite hand, it must be dribbled immediately (before the pivot foot is lifted) in order to prevent a traveling violation.

Key Elements: (see Figure 12-2a-c)

a. Begin in the triple-threat position.

b. Using a non-pivot foot, make a 6-8 in. jab-step directly at the defender.

c. Keep the "nose over the toes."

d. Pull the ball back to the hip, away from the defender.

e. If the defense does not react or steps back to cover the strong-side drive, make a crossover step using the same foot used for the first jab-step.

f. Swing the ball across the body to the opposite hand, using two hands and keeping the ball low and close to the body.

g. Pass the defender with an explosive move and drive directly to the basket.

Common Errors:

a. Standing up prior to making the move.

b. Taking a long first jab-step (more than 6-8 in.).

c. Jabbing to the side of the defender.

d. Jabbing with only the foot and leg.

e. Pulling the foot back before taking the crossover step.

f. Swinging the ball across too high or too late.

g. Failing to dribble before lifting the pivot foot.

Coaching Hints for the Triple-Threat Offensive Moves:

- Teach the moves in the order presented, since each move builds on the previous one.
- As you teach each move, break it down into steps (the key elements). Have players "walk through" the move in steps as you call them out loud. This can be done in mass formation without using a defender.
- Once the players learn the steps of the move, go over the key points and work on perfecting the finer details of the skill.
- A defender should then be added. Tell the defense how they should react to the move (i.e., take the fake or stay close) and whether to be active or passive.
- Players should practice each move in steps, at half-speed, and finally, at game-speed (see Drills 1 and 2 at the end of the chapter).
- Once players have developed the basic techniques of the moves, the defense should be instructed to vary their responses so that the offensive player learns to "read" the defender.
- Continue to re-emphasize the key points and

(a)

(b)

(c)

Figure 12-2. The crossover step.

provide your players with numerous opportunities to practice their one-on-one moves.

Players should select one or two of the individual moves presented and learn how to do them well. It is better to possess two good offensive moves than it is to have five ineffective ones! Coaches should encourage their athletes to develop a few moves and practice them often; then later, new moves may be taught and added to their "bag of tricks." Every player can be an offensive threat, if they can beat their defender one-on-one.

Shot-Fake and Jump Shot

When in shooting range and closely guarded, an offensive player can use a shot-fake to get the defender out of position and then take a jump shot over the opponent. This move works well when the player is in the block area, following an offensive rebound, or when a player has used his/her dribble and does not have the option of driving to get free for the shot.

From the shooting position, the player quickly raises the head and shoulders 2-3 in. and immediately returns to this position (the knees do not move). This "shot fake" should cause the defender to believe that a shot will be taken and to rise out of defensive position to attempt a block. In order to be effective, a shot-fake must be done with the head up and the eyes focused on the basket. The defender will not be fooled if the player is looking at him/her or at the floor! The ball should be kept in the "shooting pocket" at chest level so that it is out of the reach of the defender. The ball will rise slightly as the shoulders and body do, but the arms do not change position during the fake.

Once the defender has taken the fake, the player must go straight up and shoot a jump shot. If timed correctly, the shooter should be going up as the defender is coming down, allowing the shot to be taken over the defender. There is a strong chance that the shooter will be fouled on the shot (especially after an offensive rebound or in close to the basket) and will be awarded two free throws (or one if the basket is made).

When teaching the shot-fake, encourage players to perform the move slowly and make sure that the head and shoulders move. If the fake is done too quickly, the defense will not have time to react! As players become comfortable using the shot-fake they will tend to speed up, so have them over-emphasize the movements when first learning the move and in drills.

Key Elements:

a. Begin in good shooting position with the knees bent.
b. Keep the head up and eyes focused on the basket.
c. Make a shot-fake by raising the head and shoulders 2-3 in.
d. Keep the ball in front of the chest.
e. Return to shooting position.
f. As the defender goes up with the fake, go straight up with a jump shot.

Common Errors:

a. Faking too quickly.
b. Straightening the knees on the fake.
c. Faking with the ball too high.
d. Looking at the defender or the floor instead of the basket.
e. Jumping into the defender on the shot.

Post Play

One of the keys to good offensive play is to take high percentage shots, those close to the basket. A team that can get shots in the block area, or at the post position, will have a great advantage.

All players need to know how to get into a position to receive the ball at the low post (block) and to make a move to score once they get the ball. As a coach, you should teach every player on your team, regardless of size or playing position, the basic skills of offensive play in the post area.

Establishing Position

In youth play, the basketball is most frequently passed in to the post area from a player at the wing position. Teach your players to establish position in the block area just high of the "block" itself and outside the key when the ball is at the wing or baseline (see Figure 12-3). Establishing this position is commonly termed "posting up."

When posting up, a player must have a wide base of support and stay low and on balance.

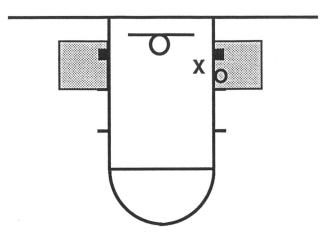

Figure 12-3. The post-up area: outside the key and high of the block.

The feet should be positioned further than shoulder-width apart with the weight on the balls of the feet. The knees must be bent to keep the buttocks low and to help the player jump and move more quickly. The body is maintained in an upright position and the arms are positioned with the elbows out and hands up. A strong post-up position should be used to keep a defender behind and to get open to receive a pass. Instruct your players to be "big" and take up as much space as possible when playing inside.

Once this position is established, the post player needs to attempt to plant the feet and hold the spot. If the player "dances around" and does not establish a stationary position outside of the key, it will be difficult for a teammate to pass to him/her.

The Target Hand

In order to signal to the passer that he/she is ready to receive a pass, the player must put up a "target hand." The hand should be positioned with the fingers spread and the palm facing the passer. The placement of the hand indicates to the passer where the post player wants to receive the ball. Instruct your players to call for the ball to the side away from the defender with the arm extended above and away from the head. (If receiving a bounce pass, the arm is extended out to the side with the fingers pointing down.) The right hand should be used as the target hand on the right side (defender is on the left), the left hand on the left side (defender is on the right). If the defender is di-

rectly behind the post player, both hands should be used as target hands and positioned at head-level.

Receiving the Ball

When the ball is passed to the target hand, the player must move the other hand to the target hand and catch the ball with both hands. The ball should then be brought to the center of the body just below the chin and held firmly with both hands with the elbows out. If the pass is not thrown directly to the target, the player will need to release the post-up position and move to meet the pass, but should assume the position again once the ball is caught.

Key Elements of Posting Up:

a. Establish position just above the block and just outside the key.
b. Assume a strong, low position with bent knees and a wide base.
c. Plant the feet and hold the spot.
d. Present a target hand with the palm facing the passer.
e. Call for the pass with the target hand away from the defender.
f. Catch the ball with two hands; then bring it into position in front of the chin with the elbows out.

Common Errors in Posting Up:

a. Standing straight up with the knees extended.
b. Posting up within the key.
c. Moving around too much ("dancing").
d. Failing to present a target hand.
e. Presenting the target hand on the defender's side.
f. Attempting to catch the ball with one hand.

Post Moves

There are many offensive moves that can be used to score from the post position. Most of these involve the basic techniques of the two moves presented or are variations of the moves. It is important that youth players learn to do these two post moves correctly, before trying to perform more complex moves.

• Square-up and shoot

After receiving the ball, the post player must turn the head quickly to one side to see where the defender is positioned, establish the foot that is furthest from the defender as the pivot foot, and then make a front pivot to square-up to the basket in shooting position. Since the player will be turning away from the defender, a shot should be taken immediately if possible. If the defender is too close, a shot-fake or drive move can be used (using one strong dribble and a power lay-up). Players must learn to turn in both directions and to make the move equally well from both the left and right sides of the basket.

• **Drop-Step Move** (see Figure 12-4)

The first step in this move is to turn the head to determine which side the defender is on and to establish the pivot foot on that side. The opposite foot is then dropped back in a step to the basket with a partial reverse pivot being performed. The foot should be planted with the knees bent and toes pointed to the backboard. The pivot foot is then lifted and the body squared to the basket. The trail leg (pivot foot) is brought up in lay-up fashion and a lay-up is shot. A power lay-up (or shot-fake and power lay-up) may be done, but the ball must be dribbled (low and close to the body) on the turn, before the trail foot is planted, or a traveling violation will be called. Players should learn this move so that they can drop-step in either direction, and can perform it equally well from both sides of the basket.

Offensive Movement Without the Ball

Along with being able to make a good move to score, strong individual offensive play also includes being able to "get open" or away from the defense, to receive a pass and to help teammates get open. Beginning players often stand in one spot waiting for the ball, making it rather easy for the defense to guard them. Proper techniques for getting open and setting and using picks need to be taught to all players and practiced often.

Getting Open

1. **Direct Cut**—The quickest method of getting open is to make a direct cut to an open area of the court. The first step of the cut is the most important! It must be a quick, explosive step that leaves the defender behind. The player then continues to cut directly to the open spot with the hands up and ready to receive a pass.

2. **The V-Cut**—If the defense is attempting to deny the ball to a player by playing tight, a cut in the shape of a "V" should be made to get the defense moving away from the area where the player wants to receive the pass (see Figure 12-5).

There are four steps to performing an effective V-cut:

1. Make a cut of at least *two to three* steps directly toward the basket.
2. Plant the forward foot, keeping the "nose over the toes" to maintain balance.
3. Turn the body back toward the original position and *explode* out in the opposite direction off of the planted foot.
4. Cut out to the open area with the hands up, ready to receive the ball.

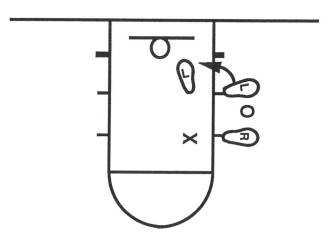

Figure 12-4. The drop-step move.

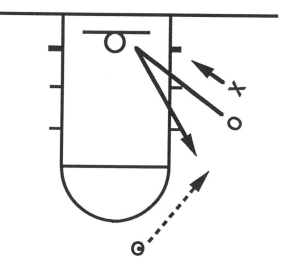

Figure 12-5. V-cut to the basket.

It is important that the initial cut be far enough to get the defense moving in that direction. Teach your players to plant the foot in the key or on the block and then explode back out.

A V-cut also may be used from various positions on the court other than the wing. In these instances, the cut is made going away from the ball, planting the foot, and then exploding back to the ball (see Figure 12-6).

3. **The L-Cut**—The L-cut is used to cut from the block area to either the wing or across the key to the opposite elbow (see Figure 12-7). The player cuts up the key toward the free throw line then comes to a brief stride-stop. This is done to "freeze" the defender. An explo-

sion step is then made out to the open area by pushing off of the foot away from that direction. The hands should be up and ready to receive the pass.

Setting Picks

A "pick" or "screen" is used to aid a teammate in getting open by blocking the path of his/her defender. A pick must be set at least one step away from the defender, and the picker must be in a stationary position with both feet planted.

The picker moves into a position one step away from and to the side of the defender so that the opponent's shoulder lines up with the middle of his/her body (see Figure 12-8). The player then plants the feet at least shoulder-width apart and assumes a strong, balanced position with the knees bent. The arms must be held close to the body and may not be used to push or hold the defender. The rules allow for girls to cross the arms flat against the chest, and for boys to place the hands in front of the groin area for protection. Players should be taught to expect contact from the defender and to establish a strong base of support and to position the arms properly to prevent possible injury.

A pick may be set for a teammate who has the ball or for a teammate cutting to the ball. Once a pick has been set, the player setting the screen must hold the position for three seconds or until the pick has been used.

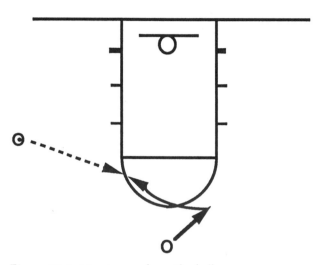

Figure 12-6. V-cut away from the ball.

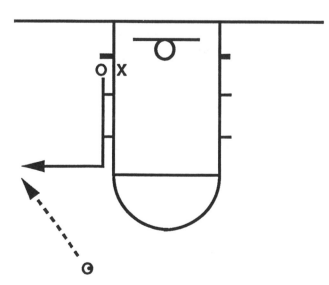

Figure 12-7. (a) L-cut to the wing.

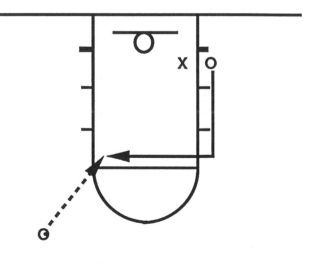

Figure 12-7. (b) L-cut to the opposite elbow.

Figure 12-8. The picker takes a stationary position one step away from the defender.

When teaching your players to set picks, emphasize the importance of safety and of establishing a stationary position with a wide base of support. Picks are an important part of team offense, but they must be set correctly in order to be effective! Have your players practice picks (and using picks) first at walk-speed and half-speed in drill situations before progressing to game-speed. This will aid them in developing good technique and help prevent injuries.

Key Elements:

a. Establish *stationary* position at least one step away from the defender.
b. Plant both feet perpendicular to the path of oncoming defender.
c. Maintain a low position with the knees flexed.
d. Keep the arms close to the body and hold (place) them in a protective position.
e. Hold the pick for three seconds or until the pick has been used.
f. Expect contact from the defender.

Common Errors:

a. Setting the pick too close to the opponent (a foul) or too far away.
b. Straightening the legs.
c. Pushing or holding with the arms.

d. Moving into the defender as he/she attempts to go around the pick.

Using the Pick

Picks may be set anywhere on the court and can be made on the ball or away from the ball. The goal is to free a player from a defender to drive or to receive a pass. Once a pick has been set, the player who is attempting to get open must *use* the screen. As the pick is set, the player should attempt to get the defender moving in the opposite direction by cutting or jab-stepping away from the pick. Then he/she needs to cut as closely as possible to the picker and "brush off" the defender on the screen. Instruct players to cut "shoulder to shoulder" with their teammate when cutting or driving off a pick. A good shoulder-to-shoulder cut should allow the player to break away from the defense and into an open area.

Key Elements: (see Figure 12-9a-b)

a. Use a V-cut or jab-step to take the defender away from the pick.
b. Wait for the pick to be set.
c. Prepare to run defender into the pick.
d. Cut or drive shoulder-to-shoulder off of the picker.

Common Errors:

a. Leaving before the pick is set.
b. Failing to take the defender away from the pick.
c. Going around the pick too wide, allowing the defender to slip through.
d. Picking up the dribble, following a pick and not taking advantage of a possible drive to the basket.

TEAM OFFENSE

Team offense needs to be presented using the "part-to-whole" method. Once you have taught your players the individual offensive techniques (getting open, offensive moves, and how to set and use picks) and the fundamental skills (footwork, dribbling, passing, and shooting), they need to be shown how to use them when playing with teammates. To do this, it is best to teach beginners in terms of two-player or three-player offensive play first, and then to incorporate those patterns into five-on-five pat-

(a)

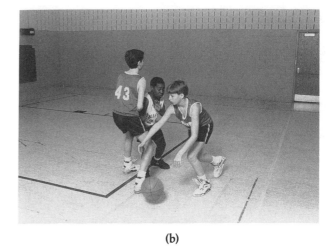

(b)

Figure 12-9. The player using the pick must cut shoulder to shoulder with the picker.

terns. Most five-player offenses can be broken down into basic two-player techniques. It is suggested in Chapter 5 that small-sided games be played when players are under the age of eleven. You will make your job much easier and avoid confusing your players if you teach them to play the two-player (or three-player) game before introducing a five-player pattern.

Two-Player Patterns

1. Give and Go (see Figures 12-10 and 12-11a-d)

The give and go may be done from any perimeter position on the court.

a. O_1 passes to O_2.
b. O_1 V-cuts and then cuts to the basket between the ball and the defender (X).
c. O_2 makes a return pass to O_1.
d. O_1 looks to shoot (lay-up or jump shot) or pass off.

2. Backdoor Cut (see Figure 12-12 and 12-13)

A backdoor cut is used when the defense is overplaying on a V-cut and attempting to deny the pass to the wing.

a. O_1 V-cuts, but cannot get open at the wing because X is overplaying.
b. O_2 signals the "backdoor" by faking a pass to O_1 at the wing.
c. O_1 reverses the direction of the cut by planting the outside foot and exploding back to the basket.
d. O_2 passes to O_1.

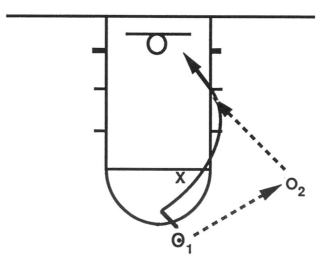

Figure 12-10. The give and go.

3. Pick and Roll (see Figure 12-14)

The pick and roll is used to get a player who is in triple-threat position open to drive and then possibly pass to the picker.

a. O_1 sets a pick on O_2's defensive player (X).
b. O_2 uses the pick and drives toward the basket.
c. After O_2 goes by, O_1 rolls to the basket by making a reverse pivot so that the back moves *away* from the direction of the ball ("opening up to the ball"—see Figure 12-15).
d. O_1 must maintain contact with X briefly and then cut to the basket calling for the ball.
e. O_2 passes to O_1.

(a)

(b)

(c)

(d)

Figure 12-11. The offensive player passes to the wing, then cuts to the basket to receive the return pass.

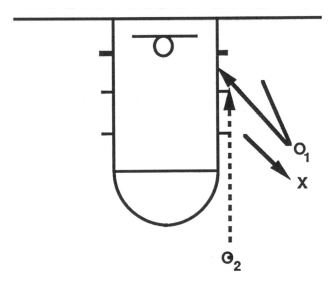

Figure 12-12. Backdoor cut.

4. Pass and Pick Away (see Figure 12-16)

This pattern involves a pass to a teammate followed by a screen set away from the ball.

a. O_1 passes to O_2 then goes away from the ball and sets a pick for O_3.
b. O_3 uses the pick to brush off the defender (X) and cuts toward the ball.
c. O_3 must cut into a shooting position and call for the ball.
d. O_2 passes to O_3.

In youth play, two-three player techniques (give and go, backdoor cut, pick and roll, and pass and pick away) serve as an effective beginning to intermediate team offense. Once players can successfully execute the basic two and three player patterns, they will gain a clear-

(a)

(b)

(c)

(d)

Figure 12-13. The wing player fakes high then cuts back to the basket, calling for the ball with the lead hand.

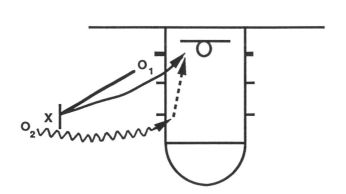

Figure 12-14. The pick and roll.

Figure 12-15. After setting the pick, the picker "opens up to the ball" to receive a pass.

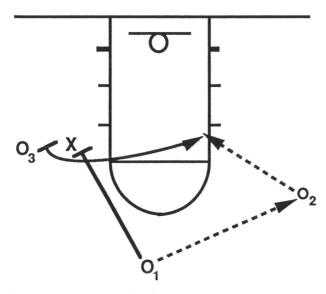

Figure 12-16. Pass and pick away.

er understanding of how these integral "pieces" fit into a more advanced five-player offense.

BASIC OFFENSIVE PRINCIPLES

The fundamentals of dribbling, passing, and shooting are very important in the game of basketball. Each player needs to develop his/her skills in order to become an offensive threat. However, basketball is ultimately a *team* game, and players need to work with their teammates to achieve the team's offensive goals.

In order to get a team to work as a unit, a coach must teach the players the principles of offensive play. These are the key elements that are needed to make any offense effective.

Floor Balance

Players must stay spread out on the court to give the offense room to maneuver. This also makes it more difficult for the opponents to play defense. To balance the floor, at least two players must remain on the weakside (away from the ball). A common error of beginning players is to crowd around the ball or to stand too close to a teammate. This allows a defender to guard two players at once and makes it difficult to pass, drive, or cut in that area.

In order to maintain court balance, offensive players are typically assigned *positions* to play. This gives players general areas of responsibility and allows them to use their skills in a role

that will best serve the team. The three primary positions are the guard, the forward, and the center. Coaches must help their athletes learn the skills required to play each of these positions. Providing younger players with varied experiences encourages a thorough understanding of the game and the abilities required to play the game.

The type of offense being played will determine where players must be to keep the floor balanced. When teaching beginners, it is suggested that the coach place tape or spots on the floor where the offensive players should begin play in order to create proper floor balance and adequate spacing (see Figure 12-17).

Take Good Shots

The goal of the offense is to score on every possession. To do this, your team needs to shoot high-percentage shots and work together to get the best shot possible. A 10-ft. shot is better than a 15-ft. shot; however, if a teammate is open at the low post, the ball should be passed and the power lay-up taken. Players must be taught to use their offensive skills to help the team get shots that have the greatest chance of going in, and to select shots that are within their shooting range.

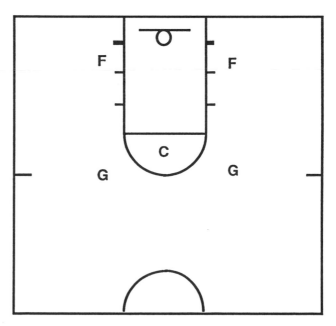

Figure 12-17. The five offensive players must be spread out on the court to maintain proper **floor balance**.

Hit the Open Player

It takes time for players to develop the ability to assess offensive opportunities and to survey the court for open teammates. With playing experience, their court awareness will improve, and players will feel more comfortable having the ball under defensive pressure.

A basic "rule" of team basketball is to always pass the ball to a teammate who is open and in a better shooting position. In order to get the best shots possible, teach your players to be *patient* when they receive the basketball and to look for the open player. A good offensive team takes advantage of every scoring opportunity!

Ball Movement

It is important to make the defense work hard by constantly forcing them to adjust their positions. One way to accomplish this is to keep the ball moving around the court area. The ball should never stay in one place for very long! Teach your players to make quick passes and to be sure they *go somewhere* when they dribble (avoid the dead dribble). Making four or five quick passes or reversing the ball to the opposite side of the key will often result in an open shot.

Move Without the Ball

Another way to keep the defense moving is for the offensive players who do not have the ball to keep moving. Many beginning players have a tendency to stand and watch the ball. This makes them easy to guard and limits the possibilities for the offense!

All five players should be active on offense. Teach your players to always look for a way to get open or to help get a teammate open. There is always something they can do: cut for the ball, clear out an area for a teammate, set a pick, or go in for the offensive rebound.

Getting Second Shots

Even the best shooters only make 40-50 percent of their shots during a game. In other words, your team will miss numerous shots and the ball will be "up for grabs" on the re-

bounds. Strong *offensive rebounding* will allow your team second (and even third or fourth) attempts to score on a possession. Emphasize to your players the importance of recognizing when a shot will be taken by your team and "crashing the boards."

SELECTING A FIVE-PLAYER PATTERN OFFENSE

The purpose of establishing a pattern offense(s) for your team to run is to keep the players organized. It provides the players with specific responsibilities and a knowledge of what their teammates will be doing; focuses players' efforts on team goals; and can help teams accomplish the basic offensive principles.

When selecting a pattern offense, a coach needs to keep several things in mind. First, remember to *keep it simple!* It is not necessary to have complex patterns or flashy plays for your team to run, especially at the youth level. A good team is one that *executes* well—a Give and Go or Pick and Roll that is done correctly will result in two points more often than a complex play that requires a lot more work!

The offense that is chosen should be one that will take advantage of the team's strengths. For instance, if your team is fairly tall and has strong inside players, you might want to use an offense that utilizes two low post players, a center, and two guards and works the ball into the key area. A good outside shooting team, or a team with quick guards, would benefit more from an offensive pattern that keeps three players on the perimeter and emphasizes ball movement and penetration to the basket. As a coach you must assess the abilities of your players, determine the strengths of your team, and then select an offensive pattern(s) that will aid your scoring efforts.

It is also important to keep in mind that *all* players should contribute to the offensive effort. Unfortunately, coaches sometimes center the offense around one or two "star" players, neglecting to involve the other members of the team. This not only makes playing basketball less rewarding for those "other" players, but it will probably backfire and end up hurting the team offensively when the defense figures out how to stop the key player(s). Remember, your goal as a coach is to provide a positive, enjoyable learning experience for all of the athletes on your team. Make sure you choose an offensive pattern that involves all five players on the court and that coincides with the skill level of the team.

Finally, make sure you don't overload your players with too many different plays to remember. You should select one or two *simple* patterns to teach your players that later can be added to or modified if needed. A team only *needs* one or two good plays if they are executed well!

There are hundreds of offensive patterns used in the game of basketball. At the end of the drills section of this chapter several basic plays have been provided that are appropriate for the youth level (see Figure 12-36 through 12-45; motion offense Figure 12-46 through 12-48).

When you introduce a new play to your team, diagram and show your players the whole pattern first so that they get an understanding of how the offense works and the scoring opportunities that will develop from proper timing and execution. Have your players walk through the pattern *without* defense to learn the sequence and timing of the different parts. Then you can break down the offense into its parts and focus on specific skills or options. Finally, develop the whole offense by having five players run through the entire offense at half- and then full-speed, and then adding passive defense and progressing to more game-like scrimmaging. By using the whole-part-whole method in teaching offensive strategies, you will help your athletes to realize the purpose for each drill, how they relate to the offense, and how they relate to their scoring opportunities. Most importantly, they will learn and execute the offense well.

ZONE OFFENSE

It is recommended that youth players be taught player-to-player offensive strategies and techniques prior to being introduced to those for playing against a zone defense. The player-to-player strategies are easy to break down for instructional purposes and carry over well to zone offensive play. Once player-to-player of-

fensive skills have been well established, coaches may begin teaching the principles of zone offense to intermediate-level players.

Principles of Zone Offense:

- Players should maintain a 12-15 ft. spacing on the perimeter.
- Good *ball movement* is needed to make the defense move. Players must pass the ball quickly; look to *reverse* the ball to the opposite side, and pass the ball back out if the defense collapses when a pass is made to the post areas.
- Penetrate and cut to the seams in the zone (the area between two defenders). Weakside players must step into the gaps to receive the ball and take the open shot.
- Players must get in triple-threat position as soon as they receive the ball.
- Dribbling should be avoided, unless it is being used to drive to the basket or to improve a passing angle to the post.
- "Overload" the zone by placing four players on one side of the key.
- Players should cut into the open areas after passing and avoid standing still.

A basic 1-3-1 zone offense is diagramed and explained at the end of the chapter following the player-to-player offenses (see Figure 12-49, 12-50, and 12-51).

THE FASTBREAK

The fastbreak is a fast paced, demanding style of play. It requires teamwork, sound fundamentals, and good conditioning. In order to run the fastbreak effectively, a team must not only be quick, but also must have strong defensive rebounding, good ball handling, and accurate passing.

There are definite advantages to using the fastbreak offense. It leads to more scoring opportunities, usually results in high-percentage shots, and is exciting to watch and play. However, if not controlled or executed properly it can produce easy scoring opportunities for the opponent and result in many turnovers and sloppy play. The fastbreak works best when players are taught to run it in an organized fashion and when it is used along with a half-court pattern offense.

Starting the Fastbreak

The objective of the fastbreak is to move the ball from the backcourt (defensive end) to the offensive end of the court as quickly as possible and beat the opponent downcourt so that your team has a 3-on-2 or 2-on-1 player advantage. Ideally this will lead to an "easy" basket scored on a lay-up, power lay-up, or open jump shot.

The key to starting the fastbreak is to secure the defensive *rebound*. A team can't break without the ball! A coach must develop the rebounding skills of the team before beginning to teach the fastbreak offense itself.

Once the rebound is made, the ball must be passed out to a guard positioned at the outlet position (see Figure 12-21) who will quickly advance it up-court. The rebounder must hold the ball securely, pivot away from the basket, and throw an overhead pass to the teammate who is cutting into position on the same side of the court as the rebounder. The player at the outlet position must yell "OUTLET!" to let the rebounder know he/she is in position. The *outlet pass* must be made quickly and accurately in order to start the fastbreak.

Getting Down Court

The outlet player must now get the ball to the *middle* of the floor so that more passing options are available. This may be done by dribbling the ball or by passing the ball to a teammate who is cutting to the middle (see Figure 12-18a-b). Passing the ball is a faster method, but if no one is ahead of him/her the outlet should take the ball to the middle on the dribble.

The other players must then *"fill the lanes"* and run downcourt expecting to receive the pass if they get ahead of the ball. One player should be in each of the three lanes, so that the players are spread out (see Figure 12-19). Players need to *stay wide* in the outside lanes until reaching the top of the key.

If a *2-on-1* break occurs, the ball should be taken down one side of the court while a teammate fills the far lane on the other side (see Figure 12-20). Again, the ball should be passed ahead if possible.

Finishing It Off

Once the ball reaches the top of the key, the middle player must make a quick decision to either continue driving to the basket for a lay-up or to pass off. The player should *challenge the defense* to stop the drive and keep going (all the way to the basket or pulling up for a short jumper) if the defenders don't come out to stop the ball. If the defense covers the ball, the player must pass off to one of his/her teammates. When teaching beginners, have the player jump stop at the top of the key before making a pass.

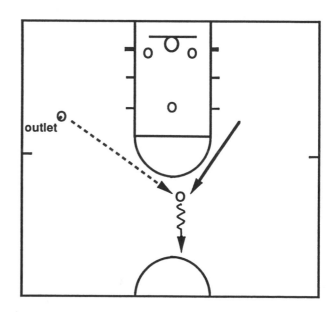

Figure 12-18a. Going to the middle on the dribble.

Figure 12-18b. Going to the middle on the pass.

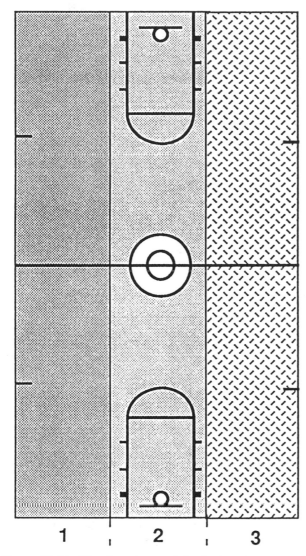

Figure 12-19. The three lanes of the fastbreak.

When the players in the outside lane reach the free throw line extended, they must *cut to the basket* at a 45-degree angle, ready to receive the pass. After receiving the ball, the player should shoot a lay-up or power lay-up (see Figure 12-21).

If the defense covers the break well, it may take an additional pass or two to get an open shot. However, remember that the rest of the defensive players are hurrying back to stop the break, so time is short! Emphasize to players that they must pass quickly and make cuts in front of the defense to get the ball. The players who are not involved in the initial break should still hustle downcourt to be *trailers*. Trailers may receive a pass at the elbow or cutting down the lane, and will be important for offensive rebounding!

When to Fastbreak

When run properly, the fastbreak is very effective. However, if there is no clear advantage over the defense or if a good shot does not open up, it is better to bring the ball back out and set up the offense. There is no reason to force a shot or to take a low-percentage shot without rebounders.

You must teach your players to recognize when to and not to fastbreak. This responsibility usually belongs to the middle player on the break or to the guards who can call for the ball and then set up the offense.

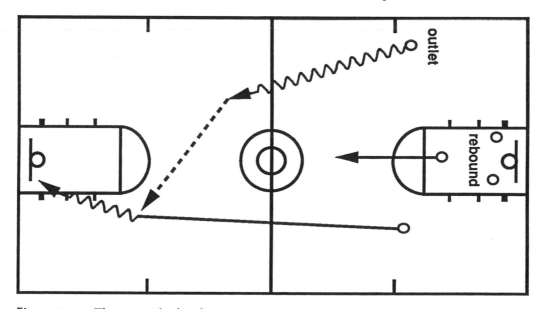

Figure 12-20. The 2-on-1 fastbreak.

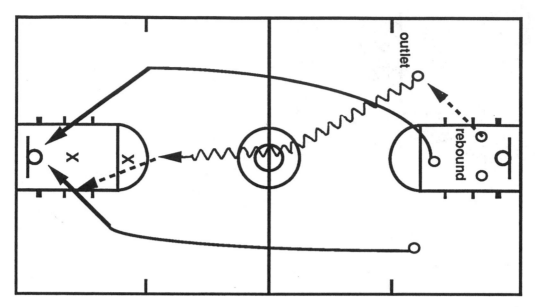

Figure 12-21. The 3-on-2 fastbreak.

Because it is a high-speed offensive style, there can be a tendency for players to get out-of-control and make a lot of turnovers. If this happens, instruct your players to slow down a little to maintain control of the ball and not to force the break. It is better to keep possession of the ball and have a chance to score using the pattern offense, than to give the opponents possession of the ball. Be sure to *praise* your players when they make good decisions!

Key Elements:

1. Secure the defensive rebound.
2. Rebounder pivots to the outside and makes a crisp outlet pass.
3. Outlet player receives the ball at the free throw line extended and takes the ball to the middle on the pass or dribble.
4. Players fill the lanes and stay wide when running down the court.
5. Middle player must challenge the defense and decide to either drive to the basket or pull up and pass off.
6. Players in the outside lane cut to the basket at a 45-degree angle when they reach the top of the key.
7. A pass is made to a cutter for a lay-up or power lay-up.
8. Players must pass and cut quickly.
9. Remaining offensive players follow the original wave of the break as "trailers" cut to the elbow area.

10. If the defense gets back too quickly or if a high-percentage shot is not available, players must make the decision to pull the ball back out and set up the offense.

Common Errors:

1. Pivoting to the inside following the defensive rebound.
2. Failing to call "outlet" for the pass.
3. Receiving the ball too high on the outlet pass (above the free throw line extended).
4. Running in lanes too narrow or close to the ball.
5. Filling the lanes behind the ballhandler.
6. Failing to dribble or pass the ball along the side of the court on a two player fastbreak.
7. Failing to dribble or pass the ball to the middle of the court on a three player break.
8. Forcing the fastbreak.
9. Throwing a pass behind the cutter.
10. Remaining offensive players fail to take position as trailers.

OUT-OF-BOUNDS SITUATIONS

During the course of a youth game, a team will need to inbound the ball from the sideline and under their own basket. A team must first be concerned with inbounding the ball as well as looking for the opportunity to score off the special inbounds play.

The special plays from out-of-bounds

should be simple and should assign each player a specific position and responsibility on the court. Most often, the best passer is assigned to inbound the ball. He/she must possess good court vision and poise. Instruct the inbounder to not look directly at the intended receiver. The player who is to inbound the ball gives a signal to initiate the play. The signal may occur before the official hands him/her the ball; or the out-of-bounds player may call the name or number of the play and slap the ball. (See Chapter 5, Figure 5-7 for the rules governing the throw-in.)

Several formations can be used to vary the out-of-bounds plays and confuse the defense. Many commonly used plays from under the basket begin in box or vertical line formations (see Figure 12-22, 12-23, 12-24, and 12-25).

When teaching inbound plays to your players, practice each option repeatedly *without* a ball first. Then progress to walk through and half speed with a ball. Lastly, add defense and practice at game speed during a scrimmage situation. The out-of-bounds plays along the sideline should be practiced from both sides of the court.

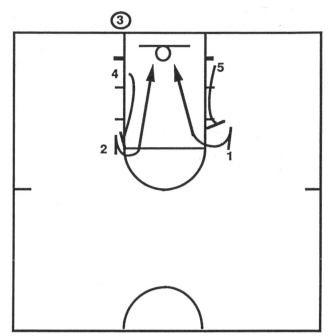

Figure 12-23. *Box Inbounds Play (odd)*
Players are positioned outside of the key area in a box formation. Players 4 and 5 (post players) begin at opposite blocks. Players 1 and 2 begin at opposite elbows. Players 4 and 5 set up picks for 2 and 1, roll and then open up to the ball looking to receive the inbounds pass. Player 3 first looks to inbound the ball to 2, 1, then 4 and 5.

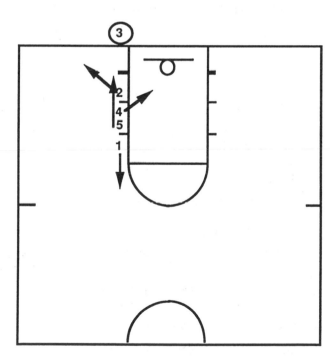

Figure 12-22. *Stack Inbounds Play*
Players are positioned ball-side above the block in a vertical line. Players 2, 4, 5, 1 move left, right, forward and back to receive the inbounds pass. Player 3 looks to pass first to 5, then 4, 2, and lastly 1 for the safety. Instruct the inbounder not to look directly at the intended receiver.

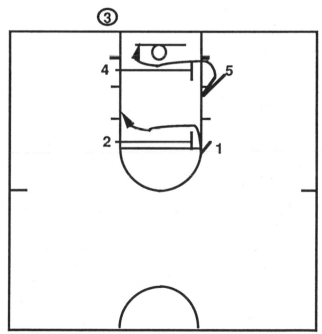

Figure 12-24. *Box Inbounds Play (even)*
Players are positioned outside of the key area in a box formation. Players 4 and 5 (post players) begin at opposite blocks. Players 1 and 2 begin at opposite elbows. Players 2 and 4 (ball-side) set cross picks for 1 and 5, roll and then open up to the ball, looking to receive the inbounds pass. Player 3 first looks to inbound the ball to 5, 4 then 1 and 2.

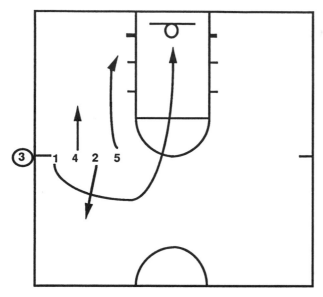

Figure 12-25. *Sideline Play*
Players are positioned in a four-player stack. Player 1 cuts off the triple-screen by 4, 2, and 5 heading straight to the basket and looking for the long pass from 3. After 1 goes by, 4 cuts to the wing, 2 cuts out toward half-court as the safety, and 5 cuts to the low post (ball-side).

OFFENSIVE DRILLS

1. Mass Individual Moves (see Figure 12-26)

Purpose: To aid in teaching the Triple-threat Offensive moves.

Procedure:

a. Divide the players into pairs and have them spread out around the three-point area. One player is on offense and faces the basket—the other player assumes defensive position between the offense and the basket. If possible, each offensive player should have a basketball.

b. The coach stands in the middle of the key and instructs the players to make one of the following moves: (1) direct drive, (2) rocker, (3) jab-step-and-go, or (4) crossover.

c. The defenders must be instructed to either drop back or hold position, depending on the move.

d. The moves may be made at "walk-through," half-, or game-speed, but *no shots* should be taken.

e. Have the players switch positions with his/her partner.

2. Two-line Offensive Moves
(see Figure 12-27)

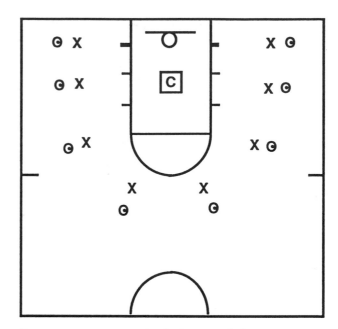

Figure 12-26 . Mass individual moves drill.

Purpose: To develop one-on-one moves from the perimeter positions.

Procedure:

a. Players form two lines at the wing positions at a basket. Balls are placed in one line, and the coach assumes the position of a defensive player on the first person (O_1) in that line (see diagram).

b. O_1 assumes triple-threat position and makes an offensive move to either shoot or drive to the basket (at walk-, ½-, or game-speed).

c. The coach may indicate a particular move that should be made *or* the actions of the defender (coach) can dictate which move O_1 will use.

d. O_1 shoots and goes to the end of the opposite line; X_1 rebounds and goes to the end of the shooting line.

e. Do the drill from both sides of the court.

Variation:
With advanced players, the rebounder (X_1) may cut over to play defense (instead of the coach) and then follow in to get the rebound.

3. Half-Court One-On-One
(see Figure 12-28)

Purpose: To develop individual offensive moves and player-to-player defense in a one-on-one situation; to strengthen offensive and defensive rebounding.

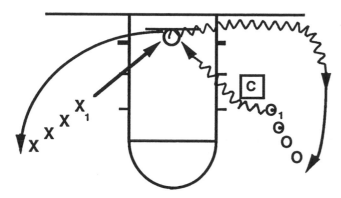

Figure 12-27. Two-line offensive moves drill.

Procedure:

a. Divide players into partners and establish two lines at half court each facing an end basket (from the right side). Both partners should be in one line and each pair should have a basketball.

b. One partner is offense (O_1) and one is defense (X_1). The defender starts about 3 ft. away from O_1 and faces the player in defensive position.

c. O_1 then drives to the basket with X_1 defending, and continues playing one-on-one until O_1 scores or X_1 secures the rebound—then O_2 and X_2 begin.

d. The coach may indicate how aggressively the defense should play or what types of shots should be taken.

e. O_1 and X_1 then go to the end of the opposite line, switch positions, and repeat the drill.

f. After each pair has done the drill three times, move the lines to the left side of the court and repeat the drill.

Variations:

This drill may also be done from the top of the key or with the defender starting next to the offense.

4. One-On-One-On-One (see Figure 12-29)

Purpose: To develop offensive and defensive one-on-one skills.

Procedure:

a. Divide the team so that six players (of similar skill level or size/position) are at a basket. One player O_1 begins at the top of the key with a ball and one plays defense X_1; the remaining players line up beneath the basket.

b. O_1 attempts to score against X_1.

IF: • a basket is made, O_1 returns to the free throw line, X_1 goes out and X_2 moves out to play defense. X_2 must come in quickly and be ready to play, as O_1 does not have to wait.

• X_1 gets a rebound or steals the ball, he/she becomes the new offensive player, O_1 goes out, and X_2 comes in on defense.

c. Points may be awarded for made baskets, rebounds, blocks, or steals.

d. The drill continues until a player scores a certain number of points or for a specific period of time (4-8 minutes).

5. Four-Spot Offensive Moves
(see Figure 12-30a-b)

Purpose: To develop the triple-threat offensive moves against defensive pressure.

Procedure:

a. Form two lines of three or four players at

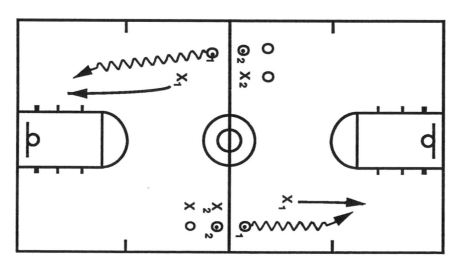

Figure 12-28. Half-court one-on-one drill.

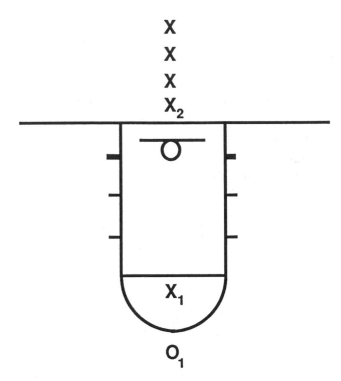

Figure 12-29. One-on-one-on-one drill.

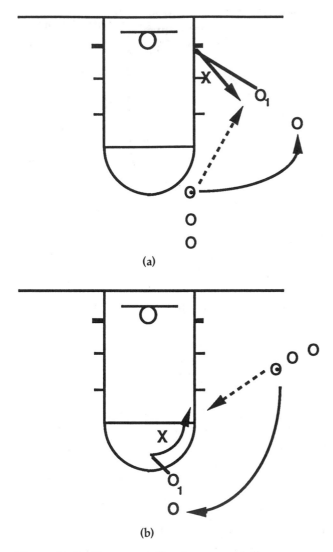

Figure 12-30. Four-spot offensive moves drill.

each basket, one at the top of the key (the passing line) and one at the wing (the shooting line).

b. The first player in the shooting line turns to become a defensive player (X) on the shooter O_1 (see Figure 12-30a).

c. O_1 makes a V-cut and receives a pass from the passing line, squares-up in triple-threat position, and attempts to score against X (who plays passive defense).

d. Any of the triple-threat moves may be used or the coach may indicate that a specific move should be made.

e. X rebounds and goes to the passing line; O_1 becomes the new defender; the passer goes to the end of the shooting line; and the next person in the shooting line becomes O_1.

f. When each player has shot three times, switch the balls to the wing and the line at the top of the key now becomes the shooting line. Repeat the same drill (see Figure 12-30b).

g. Move the lines to the left side and shoot from the other two spots (left wing and top of the key).

Variations:
For more advanced players, instruct the defense

to play aggressively and have O_1 and X play until O_1 scores or X_1 gets the rebound.

6. Block to Block (see Figure 12-31)

Purpose: To work on establishing good post-up position and to develop offensive moves from the block area.

Procedure:

a. A passer is located at each wing position with a ball; and the remaining players line up behind the backboard.

b. X_1 posts-up and receives a pass from O_1; then performs either a square-up or drop-step move, and shoots. X_1 rebounds and passes back to O_1.

c. X_1 then crosses the key, posts-up on the opposite block, and receives a pass from O_2. X_1

makes a move, shoots, rebounds, passes back to O_2, and goes to the end of the line.

d. As X_1 makes the second move, X_2 comes in and posts-up and gets the pass from O_1.

e. This rotation continues, with new players becoming the passers each time X_1 begins again.

f. Encourage players to get good position, present a target hand, make a strong move, and use a shot-fake before the shot.

7. Post Moves with Defense (see Figure 12-32)

Purpose: To develop the offensive moves from the post (block) area.

Procedure:

a. A passer stands at the wing; the shooter and defender take position on the block.

b. The shooter O_1 posts-up and receives a pass from O_2. X plays defense to one side or the other and O_1 makes either a square-up or drop-step move and shoots.

c. If possible, this drill should be done with three players to a basket—after five shots, players rotate positions.

d. If more than three players are used, rotate as follows: defense (X) to offense O_1—offense O_1 to passer O_2—passer O_2 to the end of the line—new defender (X) comes in.

e. Switch and do the drill from the opposite side of the key.

f. Have defenders box out and rebound after the shot.

8. Two-Player Offense Drills

Purpose: To develop the Give and Go, Backdoor Cut, and Pick and Roll techniques.

Procedure:

a. Two offensive and one defensive player work at a basket (another defender may be added).

b. Have the offensive players practice the pattern three times from each side of the floor against a passive defender (see the pattern descriptions in the text of the chapter for diagrams of the patterns).

c. Players should rotate positions so that each individual plays the role of shooter, passer/picker, and defender.

d. If players are learning the patterns, the defenders should be instructed to play passive defense, but may play more aggressively against more advanced players.

e. Coaches may indicate that a single pattern be used in the drill or have the players go through a series of patterns. The positioning of the offensive players may be modified so that the patterns are run from different areas of the court.

Variation:

By adding an additional offensive player (and defender, if desired), the *Pass and Pick Away* pattern may be practiced. To encourage ball movement (passing), have the players run the drill continuously without a shot being taken (the shooter should square-up to shoot, but then pass off and pick away).

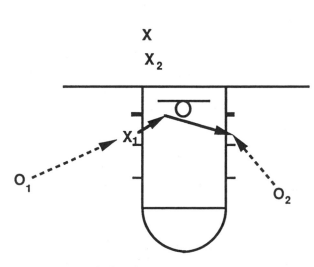

Figure 12-31. Block to block drill.

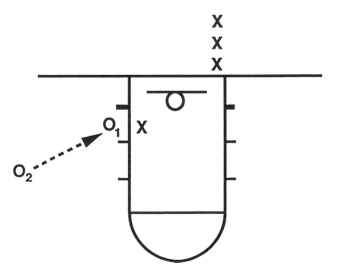

Figure 12-32. Post moves with defense drill.

9. Team 2-on-2 (see Figure 12-33)

Purpose: To develop two-player offense techniques involved in cutting for the ball, passing, driving, and shooting.

Procedure:

a. Form four single file lines—one at each elbow (the offense) and one at each junction of the lane line and the endline (the defenders).

b. One of the defenders passes the ball to the offensive player at the opposite elbow.

c. The two offensive players now attempt to score using two-player offensive techniques. The coach may indicate particular patterns or techniques that should be used, or may specify a particular player to be the shooter.

d. The defenders must call out the name of the player they will guard and move quickly to get into position.

e. Two-on-two play continues until the offense scores or the defense rebounds or steals the ball.

f. The players go to the end of the opposite lines (offense to defense—defense to offense) and four new players begin.

10. Two-on-two or Three-on-Three Scrimmage

Purpose: To practice offensive fundamentals and player to player defense in small sided game sit-

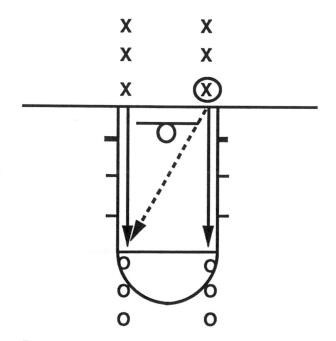

Figure 12-33. Team 2-on-2 drill.

uations; to develop two-player offensive patterns (e.g., give and go, pick and roll, etc.); and to encourage offensive movement.

Procedure:

a. Divide the players into teams of two or three. The teams should be set so that they are fairly even.

b. Two-on-two (or three-on-three) games are played at each available basket. The boundaries for play are the half-court lines and both teams will shoot at the same basket.

c. Set up a Round-Robin tournament so that each team will scrimmage all of the other teams and keep track of the win-loss record (or total points scored).

d. Rules:
   1. Games are played for three minutes.
   2. Each made basket counts as one point.
   3. Player-to-player defense must be used.
   4. After a made basket, the other team receives possession of the ball and must take the ball back beyond the free throw line before attempting to score.
   5. Referees (coaches, managers, or other players) should be used if they are available. Otherwise, players must call their own fouls. If a player is fouled while shooting, the basket is counted; on non-shooting fouls, possession of the ball is taken at the top of the key.
   6. If a game ends in a tie score, players on the two teams each shoot a one-and-one free throw to determine the winner.

e. Encourage players to work as a team and to utilize picks, V-cuts, quick passing, and the two-player patterns on offense.

f. The two teams that finish the Round Robin with the best records may play a "championship" game. Have the remaining players watch and make it a FUN activity. Be sure to praise *all* players/teams for their efforts!

11. 32/21 (see Figure 12-34a-b)

Purpose: To develop skills for conducting the 3-on-2 or 2-on-1 fastbreak and for defending against the break; to improve transition defense.

Procedure:

a. Players form three single-file lines behind the endline at one end of the court—the first two players in the centerline have a basketball. Two players take position in the

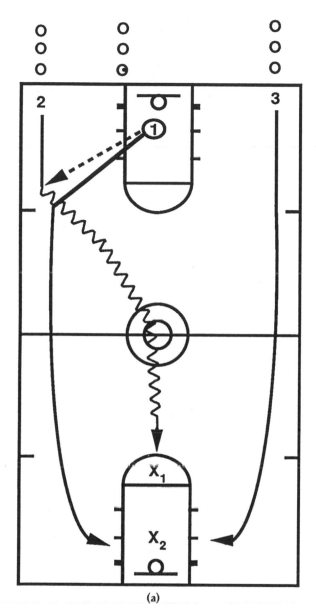

Figure 12-34. 32/21 drill.

key at the opposite end of the court as defenders.

b. Play begins with the first player in each of the three lines. The middle player (1) passes to one of the outside players cutting to the outlet position. The outlet (2) then takes the ball to the middle on the dribble, *1* fills the open lane, and *3* runs downcourt in the other lane.

c. 1, 2, and 3 then play 3-on-2, attempting to score against the two defenders (X_1 and X_2). Play continues until the offense scores or the defense gets possession of the ball (or play for one shot only).

d. X_1 and X_2 then take the ball to the other end on a 2-on-1 fastbreak. The player (*1, 2, or 3*) who took the last shot must hustle downcourt to be the "one" on defense. The other two players remain to replace X_1 and X_2 as defenders (see Figure 12-34b).

e. X_1 and X_2 attempt to score or until the defender gets the ball. Then all three go to the end of one of the lines.

f. As the 2-on-1 players take the first shot, the next three players in line begin (with the middle player passing to the outlet) and go downcourt 3-on-2.

g. Run the drill for a set period of time (10

minutes), making sure that all players have the opportunity to play all positions.

12. Continuous 3-on-2 (see Figure 12-35)

Purpose: To develop 3-on-2 offensive and defensive skills and techniques.

Procedure:

a. At least 11 players are needed for this drill. Two defenders (X) take position in each of the key areas; three offensive players (*1, 2,* and *3*) begin at half-court with the ball at the middle position; and the remaining players form lines at each of the 28 ft. hashmarks and outside of the court.

b. *1, 2, and 3* play 3-on-2 against the defenders at one end. Play continues until a basket is scored or a defender gains possession of the ball.

c. The player who scored, or the defender with the ball, then passes the ball to the first player in one of the lines at the sideline. The first players in line must step into the court and call "outlet," then the passer joins them going 3-on-2 to the other end of the court.

d. The remaining players who have just finished, either take position as one of the next defenders or fill in at the end of one of the outlet lines.

e. Play continues in this manner, with 3-on-2 being played back and forth from one end to the other. The drill may be timed, or may continue until a specified number of baskets are made.

Variation:

To encourage aggressive rebounding and to emphasize the rebound-outlet aspect of the break, play may be limited to only one shot by the offense. Then all five players crash the boards for the rebound and whoever gets it (offense or defense) passes to the outlet and continues to play 3-on-2 at the other end. A player who *HUSTLES* can continue playing indefinitely by getting rebounds and going after the ball aggressively!

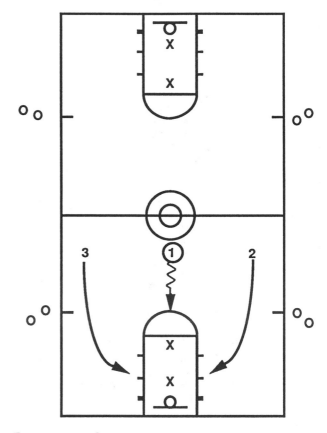

Figure 12-35. Continuous 3-on-2.

OFFENSIVE PATTERNS
Basic Player-To-Player Offense

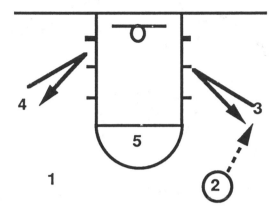

Figure 12-36. *Player-to-Player Offense*
Players 3 and 4 V-cut and pop out at the free throw line extended. Player 2 passes to 3, who squares up into a triple-threat position. If the defenders overplay, 3 and 4 use a backdoor cut to the basket for a pass.

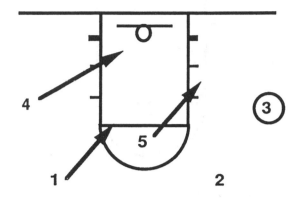

Figure 12-37. Player 3 has the option to: shoot, drive, pass to 5 or reverse the ball to 2. (The offense may be run to either side.) Any of the eight options that follow may be integrated into the basic pattern.

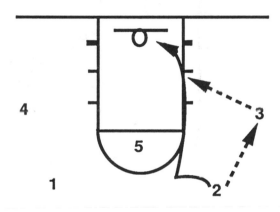

Figure 12-38. *Option #1* Give and go.

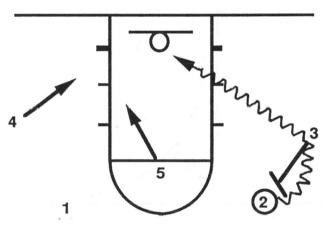

Figure 12-39. *Option #2* Pick on the ball.

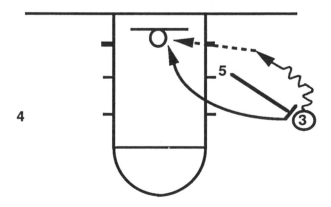

Figure 12-40. *Option #3* Pick and roll.

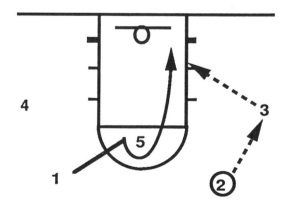

Figure 12-41. *Option #4* Opposite guard through.

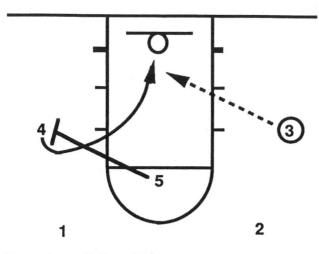

Figure 12-42. *Option #5* Pick away.

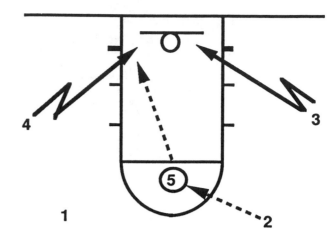

Figure 12-43. *Option #6* High post-to-wing backdoor cut.

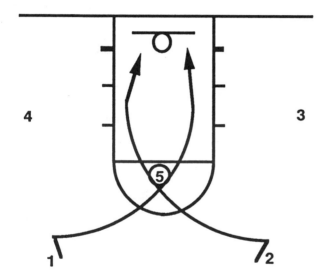

Figure 12-44. *Option #7* Scissors cut.

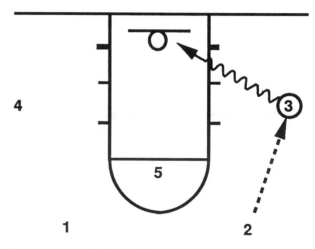

Figure 12-45. *Option #8* Clear out.
Player 3 takes the defender one-on-one and the other players follow for a possible pass or the rebound.

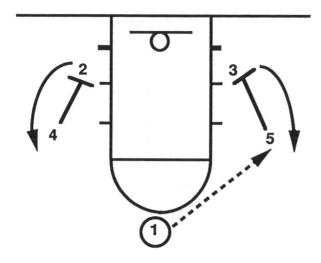

Figure 12-46. *Pick Down.*
Players 4 and 5 downpick for 2 and 3 who pop out to the wing area. 4 and 5 roll off the picks and post up at the blocks. 1 passes to 3, who looks to shoot, drive, or pass to 5.

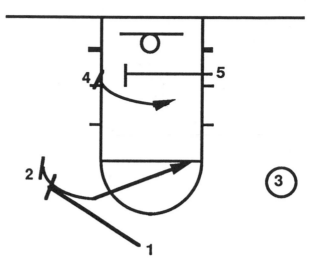

Figure 12-47. *Pick Across.*
If no pass is made, 5 picks across for 4 and 1 picks across high for 2. 3 looks for 4 and then 2.

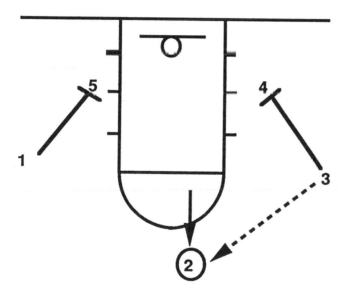

Figure 12-48. *Restart.*
If no pass is made, 2 pops out to the top of the key to receive the ball. 3 and 1 pick down and the pattern continues.

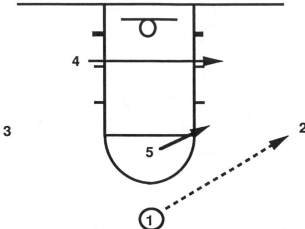

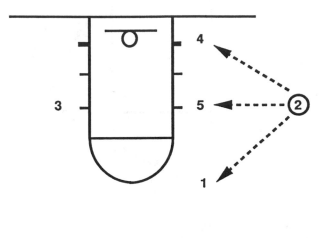

Figure 12-49. This offense establishes an overload and creates a passing triangle between the wing player and the two post players. As 1 passes to 2, 4 cuts across to the ball-side block and 5 cuts to position at the elbow. Player 3 stays weak-side and looks to cut into the seams of the defense.

Figure 12-50. Player 2 has the option to shoot, pass to either 4 or 5, or to reverse the ball back to 1.

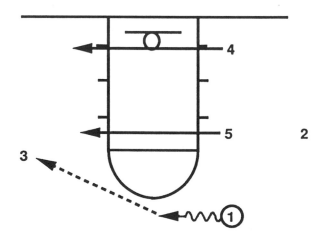

Figure 12-51. To reverse the ball, 1 passes to 3, then 4 and 5 cut across the key to form a passing triangle on the opposite side.

Offensive Strategies

PERFORMANCE AREA	SPECIFIC SKILLS	SUGGESTED EMPHASIS		
		Elem. School Beginner 8-10	Middle School Intermediate 11-13	High School Advanced 14 and up
Individual Offensive Moves	Direct drive to the basket	X	X	X
	Rocker move	X	X	X
	Jab-step and go	X	X	X
	Crossover step		X	X
	Shot-fake and jump shot	X	X	X
	Post-up position		X	X
	Post square-up and shoot		X	X
	Post drop-step move		X	X
Offensive Movement Without the Ball	Direct cut to ball	X	X	X
	V-cut	X	X	X
	L-cut	X	X	X
	Setting picks	X	X	X
	Using picks	X	X	X
Two-Player Patterns	Give and go	X	X	X
	Backdoor cut	X	X	X
	Pick and roll		X	X
	Pass and pick away		X	X
Five-Player Offense	Five-player pattern offense		X	X
	Zone offense		X	X
	Fastbreak		X	X
	Out-of-bounds situations		X	X

Offensive Strategies Drill Matrix

Drill	SKILL LEVEL		
	Beginning	Intermediate	Advanced
Mass individual moves	X	X	
Two-line offensive moves	X	X	
Half-court one-on-one	X	X	X
One-on-one-on-one	X	X	X
Four-spot offensive moves		X	X
Block-to-block		X	X
Post moves with defense		X	X
Two-player offensive drills	X	X	X
Team 2-on-2		X	X
2-on-2 (or 3-on-3) scrimmage	X	X	X
32/21 fastbreak drill		X	X
Continuous 3-on-2		X	X

13
Defensive Strategies

Karen Garchow, M.A.
Amy Dickinson, M.S.

QUESTIONS TO CONSIDER

- What are the individual and team defensive techniques used in the game of basketball?
- What sequence should be used when introducing defensive skills?
- What are the key elements and common errors of each skill?
- What drills and activities are effective in teaching defensive strategies?

INTRODUCTION

This chapter contains *individual* and *team* defensive strategies for youth play. Defensive skills are systematically arranged from player-to-player *on the ball* techniques (live and dead ball) to more advanced *off the ball* techniques (open and closed stance). Also included are coaching hints useful when teaching *team* strategies to beginning and intermediate players.

The basic principles of the zone, defending the post, and the fastbreak are presented to aid the coach in teaching the *key elements* and *common errors* of each skill.

The drill portion of this chapter contains activities that are appropriate for developing both *offensive* and *defensive* strategies. The execution of the drill may vary dependent upon the coach's intended emphasis.

For a summary of the defensive strategies and drills that are appropriate for each level of play (beginning, intermediate, and advanced), see Supplements 13-1 and 13-2.

INDIVIDUAL DEFENSE

In order to develop a team's defensive strengths, the coach must first teach his/her players the *individual* defensive skills involved in the game of basketball. Begin by stressing the "Five Points to Good Defense":

1. **Stance**
2. **Footwork**
3. **Position**
4. **Aggressiveness/desire**
5. **Team communication**

Stance

Proper body position is one of the most important fundamentals to stress when teaching defense to youth players. Prior to any other instruction, the basic defensive stance must be taught from a *stationary* position and practiced repeatedly. The defensive stance, when performed correctly, will allow players to move with improved quickness and balance.

Begin teaching the defensive stance, starting with the feet and moving upward. Instruct your players to position their feet shoulder-width apart in a slightly staggered stance. Stress that the weight be kept on the balls of the feet in order to achieve proper balance.

The body should be in a semi-crouched position with the knees flexed, back straight, and the head up. The position of the defender's arms will vary dependent upon the actions of and options available to the offensive player. However, when teaching the basic stance, instruct the defense to position the arms out at the sides with the palms facing up. Encourage your players to keep their buttocks low, as if "sitting in an imaginary chair" (see Figure 13-1). Point out that they must maintain the proper stance throughout an entire game, which requires mental and physical toughness acquired through practice.

Key Elements:

1. Position feet at shoulder width apart in a slightly staggered stance.
2. Maintain most of the weight on the balls of the feet.

Figure 13-1. Proper defensive stance with the knees flexed and buttocks low.

3. Keep knees flexed in a semi-crouched position.
4. Keep back straight, buttocks down and the head up.
5. Position arms out at the sides of the body with the palms up.

Common Errors:

1. Positioning feet closer than shoulder-width apart.
2. Standing flat-footed.
3. Standing in an erect position.
4. Leaning forward over the front foot.
5. Holding arms down at the sides of the body.
6. Looking down at the floor.

Footwork

Slide Step

Proper defensive footwork centers around teaching youth players the fundamentals of the *slide step* (also referred to as shuffling). The quick movement of the feet is one of the most important aspects of good defensive play.

Once your players have learned the basic defensive stance, progress to teaching the slide step in the lateral direction. Begin by having your players point their lead foot in the direction of the desired movement. For example, if sliding to the right, the first movement is with the right foot, sliding it approximately 12 in. to the right (see Figure 13-2).

The next move involves dragging the left foot (trail foot) to a spot near the previous position of the right foot (lead foot). A period of non-support should be maintained while moving the trail foot forward. The reverse would be true for a slide step to the left.

Instruct your athletes to guard against crossing their feet, since this causes a loss of balance and may allow the offensive player to drive past them. To help players visualize proper sliding technique, tell them to imagine that a *ruler* is placed between their feet and that their feet should never come any closer together than this distance.

Encourage your athletes to concentrate on taking short, quick steps while keeping their weight and buttocks low. The knees should remain flexed at all times (stress that no bouncing up and down is allowed—that is wasted

Figure 13-2. The first step of a defensive slide step to the right is made with the right foot, pushing off with the left.

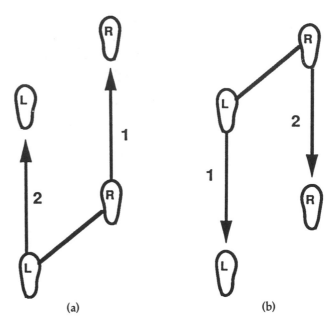

Figure 13-3. (a) Attack steps; (b) Retreat steps.

motion), and that the head should remain stationary.

Attack and Retreat Step

Next, progress to teaching the *attack and retreat step*. Explain that the attack and retreat steps are used to maintain a good defensive position when approaching or backing away from an offensive player with the ball.

Begin by having your players move forward by pointing the toe of the lead foot (*pushing* forward with this foot) and then *pulling* the trail foot behind (see Figure 13-3a). In moving backwards, players use short, quick *retreat* steps, sliding back with the rear foot first, and then the lead foot. A *retreat* step is most commonly taken after the offensive player passes the ball. Moving a step backward in the direction of the pass allows the defensive player to stop a possible cut to the basket, as well as to provide help to other teammates (see Figure 13-3b).

Emphasize that players should remain in a low, balanced defensive stance. The arms should be outstretched with the hands up while making quick changes of direction forwards and

backwards. As in the slide step, the feet should never cross.

Drop Step

Next, progress to teaching the *drop step*. Explain to your players that the drop step is used to change directions, while guarding an opponent.

Begin teaching the drop step from the basic defensive position and make certain your player's knees are flexed in a staggered stance with the left foot back.

Tell your players to imagine that they are guarding an opponent who has quickly changed directions from right to left. In order to prevent the offense from getting by them, they must quickly react and execute a drop step with the right foot. Stress that the *toe* of the right foot should point in the new direction, as the left foot pushes off to generate more power and momentum. Also practice the drop step in reverse, as the change of direction is made from left to right (see Figure 13-4).

Other key coaching points to emphasize are the opening of the hips and the swinging of the elbow (right) through in the direction of the drop step. This motion must be practiced repeatedly with beginners (in both directions) from a stationary position *without* an offensive player. Then, add the drop-step to other foot-

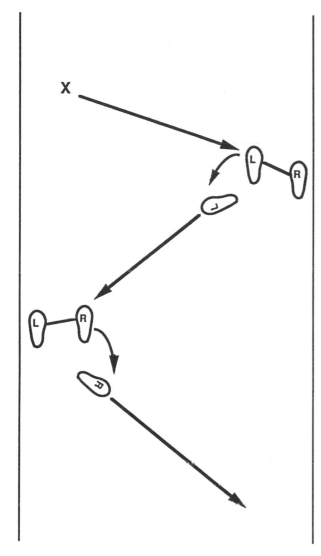

Figure 13-4. The defensive drop step.

work drills against an offensive player performing at half-speed and game-speed.

Position

Floor position is the most important (and the most difficult) aspect of defense to teach youth players. Do not begin instructing your team on proper positioning until they have learned the defensive skills of stance and footwork.

Under *general* defensive situations, certain *basic rules* apply. A defensive player must learn to:

- Maintain the proper defensive stance with their weight evenly distributed on the balls of both feet
- Maintain an arm's length distance away from

the offensive player, dependent on the player's ability and position on the floor

- Focus the eyes on the offensive player's mid-section
- Stay between the opponent and the basket
- Keep the feet moving
- Stop the offensive player from penetrating or scoring

In addition to these basic rules, there are two types of situations that can occur during player-to-player defense: guarding an opponent *with* the ball (on the ball) or guarding an opponent *without* the ball (off the ball).

Aggressiveness and Desire

Aggressiveness is one of the essential components of good defense. A coach must help his/her players develop a *positive* defensive attitude. Instill in your players that good defensive habits are developed through *hard work* and a burning desire to stop the opponent. Stress that successful defensive players do not have to be great athletes. However, to play good defense they must be aggressive and take *pride* in their individual and team defensive skills.

A few important points to share with your players are:

1. Play defense with tremendous *confidence* in yourself and in your teammates.
2. Take the *initiative* on defense. Go out to meet the offensive player under control. Believe a positive result will occur from your efforts.
3. Make your presence known with your feet, hands, arms, and voice. Disrupt the flow of the offense and force the offense to take low percentage shots.
4. *Concentrate* and play defense with *intensity!*
5. Avoid unnecessary reaching-in fouls; *pressure* the opponent to turn the ball over.
6. *Hustle* at all times! Do not rest on the defensive end of the court.

Most importantly, a coach must be *enthusiastic* about defense and reward players who demonstrate aggressiveness.

Team Communication

Talking on defense is an important defensive fundamental to teach youth players. *Team* defense depends upon each players' ability to communicate effectively using commonly understood terms. The terminology may vary slightly from team to team; however, the key lies in developing "talk" and telling your players what to say in different situations.

Offensive strategies include a variety of picks, cuts, and movements in an attempt to score. In order to execute proper defensive techniques, players must learn and practice *calling out loud* specific terms such as:

1. ball
2. dead
3. shot
4. pick right-left
5. cutter
6. switch
7. fight through
8. deny
9. got your help
10. first pass

Encourage the use of these terms at *all* times, both in practice and games. Coaches will be surprised how a common language can pull their team together, expedite the teaching process, and improve concentration.

Guarding the Player with the Ball

Begin teaching *on the ball* defensive techniques, starting with a demonstration of how to guard an offensive player who is in triple-threat position and has not dribbled. Stress these *key elements:*

1. Review proper defensive stance—"sit in your imaginary chair"
2. Stand approximately an arm's length away from the offensive player, dependent upon a player's ability and position on the court
3. Position the palm up on lead hand, other hand out at the side of the body to occupy passing lane
4. Focus eyes on the midsection of the offensive player
5. Be ready to move quickly (in either direction) in case the player drives

Dribbler Defense

Next, teach the defensive player how to *guard an offensive player who is dribbling the ball.* Since

footwork instruction precedes the teaching of dribbler defense, your players will understand how the slide, attack, retreat, and drop steps are used in "live-ball" situations.

As the offensive player dribbles the ball, either on the drive to the basket or in the open court, the defensive player must quickly drop step in the same direction to cut off the path of the dribbler. The defensive player must be in a position to slide in either direction without crossing the feet, unless they have been beat, in which case, he/she must run to re-establish position.

The most important point to stress to your players when teaching dribbler defense is to "have your head directly between the ball and the basket." A key coaching cue is *head on the ball.* This encourages the defensive player to overplay ball-side one half-step and position their lead foot to align with the middle of the offensive player's body.

The arms should be outstretched with the palms facing up. The lead hand guards against the crossover dribble, while the other hand is positioned at the side of the body to occupy the passing lane (see Figure 13-5). Instruct your players to avoid reaching-in fouls. However, if a steal is attempted, they should come at the ball with an *upward* flicking motion of the hand.

When teaching youth players proper defensive positioning, encourage a well-centered defensive stance in front of the opponent. The eyes should be focused on the ballhandler's midsection, rather than on the movement of the ball. As knowledge and skill increases, point out that the object of on-the-ball defense is to force the opponent *away from the basket.* Demonstrate how to "steer the dribbler" to the outside and pressure the ball handler to take a longer and less threatening route to where he/she wants to go (see Figure 13-6). This most likely will also result in a low percentage shot or more difficult pass into the post.

Coaching hints for more advanced dribbler defense include:

1. Force the ball handler to dribble the ball with the "non-dominant hand." *Overplay ball-side.*
2. Pressure the ball (call "Ball") and make it difficult for the offensive player to see available passing options and run the offense.
3. If the dribbler changes direction, drop-step

Figure 13-5. Proper dribbler defense with the "head on the ball."

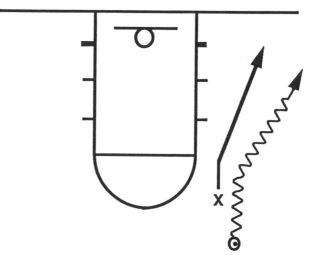

Figure 13-6. Forcing the dribbler away from the basket.

quickly and jump "ball-side" to force the opponent the other way.

4. Position your outside foot on the sideline or baseline to cut off penetration by the offensive player.

5. If the dribbler executes a reverse move, retreat step to avoid getting "hooked" by the offensive drop step.

Player-to-player defense on a dead ball

Once an offensive player picks up the ball and has stopped the dribble, the defensive player must be taught how to apply all-out pressure.

Instruct the defensive player to move towards the offensive player without making contact. Both hands are up and in front of the ball to take away more of the offensive player's vision (*swarm* the ball). The hands "trace" the path of the ball in a *windmill* fashion. The eyes of the defensive player focus on the eyes of the offensive player in order to detect a possible shot or pass attempt. Stress team communication, instruct the defensive player to call "Dead" loudly. This helps to pick up the intensity and pressure the offensive player even more.

Key Elements:

1. Call "Dead" loudly.
2. Move towards the offensive player without making contact.

3. Position both hands up and in front of the ball—"Swarm."
4. Trace the path of the ball in a *windmill* fashion.
5. Focus eyes on the offensive player's eyes.

Common Errors:

1. Failing to communicate on defense.
2. Standing further than an arm's length away from the offensive player.
3. Making contact with the offensive player's body, resulting in a foul.
4. Positioning arms down at the sides.

Defending the Shot

Defending the shot is an important "on the ball" technique that all players should master. The defensive player must guard the offensive player who is shooting the ball from a triple-threat position or off the drive.

Instruct your team that when guarding an opponent in their shooting range, they must be ready to defend against the shot at all times. Begin with a review of the defensive stance, stressing the importance of proper arm and hand position. Point out that the closer to the basket they are, the higher the lead arm should be held.

The defender must position his/her arm straight up toward the ball and not into the shooter (see Figure 13-7). Many players develop the bad habit of leaving their feet in an attempt to *block* the shot. This often results in a shooting foul or allows the offensive player to drive

Figure 13-7. Defending the shot with the arm extended up toward the ball.

around the defender while he/she is still in the air.

Encourage your players to maintain a good defensive stance between the shooter and basket; force the offensive player to shoot over the "picket fence" and outstretched arm.

Once the offensive player releases the ball, tell the defensive player to yell "Shot." This alerts four other teammates to begin boxing out for the defensive rebound. (See one-on-one shooting drills in Chapter 9 to practice proper defensive technique against the shooter.)

Guarding the Player Without the Ball

Guarding the player *without* the ball is probably the most difficult defensive technique for youth players to grasp and execute correctly. Youth coaches must stress repeatedly to begin-

ning players *to know where the ball and the opponent are at all times*. The defensive player must always be able to *see both*. Help your athletes to understand that when the offensive player is without the ball, the opponent is *still* a threat and may execute a cut to the basket or receive a pass from a teammate.

Explain to your team that a player's defensive position changes whenever the ball or the opponent moves. The exact position depends upon where on the court the opponent and the ball are located. A simple rule to share with your youth players is: *The closer your opponent is to the ball, the closer you should be to him/her.* The distance from the opponent changes relative to ball position.

Deny Defense

Begin teaching "off-the-ball" defensive techniques, starting with *deny* defense. In this position, the ball is only *one pass* away.

Demonstrate deny defense with two offensive players and one defensive player. The passer (O_1) is positioned at the point with the ball. The defensive player at the wing (X) is positioned in a *closed* stance (back to the ball) between the ball and his/her opponent (O_2) (see Figure 13-8). Instruct the defensive player to turn his/her head towards the lead shoulder, to allow for simultaneous peripheral vision of *both* ball and player.

The arm and leg closest to the ball are extended into the passing lane. The thumb of the

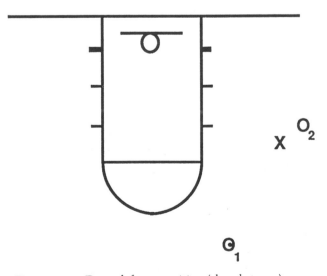

Figure 13-8. Deny defense position (closed stance).

lead hand is pointing down with the palm turned out toward the ball. As the offensive player (O₂) moves up and down the wing, the defensive player must keep his/her knees bent and move quickly in an attempt to *deny the ball* to the cutter (see Figure 13-9).

Key Elements:

1. Used on "ball-side" of court or when guarding an opponent positioned one pass away.
2. Position body in a *closed* defensive stance between the ball and the opponent.
3. Turn head towards lead shoulder, allowing simultaneous peripheral vision of ball and opponent.
4. Extend lead arm and leg into the passing lane.
5. Extend lead hand in a thumbs down position, palm facing the ball.
6. Adjust position on each and every pass.

Common Errors:

1. Denying on helpside of court or when more than one pass away.
2. Positioning the body in an *open* defensive stance.
3. Turning the head to see the opponent *only*.

Figure 13-9. To maintain deny position, the defender moves up and down the wing keeping the hand in the passing lane.

4. Keeping lead arm down at the side of the body.
5. Extending the lead hand in a thumbs-up position, palm facing the offensive player.
6. Failing to adjust defensive position with the movement of the cutter.

Helpside Defense

The defensive success of a team is dependent upon each player's ability to provide "help" for his/her teammates. Helpside defense also refers to the side of the court opposite the ballside. A player who is *two passes* away must be taught how to play proper "helpside defense" (see Figure 13-10).

Begin by sharing this simple rule with your team: *The further the ball is from the opponent, the further the defensive player can be from the opponent.* Place the ball on the other side of the court and demonstrate the *open* defensive stance. Explain that in order for the defense to see both player and ball, he/she must move away from the opponent (sag off) and open up his/her stance.

Point out how the ball, the offensive player and defensive player form three points of a triangle. The base of the triangle is a line from the ball to the offensive player (O₂). The apex is the defensive player (X) (see Figure 13-11).

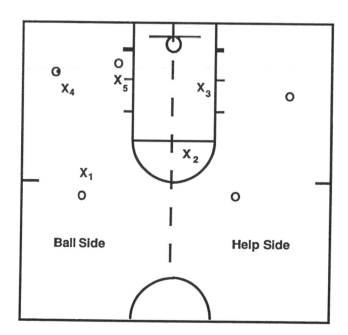

Figure 13-10. Players X_2 and X_3 are in helpside defensive position.

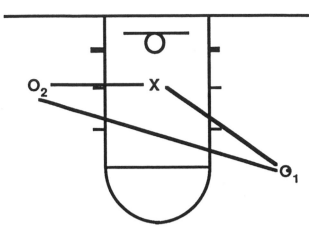

Figure 13-11. Helpside defensive triangle (open stance).

Figure 13-12. Helpside players must be in a position to see the ball and the player being guarded.

Beginners must practice pointing one hand at their opponent and the other hand at the ball. This helps them to actually visualize the triangle and move into proper helpside position. Make sure to check that the head of the defender is facing straight ahead in a position which allows simultaneous peripheral vision of the player being guarded and the ball (see Figure 13-12).

Review the following important rules for the flat triangle. *The defensive player in helpside defense must:*

1. Be close enough to the ball to stop the drive or pass.
2. Never be more than one step off the passing lane.

3. Point one hand at the opponent and the other hand at the ball.
4. Look straight ahead in a position which allows simultaneous peripheral vision of both ball and player.
5. Be in a position to give "help" to ball-side players who may have been beaten, stop penetration of the ball, and recover back to his/her own player.
6. Adjust position if the offensive player cuts to receive a pass.

The Shell Defense and Help and Recover Drills serve as excellent aids when teaching this more advanced "off-the-ball" defensive technique to your players.

Defending the Screen

Defending against the screen is as important a skill to teach your players as how to set a good screen.

Chapter 12 (Offensive Strategies) discussed how to set the two basic types of picks; the pick on the ball and the pick away from the ball. It is suggested to use many of the same drills (Two-Player Pick and Roll) to teach the defensive techniques only with the emphasis being placed on teaching the proper defense of the screen.

Often in screen drills combining offensive and defensive players, beginners get confused as to who they should pick, how they should use the pick, who should defend the pick, etc. Youth coaches can help their players learn these offensive and defensive techniques faster if they separate the two skills from one another.

Inform your team that if an opposing player is screening, the defender has three options:

1. fight over the pick
2. slide through between the screener and his/her teammate
3. switch players they are guarding

The first step in defending the screen involves *calling out the pick.* The player guarding the opponent (who is setting the screen) should say out loud "Pick-right" or "Pick-left." This alerts his/her teammate that the screen is coming and from what direction. Practice this communication repeatedly so that your defensive players begin to talk to each other instinctively.

Fighting over the pick or getting over the top

is the best way to teach youth players to defend the screen. This movement involves reacting as soon as the pick is called, staying low and well-balanced while arching the back and fighting over the top. This allows the defensive player to maintain a position between the opponent and the screen, as opposed to sliding through or switching players which allows for possible mismatches to occur. The two techniques should be introduced at a more advanced level of play.

Key Elements:

1. Call out the pick—("Pick-left," "Pick-right").
2. React as soon as the pick is called.
3. Stay low and well balanced, feel the pick coming with an outstretched arm.
4. Arch the back and step over the top of the screen.
5. Maintain a good defensive stance between the opponent and the screen.

Common Errors:

1. Failing to call out the pick.
2. Turning away from the offensive player to see the pick coming.
3. Standing up when contact is made with the picker.
4. Switching before trying to fight through the pick first.

Defending the Post

The next step in teaching individual defense is instructing players to defend the low post (block) area. Since the ballside post player is close to the basket and a definite scoring threat, the objective is to *deny* the post player the ball.

The technique of fronting is the best strategy for denying the post, since the defender completely obstructs the passing lane. However, it is recommended that beginners be taught to defend from the side first. This technique transfers well from basic deny positioning and introduces players to skills that will be used in more advanced post defense.

The basic technique of denying from the side is generally the same as deny position at the perimeter. The defender is in position between the offensive player and the ball, with an arm and leg extended into the passing lane. When guarding the post, the defender plays a

little more upright and tighter to the offensive player. The back foot is kept behind the post player so that the bodies of the two players are perpendicular (see Figure 13-13). The head is turned to watch the ball, while the rear arm and close body position are used to "feel" the movement of the player. As the post moves, the defender uses quick shuffle steps to maintain the deny position.

The post may be defended from the high side or the low side, dependent upon the location of the ball. When the ball is above the free throw line, the post should be defended on the

Figure 13-13. When defending a post player, one foot must remain behind the post and the front arm is extended into the passing lane.

high side to cut off the passing angle (see Figure 13-14). If the ball is below the free throw line, the defender should take position on the baseline side (see Figure 13-15) to force the player away from the basket and into the key where helpside defense is available.

As the ball is passed around the perimeter, the defender must switch from one side to the other. Teach your players to go *behind* the post player using quick shuffle steps to switch sides. The defender must remain close to the player and keep the knees flexed to allow for quick movements. Once on the opposite side, the arm must immediately be raised into the passing lane to prevent a pass on the switch.

If the post player does receive the ball, the defender must immediately slide behind him/her to take position between the player and the basket. Encourage players to maintain good defensive position and to be ready to defend against a drive (offensive move) or a shot. Since

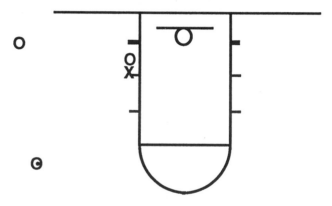

Figure 13-14. Low post defense when the ball is above the free throw line.

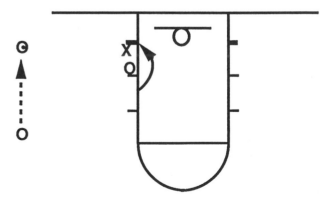

Figure 13-15. Low post defense when the ball is at the baseline (below the free throw line).

the player is in a high-percentage shooting position, the arms should be kept high to discourage the shot. If a shot is attempted, the defender must yell, "Shot!" and pivot to box out the shooter for the rebound.

Key Elements:

1. Deny on the high side when the ball is above the free throw line; on the low side when the ball is below the free throw line.
2. Establish a tight deny position with the front arm in the passing lane.
3. Keep the knees flexed and the back foot behind the post player.
4. Turn the head to watch the ball and "feel" the player move with the body and back arm.
5. Use quick shuffle steps to maintain position as the player moves.
6. To switch sides, go behind the player quickly and assume deny position with the opposite arm in the passing lane.
7. Drop into position between the player and the basket once the player receives the ball, keeping the arms up to discourage the shot.
8. Call "Shot!"; pivot and box out on the shot.

Common Errors:

1. Playing too far away from the post player.
2. Taking position on the incorrect side (high or low).
3. Failing to keep the back foot behind the player.
4. Keeping the arm down (not in passing lane).
5. Watching the player instead of the ball.
6. Going away from the player when dropping behind.
7. Failing to drop back once the player gets the ball.
8. Standing erect or with the arms down to guard against the shot.
9. Leaning on the post player (fouling).
10. Failing to box out for the rebound.

TEAM PLAYER-TO-PLAYER DEFENSE

In order for player-to-player defense to be effective, all five players must be alert, think quickly, and react to the offensive situation. Each player will need to use the individual defensive techniques (guarding the ball, deny defense, helpside defense, etc.), and must also work as part of the five-player *team* defense. Communication and teamwork are essential parts of player-to-player defense. Although each individual has a particular opponent that he/she is responsible for defending, the team needs to react as a unit to the movements of the offensive players and the ball (see Figure 13-16).

To develop good team defense, encourage your players to play aggressively and emphasize team goals ("Only allow the opponents one shot," "Don't give up lay-ups," "Everyone talks." Praise your players for good communication and for playing helpside defense, and encourage them to praise each other ("Nice help," "Stay with him/her," etc.). This will help to foster the *desire* to play tough defense and gives the team *pride* in working together to stop the opponents. Playing defense is always hard work, but it is more fun and exciting when the team unites to accept the challenge.

Coaching Hints for Teaching Player-to-Player Team Defense:

Many of the coaching hints listed below overlap the "Five Points to Good Individual Defense." It is remarkable what a team will pick up (mentally and physically from a coach's simple yet *repetitive* reminders!

Make sure to stress that defense is a *team game* and requires a team effort from all five players.

Instruct the defensive team to:

- Stay between the opponent and the basket.
- See both ball and player at all times.

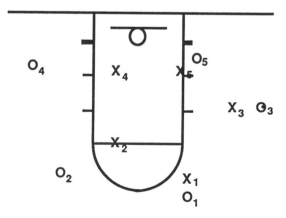

Figure 13-16. Team player-to-player defense.

- Use proper footwork and a good defensive stance to move quickly and aggressively.
- *Move* when the ball moves. All five players must adjust their defensive position on each and every pass.
- Play team defense with *desire! Deny* when you are one pass away, provide *help* when you are two passes away.
- *Talk* to your teammates on defense ("Ball," "Shot," "Pick-right," etc.).
- Force the offensive team to take low percentage shots. Prevent the shot in the lane area (i.e., lay-up, post-shot, etc.).
- Box out and rebound the ball to prevent the second or third shot.
- Play defense with intensity! Hustle at all times. Work to be the best conditioned athlete on the floor.

ZONE DEFENSE

A zone defense is a team defense in which the individual players are responsible for defending an *area* of the court and any opponents who are in that area. Generally, the players position themselves in relation to the position of the ball. As the ball moves, the zone shifts to cover the areas that are most vulnerable and the players who are scoring threats.

All the skills of player-to-player defense are needed in order to play an effective zone. The defenders must be able to guard an opponent with the ball, deny the pass, cover the cutters, and play helpside defense.

Zone defense should be taught *after* individual and player-to-player defensive techniques have been developed!

There are several reasons why a coach might want to use a zone defense. Zone defenses are designed to protect the middle of the court and the basket area. They force the opponents to take lower-percentage perimeter shots, and therefore can be very effective against poor shooting teams. A zone also provides good rebounding position, since the forward and center typically stay in the low post areas. Finally, zones can help to protect players who are in foul trouble and aid in defending a quicker or taller team.

However, keep in mind that all zones have weaknesses *and* that a good zone defense requires aggressive individual defense by all five players on the court. If players become passive when playing a zone or if an area is not covered properly, the defense becomes ineffective. Playing a tough zone defense is hard work and requires concentration, teamwork, and intensity!

There are many different types of zones. They are usually named according to the configuration of the zone (beginning at the top of the key). The 1-3-1, 2-3, and 3-2 are examples of basic zones used by many teams. Generally, a zone is strongest where there is the greatest number of players (i.e., the 3-2 is strong at the perimeter). The best zone for a team will depend on the abilities of the defensive players and on the strengths and weaknesses of the opponent.

The 2-3 is a good zone to use for introducing zone defense to youth players. It is strong near the basket and keeps three players in the low-post area to maintain the rebounding triangle. It uses two guards at the elbows, two forwards on the blocks, and a center in the middle of the key (see Figure 13-17). As the ball moves, players adjust their position by moving several steps toward the ball and guarding any offensive players in their area (see Figure 13-18).

Coaching Hints for Playing Zone Defense:

- Players must get back on defense and set up quickly.
- Each player must be in defensive position with the knees flexed, ready to move quickly. The

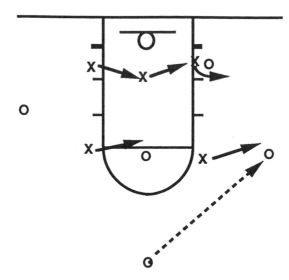

Figure 13-18. 2-3 zone defensive rotation on the pass.

arms should be up (unless guarding the ball to take away the passing lanes and make the zone look bigger.

- Players must know where the ball is at *all* times, and adjust their position quickly when it moves.
- The team must *communicate* ("Ball," "Watch the cutter," "Shot," etc.) in order to eliminate confusion and to keep all five players working together.
- Keep the zone tight and force the opponents to take outside shots. Players must be ready to stop all penetration into the key. No lay-ups should be allowed!
- Offensive players cutting to the ball must be denied. The defender should step in front of the cutter and force them to go somewhere else.
- Weakside defenders must be in a position to *see the ball* and the offensive players who are on the weakside of the zone.
- Following a shot, all five defenders must *box out* the nearest offensive player.

FASTBREAK DEFENSE

The best way to stop the opponent's fast-break is to make a quick transition from offense to defense. A good *transition defense* requires that all five players get back on defense as quickly as possible once an opponent secures the rebound. It is the responsibility of the first players back to prevent the opponent from scoring until their

Figure 13-17. Starting positions for the 2-3 zone defense.

teammates make it downcourt to help. Players should be instructed to *run* at top speed to the opposite end of the court and then turn to establish defensive position in the key area. They must protect the basket, keep the offense out of the key, and force the opponents to pass the ball as much as possible. This will delay the shot (lay-up) and give the rest of the defense time to get into position.

The most common fastbreak situations are the *2-on-1* and *3-on-2*. The responsibilities of the single defender and of a pair of defenders need to be taught in drills and practiced repeatedly (see 2-on-2 Full-Court Defense Drill; 32/21 Drill and Continuous 3-on-2 Drill in Chapter 12). Defending the break requires quick thinking, good defensive technique, hustle, and determination. Stress to your players that they must view fastbreak defense as a *challenge* and play aggressively when they are outnumbered!

2-on-1 Situations

When only one defender is in position to stop the break, the player must play defense *in the key*. As the players reach the free throw line, the defender must attempt to stop the dribbler by aggressively attacking the ball and cutting off the path to the basket. Once the player picks up the dribble, the defender immediately drops back to cover the pass to the cutter (see Figure 13-19). By doing this, the defender has prevented the lay-up and forced a lower-percentage shot to be taken. It is important that the defense box out the player nearest the basket after the shot and attempt to secure the rebound or tip the ball away from the basket.

3-on-2 Situations

When two players are defending against the fastbreak they must *communicate* and work together to stop the ball and cover the cutters. Both players must establish position in the key (tandem), one near the free throw line and the other several steps behind (see Figure 13-20).

As the ball approaches the top of the key, the front defender (X_1) yells "Ball!" He/she then steps up to stop the dribbler and force a pass. The back player (X_2) yells "First pass!" then stays in the key to protect the basket until the pass is made. If the dribble is picked up outside of the key, X_1 sags back into the key immediately to help X_2 defend the cutters.

On a pass to a cutter, the back player (X_2) goes out to defend the receiver of the pass. The front player (X_1) drops back into the key to play between the two offensive players without the ball. If additional passes occur, the same rotation continues. Once a shot is taken, both X_1 and X_2 must box out and attempt to secure the rebound or tip the ball away from the basket.

Once your players have learned the key elements for defending the 3-on-2 fastbreak, fine tune their play by teaching the following strategies:

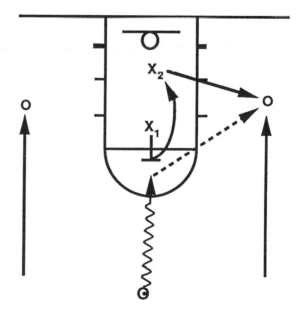

Figure 13-20. 3-on-2 defensive coverage (beginning from a tandem position).

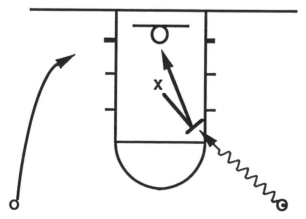

Figure 13-19. In a 2-on-1 situation, the defender steps out to stop the ball, and then drops back into the key.

- Deny all cuts into the key area—force them to take a perimeter shot.
- "Invite" players to dribble, then stop the drive and force them outside. (This will slow them down and allow time for the rest of the defense to catch up.)
- Protect the basket! Always overplay the cutter who is closest to the basket and allow the pass that will keep the ball furthest from the basket.
- When rotating positions, players must jump to the ball and/or drop back into the key ready to move quickly.
- Keep communicating—call "I got ball," "Mine," and "Shot."

DRILLS

1. Stance Drill

Purpose: To teach proper defensive stance.

Procedure:
a. Spread players out across the basketball court in mass formation facing the coach.
b. Instruct players to position feet slightly wider than shoulder-width apart with their weight resting on the balls of their feet.
c. Stress that knees are flexed with one foot slightly in front of the other for balance; the buttocks are down and the back is straight.
d. Instruct players to position arms out at the sides in either the *10 & 5* or *7 & 2* positions; the head is up and centered directly in the middle of the body.
e. Players hold this position, as the coach provides feedback on each player's defensive stance.

Variation:
For more advanced players, have your team walk *slowly* to half-court in a low defensive position.

2. Mass Defense Reaction Drill

Purpose: To improve defensive stance, movement, and agility.

Procedure:
a. Spread the players out in three lines across the basketball court in a mass formation alignment facing the coach.
b. On the command of "Stance" the players quickly get into their defensive stance and

yell out, "Defense!" The coach then checks and corrects each player's stance.
c. On the command of "Move your feet," players begin to stutter their feet using a good defensive stance with hands up.
d. The coach points forward, back, right, or left and players move quickly in the direction indicated.
e. Stress proper defensive shuffling technique: (i.e., knees flexed, trunk held erect, buttocks down low to floor, arms outstretched to sides with palms up, feet shuffling without crossing, head up).
f. Drill continues for 1-3 minutes dependent upon the physical condition and age of players. Increase duration of drill as season progresses.

Variation:
1. Coach points *up* indicating a shot, players react and yell, "Shot!" and then jump up and down with outstretched arms.
2. Coach points *down* indicating a loose ball, players react by yelling, "Ball!" and diving to the floor and getting up quickly.
3. On one whistle, players stutter feet using a defensive stance. On two whistles, the players shift one-fourth turn to the right or left. On one whistle, return to their original position. Players must be alert and react instantly to the whistle.
4. Coach calls out, "Super fast," players react by stuttering feet as quickly as possible in a stationary position for 30 seconds.

3. Lane Defensive Slide Drill

Purpose: To develop lateral, defensive quickness and improve a player's ability to change direction when moving side to side.

Procedure:
a. The player begins in the key facing the free throw line with the left foot on the lane line.
b. The body is in a semi-crouched position with the knees flexed. The feet are positioned shoulder-width apart with the weight on the balls of the feet. The arms are outstretched to the sides of the body and the head is up.
c. Using quick slide steps, the player moves across the key to touch the opposite lane line with the right foot. The first step should

be made with the right foot (the lead foot), pointing the toe in the direction of movement, followed by a drag step of the trail foot.

d. Be sure players maintain a low, balanced position, and do not cross the feet (have them work to not let feet get closer than shoulder-width apart).

e. The drill should be done for 30 seconds, with the players moving back-and-forth across the key as quickly as possible. Players count the total number of lines touched.

4. Defensive Attack and Retreat
(see Figure 13-21)

Purpose: To develop defensive quickness in forward and backward directions with either foot leading; to improve ability to change from attack to retreat and retreat to attack; to improve ability to make a quick drop step with either foot.

Procedure:

a. Players begin facing the foul line with the left foot on the left block and the right foot forward and in the lane. Position the feet shoulder width apart and distribute weight evenly on the balls of the feet. Knees should be bent to keep the body low.

b. Using short, quick attack steps with the right foot as the lead foot, players move in a forward direction and touch the middle of the foul line with the lead (right) foot. Execute a quick drop step of the trail foot (left) while pivoting on the front foot (right).

c. Players now move in a backward direction toward the right block using short, quick retreat steps, touching the right block with the right foot. The players then change directions immediately and use attack steps with the left foot leading to approach the free throw line.

d. Players repeat the pattern of attacking and retreating for 30 seconds.

e. Emphasize that players should remain in a balanced, low defensive position. Keep the arms outstretched and hands up while making quick changes of direction.

5. Defender in the Middle

Purpose: To improve passing and faking against defensive pressure.

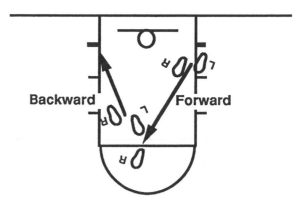

Figure 13-21. Defensive attack and retreat drill.

Procedure:

a. Two offensive players stand about 10 ft. apart, with a defender in the middle.

b. Passers use whatever pass is necessary to get the ball directly past the defense.

c. Defender remains in the middle until they touch a pass (doesn't have to gain possession), and is replaced by whomever threw it.

d. Rules: No high lob passes over the head of the defensive player. Encourage fakes, pivots, and crossover steps before every pass. Do not allow offensive players to hold the ball for more than 5 seconds.

6. Bull in the Woods (see Figure 13-22)

Purpose: To improve passing and faking techniques, and to develop decision making skills in hitting the open player.

Procedure:

a. Offensive players form a circle. One player is designated as the defensive player and stands in the center of the circle.

b. Offensive players on the outside of the circle attempt to pass to teammates without allowing the defensive player in the middle to touch the ball.

c. Offensive players may not pass to the player directly to the left or right of them.

d. The offensive player replaces the defensive player inside the circle if the ball is touched or a bad pass is thrown.

7. Push-Pull Drill (see Figure 13-23)

Purpose: To teach proper techniques for the defensive slide and the defensive attack and retreat; to improve general conditioning.

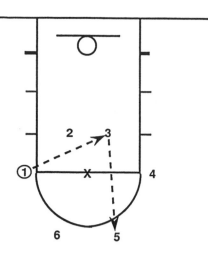

Figure 13-22. Bull in the woods drill.

Procedure:
a. Players line up at the corner of the court. Instruct players to begin in a strong defensive stance. On the whistle, the first player in the line defensive slides along the baseline to the free throw lane line.
b. The player moves forward up the free throw lane, by pointing the toe of the lead foot (*pushing* forward with this foot) and then *pulling* the trail foot behind.
c. The player defensive slides across the free throw line making certain to stay low and not to cross the feet.
d. The player retreats and moves down the lane to the baseline, then defensive slides to the sideline.
e. The player jogs full-court up the sideline and repeats the pattern as performed at the other end of the court.
f. The player finishes the drill by jogging forward up the sideline, returning to the corner of the court.
g. The next player in line begins when the player in front of him/her reaches the free throw lane.
h. Repeat this drill with players beginning in the opposite corner.

8. Zig-Zag Drill (see Figure 13-24)

Purpose: To improve defensive sliding and player-to-player defense on the ball.

Procedure:
a. One ball per two players.
b. The player with the ball starts at one end of

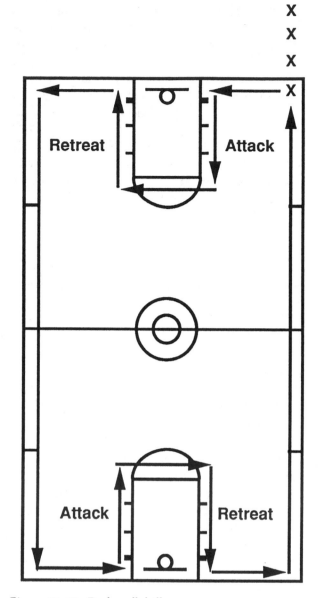

Figure 13-23. Push-pull drill.

the court and dribbles slowly three strides in each direction.
c. The defensive player (an arms length away in a defensive stance) moves his/her feet in quick sliding steps, cutting the dribbler off in each direction. When the defense gets to the spot, a boundary line, he/she must put his/her foot on the line so the offensive player has only one direction to go.
d. Stress that the defense must keep in front of the ball between the offensive player and the basket. The defensive player must keep his/her head over the ball and keep hands in a palms up position ready to steal the ball. In

early season, do not allow the steal, then later on stress "hedging hands" without careless reaching in fouls.

e. If at any time the offense beats the defense, the defense must turn, sprint, and *get in front of the ball* in order to stop the drive.

f. After reaching the opposite end of the court, the players exchange positions and come back up the opposite sideline.

Variation:

This drill can be modified by instructing your players to:

1. Use no hands. Place hands behind back and play defense with your feet.
2. Take the charge. The defensive player attempts to beat the offense to a spot and force a charge.
3. Shoot at the other end of the court. The defensive player contests the shot and blocks out.

9. Get in Front Drill (see Figure 13-25)

Purpose: To teach players to get in front to defend an opponent who is speed dribbling down court.

Procedure:

a. Divide team into partners of *equal ability* levels.

b. Player 1 stands with the ball behind the baseline near the right corner of the sideline. Player 2, the defender, stands behind his/her partner without a ball.

c. Player 1 speed dribbles to the other end of the court performing under the passive defense of player 2 who may begin chasing as soon as the dribbler moves off the baseline. Player 2 sprints to get ahead of the dribble, then turns to play defense and stop the drive.

d. When they reach the other end of the court, players 1 and 2 come back along the left sideline. Positions are switched, with player 2 speed dribbling and player 1 applying defensive pressure.

e. The next group of partners begin the drill when the players in front of them reach the half-court line.

f. This is an excellent drill to teach defensive positioning to get *in front* of the dribbler. Do not allow players to run to the side of the dribbler. If the defense is unable to catch the

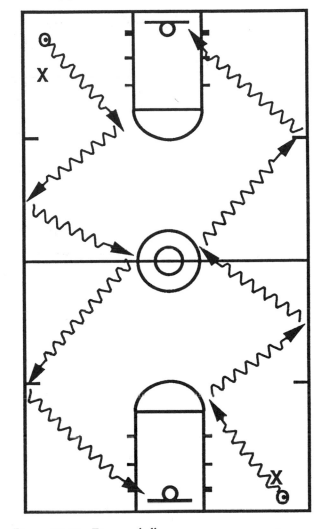

Figure 13-24. Zig-zag drill.

ball handler, teach them to come from behind the dribbler on the ball side and deflect it away.

Variation:

Player 1 may dribble in for a lay-up at the other end of the court.

10. One-on-One Full-Court Drill

Purpose: To improve defensive play on the ball, and general conditioning.

Procedure:

a. Players form two lines under one of the baskets. One player is on offense and the other is on defense.

b. The offensive player uses the whole basket-

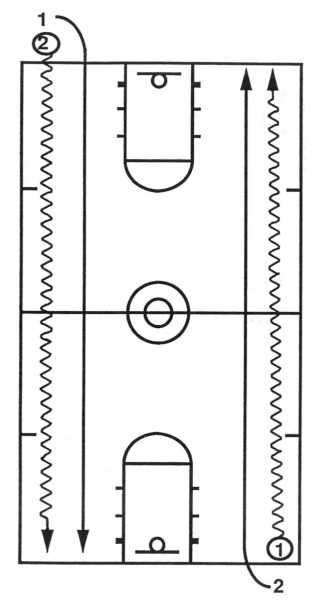

Figure 13-25. Get in front drill.

Variation:

This drill can also be run *without* a ball to practice proper defensive positioning. The coach may dictate to the offensive player to dribble at ½ or ¾ speed.

11. Rollerball Defensive Drill
(see Figure 13-26)

Purpose: To develop aggressiveness in going after loose balls and to improve defensive play on the ball.

Procedure:

a. Divide team into two lines under the basket. The coach is standing between the two lines with a basketball.

b. Match the players up according to size and position.

c. The coach rolls the ball slowly down the lane. The first player in each line quickly runs to recover the loose ball. Instruct player to *jump stop* aggressively to retrieve a loose ball.

d. The first player to retrieve the ball is on offense, the other player is on defense. The offensive player dribbles back toward the basket against the defensive pressure. Play continues (1-on-1) until the defensive player

ball court to attempt to beat the defensive player downcourt.

c. The defensive player tries to turn the offensive player as many times as possible. This is accomplished by *overplaying* the dribbler's dominant hand (ball-side). Stress "head over the ball" to the defensive player.

d. At the other end, the offensive player takes a high percentage shot and the defensive player contests the shot, yells "Shot!" and then boxes out.

e. Start the next group of two once players reach ¾ court.

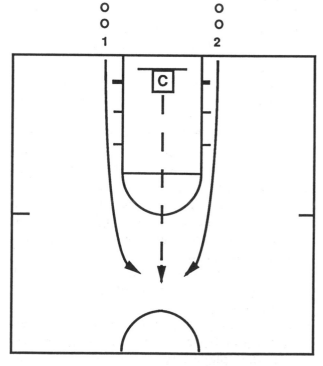

Figure 13-26. Rollerball defense drill.

rebounds the ball or the offensive player scores.

12. Deny Defense Drill (see Figure 13-27)

Purpose: To teach and develop the techniques involved in denying the pass to a player who is one pass away from the ball.

Procedure:
  a. Divide team in half. Position groups at each end of the floor.
  b. Form lines outside the sideline at the wing position.
  c. First player in line assumes defensive responsibilities and denies the wing pass to the offensive player.
  d. Entry pass can be attempted by a coach or manager at the point guard position.
  e. Instruct the defense to see both player and ball, keep arm and leg in passing lane, and use quick feet. To help the defense concentrate have them say aloud, "I see them both."
  f. Offense rotates to defense, defense to the end of the line.
  g. Continue drill in this manner on both sides of the floor.

13. Backdoor Drill (see Figure 13-28)

Purpose: To teach and develop the technique involved in defending a back cut or backdoor play.

Procedure:
  a. Same organization as Deny Defense Drill.
  b. Offensive player fakes the lead pass and attempts to create a backdoor opening.
  c. Defensive player must retreat quickly and open up to the ball at the lane area. Instruct the defense to place the inside hand down and to feel the offensive player with the outside hand.
  d. Defensive player must open to the ball and maintain a position directly in the passing lane.
  e. Defensive player resumes denial position as soon as possible, according to the further movement of the offensive player.
  f. Rotate offense to defense, defense to the end of the line.

14. Denial-Open Up Drill (see Figure 13-29)

Purpose: To teach and develop the "open-up" technique involved in defending a cutter through the key area.

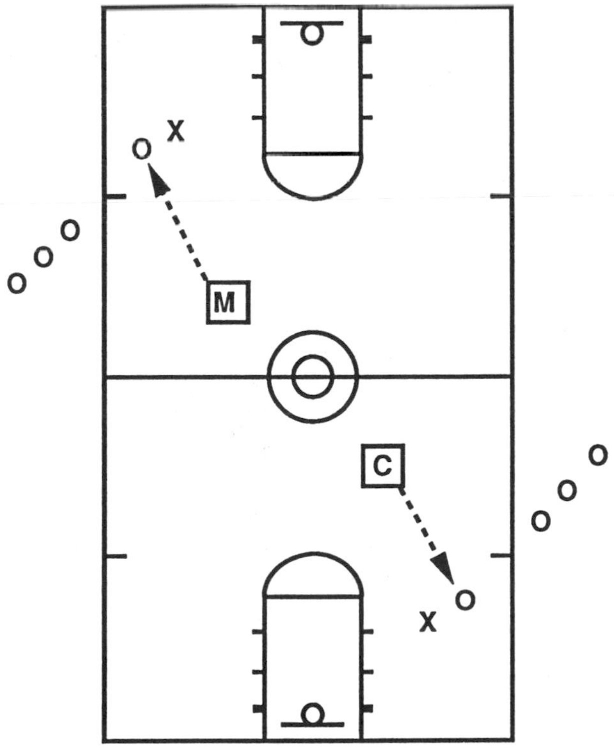

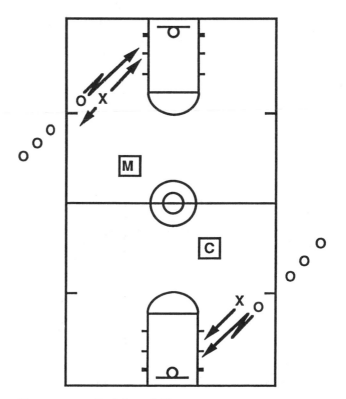

Figure 13-27. Deny defense drill.

Figure 13-28. Backdoor drill.

Procedure:
a. Same organization as Deny Defense Drill, except a manager is added on the other side of the floor.
b. The first defensive player in line denies the wing pass to the offensive player.
c. The coach then passes the ball across the court to the manager as the offensive player cuts under the basket and into the other wing.
d. Instruct the defensive player to "open up" as the offensive player goes through the lane, see the ball, and not lose contact with his/her player. When the defense gets to the ball-side block, he/she again "closes down" and starts denying.
e. Once the defensive player starts working to get open, the manager throws the ball back to the coach and the offensive and defensive players repeat the above procedure for 30 seconds to one minute or for 10 defensive denial—open up techniques.
f. Rotate offense to defense, defense to the end of the line; the first player in line comes in on offense.

15. Jump to the Ball Drill (see Figure 13-30a-b)

Purpose: To teach the defense to "jump to the ball" in order to see both the player and the ball; to teach defending the give and go cut; and to improve help and recover defense.

Procedure:
a. Divide team into three lines—offensive guards, defensive guards, and wing players.

b. O_1 passes to O_2 at the wing as X_1 jumps to the line of the ball, making sure to see both the player and the ball. Instruct X_1 to point out his/her "triangle" when he/she jumps to the ball (see Figure 13-30a).
c. O_2 drives straight for the elbow where X_1 jumps in and stops the ball. As soon as O_2 has been stopped, he/she passes back out to O_1.
d. X_1 recovers back out to O_1. O_1 now passes the ball back to O_2, and again X_1 jumps to the line of the ball.
e. O_1 jab fakes and makes an inside cut down the lane, attempting to receive the give and go from O_2. X_1 fronts O_1 all the way down the lane taking away the pass (see Figure 13-30b).
f. Rotate: Offense (O_1) to defense to wing (O_2) and out. Make sure to run this drill on both sides of the floor.

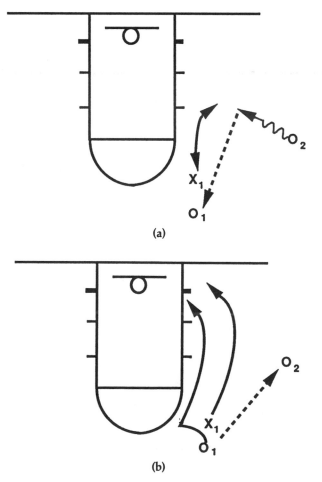

Figure 13-29. Denial—open up drill.

Figure 13-30. Jump to the ball drill.

16. Deny the Post Drill (see Figure 13-31)

Purpose: To develop deny defense at the post positions and to practice techniques for switching from high to low deny position.

Procedure:
a. Position a player on each of the blocks and at the free throw line to play stationary post players. The remaining players form a line beneath the basket.
b. X_1 begins by denying the post at the left block to the baseline side, holds position for three seconds, then goes behind and denies to the high side for three seconds.
c. X_1 then runs up to the high post and denies to the left side for three seconds, goes behind, and denies to the right side for three seconds. X_2 comes in to deny the first block player after X_1 reaches the high post.
d. Next, X_1 repeats the same procedure at the right block, starting high then going behind to deny low.
e. As players finish, they go to the end of the line. New players must be rotated in to play the post positions once X_1 reaches the front of the line.
f. Instruct the defenders to count the three seconds by saying "deny" three times and to focus on establishing a strong low position with the arm in the passing lane.

17. Help and Recover Drill (see Figure 13-32)

Purpose: To teach proper help and recover defensive techniques.

Procedure:
a. This drill involves four players, two offensive (O_1 and O_2) and two defensive (X_1 and X).
b. O_1 and O_2 are positioned at the top of the key. They begin to pass the ball back and forth as X_1 and X_2 adjust from the ball to deny defensive positions.
c. O_1 then attempts to drive the middle between X_1 and X_2. X_2 must cut off the drive and then recover back to O_2 as the ball is passed.
d. Instruct the defense to jump to the ball and to communicate by calling out "Ball," "Deny," and "I have him/her."
e. Rotate offense to defense, and defense out.
f. This drill can also be run from the wing and baseline positions.

18. 2-on-2 Full Court Defense
(see Figure 13-33)

Purpose: To teach the defensive player to get back and stop the offensive player with the ball.

Procedure:
a. Two offensive players (O_1 and O_2) are positioned on the baseline at free throw lane width apart with two defensive players (X_1 and X_2) facing them at opposite elbows.
b. The coach stands to either side of the free throw line with the ball and whichever offensive player he/she passes the ball to, that

Figure 13-31. Deny the post drill.

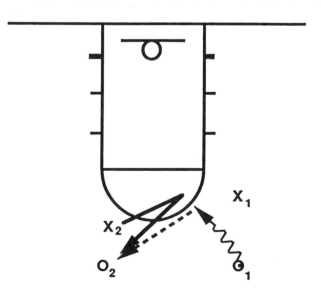

Figure 13-32. Help and recover drill.

defensive player must run and touch the endline.

c. The other defensive player (X_2) runs to other end of the court trying to stop the offensive players from scoring until the defensive help arrives.

d. Instruct X_1 to sprint back as quickly as possible and attempt to deflect a pass or cause a charging foul. Instruct X_2 to "hedge" at the offensive player with the ball causing them to pick up their dribble or commit themselves to a drive.

e. Rotate players from offense to defense, defense to a new line, and the next two players in line become the offense.

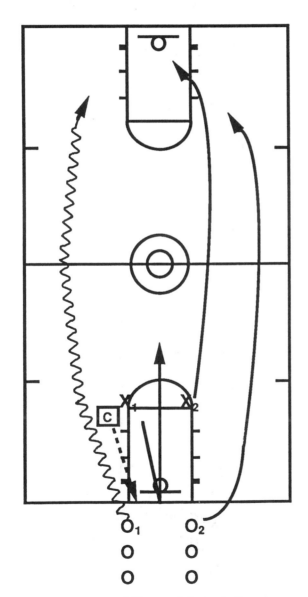

Figure 13-33. 2-on-2 full court defense drill.

19. Shell Defensive Drill (see Figure 13-34)

Purpose: To teach ball, deny, and helpside defense, at various spots on the floor; to improve communication during player-to-player *team* defense.

Procedure:

a. This is an excellent 4-on-4 half-court defense drill. Position an offensive player near each elbow and an offensive player near each wing.

b. Position defensive players according to the following helpside rules in relation to the ball:

  1. Player guarding the ball plays in a squared stance with inside foot forward.

  2. Players that are guarding an opponent *one* pass away from the ball are in a *deny* position.

  3. Players that are guarding an opponent two passes from the ball should have *one foot* in the lane and be in a position to see their player and the ball. They also must be in a position to deny an inside cut.

  4. Players guarding an opponent that is more than two passes away should have *both* feet in the lane and be in a position to see both player and ball, denying all cuts.

  5. All four defensive players must be ready to block out on all shots.

c. Stress the importance of communication; encourage players to call out loud the proper defensive position. Use the terms *ball, deny* and *help* every time the balls passed on offense.

d. Teach proper defensive positioning *without a ball* first. Then have the offensive players pass the ball around slowly (allowing time for the defense to shift correctly) and dictate to the offensive team that *no shots, cuts, or skip passes* are allowed.

20. 5-on-4 Drill (see Figure 13-35)

Purpose: To improve the defensive player's ability to recognize and defend the most dangerous offensive players; to develop communication and quick reactions; and to strengthen helpside defense.

Procedure:

a. *Five* offensive players are running a motion offense against *four* defensive players.

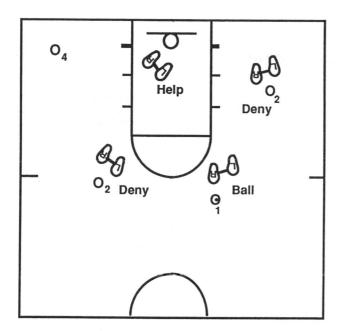

Figure 13-34. Shell defensive drill: on ball, deny, and help-side positioning.

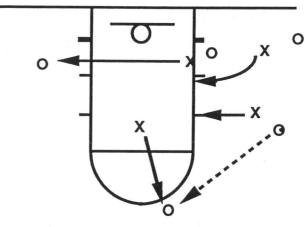

Figure 13-35. 5-on-4 drill.

b. The offensive rules are as follows: try to score, no cross court passes, keep the floor balanced, and move to the open area.

c. The defensive rules are as follows: no zones allowed, always stop the player with the ball, react quickly, communicate with teammates, and play helpside defense when positioned two passes away from the ball.

Defensive Strategies

PERFORMANCE AREA	SPECIFIC SKILLS	SUGGESTED EMPHASIS		
		Elem. School Beginner 8-10	Middle School Intermediate 11-13	High School Advanced 14 and up
Defensive Stance		X	X	
Defensive Footwork	Slide step	X	X	
	Attack and retreat step	X	X	
	Drop step	X	X	
Guarding the Player with the Ball	Dribbler defense	X	X	X
	Dead ball defense		X	X
	Defending the shot		X	X
Guarding the Player Without the Ball	Deny defense	X	X	X
	Helpside defense		X	X
	Defending the screen		X	X
	Defending the post		X	X
Team Player-to-Player Defense			X	X
Zone Defense			X	X
Fastbreak Defense			X	X

Defensive Strategies Drill Matrix

Drill	SKILL LEVEL		
	Beginning	Intermediate	Advanced
Stance drill	X		
Mass defense reaction drill	X	X	X
Lane defensive slide drill	X	X	X
Defensive attack and retreat	X	X	X
Defender in the middle	X	X	
Bull in the woods	X	X	
Push-pull drill	X	X	X
Zig-zag drill	X	X	X
Get in front drill	X	X	X
One-on-one full-court drill	X	X	X
Rollerball defensive drill	X	X	X
Deny defense drill	X	X	X
Backdoor drill		X	X
Denial-open up drill		X	X
Jump to the ball drill		X	X
Deny the post drill		X	X
Help and recover drill		X	X
2-on-2 full-court defense		X	X
Shell defense drill		X	X
5-on-4 drill		X	X

Section V
Methods of
Effective Coaching

14
Working Effectively with Parents

Martha Ewing, Ph.D.
Deborah Feltz, Ph.D.
Eugene W. Brown, Ph.D.

QUESTIONS TO CONSIDER

- How can I obtain the information and help needed from parents to do a good job?
- What is my responsibility to the parents of the players on my team?
- How can I avoid the negative influence some parents have on a team or program?
- What are the responsibilities of the players and their parents to this program?

INTRODUCTION

Support and assistance from parents can be very helpful. Some parents, however, through lack of awareness, can weaken the effects of your coaching, and thus reduce the benefits basketball can provide to their children.

These negative influences can be minimized if you tell parents:

- how you perceive your role as the coach
- the purpose and objectives of the basketball program
- the responsibilities they and their children have in helping the team run smoothly

Some parents, through lack of awareness, can weaken the effects of your coaching.

The most effective way of communicating the purposes and needs of your program is through a parents' orientation meeting. A parents' orientation meeting can be used to:

- teach parents the rules and regulations of basketball so they understand the game
- provide details about the season
- provide a setting for collecting and distributing important information

At the parents' orientation meeting, you have the opportunity to ask for their assistance and discuss other items that are specific to the team. A meeting for parents is also an excellent way for them to get to know you and each other. A face-to-face meeting and a few short remarks go a long way toward uniting coaches and parents in a cooperative endeavor that benefits the players. Many potential problems can be eliminated by good communication that begins before the first practice.

CONTENT OF A PARENTS' ORIENTATION MEETING

Parents usually have a number of questions concerning their child's basketball program.

With proper preparation and an outlined agenda, you should be able to answer most questions. A sample agenda is provided. This agenda can be supplemented with items you and/or the parents believe to be important.

Sample Agenda
Parents' Orientation Meeting

1. Introductions
2. Goals of the team and program
3. Understanding the sport of basketball
4. Dangers and risk of injury
5. Emergency procedures
6. Equipment needs
7. Athletes' responsibilities
8. Parents' responsibilities
9. Season schedule
10. Other

Each agenda item and its relationship to the basketball program is explained in the following paragraphs.

Introductions

Parents should be informed about who administers the basketball program. They should become acquainted with the coaches and the parents of the other players. As the coach, you should introduce yourself, briefly describing your background, coaching experience, and reasons for coaching.

The parents should also introduce themselves, identify where they live, and perhaps indicate how long their children have been involved in the program and the objectives that they have for their child's involvement in basketball. Learning who the other parents are makes it easier to establish working relationships for specific tasks and to initiate sharing of responsibilities (e.g., carpooling and bringing refreshments to games).

Finally, the purpose of the meeting should be explained to communicate important information about each agenda item. If handouts are available, they should be distributed at this time. We suggest that at least one handout, an agenda, be distributed to provide order to the meeting, a sense of organization on your part, and a place for parents to write notes.

Information about the players and their families should be collected (see Supplement 14-1). A team roster and telephone tree (see Supplement 14-2) could be compiled from the information collected, then typed and distributed to each of the families at another time.

Goals of the Team and Programs

The goals of the sponsoring organization, as well as your personal goals, should be presented. Parents then will be able to judge whether those goals are compatible with their beliefs regarding what is appropriate for their child. Goals that have been identified by young basketball players as most important are:

- to have fun
- to improve skills and learn new skills
- to be on a team and to make new friends
- to succeed or win

Most educators, pediatricians, sport psychologists, and parents consider these to be healthy goals that coaches should help young athletes achieve. Parents should be informed of the primary goals of the team and the amount of emphasis that will be placed on achieving these goals.

Parents should be informed of the primary goals of the team.

Other areas that should be addressed are your policies on eliminating players, the consequences of missing practices, and recognizing players through awards. You may be asked to answer many questions about how you will function as a coach. Some examples are:

- Will players be allowed to compete if they missed the last practice before a game?
- Will players be excluded from contests or taken off the team if they go on a two-week vacation?
- Will players receive trophies or other material rewards?
- How much emphasis will be placed on rewards?
- Are the rewards given only to good performers or are they given to all participants?

Chapter 15 discusses the issue of appropriate use of rewards. You may wish to comment on several points explained in Chapter 15 as you address this issue.

Understanding the Sport of Basketball

Many times spectators boo officials, shout instructions to players, or contradict the coach because they do not know the rules or strategies of basketball. This is particularly true if the rules of play have been modified for younger age groups. Informing parents about basic rules, skills, and strategies may help those who are unfamiliar with basketball and will prevent some of this negative behavior.

The information may be presented in the form of a film, brief explanation, demonstration of techniques, and/or interpretations. In addition, parents could obtain copies of Section II "Rules of Play" to learn more about the rules of the game. If you'd rather not use the meeting to cover this information, you could invite parents to attend selected practice sessions where a demonstration and/or explanation of positions, rules, and strategies will be presented to the team.

Dangers and Risk of Injury

Parents should be told what they can expect in terms of possible injuries their child may incur in basketball. As noted in Chapter 2, failure to inform parents of potential injuries is the most frequent basis for lawsuits involving coaches and players.

Tell them, for example, that generally the injuries are confined to sprains, bruises, and contusions, but that there is a possibility for broken bones, concussions, and catastrophic injuries. Supplement 14-3 provides information on sites of injuries in youth basketball. This information should be reviewed with parents. Let them know if a medical examination is required before their child's participation. If so, what forms or evidence of compliance is acceptable, to whom it must be provided, and when it is due.

Parents should be told what they can expect in terms of possible injuries in youth basketball.

Tell the parents what will be done to prevent injuries and assure them that the playing/practice area and equipment will be checked to help keep players safe and free from exposure to hazards.

Lastly, the program's policy of accident insurance should be described. Inform parents if the program maintains athletic accident coverage or whether parents are required to provide insurance coverage for injuries that happen during their child's athletic participation.

Emergency Procedures

Have the parents provide you with information and permission necessary for you to function during an emergency. The Athlete's Medical Information Form (Supplement 14-4) and Medical Release Form (Supplement 14-5) were designed for these purposes. You should have the parents complete these forms and keep them with you at all team functions. These forms will provide you with information to guide your actions in an emergency.

Equipment Needs

Explain what equipment the players need and where it can be purchased. Advice on the quality of particular brands and models and an indication of how much parents can expect to pay for specific items is also welcomed by the parents.

If an equipment swap is organized, tell them where and when it will be held. A handout describing proper equipment should be provided. Supplement 14-6 provides a list and guidelines for the selection of basketball equipment. This supplement could be reproduced and used as a handout to the parents for properly outfitting their child.

Athletes' Responsibilities

The "Bill of Rights for Young Athletes," (Martens and Seefeldt 1979) reminds adults that the child's welfare must be placed above all other considerations. Children and their parents must realize, however, that along with rights, they must meet certain responsibilities. Young athletes must be responsible for:

- being on time at practices and games with all of their equipment
- cooperating with coaches and teammates
- putting forth the effort to condition their bodies and to learn the basic skills
- conducting themselves properly and living with the consequences of inappropriate behavior

These responsibilities should be discussed so parents may help reinforce them at home.

Parents' Responsibilities

Parents of young athletes must assume some responsibilities associated with their child's participation on the basketball team. This should be discussed at the parents' orientation meeting. Martens (Martens 1978) has identified a number of parental responsibilities. You may wish to cover all or a portion of the following responsibilities in the parents' orientation meeting.

- Parents should learn what their child expects from basketball.
- Parents should decide if their child is ready to compete and at what level.
- Parents should help their child understand the meaning of winning and losing.
- Parents are responsible for disciplining their child and ensuring that their child meets specific responsibilities for participating on the basketball team.
- Parents should not interfere with their child's coach and should conduct themselves in a proper manner at games.

Parents should also be sensitive to fulfill the commitment they and their child have made to the team. This often requires that parents displace other important tasks in order to get their child to practice on time, publicly support the coach, encourage players to give their best effort, reward players for desirable efforts, and participate in the social events of the team.

Children and their parents must assume certain responsibilities.

If called upon, parents should be willing to assist the coach to carry out some of the many tasks required to meet the needs of the team. If you, as the coach, can anticipate and identify tasks with which you will need assistance, these should be presented to the parents at the orientation meeting.

It is surprising how many parents will volunteer to help you if the tasks are well-defined. See Supplement 14-7 for a description of some qualifications required of assistants and some possible responsibilities. You may not be able to

anticipate all the tasks. However, by developing an expectation of shared cooperation at the orientation meeting, parents who are not initially called upon for assistance are more likely to provide help as the need arises.

One conflict that sometimes arises results from parents falsely assuming your responsibility as coach. They may attempt to direct the play of their child and/or others during practices and games. This type of action by a parent undermines your plans for the team. It may also create a conflict in the mind of the athlete as to which set of instructions to follow.

You must inform parents that their public comments should be limited to praise and applause and that you will be prepared to coach the team. There are many ways to coach young athletes and different strategies that can result in success. You should inform parents that, if they disagree with your coaching, you will be open to their suggestions when they are presented in private.

Season Schedule

Fewer telephone calls and memos will be needed later in the season if you prepare and distribute a schedule of events for the season at the orientation meeting. The most efficient way to provide parents with the entire season schedule is with a handout.

The schedule should inform the parents about the length of the season; the dates, sites, and times when practices and games will be held; lengths of practices and games; number of games; number of practices; and other events for the season. Maps and/or instructions about where team events will occur are often helpful.

GETTING PARENTS TO ATTEND AN ORIENTATION MEETING

After you have received your team roster and, if possible before the first practice, you should make arrangements to schedule a parents' orientation meeting. If you do not personally have sufficient space to accommodate the parents, a room in a neighborhood school usually can be scheduled free of charge for an orientation meeting.

Before scheduling the time and date for the meeting, the parents should be asked about the times that they could attend. This information, as well as items of parental concern for an agenda, can be obtained through a telephone conversation with the parents. Once the time and date have been determined, the parents should be notified about this information by telephone or brief letter.

If a letter is sent, the agenda for the meeting should be included. If possible, this notification should occur about two weeks before the meeting and should be followed by a courteous telephone reminder on the night before the meeting.

In your communication with the parents, you should stress the importance of the meeting and the need for each family to be represented at the meeting.

ORGANIZING THE PARENTS' ORIENTATION MEETING

If you are well-prepared and organized, conducting a parents' orientation meeting will be an enjoyable and useful event. Before this meeting, you should complete the agenda and write down key points you plan to communicate under each item. Next, assemble the handouts that will be distributed at the meeting. At the very least, the handouts should include an agenda for the parents to follow.

Other suggested handouts and forms for distributing and collecting information include: Information on common basketball injuries, medical examination form (if provided by your program), accident insurance form and information (if provided through your program), athletic medical information form, medical release form, description of proper equipment, list of team assistants and responsibilities, season schedule, telephone tree, and player and parent roster. The items in Supplements 14-1 through 14-7 are suitable for duplication (permission is granted) and could be distributed at the orientation meeting.

FOLLOW-UP ON THE PARENTS' ORIENTATION MEETING

After having conducted the parents' orientation meeting, you should contact the families who were unable to attend and briefly inform them about what was discussed. They should be given the handouts that were distributed at the meeting, and you should collect whatever information is needed from them. Once your records are completed, you may compile additional handouts (e.g., telephone tree).

Keep the lines of communication open between you and the parents.

No matter how many questions you answer at the parents' orientation meeting, it will not solve all of the problems. Thus, it is important to keep the lines of communication open. You should indicate your willingness to discuss any problems that were not discussed at the first meeting. This might be done with a telephone call or at a conference involving the coach and parent, or the coach, parent, and athlete. Immediately before or after a practice is often an appropriate time to discuss major issues with parents. You could even have another meeting for parents midway through the season to provide an update on the team's progress, to discuss any problems, or to listen to parent's comments. By inviting parents to talk with you, they will become a positive rather than negative influence on the players and the team.

SUMMARY

Parents can be an asset to your program, but some parents can have a negative influence on your program. Communicating to parents about how you perceive your role as the coach, the purpose of the basketball program, and the responsibilities that they and their children have to the basketball program can minimize these negative influences. The most effective way to communicate this information is through a parents' orientation meeting. The time and effort you put into developing a well-organized meeting will save you considerably more time and effort throughout the season.

In a parents' orientation meeting, you have the opportunity to explain to parents that they have responsibilities to you and the team, such as deciding if their child is ready to compete, having realistic expectations, disciplining, and not interfering with coaching or playing. Children's responsibilities of promptness, cooperation, commitment, and proper conduct can also be outlined for parents.

In addition, other agenda items can be discussed and information can be gathered at a parents' orientation meeting that may make your job run more smoothly throughout the season. Be sure to discuss such items as danger and risk of injury, equipment needs, emergency procedures, and the season schedule.

The agenda items outlined in this chapter may not cover all the issues you need to address with the parents of your players. Therefore, you must organize a specific meeting that meets the needs of your team.

REFERENCES

Martens, R. (1978). *Joys and sadness in children's sports.* Champaign, IL: Human Kinetics Publishers
Martens, R. & Seefeldt, V. (Eds.). (1979). *Guidelines for children's sports.* Reston, VA: AAHPERD.

SUGGESTED READINGS

American College of Sports Medicine, American Orthopaedic Society for Sports Medicine & Sports Medicine Committee of the United States Tennis Association. (1982). *Sports injuries— An aid to prevention and treatment.* Coventry, CT: Bristol Myers Co.
Foley, J. (1980). *Questions parents should ask about youth sports programs.* East Lansing, MI: Institute for the Study of Youth Sports.
Jackson, D. & Pescar, S. (1981). *The young athletes' health handbook.* New York: Everest House.
Micheli, L.J. (1985). Preventing youth sports injuries. *Journal of Health, Physical Education, Recreation and Dance, 76*(6), 52-54.
Mirkin, G. & Marshall, H. (1978). *The sportsmedicine book.* Waltham, MA: Little Brown, & Co.

Supplement 14-1.

Team Roster Information

	Player's Name	Birth Date	Parents' Names	Address	Phone #'s Home/Work
1.		/ /			
2.		/ /			
3.		/ /			
4.		/ /			
5.		/ /			
6.		/ /			
7.		/ /			
8.		/ /			
9.		/ /			
10.		/ /			
11.		/ /			
12.		/ /			
13.		/ /			
14.		/ /			
15.		/ /			
16.		/ /			
17.		/ /			
18.		/ /			

Telephone Tree

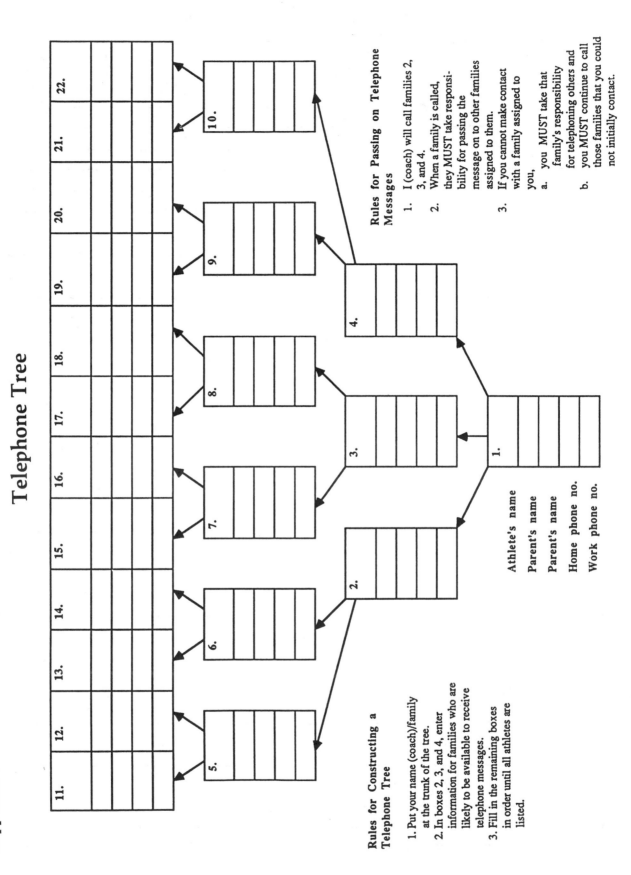

Rules for Constructing a Telephone Tree

1. Put your name (coach)/family at the trunk of the tree.
2. In boxes 2, 3, and 4, enter information for families who are likely to be available to receive telephone messages.
3. Fill in the remaining boxes in order until all athletes are listed.

Rules for Passing on Telephone Messages

1. I (coach) will call families 2, 3, and 4.
2. When a family is called, they MUST take responsibility for passing the message on to other families assigned to them.
3. If you cannot make contact with a family assigned to you,
   a. you MUST take that family's responsibility for telephoning others and
   b. you MUST continue to call those families that you could not initially contact.

Athlete's name

Parent's name

Parent's name

Home phone no.

Work phone no.

Sites of Injuries in Youth Basketball

Age Group[a]

	Total	0-4 Years		5-14 Years		15+ Years	
		Number	Percent	Number	Percent	Number	Percent
Head and Face	57,833	322	(78%)	11,386	(12%)	46,125	(14%)
Shoulder and Trunk	24,810	----	-------	3,977	(4%)	20,833	(6%)
Arms and Hands	116,340	91	(22%)	45,896	(50%)	70,353	(22%)
Legs and Feet	220,306	----	-------	31,382	(34%)	188,924	(58%)
Other	1,423	----	-------	188	-------	1,235	-------
Totals	420,712 (100%)	413 ----	(100%)	92,829 (22%)	(100%)	327,470 (78%)	(100%)

		Total All Ages	Age Group 5-14 Years
A.	Medically attended injuries, 1980	1,180,300	295,300
B.	Hospital emergency room-treated injuries, 1980	421,000	92,900

a Distribution of Estimated Basketball-Related Injuries Treated in U.S. Hospital Emergency Rooms, by Body Part Injured and Age Group of Victim, 1980.

Source: National Electronic Injury Surveillance System, U.S. Consumer Product Safety Commission/EPHA

Supplement 14-4.

Athlete's Medical Information
(to be completed by parents/guardians and athlete)

Athlete's Name: _____ Athlete's Birthdate: _____

Parents' Names: _____ Date: _____

Address: _____

Phone No's.: (____)_____ (____)_____ (____)_____
             (Home)   (Work)   (Other)

Who to contact in case of emergency (if parents cannot be immediately contacted):

Name: _____ Relationship: _____

Home Phone No.: (____)_____ Work Phone No.: (____)_____

Name: _____ Relationship: _____

Home Phone No.: (____)_____ Work Phone No.: (____)_____

Hospital preference: _____ Emergency Phone No.: (____)_____

Doctor preference: _____ Office Phone No.: (____)_____

MEDICAL HISTORY

Part I. Complete the following:

	Date	Doctor	Doctor's Phone No.
1. Last tetanus shot?	_____		
2. Last dental examination?	_____	_____	_____
3. Last eye examination?	_____	_____	_____

Part II. Has your child or did your child have any of the following?

General Conditions:	Circle one		Circle one or both		Injuries:	Circle one		Circle one or both	
1. Fainting spells/dizziness	Yes	No	Past	Present	1. Toes	Yes	No	Past	Present
2. Headaches	Yes	No	Past	Present	2. Feet	Yes	No	Past	Present
3. Convulsions/epilepsy	Yes	No	Past	Present	3. Ankles	Yes	No	Past	Present
4. Asthma	Yes	No	Past	Present	4. Lower legs	Yes	No	Past	Present
5. High blood pressure	Yes	No	Past	Present	5. Knees	Yes	No	Past	Present
6. Kidney problems	Yes	No	Past	Present	6. Thighs	Yes	No	Past	Present
7. Intestinal disorder	Yes	No	Past	Present	7. Hips	Yes	No	Past	Present
8. Hernia	Yes	No	Past	Present	8. Lower back	Yes	No	Past	Present
9. Diabetes	Yes	No	Past	Present	9. Upper back	Yes	No	Past	Present
10. Heart disease/disorder	Yes	No	Past	Present	10. Ribs	Yes	No	Past	Present
11. Dental plate	Yes	No	Past	Present	11. Abdomen	Yes	No	Past	Present
12. Poor vision	Yes	No	Past	Present	12. Chest	Yes	No	Past	Present
13. Poor hearing	Yes	No	Past	Present	13. Neck	Yes	No	Past	Present
14. Skin disorder	Yes	No	Past	Present	14. Fingers	Yes	No	Past	Present
15. Allergies	Yes	No			15. Hands	Yes	No	Past	Present
Specify:_____			Past	Present	16. Wrists	Yes	No	Past	Present
_____			Past	Present	17. Forearms	Yes	No	Past	Present
16. Joint dislocation or					18. Elbows	Yes	No	Past	Present
separations	Yes	No			19. Upper arms	Yes	No	Past	Present
Specify:_____			Past	Present	20. Shoulders	Yes	No	Past	Present
_____			Past	Present	21. Head	Yes	No	Past	Present
17. Serious or significant illnesses not included above	Yes	No			22. Serious or significant injuries not included above	Yes	No		
Specify:_____			Past	Present	Specify:_____			Past	Present
_____			Past	Present	_____			Past	Present
18. Others:_____			Past	Present	23. Others:_____			Past	Present
_____			Past	Present	_____			Past	Present

Part III. Circle appropriate response to each question. For each "Yes" response, provide additional information.

	Circle one	Additional information
1. Is your child currently taking any medication? If yes, describe medication, amount, and reason for taking.	Yes No	_____ _____
2. Does your child have any allergic reactions to medication, bee stings, food, etc.? If yes, describe agents that cause adverse reactions and describe these reactions.	Yes No	_____ _____ _____
3. Does your child wear any appliances (e.g., glasses, contact lenses, hearing aid, false teeth, braces, etc.)? If yes, describe appliances.	Yes No	_____ _____ _____
4. Has your child had any surgical operations? If yes, indicate site, explain the reason for the surgery, and describe the level of success.	Yes No	_____ _____ _____
5. Has a physician placed any restrictions on your child's present activities? If yes, describe restrictions.	Yes No	_____ _____
6. Does your child have any existing and/or past medical or emotional conditions that require special concern and attention by a sports coach? If yes, explain.	Yes No	_____ _____ _____
7. Does your child have any deformities (e.g., abnormal curvature of the spine, heart problems, one kidney, blindness in one eye, one testicle, etc.)? If yes, describe.	Yes No	_____ _____ _____
8. Is there a history of serious family illnesses (e.g., diabetes, bleeding disorders, heart attack before age 50, etc.)? If yes, describe illnesses.	Yes No	_____ _____ _____
9. Has your child lost consciousness or sustained a concussion?	Yes No	_____ _____
10. Has your child experienced fainting spells or dizziness while exercising?	Yes No	_____ _____

Part IV. Has your child or did your child have any of the following personal habits?

Personal Habit	Circle one	Circle one or both	Indicate extent or amount
1. Smoking	Yes No	Past Present	_____
2. Smokeless tobacco	Yes No	Past Present	_____
3. Alcohol	Yes No	Past Present	_____
4. Recreational drugs (e.g., marijuana, cocaine, etc.)	Yes No	Past Present	_____
5. Steroids	Yes No	Past Present	_____
6. Others Specify: _____	Yes No	Past Present	_____
_____	Yes No	Past Present	_____
_____	Yes No	Past Present	_____

Part V. Please explain below any "Yes" responses in Parts II, III, and IV or any other concerns that have present implications for my coaching your child. Also, describe special first aid requirements, if appropriate. An additional sheet may be attached if necessary.

_____

_____

_____

_____

_____

_____

Medical Release Form

I hereby give permission for any and all medical attention necessary to be administered to my child in the event of an accident, injury, sickness, etc., under the direction of the people listed below until such time as I may be contacted. My child's name is _____.
This release is effective for the time during which my child is participating in the _____
_____ basketball program and any tournaments for the 19___/19____
season, including traveling to or from such tournaments. I also hereby assume the responsibility for payment of any such treatment.

PARENTS' OR GUARDIANS' NAMES: _____

HOME ADDRESS: _____

	Street	City	State	Zip

(_____)_____(W)

HOME PHONE: (_____)_____ (_____)_____(W)

INSURANCE COMPANY: _____

POLICY NUMBER: _____

FAMILY PHYSICIAN: _____

PHYSICIAN'S ADDRESS: _____ PHONE NO. (_____)_____

In case I cannot be reached, either of the following people is designated:

COACH'S NAME: _____ PHONE NO. (_____)_____

ASS'T. COACH OR OTHER: _____ PHONE NO. (_____)_____

SIGNATURE OF PARENT OR GUARDIAN _____

SUBSCRIBED AND SWORN BEFORE ME THIS _____ OF _____, 19____

SIGNATURE OF NOTARY PUBLIC _____

Working Effectively with Parents

Guidelines for Selecting Basketball Equipment

• Ball

There are a variety of basketballs available for purchase in sporting goods and department stores. The balls vary in size, weight, and material.

Basketballs are currently manufactured in junior, intermediate, women's, and men's sizes. They range in circumference from 28.5 to 30 inches and in weight from 18 to 22 ounces. Construction of the ball may include leather (for indoor use only), synthetic leather, or rubber.

Basketballs should be selected for their compatibility with the physical characteristics and needs of the youth player. Smaller and lighter-weight balls permit younger players to dribble, pass, and shoot with more accuracy and help to eliminate injuries. A "junior" size or official women's size ball should be used for youth play.

• Shoes

Shoes are the most important article of personal equipment for a youth basketball player. The shoes should fit well and provide proper ankle and arch support. High-topped basketball shoes are recommended because they provide extra ankle stability and may help to prevent ankle sprains.

• Clothing

Unless uniforms are provided, typical attire (T-shirt, shorts/sweats, and athletic socks) will function well for youth basketball. Clothing should not inhibit easy movement or "get in the way" of the player. Wearing two pairs of socks, the one next to the skin being cotton, may prevent blisters.

• Athletic Supporter For Boys

• Athletic Support-Bra For Girls

Descriptions of Team Assistants and Their Responsibilities

Assistant coach—aids the coach in all aspects of coaching the team during practices and games.

Team manager—keeps game statistics, completes line-up cards, and makes arrangements for practice sites and times; works approximately one hour per week.

Team treasurer—collects fees from players, identifies sponsors, maintains financial records; works approximately five hours at the beginning of the season and a few hours throughout the remainder of the season.

Team doctor/nurse/paramedic—establishes a plan to respond to possible emergencies for each practice and game site, prepares and updates a medical kit, assists the coach in responding to injured players by providing first aid, collects and organizes completed medical history forms and reviews these with the coach, maintains records of completed on-site injury reports and completes a summary of season injuries, delegates other parents to bring ice to games for initial care of certain injuries; works approximately five hours at the beginning of the season and approximately 1/2 hour per week throughout the remainder of the season. Note that only a certified medical doctor, trainer, nurse, or paramedic should assume some of these defined responsibilities. See Section VI, Chapter 23, for more details.

Team social coordinator—plans team party and team social functions; works approximately five hours per season.

Team refreshments coordinator—contacts parents to assign them the shared expense and responsibilities of providing refreshments at all games (see Section VI, Chapter 22) works approximately two hours per week.

Team secretary—prepares and duplicates handouts, types, sends out mailings; works approximately 10 hours per season.

*Note that these are only suggestions for assistants and their responsibilities. The way you organize your team may result in the need for different and/or additional assistants.

15
Motivating Your Players

Martha Ewing, Ph.D.
Deborah Feltz, Ph.D.

QUESTIONS TO CONSIDER

- Why do children play basketball?
- What techniques can you use to minimize the number of "dropouts" from your team?
- What are the four elements of "positive" coaching?
- What can you do to help your players set realistic goals for themselves?

INTRODUCTION

The key to understanding your athletes' motivation is to understand each of their needs. As a coach, you play an important role in determining whether an athlete's needs are fulfilled. Previous research indicates that motivation will be high and young athletes will persist in a sport if their needs are met by that sport. But what are those needs and why do children desire to participate in sports?

WHY YOUNG ATHLETES PARTICIPATE IN BASKETBALL

In order to help your players maintain or improve their motivation in basketball, you must understand why they participate and why some of them stop participating. Based on interviews with young athletes who participated in a variety of sports, the following reasons for playing were identified and are listed in the order of their importance.

1. To have fun
2. To improve skills and learn new ones
3. For thrills and excitement
4. To be with friends or make new friends
5. To succeed or win

While these research findings provide some insight as to why most children play basketball, they are only general guidelines. The best information available to you is to learn from the athletes on your team why they are participating in the basketball program.

To improve your players' motivation, you must know why they participate in basketball.

WHY YOUNG ATHLETES DROP OUT OF BASKETBALL

Knowing why some youngsters stop playing basketball can help you find ways to encourage them to continue playing. From a survey of 1,773 young athletes (Youth Sports Institute

1977) who dropped out of basketball and other sports, we learned that the reason for dropping out was that they did not achieve the goals they set when they initially enrolled to play.

This is not surprising if you consider that their reasons for getting involved in sports represent goals that can only be achieved through participation. When these goals are not being met, withdrawal occurs. Some of the reasons most often cited for dropping out of sports are discussed in the following paragraphs.

Other Interests

Children are often very good at assessing their relative ability in various activities. They may "shop around" and participate in several sports and other activities before deciding which ones provide them the greatest chance of being successful.

Dropping basketball to achieve in other activities such as music, soccer, swimming, dance, and scouting is acceptable. When children tell you or their parents that they want to pursue other activities, they should be encouraged to do so but welcomed to return to basketball later if they desire.

Work

Many children who would like to participate in basketball discontinue because their help is needed at home or they desire to obtain a job. If it is possible, practices and games should be arranged at times that allow all individuals to stay involved. Attempt to find a creative alternative so that having a job does not preclude participation in basketball. Although much can be learned from work, the lessons that can be learned in sport are also valuable.

Another compelling reason for sports participation during childhood is that this experience may be a prerequisite for successful performance in later years. However, children who find that they must discontinue their participation should be assured that they may return to basketball at a later time.

No Longer Interested

For many children, playing basketball is a prestigious achievement. However, once they get involved, some may determine that basketball is not as glamorous as it first appeared. Although these children may have enjoyed their sport experience, they may decide that other interests are more important and/or enjoyable.

Children with interests in other activities should not be forced by parents or pressured by coaches and peers to continue participation in a basketball program. Doing so often transforms a normally well-behaved child into one who becomes a discipline problem. Parents and coaches should give children a chance to explore other activities and return to basketball if they so decide.

Not Enough Playing Time

Children sign up for basketball because they anticipate the enjoyment and skill development that will result from their involvement. Many young athletes who cited "not playing enough" as a reason for dropping out were telling coaches that they needed more playing time to achieve their goal. These children are not usually asking to be starters or even to play the majority of the time. However, to be told indirectly that they aren't good enough to play during a game can be devastating to a child's feelings of self-worth. Coaches of young athletes need to ensure that a fair and equitable pattern of play occurs both during practices and games.

Skills Were Not Improving

Young athletes want to learn skills and see themselves improving in those skills. Coaches need to recognize that each athlete is different in his/her skill level. Instruction should be designed to help each athlete on the team improve in performance abilities.

It is important to show athletes how they have improved. Too often, young athletes compare their skills to the skills of other athletes rather than their own past performances. This type of comparison is destructive to the self-esteem of unskilled players. Players of all ability levels should be taught to evaluate their performance based on the progress they are making.

Young athletes expect to see improvement in their skills if they are to remain in basketball.

Did Not Like the Coach

This reason for dropping out may be another way for athletes to tell coaches that they were not playing enough and their skills were not improving. In a study of youth sport participants, the athletes who did not like the coach said they did not like being yelled at, thought the coaches played only their favorite players, and did not think the coaches were fair.

To be effective, coaches must treat young athletes with the same respect that coaches expect from the athletes. It is not necessary or effective to yell at athletes to communicate with them. Avoid all sarcastic and degrading comments. Use a positive approach to create an enjoyable and motivating environment for players to learn and have fun playing the game.

HOW TO HELP MOTIVATE YOUR PLAYERS

Athletes are most highly motivated when they obtain what they seek from their participation in sport. Therefore, motivational techniques that you select should be based on the reasons athletes have for joining the team. The following strategies may help you improve your players' motivation.

Know Why Your Athletes Are Participating

Young athletes differ in their personalities, needs, interests, and objectives for playing basketball. You must, therefore, get to know your athletes as individuals to determine why they participate. One way to accomplish this is through a team meeting at the start of the season.

Ask your players why they are participating and what their personal objectives are for the season. They may be asked this question before, during, and after practices and special events or whenever you have a chance to talk one-on-one with your players.

Help Your Athletes Improve Skills and Learn New Skills

Skill improvement is a very important reason for joining a basketball team. Therefore, practice sessions should focus on skill develop-

ment, with regular opportunities for players to measure their progress. In addition, you can help athletes set performance goals that are appropriate for them. For example, as young players first learn to dribble the basketball, they should practice controlling the ball at a slow pace. More advanced players should be encouraged to practice at a faster pace, to develop dribbling, passing, and shooting with both hands, and to practice dribbling while guarded by a defensive player. As players improve, they can understand and measure their progress both in practice and in game situations.

Make Practices and Games Enjoyable

As indicated by various studies, young athletes want to have fun. This means they want to play; they do not want to sit on the bench or stand in long lines waiting their turn at a drill. One of the best ways to ensure that practices are enjoyable is to use short, snappy drills that result in all players being involved most of the time. You can also keep your players' interest by incorporating new and challenging drills. Your players may even be able to invent useful drills of their own.

Having a chance to display their skills during a game is an excellent motivator of young athletes.

In games, too, all players can be involved, even if they are sitting on the bench. Team members can be watching the individuals who are playing similar positions to learn from their good techniques or their mistakes. They can also watch for strategies used by the other team. Most importantly, however, they should all have a chance to play in every game. The knowledge that they will have a chance to display their skills during the course of the contest is a primary source of motivation before and after the experience. Players who sit on the bench, unable to test their skills in a game, are not likely to have fun.

Allow Players to be with Their Friends and Make New Friends

Many athletes view their basketball participation as a chance to be with their friends while doing something they enjoy. Allowing your players to have fun with their friends does not mean your practices have to be disruptive. You can encourage an esprit de corps within the team. Social activities, such as a mid-season pizza party, require more time on your part but may foster rewarding friendships among players and coaches.

Remember, many of your players' friends may be on opposing teams. Encourage athletes to continue their friendships with players on opposing teams and even develop new friendships with opponents.

Help Players Understand the Meaning of Success

Children learn at an early age to equate winning with success and losing with failure. If athletes win a game, they feel good or worthy. If they lose, they feel incompetent or unworthy. This attitude toward winning can be discouraging to players, unless they are always winning. One of your most important roles, therefore, is to help your players keep winning in perspective. One way to accomplish this is to help your players understand that winning a game is not always under their control. For example, after losing a game, you may explain the loss to your team: "We ran the offense well today, but their team played very good defense, so we didn't get as many points as we expected."

Your players also need to know that, although striving to win is an important objective in basketball, being successful in basketball also means making personal improvements and striving to do one's best. This attitude can be developed by:

- encouraging maximum effort during practices and games
- rewarding effort
- helping players set important but realistic goals that they can attain and thus feel successful when they are achieved

In helping your players understand the meaning of success, it is also important not to punish them when they fail, particularly if they gave a maximum effort.

Your coaching approach is the factor with the greatest influence on player motivation.

Use the Positive Approach to Coaching

Probably the most important factor that influences your players' motivation is the approach you take in coaching. There are many different styles or approaches used by coaches, but most fall into either of two categories: the negative approach and the positive approach.

- ### Negative Approach

The negative approach is the most visible model of coaching. The negative approach, demonstrated by some professional, college, and even high school coaches, is often highlighted in the media. This approach is one in which the coach focuses on performance errors and uses fear, hate, and/or anger to motivate players.

The negative approach doesn't work very well with young athletes. Constant criticism, sarcasm, and yelling often frustrate young athletes, deteriorate their self-confidence, and decrease their motivation. Remember that young athletes are just beginning to develop their skills, and they have fragile self-concepts.

Focus on correct aspects of performance and use liberal amounts of praise and encouragement.

- ### Positive Approach

The positive approach, in contrast, is one where the coach focuses on the correct aspects of performance and uses plenty of encouragement and praise for the tasks that players perform correctly. When errors occur, a coach who uses the positive approach corrects mistakes with constructive criticism.

A positive, supportive approach is essential when coaching young athletes if high levels of motivation are to be maintained. Key principles for implementing a positive approach to coaching are listed and explained in the following paragraphs.

Key Principles for Implementing a Positive Approach to Coaching (Smoll & Smith 1979)

- ### Be liberal with rewards and encouragement.

The most effective way to influence positive behavior and increase motivation is through the frequent use of encouraging statements and rewards. The single most important difference between coaches whom young athletes respect most and those they respect least is the frequency with which coaches reward them for desirable behaviors.

The most important rewards you can give are free. They include a pat on the back, a smile, applause, verbal praise, or a friendly nod. The greater your use of encouraging statements and rewards, the more your players will be motivated.

• **Give rewards and encouragement sincerely.**

For rewards to be beneficial, they must be given sincerely. It will mean little to your players to tell them they played well if, in fact, they played poorly. This does not mean that you should not give them positive feedback about their performance when they make mistakes. You can point out their errors and at the same time praise them for the plays they performed well. It is important to be positive but also honest.

• **Reward effort and correct technique, not just results.**

It is easy to praise a player who just made a basket, but it is less natural to praise a player who tried hard but missed the shot. Sometimes, too, we forget to reward correct technique when it does not result in scoring goals. It is important, however, to reward players' efforts and the use of correct technique if you want this behavior to continue. An excellent drive to the basket that is stopped by a defensive player who makes a spectacular block should be recognized as if the shot was made. Occasionally, spend a few extra minutes with the lesser skilled players, before or after practice, to help them learn the correct techniques. This extra attention and caring will greatly increase their motivation to keep trying.

• **Have realistic expectations.**

Base your rewards and encouragement on realistic expectations. Encouraging your basketball players to strive for NBA standards, without the feelings of success associated with achieving the many levels of performance leading to such standards, will probably make them feel as though they have failed. It is much easier for you to give honest rewards when you have realistic expectations about your players' abilities.

Help Players Set Goals

Young athletes learn from parents and coaches that success is equated with winning and failure is equated with losing. Adopting this view of success and failure confuses the players. Let's take, for example, the play of Mary and Kara, members of the winning and losing teams, respectively.

Both girls played about half of the game. Mary's unsporting conduct was noticed quickly by the referee. After her third personal foul, the referee cautioned her about her unnecessary rough play. Early in the third quarter, she pushed an opponent who was attempting a lay-up and was disqualified from further play due to the flagrant foul. Kara, on the other hand, masterfully used her practiced skills to assist her teammates in scoring and scored her first basket of the season. However, since Mary was a member of the winning team, she was able to "laugh-off" her behavior and revel in the success of her team. On the other hand, Kara felt that her efforts were insignificant and worthless and joined her teammates in the disappointment of a 36-28 loss.

As adults, we recognize the inaccuracy of these perceptions. But, our actions at the end of a contest may tell our players that a winning score is what really matters.

Equating success with winning and failure with losing results in mixed messages to the athlete.

Athletes need a way to compare their current performances with their past performances to determine whether they are successful. This can be accomplished through goal setting. You as a coach can help each of your athletes establish individual goals. By doing this, each athlete can regain control over personal success or failure. In addition to removing the mixed messages, remind your players that there are some factors that are out of their control that may determine the outcome of a game. For example, the person your athlete is defending may be playing the best game of his/her career. Although your athlete is playing very well, there is just no stopping the opposing player. Or, due to injury or illness, a player is forced to play an unfamiliar position. These examples highlight the need to establish goals for personal improvement that are consistent with the objective of winning, but not entirely dependent on their achievement, to maintain player motivation. There are several guidelines for goal setting that can markedly help performance.

Guidelines for Goal Setting

• Success should be possible for everyone on the team.

When implementing a goal setting program, each athlete must experience some success. In other words, each athlete should perform at a level that demands a best effort for the existing conditions. Help each athlete realize that effort equals success by focusing rewards on such efforts.

• Goals under practice conditions should be increasingly more challenging and goals during competition should be more realistic.

When you set up drills to work on passing or shooting, help your players set goals for practice that will challenge each of them to exceed a previous effort. For example, when practicing shooting, you may ask your "star" to make seven out of 10 shots in practice, while another player may be challenged with four out of 10. You should not expect the same level of performance in a game because neither you nor the players control all the factors. With this approach, motivation at practice is increased and players have a realistic chance of experiencing self-worth in a game.

• Goals should be flexible.

If goal setting is to be effective, goals must be evaluated frequently and adjusted depending on the athlete's success ratio. If an athlete is achieving the set goal, raise the goal to provide a greater challenge and motivation. If the goal is too difficult and the athlete is feeling frustration or failure, the goal should be lowered rather than have the athlete continue to experience failure. Having to lower the level of a goal may also be frustrating. Therefore, it is important to be as accurate as possible when initially setting goals for individual players.

• Set individual goals rather than team goals.

In general, team goals should not be made. This is because team goals are not under anyone's control, and they are often unrealistic. It is too difficult to assess accurately how a team will progress through a season. Will your team improve faster than other teams, at the same pace, or be a latecomer? If you set winning a certain number of games (e.g., eight of 10 games) as a goal and the team loses their first three games, you cannot achieve the goal even by winning the remaining seven games. This will only cause greater discouragement among team members. Work on individual improvement through goal setting, and let the team's improvement reflect the individual's improvement.

Goal setting can be very effective in improving a player's performance, confidence, and self-worth. To be effective, however, you must know your players well enough to know when they are setting goals that are challenging, controllable, and realistic. In addition, goals must be adjusted to ensure feelings of self-worth.

DEALING WITH COMPETITIVE STRESS

Some coaches believe the best way to motivate a team for competition is to get them "psyched-up" before the game. With young athletes, however, getting psyched-up is not usually the problem; rather, the problem for them is getting "psyched-out."

Competitive stress in young athletes can originate from many sources—the athlete, the teammates, the coach, and the parents. When young athletes were asked what caused them to worry, among the most frequently given answers were:

1. improving their performance
2. participating in championship games
3. performing up to their level of ability
4. what their coach and parents would think or say

Thus, young basketball players are most likely to be worried about performance failure. This worry about failure may increase players' anxieties, which, in turn, may cause poor performance, and eventually may decrease motivation. Figure 15-1 illustrates this cycle.

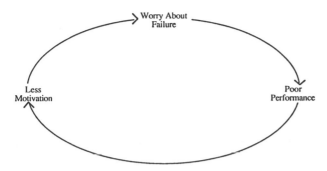

Figure 15-1. A cyclic representation of performance failure.

A good way to help your players avoid the effects of competitive stress is to reduce their fear of failure. This can be achieved by encouraging them to enjoy the game and to do their best. When your players lose or make a mistake, do not express displeasure; rather, correct their mistakes in a positive way by using the following sequence:

1. Start with a compliment. Find some aspect of the performance that was correct.
2. Tell the player what was wrong and how to correct it.
3. Give another positive statement such as, "Everyone makes mistakes. Keep working at it and you will get it."

This approach allows players to keep practicing their skills without the fear of making a mistake. The following guidelines may be helpful in preventing competitive stress.

Guidelines for Preventing Competitive Stress

- Set realistic goals.
- Use the positive approach when correcting mistakes.
- Eliminate the type of "pep talks" that communicate overemphasis on the game and the outcome.

APPROPRIATE USE OF TEAM TROPHIES, MEDALS, AND OTHER AWARDS*

Anyone who has ever attended a post-season basketball team party is aware that pre-

*Much of the material presented in this section has been adapted from Gould (1980).

senting trophies and awards is a common practice. Young athletes may receive any number of external awards, ranging from small ribbons to large trophies. However, whether it is appropriate to give children these awards is a controversial issue.

The advocates of awards such as medals, trophies, ribbons, certificates, and jackets indicate that they increase the children's desire and motivation to participate. Critics, in contrast, suggest that giving rewards to young athletes for activities in which they are already interested turns play into work and decreases their desire to participate. What is the answer: Awards or no awards?

While the advocates and critics of this issue would have us view it as a simple one, researchers have found that no simple answer exists. The purpose of this section is to provide you with information on how and in what situations external rewards influence young athletes' self-motivation to participate in sports.

Understanding Rewards

An activity is defined as intrinsically motivating if an individual engages in that activity for personal interest and enjoyment, rather than for external reasons such as receiving a trophy, money, or publicity. In essence, young athletes are intrinsically motivated when they play for the sake of playing. Until recently, coaches assumed that if external rewards are given for activities that are already intrinsically motivating, the result will be a further increase in intrinsic motivation.

However, research has shown that this is not always the case. The presentation of extrinsic rewards for an already self-motivated activity may result in reduced intrinsic motivation. The following adapted story (Casady 1974) illustrates how rewards can undermine intrinsic motivation.

An old man lived next to an open field that was a perfect location for the neighborhood children's "pick-up" baseball games. Every afternoon the children would come to the field, choose sides, and engage in a noisy game. Finally, the noise became too much for the old man, so he decided to put an end to the games. However, being a wise old man who did not want to stir up trouble in the neighbor-

hood, he changed the children's behavior in a subtle way.

The old man told the children that he liked to hear them play, but because of his failing hearing, he had trouble doing so. He then told the children that if they would play and create enough noise so he could hear them, he would give each of them a quarter.

The children gladly obliged. After the game, the old man paid the children and asked if they could return the next day. They agreed, and once again they created a great deal of noise during the game. However, this time the old man said he was running short of money and could only pay them 20 cents each. This still satisfied the children. However, when he told them that he would be able to pay only 5 cents on the third day, the children became angry and indicated that they would not come back. They felt that it was not worth the effort to make so much noise for only 5 cents apiece.

In this example, giving an external reward (money) for an already intrinsically motivating activity (playing baseball and making noise) resulted in decreased intrinsic motivation in the children. Hence, when the rewards were removed, the amount of participation decreased.

An increasing number of individuals have suggested that this phenomenon also occurs in organized youth sports such as basketball. In many programs, young athletes are presented with a substantial number of external awards (trophies, jackets, ribbons, etc.) for participating in an already desirable activity. Critics of external awards feel that giving these rewards decreases the youngsters' intrinsic motivation and when the rewards are no longer available, they no longer participate. Thus, external rewards may be one cause of discontinued participation in basketball.

Effects of Intrinsic Awards

There are two aspects of every reward that can influence a young athlete's intrinsic motivation (Deci 1975). These are:

1. the controlling aspect of the reward
2. the informational aspect of the reward

● **Controlling Aspects of Rewards**

Extrinsic rewards can decrease intrinsic motivation when they cause players to perceive

that their reasons for participation have shifted from their own internal control to factors outside (or external to) themselves. This was illustrated clearly in the story of the old man and the children. The children's reasons for playing shifted from internal factors (fun and self-interest) to external factors (money). Then, when the rewards were diminished, they no longer wanted to play. In essence, the children were no longer participating for the fun of it but were participating solely for the reward. If young basketball players are made to feel that their primary reason for participating is to receive a trophy or a medal to please their parents, their intrinsic motivation will probably decrease.

● **Informational Aspects of Rewards**

External rewards can also communicate information to individuals about their competence and self-worth. If the reward provides information that causes an increase in a child's feelings of personal worth and competence, it will increase intrinsic motivation. If it provides no information about self-worth or competence or reduces these feelings about oneself, it will decrease intrinsic motivation.

Seek to elevate feelings of self-worth in the awards you give.

A "Most Improved Player" award is a good example of how material rewards can enhance motivation. This award usually tells the player that he/she has worked hard and learned a lot. This award would probably increase intrinsic motivation. Constant failure and negative feedback, however, would decrease a young player's feelings of competence and self-worth and, in turn, would decrease intrinsic motivation. Consequently, you must help children establish realistic goals. When rewards are given, they should be based upon some known criteria (performance, effort, etc.). This helps to ensure that rewards provide the recipients with information to increase feelings of self-worth and competence.

● **Informational Versus Controlling Aspects of Rewards**

Because most rewards in children's athletics are based upon performance, thus conveying information about the recipient's self-worth, giving external rewards should never undermine intrinsic motivation. However, this may not always be true. Even though external rewards may convey information about a child's sense of personal competence, the child may perceive the controlling aspect as being more important than the information conveyed (Halliwell 1978). Thus, instead of increasing the young athletes' intrinsic motivation, the extrinsic rewards undermine children's interest in sports by causing them to perceive their involvement as a means to an end. They are pawns being "controlled" by the pursuit of winning the reward.

Practical Implications

Extrinsic rewards have the potential to either increase or decrease intrinsic motivation. Two key factors determine which will occur:

1. If children perceive their basketball involvement as being controlled primarily by the reward (e.g., they are participating only to win the trophy or to please Mom or Dad), intrinsic motivation will decrease. In contrast, if children feel they are controlling their involvement (playing because they want to), then intrinsic motivation will increase.
2. If the reward provides information that increases the young players' feelings of self-worth and competence, intrinsic motivation will increase. If, however, the reward provides no information at all or decreases a person's feelings of competence or self-worth, then intrinsic motivation will decrease.

These findings have important implications for you as the coach. Be very careful about using extrinsic rewards! These rewards should be relatively inexpensive and not used to "control" or "coerce" children into participation in already desirable activities. Moreover, because you play such a vital role in determining how children perceive rewards, you must keep winning in perspective and stress the non-tangible values of participation in basketball (fun and personal improvement) as opposed to participating solely for the victory or the reward.

The frequent use of inexpensive or "free" rewards will increase player motivation.

One way to increase intrinsic motivation is to give your players more responsibility (more internal control) for decision making and for rule making (Halliwell 1978). This could be done by getting input from your athletes about making team rules or letting them help organize practices. Younger players could be selected to lead a drill or favorite warm-up exercise and given some playing time at positions they desire. Older, more experienced players could help conduct practices and make actual game decisions (allowing players to call some plays without interference, for example).

Intrinsic motivation can also be increased by ensuring that when external rewards are given, they provide information that increases your players' feelings of self-worth and competence. The easiest way to accomplish this is to have realistic expectations of the players. Not all children will have a winning season or place first in the tournament. However, some realistic goals can be set with each athlete in terms of improved personal skills, playing time, etc., and the players can be rewarded for achieving their goals. This could be accomplished through the use of "Unsung Hero" and/or "Most Improved Player" awards.

These "official" rewards are not nearly as important, however, as the simple ones that you can give regularly. Remember, some of the most powerful rewards are free (pat on the back, friendly nod, or verbal praise). These rewards should be frequently used to acknowledge each athlete's contribution to the team, personal improvement, or achievement of a personal goal.

Finally, remember that the rewards must be given for a reason that has meaning to your players. Rewards not given sincerely (not based upon some criteria of success) may actually decrease intrinsic motivation. Therefore, coaches must set realistic, attainable goals and reward children when they attain those goals.

SUMMARY

Children play basketball because they want to improve their skills, have fun, be with friends, and be successful. Children who drop out of basketball typically do so because one or more of their goals was not met. You can maximize your players' desire to participate, and help prevent them from dropping out, by getting to know them as individuals.

Learn why they are participating. Focus on skill development in practice sessions and make sure the practices are enjoyable. Allow time for friendships to develop by creating a cordial environment both on and off the court. Help players understand the meaning of success and have them set realistic goals.

Using a positive approach to coaching is the most effective way to improve players' performance. Positive coaching also makes playing and coaching more enjoyable. Be sure to reward effort and correct techniques in addition to the results that meet your expectations.

Having realistic expectations of players' performances will provide more opportunities to give rewards. However, when players make mistakes, use the positive approach to correcting errors. The positive approach involves issuing a compliment, correcting the error, and then finishing with another positive statement. Using a positive approach and helping players reach their goals are effective ways to motivate your players toward maximum performance.

Extrinsic rewards have the potential to either increase or decrease intrinsic motivation.

Extrinsic rewards are most effective when they are kept in perspective, are inexpensive, and are used to reflect improvements in personal competence. The non-tangible values of participation in basketball should be stressed, as opposed to participating only for winning or for the reward.

REFERENCES

Casady, M. (1974). The tricky business of giving rewards. *Psychology Today*, 8(4): 52.

Deci, E.L. (1975). *Intrinsic motivation*. New York: Plenum.

Gould, D. (1980). *Motivating young athletes*. East Lansing, MI: Institute for the Study of Youth Sports.

Halliwell, W. (1978). Intrinsic motivation in sport. In W.F. Straub (Ed.), *Sport psychology: An analysis of athlete behavior*. Ithaca, NY: Movement Publications.

Smoll, F.L. & Smith, R.E. (1979). *Improving relationship skills in youth sport coaches*. East Lansing, MI: Institute for the Study of Youth Sports.

Youth Sports Institute (1977). *Joint legislative study on youth sports program, phase II*. East Lansing, MI: Institute for the Study of Youth Sports.

SUGGESTED READINGS

Orlick, T. (1980). *In pursuit of excellence*. Ottawa, Ontario: Coaching Association of Canada.

Singer, R.N. (1984). *Sustaining motivation in sport*. Tallahassee, FL: Sport Consultants International, Inc.

Smoll, F.L., & Smith, R.E. (1979). *Improving relationship skills in youth sports coaches*. East Lansing, MI: Institute for the Study of Youth Sports.

16
Communicating With Your Players

Martha Ewing, Ph.D.
Deborah Feltz, Ph.D.

QUESTIONS TO CONSIDER

- How can you send clear messages to your players?
- What is the positive approach to communication?
- What are the characteristics of a good listener?
- How can good communication skills improve your ability to coach?

INTRODUCTION

The most important skill in coaching is the ability to communicate with your players. It is critical to effectively carry out your roles of leader, teacher, motivator, and organizer. Effective communication not only involves skill in sending messages but skill in interpreting the messages that come from your players and their parents.

SENDING CLEAR MESSAGES

Any means you use to convey your ideas, feelings, instructions, and/or attitudes to others involves communication. Thus, when communicating with your players, your messages may contain verbal as well as nonverbal information. Nonverbal messages can be transmitted through facial expressions such as smiling, or through gestures and body movements.

When you send messages to your players, you may, without thinking, send unintentional nonverbal information as well as your intentional verbal message. If your nonverbal message conflicts with what you say, your message will probably be confusing. For example, when you tell your players that they have done a good job and let your shoulders slump and heave a heavy sigh, don't be surprised if your players are less receptive to your next attempt at praise.

Another example of mixed messages occurs when you tell your players they should never question officials' calls and then you denounce an official's decision. If the need should arise to question an official's call, you should ask the official for clarification in a professional manner.

Using a Positive Approach to Communicate

Communication is more effective when you use the positive approach. The positive approach to communication between you and your athletes involves establishing:

- mutual trust
- respect
- confidence
- cooperation

277

Essential Factors in Sending Clear Messages

• Getting and Keeping Attention

Getting and keeping your athletes' attention can be accomplished by making eye contact with them; avoid potential distractions but be enthusiastic, and emphasize the importance of what you have to say. For example, when you want to instruct your players on a new skill, organize them so everything you do is visible to them. Be sure that they are not facing any distractions, such as children playing at the other end of the court. It is also helpful to use a story, illustration, or event that will highlight the importance or focus attention on the instruction that is to follow.

• Using Simple and Direct Language

Reduce your comments to contain only the specific information the player needs to know. For example, when a player makes a mistake in a pass-and-shoot drill, make sure your feedback is simple, focuses on one error at a time, and contains only information that the player can use to correct the mistake. Keep information simple and specific.

The positive approach to communication is an essential element of good coaching.

• Checking With Your Athletes

Make certain that your players understand what you are saying. Question them so you will know if they understood the key points of your message. For example, let's say you are trying to explain how to run the three-on-two passing-and-shooting drill. After showing them the drill, you can save time and frustration by asking your players before they practice the drill where they should pass the ball, what openings they should look for to decide if they should shoot or pass, and where they should move after passing or shooting the ball. If your athletes cannot answer these questions, they will not be able to participate effectively in the drill.

• Being Consistent

Make sure your actions match your words. When a discrepancy occurs between what you say and what you do, players are affected most by what you do. "Actions speak louder than words." You need to practice what you preach if you wish to effectively communicate with your players and avoid the loss of credibility that comes with inconsistent behaviors.

• Using Verbal and Nonverbal Communication

Your athletes are more likely to understand and remember what you have said when they can see it and hear it at the same time. Using the previous example, simultaneously demonstrating the three-on-two drill while explaining the key points will result in clearer instructions.

BEING A GOOD LISTENER

Remember, too, that you must be a good listener to be an effective communicator. Communication is a two-way street. Being receptive to your players' ideas and concerns is important to them and informational to you.

Part of good coaching involves listening to your players.

By listening to what your athletes say and asking them how they feel about a point, you can determine how well they are learning. Their input provides you the opportunity to teach what they do not understand.

Essential Factors in Good Listening Skills

• Listening Positively

Players want the chance to be heard and to express themselves. You can encourage this by using affirmative head nods and occasional one- to three-word comments (e.g., "I understand.") while you're listening. The quickest way to cut off communication channels is by giving "no" responses or negative head nods.

• Listening Objectively

Avoid prematurely judging the content of a message. Sincerely consider what your players have to say. They may have good ideas! A good listener creates a warm, non-judgmental atmosphere so players will be encouraged to talk and ask questions.

• Listening With Interest

Being a good listener means being attentive and truly interested in what your players have to say. Look and listen with concern. Listen to what is being said and how it is being said. Establish good eye contact and make sure your body also reflects your interest in your player's message. Be receptive to comments that are critical of you or your coaching. Criticism is the most difficult communication to accept, but it is often the most helpful in improving our behavior.

- **Checking for Clarity**

  If you are uncertain of what your athletes are communicating to you, ask them what they mean. This will help to avoid misinterpretation.

Being receptive to your players' thoughts and comments is important to them, and it also provides you with essential information.

SUMMARY

The ability to communicate with your players is critical in your role as a coach. It is a skill that involves two major aspects: speaking and listening. Coaches who are effective communicators get and keep the attention of their players, send clear and simple messages, and check to make sure their message is consistent with their actions. They also have good listening skills, which involve listening positively, helpfully, objectively, and with concern.

SUGGESTED READING

Martens, R. (1987). *Coaches guide to sport psychology.* Champaign, IL: Human Kinetics.

17
Maintaining Discipline

Martha Ewing, Ph.D.
Deborah Feltz, Ph.D.

QUESTIONS TO CONSIDER

- What is the best way to prevent misbehavior?
- Should players be involved in establishing team rules?
- How should team rules be enforced?
- What are the key points of an effective plan for handling misconduct?

INTRODUCTION

Coaches often react to their athletes' misbehaviors by yelling, lecturing, or using threats. These verbal techniques are used because we often do not know what else to do to regain control. Many discipline problems could be avoided, however, if coaches anticipated misbehavior and developed policies to deal with them.

Harsh comments may prevent misbehavior, but they often create a hostile, negative environment that reduces learning and motivation.

PLAN FOR SOUND DISCIPLINE

Although threats and lectures may prevent misbehavior in the short term, they create a hostile, negative atmosphere. Typically, their effectiveness is short-lived. Hostility between a coach and team members neither promotes a positive environment in which it is fun to learn the game of basketball nor motivates the players to accept the coach's instructions.

Sound discipline involves a two-step plan that must be in place before the misbehaviors occur. These steps are: (1) define team rules, and (2) enforce team rules.

Athletes want clearly defined limits and structure for how they should behave. You can accomplish this without showing anger, lecturing, or threatening. As the coach, it is your responsibility to have a systematic plan for maintaining discipline before your season gets under way. If you have taken the time to establish rules of conduct, you will be in a position to react in a reasonable manner when children misbehave.

Athletes want clearly defined limits and structure for how they should behave.

Define Team Rules

The first step in developing a plan to maintain discipline is to identify what you consider to be desirable and undesirable conduct. This list can then be used to establish relevant team rules. A list of potential behaviors to consider when identifying team rules is included in Table 17-1.

Your players (especially if you are coaching individuals who are 10 years of age or older) should be involved in establishing the rules for the team. Research has shown that players are more willing to live by rules when they have had a voice in formulating them (Seefeldt et al. 1981). This can be done at a team meeting, early in the season. The following introduction has been suggested (Smoll & Smith 1979) to establish rules with players:

"I think rules and regulations are an important part of the game because the game happens to be governed by rules and regulations. Our team rules ought to be something we can agree upon. I have a set of rules that I feel are important. But we all have to follow them, so you ought to think about what you want. They should be your rules, too."

Rules of conduct must be defined in clear and specific terms. For instance, a team rule that players must "show good sportsmanship" in their games is not a very clear and specific rule. What, exactly, is showing good sportsmanship? Does it mean obeying all the rules, calling one's own fouls, or respecting officials' decisions? The Youth Sports Institute has adopted a code of sportsmanship which defines sportsmanship in more specific terms (Seefeldt et al. 1981). This code has been reprinted in Table 17-2. You may wish to use some of the items listed as you formulate your team rules.

Players are more willing to live by rules when they have had a voice in formulating them.

Remember, you are a part of the team and you should live by the same rules. You should demonstrate the proper behaviors so the children will have a standard to copy. As a coach, you must also emphasize that behaviors of coaches as seen on television (such as screaming, throwing chairs, and belittling and embarrassing players) are also examples of undesirable conduct!

Enforce Team Rules

Not only are rules needed to maintain discipline, but these rules must be enforced so reoccurrences are less likely. Rules are enforced through rewards and penalties. Players should be rewarded when they abide by the rules and penalized when they break the rules. The next step, therefore, in developing a plan to maintain discipline, is to determine the rewards and penalties for each rule. Your players should be asked for suggestions at this point because they will receive the benefits or consequences of the decisions. When determining rewards and penalties for the behaviors, the most effective approach is to use rewards that are meaningful to your players and appropriate to the situation. Withdrawal of rewards should be used for misconduct. A list of potential rewards and penalties that can be used in basketball is given in Table 17-3.

Table 17-1. Examples of desirable and undesirable behavior to consider when making team rules.

Desirable Behavior	Undesirable Behavior
Making every effort to attend all practices and games except when excused for justifiable reasons	Missing practices and games without legitimate reasons
Being on time for practices and games	Being late or absent from practices and games
Attending to instructions	Talking while the coach is giving instructions
Concentrating on drills	Not attending to demonstrations during drills
Treating opponents and teammates with respect	Pushing, fighting, and/or using abusive language with opponents and teammates
Giving positive encouragement to teammates	Making negative comments about teammates
Avoiding fouls	Intentionally fouling during the game
Bringing required equipment or uniform to practices and games	Forgetting to bring required equipment or uniform to games and practices
Reporting injuries promptly	Waiting till after the team roster is set to report an injury
Helping to pick up equipment after practices	Leaving equipment out for others to pick up

Table 17-2. Youth sportsmanship code

Area of Concern	Sportsmanlike Behavior	Unsportsmanlike Behavior
Behavior toward officials	No technical fouls	Arguing with officials
	When questioning officials, do so in the appropriate manner (e.g., lodge an official protest, have only designated individuals such as a captain address officials)	Swearing at officials
	Treat officials with respect and dignity at all times	Technical fouls
	Thank officials after game	
Behavior toward opponents	Treat all opponents with respect and dignity at all times	Arguing with opponents
	Talk to opponents after the game	Making sarcastic remarks about opponents
		Making aggressive actions toward opponents
Behavior toward teammates	Give only constructive criticism and positive encouragement	Making negative comments or sarcastic remarks
		Swearing at or arguing with teammates
Behavior toward spectators	No talking	Arguing with spectators
		Making negative remarks/swearing at spectators
Behavior toward coach	Share likes and dislikes with the coach as soon as possible	
Rule acceptance and infraction	Obey all league rules	Intentionally violating league rules
		Taking advantage of loopholes in rules (e.g., everyone must play, so coach tells unskilled players to be ill on important game days)

Table 17-3. Examples of rewards and penalties that can be used in basketball.

Rewards	Penalties
Being a starter	Being taken out of a game
Playing a desired position	Not being allowed to start
Leading an exercise or part of it	Sitting out during practice: • until ready to respond properly • a specific number of minutes • rest of practice or sent home early
Praise from you • in team meeting • to media • to parents • to individual	Dismissed from drills: • for half of practice • next practice • next week • rest of season
Decals	Informing parents about misbehavior
Medals	
Certificates	

The best way to motivate players to behave in an acceptable manner is to reward them for good behavior. When appropriate behavior is demonstrated, comment accordingly or be ready to use nonverbal interactions such as smiling or applauding. Some examples are:

- "We only had nine fouls in that game, that's the fewest we ever had. Way to be!"
- "I know you are all very disappointed in losing this game. I was real proud of the way you congratulated and praised the other team after the game."
- "Do you realize that for our first five practices everyone was dressed and ready to play at 3 o'clock, our starting time? That helped make the practice go better. Keep it up! Let's see if we can make it a tradition!"

Penalties are only effective when they are meaningful to the players. Examples of ineffective penalties include showing anger, giving a player an embarrassing lecture, shouting at the player, or assigning a physical activity (e.g., running laps or doing push-ups). These penalties are ineffective because they leave no room for positive interactions between you and your players. Avoid using physical activity as a form of punishment; the benefits of basketball, such as learning skills and improving cardiovascular fitness, are gained through activity. Players should not associate these types of beneficial activities with punishment.

Rewards and penalties that are meaningful to your players and appropriate to the situation are most effective.

Sometimes it is more effective to ignore inappropriate behavior if the infractions are relatively minor. Continually scolding players for minor pranks or "horseplay" can become counterproductive. If team deportment is a constant problem, the coach must ask, "Why?" Misbehavior may be the players' way of telling the coach that they need attention or that they do not have enough to do. Coaches should check to see if the players are spending a lot of time standing in lines while waiting a turn to practice. Try to keep your players productively involved so they don't have time for inappropriate behavior. This is accomplished through well-designed practice plans. A lack of meaningful basketball activity in your practices could lead to counterproductive or disruptive behavior.

Misbehavior may be the players' way of telling the coach that they need attention or do not have enough to do.

When the rules for proper conduct have been outlined and the rewards and penalties have been determined, they must then be stated clearly so the players will understand them. Your players must understand the consequences for breaking the rules and the rewards for abiding by the rules. Violators should explain their actions to the coach and apologize to their teammates. You must also follow through, consistently and impartially, with your application of

rewards for desirable conduct and penalties for misconduct.

Nothing destroys a plan for discipline more quickly than its inconsistent application. Rules must apply to all players equally and in all situations. Thus, if your team is in a championship game and your star player violates a rule that requires that he or she not be allowed to start, the rule must still be enforced. If not, you are communicating to your players that the rules are not to be taken seriously, especially when the game is at stake.

It is impossible to predetermine all rules that may ultimately be important during the season. However, by initiating several rules early in the season, a standard of expected behavior will be established. Positive and negative behaviors that are not covered by the rules can still be judged relative to these established standards and appropriate rewards or punishment can be given.

Key Points to An Effective Discipline Plan

- Specify desirable and undesirable conduct clearly in terms of rules.
- Involve players in establishing the team rules.
- Determine rewards and penalties for rules that are meaningful to players and allow for positive interaction between you and your players.
- Apply rewards and penalties consistently and impartially.

SUMMARY

Although threats, lectures, or yelling may deter misbehavior in the short term, the negative atmosphere that results reduces long-term coaching effectiveness. A more positive approach to handling misbehavior is to prevent it by establishing, with player input, clear team rules and enforcement policies. Use fair and consistent enforcement of the rules primarily through rewarding correct behaviors rather than penalizing wrong behaviors.

REFERENCES

Seefeldt, V. et al. (1981). *A winning philosophy for youth sports programs.* East Lansing, MI: Institute for the Study of Youth Sports.
Smoll, F., & Smith, R.E. (1979). *Improving relationship skills in youth sport coaches.* East Lansing, MI: Institute for the Study of Youth Sports.

18
Developing Good Personal and Social Skills

Annelies Knoppers, Ph.D.

QUESTIONS TO CONSIDER

- Which personal and social skills should youth basketball coaches attempt to foster?
- Why are personal and social skills important?
- How can a coach bolster the self-esteem of athletes?
- How important is fun in youth sports?
- What can a coach do to ensure that sport participation is an enjoyable experience for athletes?
- What strategies can be used to help young athletes develop positive interpersonal skills?
- What is sportsmanship and how can it be taught?

INTRODUCTION

Youth sport experiences can play, and often do play, a crucial role in the development of personal and social skills of children. The learning of these skills is different from that of physical skills in the following ways:

- Athletes will learn something about these skills whether or not we plan for such learning. If we do not plan for this learning, however, it is possible that the sport experience will be a negative one for some of the athletes. If we do plan, then it is more likely that the sports experience will be positive. Obviously then, this is different than the learning of physical skills. If you don't teach your players to do a specific sport skill, they will not learn anything about these skills. In contrast, at every practice and game, players are learning something about the personal and social skills regardless of planning.
- You as the coach continually model these skills. You may never have to model certain physical skills, but personal and social skills always show.
- The learning of these skills is also different from learning physical skills in that you cannot design many drills for the personal and social skills. These skills are a part of every drill and experience.

Coaches, therefore, can have an influence on children that goes well beyond the sport setting. The extent of this influence is increased when:

- the coach and athletes work together over a long period of time

- the athletes are participating in sport because they want to
- the coach is respected and liked by the athletes

Research has also shown that many parents want their children to participate in sports so their daughters and sons can develop personal and social skills through their sport experiences. Thus, coaches can and should work on the development of these skills in athletes.

The basic skills on which a beginning coach should focus are: self-esteem, fun in sport, interpersonal skills, and sportsmanship. Although self-esteem and interpersonal skills are not solely developed through sport, sport experiences can play a crucial role in the enhancement of these skills. In contrast, having fun in sport and showing sportsmanlike behavior are elements specific to the sport setting. Therefore, the coach is often held responsible for their development.

Regardless of the type of personal and social skills emphasized, the more coaches are liked and respected by the athletes and the more they work to create a positive atmosphere, the more likely it is they will influence the development of those skills in their players. The development of these skills is also likely to be enhanced when there is respect for teammates, opponents, officials, the spirit and letter of the rules, and the sport. Consequently, coaches who are very critical when athletes practice and compete, who are angry after a game or after errors, or who will do anything for a win, should change their ways or get out of coaching. Coaches who are unhappy or angry with athletes who make mistakes or lose contests retard the development of personal and social skills.

PERSONAL AND SOCIAL SKILLS

Self-Esteem

Self-esteem is the extent to which an individual is satisfied with oneself, both generally and in specific situations. The level of your athletes' self-esteem will affect their performance, relationships with others, behavior, enjoyment, and motivation. Thus, self-esteem plays a large part in the lives of your athletes as well as in your own life.

All of the players on your team will have feelings about themselves and their ability to do the things you ask of them. Those feelings were developed through experience. They will tend to behave in a way that reflects how they feel about themselves, making that behavior a self-fulfilling prophecy.

The level of self-esteem in young athletes influences their performance level.

Examples

If Sam feels clumsy when playing the point guard position, he is likely to mishandle the ball frequently, which reinforces for him that he is clumsy.

If adults or kids always laugh at Susan's dribbling technique, then she may be very self-conscious about dribbling and always pass the ball.

A combination of a sense of failure and the derisive or negative comments from others can, therefore, lower self-esteem. Luckily, the level of self-esteem is not something that is fixed forever. It can be changed, not overnight nor with a few comments, but over a period of time with a great deal of encouragement. Consequently, enhancing levels of self-esteem requires consistent and daily planning by a coach. Positive changes in the self-esteem of players come about through the implementation of a coaching philosophy that places a priority on this change. Mere participation in sport will not automatically enhance Susan's self-esteem; her coach must plan for experiences and develop strategies that promote self-esteem.

- **Show Acceptance of Each Athlete**

Showing acceptance of each athlete means you must take a personal interest in each of your players regardless of their ability, size, shape, or personality. You need to be sensitive to individual differences and respect those differences. Coaches have to accept their athletes as they are. This does not mean that you have to accept or condone all their behaviors and actions. It means you should still show an interest in Tom even though he seems to whine a lot. You can talk with him about his whining, but you still should give him the same amount of attention as the other players, praise him for good behavior, encourage his effort, chat with him about his non-sport life, and compliment him when he does not whine.

You also can show your acceptance of each player by demonstrating an interest in them as people, not just as athletes. Show an interest in their school life and their family as well as in the things they like and dislike. Take the time to make each athlete feel special as both a player and a person. All athletes should know that without them the team would not be such a great place to be.

- ## React Positively to Mistakes

In practice, be patient. Don't get upset with errors. Instead, focus on the part of the skill that was correctly performed and on the effort made by the player. Give positive suggestions for error correction. Helpful hints on how to do so are given in Chapter 4. Often in games, it is best to let mistakes go by without comment; simply praise the effort and the part of the skill that was performed correctly.

Kids usually know when they make mistakes and do not need an adult to point them out publicly. A coach who constantly corrects errors publicly not only embarrasses the players but may also be giving them too much information. Ask them privately if they know why the error occurred. If they know, then no correction needs to be given. Encourage them also to ask for help when they need it: "Coach, why did I miss that shot?" This type of questioning encourages self-responsibility and ensures that an athlete is ready to respond to your helpful suggestions.

- ## Encourage Athletes

Encouragement plays a vital role in building self-esteem. Coaches can never encourage their athletes enough. Athletes benefit most from coaches who are encouraging. Also, athletes who have supportive coaches tend to like sports more and are more likely to develop a positive self-image in sports. Encouragement is especially crucial for athletes who have low self-esteem, who have difficulty mastering a skill, who make crucial errors in a game, who are not highly skilled, and who are "loners." Encouragement conveys to athletes that the coach is on their side, especially if that encouragement is individualized.

Appropriate Times for Encouragement

- when a skill performance is partially correct
- when things aren't going well (the more discouraging the situation, the more encouragement is needed)
- right after a mistake; focus on the effort, not the error
- when any effort is made to do a difficult task
- after each game and practice; do not let players leave feeling upset or worthless

How to Give Encouragement

In general, give encouragement by publicly naming the athlete so that recognition is directly received for the effort. If an athlete is struggling with something personal, then encourage the athlete privately.

- Publicly acknowledge each athlete's effort and skill as they occur
- Recognize each athlete as they come off the court in either a verbal way: "Good hustle in going for that ball, Joan!" or in a nonverbal way: a smile, pat on the back, or wink
- Praise players who encourage each other
- Monitor your behavior or have someone else observe a practice or game
- Be sincere; make the encouragement both meaningful and specific

Examples

After a player fails to catch a pass, instead of saying "Nice try, John!" say "Way to get open, John! Good hustle!"

After a player fell, instead of saying "I'm sorry you fell, Sue!" say "Way to get back up on your feet so quickly, Sue! I like your determination!"

Before a game, instead of saying "Play well in this game, OK?" say "I want all of you to try to do a little better than you did in the last game. I know you can do it!"

Additional Tips for Enhancing Self-Esteem

- Credit every player with the win
- Applaud physical skills (or parts of them) that were performed correctly
- Praise the use of appropriate social skills and effort
- Be more concerned that each player gets a

substantial amount of playing time than whether or not the team wins

- Give special and more attention in practices and games to nonstarters
- Give athletes responsibilities; ask for help in setting up team rules and in creating new drills
- Never call athletes by degrading names; poke fun at their physiques, abilities, or gender; or use ethnic, racial, or gender stereotypes or slurs

Examples

Instead of saying (in a derogatory manner), "John runs like a girl!" say "John needs to improve his running."

Instead of saying (in a derogatory manner), "You played like a bunch of sissies!" say "We're going to have to work on being a bit quicker and more assertive!"

Instead of saying, "Paul really looks funny the way he runs down the court!" say "Of all the kids on this team, Paul seems to show the most determination in getting down the court. Good for him!"

FUN IN SPORT

One of the main reasons why youngsters participate in sport is to have fun. Conversely, if they do not enjoy being on the team, players are more likely to drop out. Fun, therefore, is a crucial element in participation. Even though fun occurs spontaneously in sport, each coach should plan carefully to ensure that each athlete is enjoying the sport experience. The following ideas, when put into practice, increase the likelihood that the athletes and you will enjoy the team experience.

A primary reason young athletes participate in sports is to have fun.

- Conduct well-organized practices. Plan so all of the players have the maximum amount of physical activity that is feasible in conjunction with your objectives for a practice. Try to eliminate standing in line and waiting for turns as much as possible. If you have a large group, use the station method to keep all the players busy (see Chapter 4).

- Select drills that are suitable for the skill level of the players.
- Create enjoyable ways of learning skills; use innovative drills and games for practicing fundamental skills; and ask the players for suggestions and innovations.
- Watch the players' faces; if you see smiles and hear laughter, your players are enjoying practice!
- Project fun yourself; tolerate some silliness; avoid sarcasm; and be enthusiastic!
- Use games or drills that end when each person has won or has performed a skill correctly a specific number of times.
- Give positive reinforcement.
- Encourage athletes to praise, compliment, and encourage each other; do not allow them to criticize each other nor use degrading nicknames.
- Make sure athletes regularly change partners in drills.
- Allow each child to learn and play at least two positions, if possible, and to play a lot in every game.
- Keep the atmosphere light; don't be afraid to laugh and to gently joke .
- Smile; show that you enjoy being at practice or at the games. Say, "I really enjoyed this practice!" or "This is fun!"
- Take time to make each athlete feel very special. "The team could not function as well as it does without YOU!"

INTERPERSONAL SKILLS

Since sport involves teammates, opponents, officials, and coaches, it can be a great place to develop good interpersonal, or people, skills. Sport, however, can also be a place where athletes learn poor interpersonal skills. The type of skills that the athletes learn depends on the coach. If you, for example, praise Deb because she encouraged Donna, then you are reinforcing a positive interpersonal skill and creating a cooperative environment. If you say nothing when you hear Mike call one of the Hispanics on the team Chico, then you are reinforcing a racial slur and an inequitable climate. Just as youngsters need to be taught the proper technique for shooting a lay-up, they also need to be taught how to relate to others in a way that bolsters self-esteem and sensitivity.

• The Coach as Model

If you want your athletes to develop good people skills, you must consistently model the skills you wish them to develop. If you explain to them that they are not to yell and scream at each other and yet you yell and scream at them, you are giving a conflicting message: "Do as I say, not as I do." Similarly, if you state that your athletes may never criticize each other because it shows lack of respect and yet you criticize officials, you are sending a mixed message.

The greater the inconsistencies in your messages (that is, between what you say and what you do), the less likely that the players will develop good people skills. When you send mixed messages, players are likely to ignore what you say and imitate your behavior. Thus they will yell, scream, and criticize if you yell, scream, and criticize. As part of practice and game plans, therefore, you should give serious thought to the type of behaviors you wish your athletes to show to each other, opponents, officials, and coaches.

The overriding principle that should guide your planning and behavior is to show respect and sensitivity to all others without exception.

What does respectful behavior look like? According to Griffin and Placek, a player who shows respect for others:

- follows rules
- accepts official's calls without arguing
- compliments good play of others including that of opponents
- congratulates the winner
- plays safely
- says "my fault" if it was
- accepts instruction
- will hold back rather than physically hurt someone
- questions coach and officials respectfully

Players show sensitivity to the feelings of others when they:

- pair up with different teammates each time

- cheer teammates on, especially those who are struggling
- help and encourage less skilled teammates
- stand up for those who are belittled or mocked by others
- are willing to sit out sometimes so others can play
- feel OK about changing some rules so others can play or to make the competition more even
- refrain from using abusive names, stereotypic slurs, and from mocking others

The above behaviors are those you must model, teach, discuss, and encourage to enhance the people skills of your players. When you "catch" your players using these skills, praise them! Praise as frequently, if not more, the use of these skills as you would praise correct physical performance.

However, modeling, teaching, discussing, and encouraging these behaviors is not enough. You must also intervene when players use poor interpersonal skills. If you see such actions and ignore them, you are giving consent and approval.

When should you intervene? Griffin and Placek suggest that you should act when a player:

- criticizes teammates' play
- yells at officials
- pushes, shoves, or trips teammates or opponents
- hogs the ball
- gloats and rubs it in when the team wins
- baits opponents, e.g., "you're no good"
- bosses other players
- will hurt someone just to win
- makes fun of teammates because of their shape, skill, gender, race, or ethnic origin
- calls others names, like "wimp," "stupid," "klutz," etc.
- blames mistakes on others
- complains to officials
- shares a position unwillingly
- ignores less skilled players
- complains about less skilled players
- gets into verbal or physical fights
- uses racial, ethnic, or gender slurs

Obviously, the lists of desirable and undesirable behaviors could be much longer. Their overall theme suggests that everyone should show respect and sensitivity to all people. This includes coaches, officials, teammates, and opponents. Coaches should be firmly committed to this "people principle" and should try to express it in their coaching.

• Tips for Enhancing People Skills

- Explain the "people principle" and establish a few basic rules as examples of the principle (e.g., praise and encourage each other).
- Discuss how you feel when you are encouraged and when you are hassled. Ask them how they feel.
- Praise behavior that exemplifies the "people principle."
- Work to eliminate stereotypic grouping of players for drills; don't let players group themselves by race, gender, or skill level. They should rotate so all will have a chance to work with everyone else.
- Call the entire team's attention to an undesirable behavior the first time it occurs and explain or ask why that behavior does not fit the "people principle."
- Talk to the team about the use of racial jokes and slurs such as calling a Native American "Chief," an Asian American "Kung Foo," and an Hispanic "Taco," and the derogatory use of gender stereotypes such as "sissies," "playing/throwing like a girl," and "wimp." Explain how these behaviors convey disrespect and insensitivity and cannot be tolerated. Remember, too, that often these verbalizations by players echo those they have heard used by adults.
- Assign drill partners on irrelevant characteristics such as birthday month, color of shirt, number of siblings, etc.
- Stress the "one for all and all for one" concept.
- Monitor your own behavior.

SPORTSMANSHIP

Sportsmanship is a familiar term that is difficult to define precisely. When we talk about sportsmanship, we usually are referring to the behavior of coaches, athletes, and spectators in the competitive game setting, especially in stressful situations. Thus, it is easier to give exam-

ples of sportsmanlike and unsportsmanlike behaviors than to define sportsmanship. For some examples, see Table 17-2 in Chapter 17.

• Displaying Sportsmanship

Treatment of Opponents

Sportsmanlike behaviors

- At the end of the game, athletes shake hands sincerely with their opponents and talk with them for a while.
- An opponent falls and Joan helps her back on her feet.
- John forgets his game shoes and the opposing team lends him a pair.
- A team brings orange slices and shares them with their opponents.
- After the game, a coach praises the play of both teams.

Unsportsmanlike behaviors

- Joan stomps away in disgust after her team loses.
- An athlete verbally hassles an opponent, saying "You dummy! We're going to run right over you!"
- A player swears after the opponents score.
- After a player on the Stars is tripped by an opposing player, the Stars players decide they have to "get physical" too.

Treatment of Officials

Sportsmanlike behaviors

- The Stars coach saw a Blazers player touch the ball last before it went out of bounds. When the ball is awarded to the Blazers, because the official thought the ball was touched last by a player on the Stars, the Stars coach says nothing.
- The only Stars player who asks the official to explain a call is the captain. When other Stars players have a question, they ask the captain to speak for them.
- When the captain or coach speaks to an official, they do so in a respectful and courteous manner.

Unsportsmanlike behaviors

- The coach of the Stars throws the clipboard to the floor after an official misses a call.

- When an official makes two calls in a row against the Blazers, the coach yells "Homer!"

Reaction to Rules

Sportsmanlike behaviors

- Since league rules permit only one practice per week, the coach of the Tigers holds only one practice and schedules no "secret" practices.
- One league requires that all its players play an equal amount of time. Although some coaches ask lesser skilled players to "be sick" on important game days, the coach of the Panthers continually stresses that all players are expected and needed for every game.

Unsportsmanlike behaviors

- The players on the Eagles are taught by their coach how they can break the rules without being detected.
- In order to get play stopped, the coach of the Falcons tells an athlete to fake an injury.
- Sue elbows Joan whenever the official is not looking in their direction.

• Creating a Positive Climate

Because one of the goals of youth sports is to teach sportsmanship, a coach should know in which situations unsportsmanlike actions are most likely to occur. Often these situations are under the control of the coach and by changing them, the likelihood of unsportsmanlike behavior occurring decreases.

Situations when unsportsmanlike behavior is most likely to occur are those in which coaches, parents, and athletes view:

- competition as war rather than as a cooperative, competitive game;
- opponents as enemies rather than as children playing a game;
- abusive language towards opponents and officials as "part of the game" rather than as disrespectful and intolerant behavior;
- errors by officials as proof that they favor the other team rather than as evidence that officials make mistakes, too;
- winning as the only important part of the game rather than as being only a part of the game; and

- every game as serious business rather than as a playful, fun-filled, and skillful endeavor.

Obviously then, a coach can decrease the likelihood of the occurrence of unsportsmanlike behavior by viewing youth sport as a playful, competitive, cooperative activity in which athletes strive to be skillful and to win and yet know that neither winning nor perfect performance are required. This type of attitude creates a positive climate and tends to enhance sportsmanship.

• Teaching Sportsmanship

Stress-filled situations are the second type of condition under which unsportsmanlike behaviors tend to occur. These situations are created by the game rather than by the coach. As a coach, therefore, you must teach the athletes how they should behave in these situations. Sportsmanship can be taught.

Role Modeling

Often the behavior of athletes in a stress-filled situation reflects that of their coach. If you stay calm, cool and collected when the score is tied in the championship game, so will your players. To do so, however, you need to keep the game in perspective which you can do by answering "no" to the following questions:

- Will the outcome of the game matter a month from now?
- Will it shake up the world if our team wins or loses today?
- Is winning more important than playing well and having fun?

Once you begin to answer "yes" to these questions, the game has become so important to you that you will be more likely to snap at the players and argue with the officials. Perhaps then you should ask yourself whether you should stay in youth sport.

On the other hand, if you can answer "no" to the above questions, you are probably approaching the game from a healthy perspective and are more likely to stay calm, cool, and collected and exhibit good sportsmanlike behavior.

Using the "People Principle"

If children are to behave in a sportsmanlike manner, they must be told specifically what is expected of them and must be praised for doing so. The "people principle" that was described in an earlier section requires all to show respect and sensitivity to others.

The "people principle" is the basic guideline for sportsmanlike behavior.

Use Praise

When athletes follow the "people principle," they should be praised.

Examples

Sally helps her opponent back up to her feet. Coach immediately says, "Way to be, Sally!"

You know Johnny thinks the official made a mistake, but Johnny says nothing. You immediately say, "Way to stay cool, Johnny!"

Eliminate Unsportsmanlike Behaviors

Ideally, when an athlete behaves in an unsportsmanlike way, you should say something immediately, and if possible, pull the child aside. Firmly indicate:

- that the behavior was inappropriate
- how it violates the "people principle"
- that you expect everyone to follow this principle
- that the athlete will be in trouble if the behavior is repeated
- that you know the athlete will try hard not to do it again

If the behavior is repeated, remind the athlete of the previous discussion and give an appropriate penalty. For examples of penalties see Chapter 17.

If athletes are to develop sportsmanship, you must not tolerate any unsportsmanlike actions. Sometimes it is easy to ignore a youngster's outburst because you feel the same frustration. By ignoring it, however, you are sending the message that at times such behavior is acceptable. Consequently, athletes will not acquire a clear sense of sportsmanship.

Discuss Sportsmanship

Young athletes need to have time to discuss sportsmanship because it is so difficult to define precisely. Team meetings before or after a practice provide a good opportunity for discussion. The following tips should help you facilitate such a discussion:

- Ask opening questions such as "Who can give an example of sportsmanlike behavior? Unsportsmanlike behavior? Why is one wrong and not the other?"
- Read the examples from this section of both types of behaviors and ask the athletes to label them as sportsmanlike and unsportsmanlike. Ask them to explain their reasoning.
- Encourage role playing. "What would it be like to be an official who is trying to do what's best and to have a coach or players yelling at you?"
- Discuss the relationship between the importance attached to winning and sportsmanship.
- Point out examples from college and professional sports. Ask the players to classify the behaviors and to give a rationale.

During these discussions, refrain from lecturing. Think of yourself as a facilitator who attempts to encourage discussion and an exploration of the "people principle."

The extent to which your athletes display or react to sportsmanlike or unsportsmanlike behavior will determine the frequency with which you should hold such discussions at practice. To reinforce these discussions, you should point out examples of both types of behaviors at the brief team meeting after some game. Publicly praise each player who acted in a sportsmanlike manner and remind those who acted otherwise of your expectations. Remember also to continually examine your own behaviors to ensure that you are demonstrating the type of actions in which you want your players to engage.

SUMMARY

The extent to which athletes develop personal and social skills through the sport experience depends a great deal on you. Just as physical skills cannot be mastered without planned and directed practice, neither can personal and social skills be developed without specific strategies and guidelines. If a coach does not plan such strategies nor set guidelines for the development of these skills, then the sports experience may be a negative one for the athletes.

They may lose self-esteem, develop a dislike for sport participation, and drop out. Conversely, those athletes who feel good about themselves, their teammates, and the sports experience are more likely to stay in sport. Thus a coach has a responsibility to develop these skills.

REFERENCES

Berlage, G. (1982). Are children's competitive team sports socializing agents for corporate America? In A. Dunleavy et al. (Eds.), *Studies in the sociology of sport*. Fort Worth, TX: Texas Christian University Press.

Coakley, J. (1986). *Sport in society* (3rd ed.). St. Louis, MO: Times/Mirror Mosby.

Griffin, P., & Placek, J. (1983). *Fair play in the gym: Race and sex equity in physical education*. Amherst, MA: University of Massachusetts.

SUGGESTED READINGS

Martens, R. (Ed.). (1978). *Joy and sadness in children's sports*. Champaign, IL: Human Kinetics.

National Coaching Certification Program (NCCP I). (1979). *Coaching theory, level one*. Ottawa, Ontario: Coaching Association of Canada.

National Coaching Certification Program (NCCP II). (1979). *Coaching theory, level two*. Ottawa, Ontario: Coaching Association of Canada.

Orlick, T., & Botterill, C. (1975). *Every kid can win*. Chicago: Nelson Hall.

Tutko, T., & Burns, W. (1976). *Winning is everything and other American myths*. New York: Macmillan, Inc.

Yablonsky, L., & Brower, J.J. (1979). *The little league game*. New York: Times Books.

19
Evaluating Coaching Effectiveness

Paul Vogel, Ph.D.

QUESTIONS TO CONSIDER

- Why evaluate coaching effectiveness?
- What should be evaluated?
- Who should evaluate it?
- What steps can be used to conduct an evaluation?

INTRODUCTION

No individual can coach with 100 percent effectiveness. While beginning coaches who have had no formal coaching education programs, sport-specific clinics, or prior coaching experience are particularly susceptible to using ineffective techniques, experienced professionals have their weaknesses as well. To determine where both strengths and weaknesses exist, beginning as well as experienced coaches should conduct systematic evaluations of their effectiveness.

All coaches can significantly improve their coaching effectiveness by completing an evaluation and then acting on the results.

At least two evaluation questions should be asked:

1. Was the coaching effective in achieving its purpose?
2. What changes can be made to improve the quality of coaching?

The evaluation described herein provides a relatively simple procedure for estimating the effects of your coaching efforts. It will also help you identify ways to improve your techniques.

WHAT SHOULD BE EVALUATED?

Evaluation should be based on more than whether or not you're a good person, worked the team hard, or even had a winning season. The important issue is whether or not you met the objectives identified for your players at the beginning of the season (see Chapter 3), including technique, knowledge, tactics, fitness, and personal-social skills. The worksheet in Figure 19-1 (also included in reproducible form in Supplement 19-1) provides an example of how you can identify what should be evaluated.

Coaching effectiveness should be judged by the degree to which players meet their objectives.

For a discussion on how to use Supplement 19-1, see Step 2: Collect the Evaluation Data.

WHO SHOULD EVALUATE?

Initially, you should evaluate your own effectiveness. To ensure a broader and more objective evaluation, however, you should have others participate in the evaluation. For example, by using the worksheet illustrated in Figure 19-1, you might rate the majority of your players as achieving one or more objectives in the areas of sport skills, knowledge, tactics, fitness, and personal-social skills. Another person, however, may feel that what you thought was appropriate was in fact an inappropriate technique, an incorrect interpretation of a rule, an improper tactic, a contraindicated exercise, or an improper attitude. Obtaining such information requires courage on your part but it often yields important information to help you improve your coaching effectiveness.

Self-evaluation is a valuable means for improving your coaching effectiveness.

To obtain the most useful second party information, use individuals who meet the following three criteria:

1. They are familiar with your coaching actions.
2. They know the progress of your players.
3. They are individuals whose judgment you respect.

A person fulfilling these criteria could be an assistant coach, parent, official, league supervisor, other coach, local expert, or even one or more of your players.

The evaluation form illustrated in Supplement 19-2 provides another way to obtain information relative to coaching effectiveness as perceived by others. This form can be used for individual players (one form per player) or for the team as a whole (one form for the entire team). The purpose of the form is to obtain information that will reveal areas of low ratings. Follow-up can be completed in a debriefing session with the rater to determine the reasons for low ratings and to identify what can be done to strengthen the ratings. Debriefing sessions with this type of focus have proven to be highly effective in identifying ways to improve programs and procedures.

WHAT STEPS CAN BE USED TO CONDUCT AN EVALUATION?

Four steps can be used to complete an evaluation of your coaching effectiveness. These are:

1. Identify the objectives
2. Collect evaluation data
3. Analyze the evaluation data to identify reasons why some coaching actions were ineffective
4. Implement the needed changes

Step 1: Identify Objectives

The form illustrated in Supplement 19-1 can be used to identify the objectives you have for your players. Simply list the specific sport skills, knowledges, tactics, fitness abilities, and personal-social skills that you intend to develop in your players. Completion of this step clearly identifies what you believe is most important for your players to master and it provides a basis for later evaluation.

A prerequisite to conducting an evaluation of coaching effectiveness is to clearly identify the objectives that you want your players to achieve.

Once the objectives are identified, the remaining evaluation steps can be completed. This step also provides a good opportunity for you to obtain information from others regarding the appropriateness of your season's objectives for the age and experience level of your players.

Let your players know what the objectives are. Research shows that when players know what they need to learn, they experience improved achievement.

Step 2: Collect the Evaluation Data

The primary source of evaluative data should be your self-evaluation of the results of all or various parts of the season. However, assessments by others, combined with self-assessment, are more valuable than self-evaluation alone. Both approaches are recommended.

• Completing the Coach's Assessment of Player Performance

After you have identified objectives and

Coach **CANDY JONES**   Season **WINTER**   Date **MARCH 20, 1992**

EVALUATION QUESTION: Did significant, positive results occur on the objectives included in the performance areas listed below?

CATEGORIES SEASON OBJECTIVES	ROSTER Jane	Janice	Alice	Frankie	Bonnie	Carol	Kate	Patty	Amy	Marcia	Karen	Sue								Total (% yes)	Other notes
DRIBBLING																					
STATIONARY	Y	Y	N	Y	Y	Y	Y	N	Y	Y	Y	Y								91	EXCELLENT
WITH PIVOT	Y	Y	N	Y	Y	Y	Y	N	Y	Y	Y	Y								91	EXCELLENT
QUICK STOP	Y	Y	Y	N	Y	Y	N	N	Y	N	Y	Y								83	EXCELLENT
CROSS-OVER	N	Y	N	Y	Y	N	N	Y	N	Y	N									66	FAIR
BEHIND-THE-BACK	N	Y	N	N	Y	N	N	N	Y	N	Y	N								33	NEEDS WORK
REVERSE	N	Y	N	N	Y	N	N	N	Y	N	Y	N								33	NEEDS WORK
PASSING																					
CHEST	Y	Y	Y	Y	N	Y	Y	N	Y	Y	N	Y								75	FAIR
OVERHEAD	Y	N	Y	Y	N	Y	Y	N	Y	Y	N	Y								66	FAIR
ONE HANDED	Y	N	Y	Y	Y	Y	Y	N	Y	Y	N	Y								75	FAIR
BOUNCE	N	Y	Y	Y	Y	Y	Y	N	Y	N	N	N								58	NEEDS WORK
SHOOTING																					
TWO HANDED SET	Y	Y	N	N	Y	N	N	N	Y	N	Y	N								42	NEEDS WORK
ONE HANDED SET	Y	Y	N	N	Y	N	N	N	Y	N	Y	N								42	NEEDS WORK
JUMP	Y	Y	Y	Y	Y	Y	N	N	Y	N	Y	N								66	FAIR
LAY-IN	Y	N	Y	Y	Y	Y	Y	Y	Y	Y	Y	N									
REBOUNDING																					
OFFENSIVE	Y	N	Y	Y	N	Y	Y	Y	N	Y	N	N								58	NEEDS WORK
DEFENSIVE	Y	N	Y	Y	N	Y	Y	Y	Y	N	N	N								58	NEEDS WORK
SCREEN																					
SETTING	Y	Y	Y	Y	Y	Y	Y	Y	Y	Y	N	N								83	EXCELLENT
USING	Y	Y	N	Y	Y	Y	Y	N	Y	N	N	N								58	NEEDS WORK
JUMP BALL	Y	Y	Y	Y	N	Y	N	Y	Y	Y	Y	N								75	FAIR
DEPORTMENT	Y	Y	Y	Y	Y	Y	Y	Y	Y	Y	N	N								83	GOOD
Total (% yes)	80	75	60	75	75	75	60	30	90	55	55	30									

EVALUATIVE RESPONSES: Record your assessment of player outcomes for each objective by answering the evaluative questions with a "Y" ("YES") or "N" ("NO") response.

Figure 19-1. Coach's Evaluation of Player outcomes.

entered them in the first column of the "Coach's Evaluation of Player Outcomes" form, enter the names of your players in the spaces on the top of the form. Next, respond either Y (Yes) or N (No) to the question, "Did significant improvements occur?" as it relates to each season objective for each player.

Your decision to enter a Y or N in each space requires you to define one or more standards. For example, all of your players may have improved on a particular season objective but you may feel that several of those players did not achieve enough to receive a Y. However, an N may also seem inappropriate. To resolve this difficulty, clarify the amount of player achievement for each objective that you are willing to accept as evidence of a significant positive improvement. There is no exact method of determining how much gain is enough; therefore, you need to rely on your own estimates of these standards. The procedures suggested on the following pages of this chapter allow for correction of erroneous judgments. It is also possible to use a scale to further divide the response options: 0 = none, 1 = very little, 2 = little, 3 = some, 4 = large, and 5 = very large. Given ratings of this type, you may establish 4 and/or 5 ratings as large enough to be categorized as a Y and ratings of 3 or less as an N.

It is important to remember that players who begin the season at low levels of performance on various objectives have the potential for more improvement than players who are near mastery. Players who begin the season at high levels of performance often deserve Y rather than N for relatively small gains.

Injury, loss of fitness, or development of inappropriate sport skills, knowledge, tactics, or personal-social skills are detrimental effects that can occur and should be identified. In this situation the appropriate entry is an N circled to distinguish it from small or slight gains.

You must decide if your players achieved significant gains on the outcomes you intended to teach.

Completion of the coach's evaluation form will reveal your perception of the degree to which your players achieved important objectives. By looking at one objective across all players as well as one player across all objectives, patterns of your coaching effectiveness will emerge. (This is explained in more detail in Step 3.)

- **Obtaining Information from Selected Other Persons**

To obtain information from others about your coaching effectiveness, use the form illustrated in Supplement 19-2. Remember, the form can be used for individual players or for an entire team. Note that the estimates of performance are relative to other players of similar age and gender participating in the same league. When using the form to rate individual players, ask the evaluator to simply place a check in the appropriate column (top 25 percent, mid 50 percent or bottom 25 percent) for each performance area. When using the form to rate the entire team, estimate the number of players judged to be in each column.

Ratings of players' performance at the end of the season (or other evaluation period) are not very useful without knowing your players' performance levels at the beginning of the season. Changes in performance levels are the best indicators of your coaching effectiveness. To determine change in players' performance, it is necessary to estimate performance before and after coaching occurred. Pre and post ratings may be difficult to obtain, however, because of the time it requires of your raters.

A good alternative is to have the evaluators record pre and post ratings at the end of the evaluation period. For example, if three of your players were perceived to be in the top 25 percent of their peers at the beginning of the season and seven players were perceived to be in that performance category at the end of the season, the net gain in performance would be 4. Your desire may be to have all of your players move into the top 25 percent category during the course of the season. Such a desire is, however, probably unrealistic. Having 50 percent of your players move from one performance level to the next would be an excellent achievement.

It would be nice to look at your evaluations of player performance and the evaluations of their performance by others and see only Y responses or ratings in the top 25 percent. Such a set of responses, however, would not be helpful for improving your coaching effectiveness. An excessive number of high ratings probably signals the use of a relaxed set of standards.

All coaches vary in their ability to change behavior across stated outcome areas and across various individual players on a team. The incidences where individual players do not attain high ratings on various objectives are most useful to reveal principles of coaching effectiveness that are being violated. Accordingly, use standards for your self-ratings (or for the ratings by others) that result in no more than 80 percent of the responses being Y on the "Coach's Evaluation of Player Outcomes" or moving from one category of performance to another when rated by others. As you will see in Step 3, ratings that are more evenly distributed among the response options are the most helpful for determining how your effectiveness may be improved.

Use of the form "Evaluation of Player/Team Performance Relative to Others" (Supplement 19-2) provides you with an estimate of changes in player performance as viewed by other persons whose judgment you respect. The relatively broad performance areas upon which the evaluation is based does not, however, provide enough detailed information to fully interpret the data obtained. Simply stated, more information is needed. Additional information can be obtained by using the technique of debriefing.

A debriefing session, based upon the information included in the completed evaluation form, provides a good agenda for discussing potential changes in your coaching procedures with the person who completed the evaluation. The debriefing should include these elements:

- Thank the individual for completing the evaluation form and agreeing to discuss its implications.
- Indicate that the purpose of the debriefing session is to identify both strengths and weaknesses, but that emphasis should be focused on weaknesses, and how they may be improved.
- Proceed through the outcome areas and their corresponding ratings, seeking to understand why each area resulted in large or small gains. For example, if a disproportionate number of the players were rated low relative to their

peers on offensive skills, and there were very small gains from the beginning to the end of the evaluation period, you need more information. Attempt to determine what offensive skills were weak and what might be changed to strengthen them in the coming season.

- In your discussion, probe for the things you can do (or avoid doing) that may produce better results. Make a special attempt to identify the reasons why a suggested alternative may produce better results.
- Take careful notes during the discussion. Record the alternative ideas that have good supporting rationales and how they might be implemented.

The information collected in this way is invaluable for helping to identify good ideas for increasing your ability to help players achieve future season objectives.

Coaching strengths are pleasing to hear, but identified weaknesses are more helpful for improving effectiveness.

Step 3: Analyze the Data

The first step necessary to analyze the information collected is to total the number of Y responses entered for each player across all season objectives.

From a coaching improvement viewpoint, it is necessary to have a mixture of Y and N responses across both the objectives and players. It is important that no more than 80 percent of your ratings be Y responses on the coaches' self-evaluation form. Tell other raters that no more than 80 percent of the players can be listed as showing improvement from one performance level to another in their pre/post estimates. It may be necessary to "force" the appropriate number of Y and N responses to meet this requirement.

When you have met the criteria of no more than 80 percent positive answers, divide the number of Y responses by the total number of objectives and enter the percent of Y responses in the row labeled "Total" for each player. Similarly sum the number of Y responses across players for each objective and enter the percent of Y responses in the column labeled "Total" for each season objective.

The pattern of Y and N responses that emerges from "forced ratings" can be very helpful in identifying the season's objectives and/or the kinds of players for which your coaching is most or least effective. By looking at the characteristics of the players who obtained the highest ratings versus those that achieved the lowest ratings, you may obtain good insight into things you can change to be more effective with certain kinds of players. This same type of comparison provides similar insight into how to be more effective in teaching certain objectives.

The real benefits of this kind of analysis come with evaluating the reasons why no or few players received Y responses. Answers to these "Why?" questions reveal changes you can make to improve your coaching effectiveness.

To help you determine why you were (or were not) successful with your coaching in certain player performance areas, a "Checklist of Effective Coaching Actions" was developed (Supplement 19-3). It provides a number of items you can rate that may help you identify ways to increase your coaching effectiveness. For example, if several of your players made insufficient progress in the offensive technique of setting screens, you could review the checklist to help determine coaching actions you used (or did not use) that may be related to helping players of similar skill level, fitness, or qualities of character. As you identify coaching actions that may have detracted from player improvement, note these and then alter your subsequent coaching actions accordingly.

• **Interpreting Unmet Expectations**

The above suggestions provide a systematic method for you to identify ways to improve your coaching ability. There are, however, other ways to interpret lack of achievement. The first and foremost (and nearly always incorrect) is to blame lack of performance on lack of talent or lack of player interest.

Be sure to consider all possibilities for self improvement before accepting other reasons for unmet expectations.

Effective coaches can improve the ability of their players, even those with only average abilities. The most helpful approach you can use to improve your coaching effectiveness is to assume that when the performances of your players do not meet your expectations, the solutions to the problem will be found in your coaching actions. This assumption may prove to be wrong, but you must be absolutely sure that you have considered all possibilities for self-improvement before accepting other reasons for unmet expectations.

If you determine that insufficient players' achievement is not likely to be due to ineffective coaching, it is possible that the expectations you hold for your players is unrealistic. Remember, motivation is enhanced when players perceive that they are improving. Expectations that are too high can have a negative effect on motivation and improvement. Reasonable expectations divided into achievable and sequential steps will result in appropriate standards of performance.

Allotment of insufficient time for teaching and learning the objectives selected for the season can also result in poor players' achievement, even when performance expectations and other coaching actions are appropriate. Players must have sufficient time to attempt a task, make errors, obtain feedback, refine their attempts, and habituate the intended actions before it is reasonable to expect them to demonstrate those actions in competition. Attempting to cover too many objectives within limited practice time is a major cause of insufficient achievement.

If the changes identified to improve coaching effectiveness are not implemented, evaluation is a waste of time.

Step 4: Act on the Needed Changes

The primary reason for conducting an evaluation of your coaching effectiveness is to learn what can be done to improve the achievement levels of your players. Identifying the changes that will lead to improvements, however, is a waste of time if those changes are not implemented. Improvements can occur in planning, instruction, motivation, communication, knowledge of the game, and evaluation. Regardless of your level of expertise, by systematically evaluating your coaching actions, you can find ways to become more effective and more efficient.

SUMMARY

By systematically evaluating players' performance on the intended outcomes of the season, you can estimate the effectiveness of your coaching actions. Limited achievement of players in some performance areas can signal a need to change some coaching actions. Use of the forms and procedures outlined in this chapter will reveal changes you can make to improve your coaching effectiveness. By taking action on the changes that are identified, you can make significant steps toward becoming a more effective and efficient coach.

Supplement 19-1.

Coach's Evaluation of Player Outcomes

Coach _____ Season _____ Date _____

EVALUATION QUESTION:	Did significant, positive results occur on the objectives included in the performance areas listed below?		Total (% yes)
SEASON OBJECTIVES	Players		Notes
Total (% yes)			
EVALUATIVE RESPONSES:	Record your assessment of player outcomes for each objective by answering the evaluative questions with a "Y" ("YES") or "N" ("NO") response.		

Evaluation of Player/Team Performance Relative to Others

Evaluator: _____ Player/Team _____ Season _____

EVALUATION QUESTION:	In comparison with other players in this league, how does the player (or team) listed above perform in the areas listed below?						
PERFORMANCE AREAS	**PLAYER OR TEAM PERFORMANCE LEVELS**						**COMMENTS**
	SEASON START			**SEASON END**			
	TOP 25%	MID 50%	BOTTOM 25%	TOP 25%	MID 50%	BOTTOM 25%	

INDIVIDUAL EVALUATION:
 For each performance area, place a check in the top, mid or bottom column to indicate the start and end of the season performance level of the player.

TEAM EVALUATION:
 For each performance area estimate the number of players (% or actual numbers) in the top, mid or bottom performance levels at the start and end of the season.

Checklist of Effective Coaching Actions[1]

Introduction

This checklist can be used to identify coaching actions that may be related to player achievement (or lack of achievement) of objectives. It, therefore, serves as an aid to identify the reason(s) why a player(s) did not achieve one or more of your expected outcomes. To use the checklist in this way, read the items in each content category (i.e., coaching role, organization, effective instruction) and ask yourself the question, "Could the coaching actions (or inactions) implied by this item have contributed to the unmet expectation?" Answer the question by responding with a 'Yes' or 'No.' If you wish to rate the degree to which your actions (inactions) were consistent with the guidelines implied by the items, use the 5 point rating scale described below. Items which result in "No" or low ratings suggest that you are in discord with effective coaching practices. The process of seeking answers to specific concerns identified by your reaction to checklist items is an excellent way to obtain information most likely to help you become more effective as a coach.

Directions

Rate the degree to which you incorporate each of the following items into your coaching activities. Check "Yes" or "No" or use the following 5 point scale where: 1 = Strongly Disagree, 2 = Disagree, 3 = Neutral, 4 = Agree, 5 = Strongly Agree.

Item	Rating		
	Disagree		Agree
Coaching Role			
1. My primary purpose for coaching was to maximize the benefits of participation for <u>all</u> of the players.	(NO)	1 2 3 4 5	(YES)
2. The beneficial (individual techniques, knowledge, tactics, fitness, attitudes) and detrimental (time, money, injury, etc.) of participation were constantly in mind during planning and coaching times.	(NO)	1 2 3 4 5	(YES)
3. I communicated through actions and words that I expected each player to succeed in improving his/her level of play.	(NO)	1 2 3 4 5	(YES)
Organization			
4. I completed a plan for the season to guide the conduct of my practices.	(NO)	1 2 3 4 5	(YES)

[1] Modified from: Vogel, P.G. (1987). Post season evaluation: What did we accomplish? In V.D. Seefeldt (ed.) *Handbook for youth sport coaches*. Reston, VA: American Alliance for Health, Physical Education, Recreation and Dance.

5. Performance expectations set for the   (NO)   1   2   3   4   5   (YES)
    players were realistic and attainable.

6. I conscientiously decided which   (NO)   1   2   3   4   5   (YES)
    objectives must be emphasized in the
    pre, early, mid, and late season.

7. Objectives for developing my practices   (NO)   1   2   3   4   5   (YES)
    were drawn from those identified and
    sequenced from pre to late season.

8. The amount of total practice time allo-   (NO)   1   2   3   4   5   (YES)
    cated to each season objective was
    sufficient.

9. My practices would be characterized   (NO)   1   2   3   4   5   (YES)
    by others as orderly, safe, businesslike,
    and enjoyable.

10. Objectives were broken down as neces-   (NO)   1   2   3   4   5   (YES)
    sary to allow players to achieve them in
    several small steps.

Knowledge of the Sport

11. I am familiar with the rationale for   (NO)   1   2   3   4   5   (YES)
    each season objective selected and
    clearly communicated to my
    players its purpose and described
    how it is to be executed.

12. I was able to identify the key elements   (NO)   1   2   3   4   5   (YES)
    of performance necessary for achieve-
    ment of each season objective.

Effective Instruction

13. I clearly communicated (by word and/or   (NO)   1   2   3   4   5   (YES)
    example) the key elements to be learned
    for each objective included in a practice.

14. Practice on an objective was initiated   (NO)   1   2   3   4   5   (YES)
    with a rationale for why the objective
    is important.

15. Instruction did not continue without   (NO)   1   2   3   4   5   (YES)
    players' attention.

16. Practice on an objective provided each   (NO)   1   2   3   4   5   (YES)
    player with many practice trials and
    with specific and positive feedback.

17. During practice, I regularly grouped the   (NO)   1   2   3   4   5   (YES)
    players in accordance with their differ-
    ent practice needs on the season's
    objectives.

18. I used questions to determine if the   (NO)   1   2   3   4   5   (YES)
    players understood the objectives
    and instruction.

19. The players sensed a feeling of control over their own learning which resulted from my emphasis of clearly identifying what they needed to learn and then encouraging maximum effort.   (NO)   1   2   3   4   5   (YES)

20. My practices were pre-planned and clearly associated the use of learning activities, drills, and games with the season objectives.   (NO)   1   2   3   4   5   (YES)

21. I evaluated my practices and incorporated appropriate changes for subsequent practices.   (NO)   1   2   3   4   5   (YES)

Motivation

22. My practices and games resulted in the players achieving many of their goals for participation.   (NO)   1   2   3   4   5   (YES)

23. I taught the players how to realistically define success in terms of effort and self improvement.   (NO)   1   2   3   4   5   (YES)

24. An expert would agree, upon observing my practices, that I use a positive, rather than negative, coaching approach.   (NO)   1   2   3   4   5   (YES)

Communication

25. There was no conflict between the verbal and non-verbal messages I communicated to my players.   (NO)   1   2   3   4   5   (YES)

26. I facilitated communication with the players by being a good listener.   (NO)   1   2   3   4   5   (YES)

27. Accepted behaviors (and consequences of misbehavior) were communicated to players at the beginning of the season.   (NO)   1   2   3   4   5   (YES)

28. Players were involved in developing or confirming team rules.   (NO)   1   2   3   4   5   (YES)

29. Enforcement of team rules was consistent for all players throughout the season.   (NO)   1   2   3   4   5   (YES)

Involvement with Parents

30. Parents of the players were a positive, rather than negative, influence on player's achievement of the season objectives.   (NO)   1   2   3   4   5   (YES)

31. I communicated to the parents my responsibilities and the responsibilities of parents and players to the team.   (NO)   1   2   3   4   5   (YES)

Conditioning

32. The intensity, duration, and frequency of the physical conditioning I used was appropriate for the age of the players.　　(NO)　1　2　3　4　5　(YES)

33. I routinely used a systematic warm-up and cool-down prior to and after practices and games.　　(NO)　1　2　3　4　5　(YES)

34. The physical conditioning aspects of my practices appropriately simulated the requirements of the sport.　　(NO)　1　2　3　4　5　(YES)

Injury Prevention

35. I followed all recommended safety procedures for the use of equipment and facilities.　　(NO)　1　2　3　4　5　(YES)

36. I did not use any contraindicated exercises in my practices.　　(NO)　1　2　3　4　5　(YES)

Care of Common Injuries

37. I established and followed appropriate emergency procedures and simple first aid as needed.　　(NO)　1　2　3　4　5　(YES)

38. I had a well stocked first aid kit at each practice and game, including players' medical history information and medical release forms.　　(NO)　1　2　3　4　5　(YES)

Rehabilitation of Injuries

39. None of the players experienced a recurrence of an injury that could be attributed to inappropriate rehabilitation.　　(NO)　1　2　3　4　5　(YES)

Evaluation

40. I completed an evaluation of player improvement on the season objectives.　　(NO)　1　2　3　4　5　(YES)

41. I identified the coaching actions (or inactions) that appeared most closely related to unmet player expectations.　　(NO)　1　2　3　4　5　(YES)

42. I made the changes in coaching action needed to improve my coaching effect-iveness.　　(NO)　1　2　3　4　5　(YES)

Section VI
Sports Medicine and Training

20
Conditioning Youth Basketball Players

Jean Foley, Ph.D.
Paul Vogel, Ph.D.
Eugene W. Brown, Ph.D.
Karen Garchow, M.A.

QUESTIONS TO CONSIDER

- What are the energy production systems and how important are they to performance in basketball?
- What are muscular strength, power, endurance, and flexibility and how important are they to performance in basketball?
- What are the five principles of training that should be used when conditioning youth basketball players?
- What are interval training, circuit training, and weight training and how can they be used to enhance the conditioning of your athletes?

INTRODUCTION

Aerobics, anaerobics, strength, power, and endurance are some of the many terms that may lend confusion to your understanding of sport conditioning. The goals of this chapter are to provide you with an understanding of the basic principles of conditioning and how these principles apply to basketball. The information will provide you with a more detailed understanding of the process involved in conditioning so that you can appropriately integrate these concepts into your coaching.

Sport conditioning is the participation in physical activity, intended to enhance the energy production and muscular systems of the body, which may supplement and improve the performance of learned sport skills in future play.

ENERGY PRODUCTION SYSTEMS

Anyone who has played or watched basketball knows that much energy is required to participate in the game. Sport scientists have discovered that the body can produce energy for physical activity by two different systems—

the aerobic system and the anaerobic system. Muscle cells, which use the energy, can only store enough reserves for a few seconds of all-out exercise. When this immediate energy supply is used up, new energy is generated by one of these two energy "refill" systems.

Aerobic System

The aerobic system is sometimes called the "endurance" system. In this system, food, the body's fuel, is converted into energy in the presence of oxygen. The aerobic system functions during long-duration, low-intensity exercise. This type of activity allows the body plenty of time to react effectively to the energy needs of the working muscle.

The aerobic system is very efficient because it converts fuel into energy with relatively little waste and produces little unnecessary heat. The aerobic system can function for extended periods of time because it can produce energy from fats, carbohydrates, and protein.

Protein is not a major source of energy for exercise except in cases of extreme starvation.

Carbohydrates are stored in a limited supply in the muscles and liver, and can be used for both aerobic and anaerobic work.

Fats can be used only by the aerobic system. The virtually unlimited supply of this fuel, stored as adipose tissue or fat, is the basis for the long-term functioning of the aerobic system.

In basketball, conditioning the aerobic system is a necessary base for energy system conditioning. The reasons for this are twofold:

1. Basketball has an endurance component.

The basketball player with a well-conditioned aerobic system is not as susceptible to fatigue toward the end of a contest. The delayed onset of fatigue in an aerobically fit athlete can also be a factor in determining how much high quality work can be accomplished during lengthy practice sessions and games.

2. The body learns to "spare" carbohydrates.

As the aerobic system is trained, the body learns to use more fat for fuel and to conserve carbohydrates for high-intensity (anaerobic) activities.

Anaerobic System

High-speed or sprint-type activities require a refilling of the muscle cells' energy supplies at a faster rate than is possible by the aerobic system. In this situation, energy production switches over to a special, faster operating system that converts carbohydrates into energy without using oxygen. This system is called anaerobic, meaning "without oxygen." As with any emergency procedure, there are trade-offs that must be made. In order to gain the advantage of quicker replenishment of energy supplies, the anaerobic system suffers two limitations:

1. Reduced energy yield.

For each sugar (carbohydrate) unit consumed, the anaerobic system can produce only three basic energy units. On the other hand, the aerobic system can produce 39 energy units from each sugar unit. Therefore, the aerobic system yields 13 times more energy (per fuel unit utilized) than the anaerobic system.

2. Lactic-acid build-up.

The anaerobic system produces a byproduct called lactic acid that is not produced by the aerobic system. This chemical quickly builds up in fast-working muscles, causing temporary fatigue, discomfort, and impaired performance. The only way the body can get rid of lactic acid is to slow down and use the aerobic system to convert the lactic acid into usable fuel.

The anaerobic system can produce energy at high speed for about 30 to 90 seconds or at a moderate speed for about 90 seconds to three minutes before the oxygen debt forces the body to slow down so it can switch to the aerobic system. After a recovery period, the anaerobic system can be turned on again to give another short burst of high-speed work. This alternating of sprint work and recovery periods can be continued only until the body's stores of carbohydrates are used up or until the lactic acid removal system can no longer keep up with the rate of anaerobic work.

The energy production system responds to anaerobic training in three major ways:

1. By learning to tolerate larger amounts of lactic acid

The body physiologically adapts to tolerate larger amounts of lactic acid. Therefore, high-intensity work can be maintained for longer periods of time.

2. By reducing the recovery period

The body adapts by reducing the recovery time required before the anaerobic system can be used again.

3. By increasing the rate at which the anaerobic system can operate

Training adaptations increase the speed at which the system can produce energy.

A summary of the two energy production systems is presented in Table 20-1.

Table 20-1. Energy Production Summary.

Energy Production Systems	Characteristics
Aerobic	• produces energy from fuel with oxygen • can use fats, carbohydrates, or protein for fuel • high energy yield per fuel unit • no lactic acid produced • slow rate of energy production
Anaerobic	• produces energy from fuel without oxygen • can only use carbohydrates for fuel • low energy yield per fuel unit • produces lactic acid as a byproduct • fast rate of energy production

USE OF THE ENERGY SYSTEMS IN BASKETBALL

Now that the basic principles of the energy production systems have been presented, let's look at the sport of basketball and determine where its requirements fit on the energy scale from aerobic to anaerobic. In analyzing the relative importance of the two energy systems in basketball, the main concept to keep in mind is that performance time and effort determine the extent to which the aerobic, anaerobic, or both systems are called upon.

Basketball generally can be considered a sport that places a relatively high demand on the anaerobic system and a moderate demand on the aerobic system. The anaerobic system is used during high-intensity work such as sprinting down the court. The aerobic system is used during recovery between the short bursts of activity and during longer periods of low-intensity work. Thus, it is important to condition both of these energy systems to be prepared best for the various demands of basketball.

MUSCULAR SYSTEM

In addition to requiring large amounts of energy, basketball calls upon the muscles to produce forces for various activities. Shooting the ball requires upper arm strength while jumping requires explosive power by the legs so rebounds can be effectively snatched from opponents.

Muscles can produce force only by shortening or contracting. All muscle forces, therefore, are pulling forces and not pushing forces. For example, if you forcefully bend (flex) your knee, the muscles in the back of the thigh (hamstrings) are active. On the other hand, forcefully straightening (extension) the knee results in contraction of the muscles in the front of the thigh (quadriceps). Almost all muscles in the body operate in this paired fashion. As one muscle (or muscle group) shortens to pull a body part in a particular direction, the paired muscle (or muscle group) relaxes and allows the movement to take place. To cause movement in the opposite direction, the muscles simply reverse their roles. If it is desirable to hold a body part in a fixed position, both muscles in the pair exert force to stabilize the joint.

When planning to condition the muscular system for basketball, several factors need to be addressed. In addition to the "muscle pair" concept, the components of muscular power, endurance, and flexibility; age and ability level of the players; and the specific muscular needs for participation in the sport must be carefully considered. These factors are covered in the sections that follow.

Muscular Power

The force that a muscle can apply is called muscular strength. In basketball, many of the movements not only require large muscular forces, but these forces must be exerted during short periods of time. This concept of rate of application of muscular force is called muscular power.

Muscular Endurance

Power is the high-intensity component of muscular conditioning. There is also a low-intensity aspect, the muscular endurance component. Muscular endurance refers to the ability of a muscle to exert a sub-maximal force for a prolonged period of time.

Scientists have shown that there are actually different types of muscle fibers within a muscle. Some of these fibers, called fast-twitch or white fibers, are used primarily for brief, powerful muscular movements. Other fibers, called slow-twitch or red fibers, are mainly used for longer, low-intensity movements. As with the aerobic and anaerobic energy systems, the power and endurance components of the muscular system require different types of conditioning.

Flexibility

Flexibility refers to the range of motion of a joint or the range through which the muscle groups can move the bones of a joint without causing injury.

Stretching exercises, used as part of a conditioning program to maintain or increase flexibility, are often ignored by coaches and athletes. However, flexibility exercises are an important component of a basketball conditioning program. They may reduce the occurrence of certain injuries and enhance the performance of certain techniques.

• Reducing injury potential

When muscles are worked hard, there is a temporary breakdown in their tissue. This breakdown is quickly repaired, but the muscle fibers become shortened unless they are stretched. A shortened, inflexible muscle on one side of the joint won't be able to readily stretch when its muscle pair on the opposite side of the joint fully contracts. The result may be a muscle tear (strain) or damage to the connective tissues of the joint (sprain). Flexibility exercises may reduce the occurrence of these types of injuries.

• Enhancing performance

Lack of flexibility may inhibit or prevent the performance of certain techniques. For example, limited trunk flexibility may retard a player's ability to make a long inbounds pass. This is only one of the many examples of the influence of flexibility on performance.

USE OF THE MUSCULAR SYSTEM IN BASKETBALL

Picture again a typical game of basketball. How would you rate the three muscular factors of power, endurance, and flexibility in terms of their importance to successful performance? (See Figure 20-1.) Clearly, most of the actions in basketball can be characterized as powerful movements. Along with powerful, high-force actions comes a high risk of injury, so flexibility should also be a high priority in conditioning for basketball. Finally, for the same reasons aerobic fitness is necessary in conditioning the energy systems for basketball, a muscular endurance base is required by the repetitive nature of the movements.

How to Condition for Basketball

Now that we have examined conditioning, we can turn to the problem of how to develop programs to promote the kind of conditioning needed for basketball.

You should now have a basic knowledge of the underlying concepts of conditioning. The contrasts between the aerobic and anaerobic ends of the energy production continuum have been described. Three critical aspects of the muscular system continuum (power, endurance, and flexibility) have been explained. Both the energy production systems and the muscular system have been analyzed in relation to their specific applications to basketball. Now we come to the practical application of this information. How can you as a coach use the discoveries of the sport scientists to develop better basketball players?

Five Principles of Training

The following five principles of training should be used as guidelines for conditioning

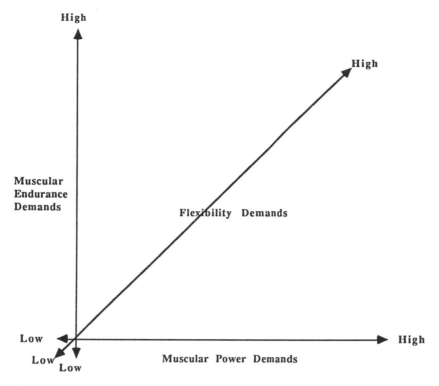

Where should the various positions in basketball be placed?

Figure 20-1. Graph showing the continuum of the muscular system demands.

both the energy production and muscular systems.

1. Warm-Up/Cool-Down

Before beginning a training session or game, use jogging, calisthenics, basketball-specific exercises, and stretching to prepare the body for more strenuous activity. A program for accomplishing this goal, as well as cooling down the body after strenuous exercise, is outlined in Supplement 20-1. Warm-up activities increase the breathing rate, heart rate, and muscle temperature to exercise levels. Warm-up also causes cartilage pads in the joints to absorb fluids, thereby increasing their shock-absorbing capabilities. It is a period in which the athlete becomes more aware of his/her surroundings (the court, bleachers, etc.) and gradually reacquainted with the demands of more vigorous activity to follow. Providing the opportunity for your athletes to become aware of their surroundings and sensitive to the demands of the sport are

important factors in reducing the potential for injury.

Proper warm-up can thus improve performance and reduce the likelihood of injury to the athlete. Note that the warm-up should not be used as a conditioning period. Having your players exercise too hard during warm-ups defeats the purpose of this period and may cause, rather than prevent, injuries. Stretching exercises are appropriate after a warm-up.

As the age of the athlete group increases, a greater amount of time is needed to warm-up for exercises. Seven-year-olds may only need five minutes to warm up, whereas 18-year-olds may need as much as 10 to 15 minutes of warm-up exercises. It is, however, important to include a warm-up interval before practices and games even with the youngest athletes because this proper approach to training is more likely to persist as they grow older.

After a workout session or game, the body should be cooled down. This process should include light, aerobic activity (e.g., jogging) to help the body clear out any remaining lactic acid from the muscles and to reduce the pooling of blood in the extremities. This will reduce soreness and speed the recovery process in preparation for the next day's activities. The cool-down should also be followed by stretching exercises, as emphasized earlier, to help maintain flexibility.

2. Overload

In order to cause a change to take place in the energy production and muscular systems, a stress must be applied to these systems. Repeatedly demanding more than usual of a bodily system causes the system to respond by changing to a state in which it can more easily handle that stress. Overload does not mean placing an impossibly heavy work load on the system, but rather, asking the system to work harder than it is normally accustomed to doing, without reaching a work load at which injury may occur.

Regulation of the overload is the basis of all conditioning programs.

There are five factors that can be manipulated to produce an exercise overload within a workout:

• *Load*

This is the resistance to muscular force. It can be the body, a body part, or any object, such as a weight, which is to be moved. Systematic variation of resistance (load) can be used to create an exercise overload to enhance the development of muscular strength.

• *Repetitions*

This is the number of times muscular force is applied in moving a load. Conditioning of the aerobic energy-production system and enhanced muscular endurance result from progressively increasing the number of repetitions of muscular contraction.

• *Duration*

This is the length of time muscular force is applied in performing a set (bout) of repetitions. Similar to a systematic increase in repetitions, increasing duration of exercise can be used to

enhance the aerobic energy-production system and muscular endurance.

• *Frequency*

The rate of exercise (number of repetitions for a given time unit) is the frequency. As frequency increases, exercises shift from having a conditioning effect on the aerobic energy-production system and muscular endurance to having a conditioning effect on the anaerobic energy-production system and muscular power.

• *Rest*

The recovery interval between bouts of exercise, during which a muscle or muscle group is moderately inactive to inactive, is the rest period.* Note that rest for the anaerobic system also may occur when the frequency of exercise is reduced so the demands of the exercise are placed upon the aerobic system.

3. Progression

The overload principle must be applied in progressive stages. Conditioning must start with an exercise intensity the body can handle, allowing time for recovery from the physical stress before progressing to an increased work level. Overloading your athletes too rapidly or failing to allow sufficient time for them to recover between workouts can cause injury or illness rather than enhance their fitness.

A good example to keep in mind is the method by which muscles get stronger. A training overload actually causes a temporary breakdown of the muscle fibers, which are then repaired to an even stronger state. If the muscles are overloaded again before the repair period is over, the result may be further damage instead of adaptation. Coaches should be familiar with the signs of overtraining as outlined in Chapter 22 and should monitor their athletes closely to make sure they are progressing at a rate their bodies can handle.

4. Specificity

In order to activate the energy production systems, the muscular system must also be ac-

*Longer rests are required for short, high-intensity exercise bouts. Shorter rests are required for long, low-intensity exercise bouts.

tivated. Even though this relationship exists, it is important to carefully consider the desired nature of conditioning when selecting physical activity to achieve these goals.

Physical exercises have specific conditioning effects. Stretching the hip joints will have little, if any, influence on increasing the power of the muscles that move these joints. Exercises to strengthen the calf muscles will not increase the strength of the stomach muscles. Similarly, a well-conditioned gymnast is not likely to possess the type of fitness required for basketball. Thus, when planning a conditioning program, it is important to first assess the demands of basketball on your players in order to select exercises and manipulate the overload factors to help condition your players to meet these specific demands.

The specific components of the energy and muscular systems can be conditioned by application of the following general guidelines to overload these systems. However, these guidelines must be applied in conditioning the energy and muscular systems associated with the specific demands of basketball.

Training the Energy Production Systems

- Aerobic system—use endurance activities involving moderate exercise intensity of large body segments or the whole body. Some examples include running and dribbling the basketball, swimming laps, running, and bicycling long distances. Running and dribbling the basketball is more desirable for basketball than the other aerobic activities because it has a more specific training effect for the sport.

- Anaerobic system—use "sprint" type activities involving very intense exercise of large body segments or the whole body. The same exercises, as listed for aerobic training, are appropriate activities for anaerobic training. However, distances must be reduced and the intensity increased. Again, sprint dribbling would have a more specific training effect for basketball. By dribbling, players would be concomitantly developing their techniques along with anaerobic conditioning.

Training the Muscular System

- Power—use exercises, by specific muscle groups, involving the rapid application of relatively large forces and few repetitions.
- Endurance—use exercises, by specific muscle groups, involving the application of relatively small forces and many repetitions.
- Flexibility—use slow and sustained (six to 30 seconds) stretching of specific muscle groups to the point of slight discomfort. Don't bounce!

5. Reversibility

It is not enough to plan and carry out a developmental conditioning program. Once an athlete's body attains a certain fitness level, a maintenance program is necessary to prevent the conditioning benefits from being lost.

Studies on athletes have shown that even starting players will experience a decrease in fitness level during the competitive season unless provisions are made to maintain conditioning throughout the season. The maintenance program does not have to be as frequent or as intense as the build-up program, but without a minimal program of this type, the hard-earned fitness will gradually be lost.

METHODS FOR CONDITIONING

Regulation of the exercise overload is the basis for all conditioning programs. As previously stated, this can be accomplished by manipulating the factors of load, repetition, duration, frequency, and rest. There are three distinct training methods that can be used to effectively manipulate these factors to enhance conditioning. These methods are *interval training, circuit training,* and *weight training.*

1. Interval Training

This type of training was first used in training runners. Interval training, however, has been used in many sports, including basketball. Interval training involves a period of vigorous exercise followed by a recovery period. It functions by using aerobic and anaerobic activities to condition the energy production systems. By gradually increasing the duration, intensity, and number of exercise bouts and by decreasing the rest interval between bouts, an overload can be achieved.

Interval training can be adapted to basketball by alternating bouts of intense practice on basic skills, such as dribbling, with recovery periods. In fact, a series of practice sessions can be structured with an interval training basis. The first session would consist of relatively low-intensity exercises of short duration with relatively long rest intervals; whereas, in subsequent practice sessions, the exercise intensity and duration would be increased and the number and duration of rest intervals would be decreased. It should be noted that in interval training, rest periods can be used for rest, water breaks, strategy sessions, team organization, and light aerobic activity.

The specific conditioning components enhanced by an interval training program depend upon the nature of the exercises included in the program. A systematic interval training program can improve the energy production systems (aerobic and anaerobic) as well as the strength and endurance of specific muscle groups that are exercised. A year-round interval training program for highly skilled and motivated players who are 14 years of age or older is included in Supplement 20-2.

2. Circuit Training

This type of training involves participation in a variety of activities in rapid succession. These activities are conducted at various locations (stations) around the basketball court. The team is divided so that an equal number of players are at each station. When the circuit begins, all players attempt to perform their best at the tasks assigned to each station within a set time. Successive stations should differ in the demand they place on the body. For example, an intense arm exercise should not be followed by a shooting drill. Recovery occurs as the groups rotate, within a specified time interval, to the next station and as subsequent stations differ in their demands upon the body.

In circuit training an exercise overload is produced by:

- increasing the number of stations in the circuit
- increasing the number of repetitions or work intensity at one or more stations
- increasing the time for exercise at each station
- increasing the number of times the circuit is completed
- decreasing the recovery period between stations

The variety of activities that can be included in a circuit provides the opportunity to be flexible in creating different and specific exercise overloads as well as simultaneously enhancing skill. Supplement 20-3 contains an example of a basketball training circuit and recording form, which can be photocopied as is, as well as a blank form upon which you can implement your own training circuit to meet the specific needs of your players.

3. Weight Training

This type of training involves the lifting of weights to produce an exercise overload. In weight training, a variety of sub-maximal lifts are performed to produce increased strength, power, and endurance in the specific muscle groups that are exercised. In general, weight training involves applying the "Five Principles of Training" to produce increases in muscular strength.

Following the "Five Principles of Training," the first part of a weight training routine is the warm-up and stretching program. The weight resistance is the overload, which is increased in a progression as the athlete's workout record indicates gains in strength. Analysis of the strength requirements of basketball (specificity) has resulted in the list of exercises outlined in Supplement 20-2. The cool-down and post-lifting stretching routine decreases muscle soreness and prevents loss of flexibility. Finally, once strength gains are achieved, the maintenance program must be used to avoid reversal of strength increases acquired during the developmental program.

In weight training, an exercise overload can be produced by varying the:

- exercise load
- number of repetitions per set

- frequency of exercise during each set
- number of sets
- length of rest interval between exercise sets

The exercise load determines the number of repetitions of an exercise an athlete can perform during each set. Generally, no fewer than eight repetitions per set of each exercise are recommended when attempting to increase muscular strength for basketball. However, if increased muscular endurance is the goal of a particular weight training exercise, (a) the load should be decreased to permit a much greater number of repetitions, (b) the number of sets should be increased to three or more, and (c) the rest intervals between sets should be decreased. On the other hand, if increase in muscular power is the goal, this can be achieved by rapidly and repeatedly lifting a relatively heavy load eight to 12 repetitions per set.

It should be noted that it is possible to train some muscle groups to increase power and others to increase endurance. The degree to which either component increases depends upon the specific nature of the overload condition.

Several factors should be carefully considered before engaging your players in a weight training program. These factors include:

- Age of the athletes

A weight training program for basketball is not recommended for players under 14 years of age.

- Level of interest

A weight training program is not an essential element for participants in a recreational league. However, a weight training program can be beneficial to highly skilled players who are interested in participating in a very competitive league.

- Availability of facilities and equipment

Sites and equipment for weight training may not be accessible. Before encouraging your athletes to participate in a weight training program, some investigation of availability is needed.

- Availability of qualified adults

Before encouraging your players to participate in a particular weight training program, a qualified adult must be available to supervise the weight room and to provide instruction in proper spotting and performance techniques for each of the suggested exercises.

Because of the great variety of weight training equipment and the availability of many books and guides to weight training, only general guidelines are presented here. A suggested program of weight training exercises appropriate for the highly skilled basketball player who is 14 years of age or older is included in Supplement 20-2. These exercises can be done using either free weights or weight machines. The guidelines given cover training schedules and how to fit a weight training program into the overall plan of the season. Specific techniques and explanations of weight training exercises can be found in manuals available in most local bookstores. Some references are:

- *Strength Training by the Experts* by Daniel P. Riley (2nd edition, Leisure Press, 1982). Covers a variety of equipment, including free weights, Nautilus, and Universal. Explains which muscle groups are used in each exercise.
- *Weightlifting for Beginners* by Bill Reynolds (Contemporary Books, 1982). Designed primarily for free weights and at-home weight training.

ECONOMICAL TRAINING

The relative importance of conditioning for basketball must be put into perspective with the importance of meeting the cognitive, psychosocial, strategy, and sport techniques needs of your players. As a basketball coach, you must address all of these needs, to varying degrees, during practices and games. However, because of the limited amount of time available to meet the needs of your players, whenever possible, you should plan activities that simultaneously meet needs in more than one area. This approach is referred to as economical training. If practice sessions are carefully planned, it is possible to devise activities that simultaneously meet needs in more than one area. For example, the intensity, duration, and structure of a dribbling drill could be organized to enhance components of conditioning and strategy, as well as techniques of dribbling.

It is easier to get 14-year-olds in condition to play than it is to make up for the years in which they were not taught the techniques of the game.

The concept of economical training is presented here because many coaches erroneously set aside blocks of time within their practices for conditioning-only activities. Push-ups, sit-ups, sprints, and distance running are typical of what is included in these conditioning-only blocks of time. With youth players who have not achieved a high level of mastery of the techniques of the game, conditioning-only activities are not recommended. Practice time needs to be spent on learning the techniques and strategies of the game of basketball, with conditioning an accompanying outcome as the result of planned economical training. As players develop a higher level of mastery of the techniques of basketball, conditioning-only activities could be included in practices. However, they should be made as closely related to basketball as possible.

SUMMARY

In this chapter you have learned how the energy and muscular systems work, how they are used in basketball, and how to condition these systems. Although separate conditioning-only workouts were not recommended for the under-14 age group, guidelines were given for incorporating the principles of training into the regular practices for the double purpose of skill improvement and enhanced conditioning (economical training). Athletes begin to require and benefit from supplementary programs for conditioning the energy and muscular systems around the age of 14. Examples of such programs have been provided, with guidelines for varying the training at different points in the year. Suggested schedules and workout routines to guide this training are provided in the supplements.

A basic knowledge of the scientific principles of physical conditioning will help you design effective practices and training sessions. It will also help you communicate to your athletes the importance of each type of conditioning activity you use. Conveying this understanding to your players will not only make them more knowledgeable, but will also help them develop good lifelong habits and attitudes towards exercise and fitness.

SUGGESTED READINGS

Fox, E.L. (1979). *Sports physiology*. Philadelphia: W.B. Saunders.
Lamb, D.R. (1984). *Physiology of exercise* (2nd ed.). New York: Macmillan.
Sharkey, B. (1984). *Physiology of fitness* (2nd ed.). Champaign, IL: Human Kinetics Publishers.
Stone, W.V., & Knoll, W.K. (1978). *Sports conditioning and weight training*. Boston: Allyn and Bacon.

Supplement 20-1.
Warm-Up, Cool-Down, and Stretching Activities for Basketball

Introduction

The players' preparation for each practice and game should begin with a warm-up session and should be followed by a cool-down period. Warm-up and cool-down activities should be conducted at light to moderate intensities and should be followed by stretching exercises.

Warm-Up

Warm-up activities should be performed to increase the breathing rate, heart rate, and muscle temperature to exercise levels. These are done to prepare the body for the demands of subsequent strenuous activities. Additionally, warm-ups enhance the players' awareness for their surroundings. Warm-ups can also be used as a valuable introduction in setting the tone of the players' attitude toward the activity to follow. Warm-ups for sport should involve the regions of the body upon which more intense exercise demands will be placed during training for and participation in the sport. Thus, with basketball, virtually all regions of the body should be prepared. The following categories included some examples of warm-ups that can be used for basketball.

Light Aerobic/General Warm Ups

- Jogging
- Jogging in place
- Jumping jacks

Light Aerobic/Basketball-Specific Warm-ups

- Jogging while dribbling the ball
- Partner passing drills using various types of passes

Body Region-Specific Warm-ups

- Neck rolls—The head is rolled from shoulder, to chest, to opposite shoulder, and the procedure is reversed and repeated. (Note: Do not make complete head circle. There is potential for compression of the vertebrae when the neck is hyperextended.)
- Shoulder circles—With arms horizontal and to the side of the body, small circular rotations of the arms are made. These circles are gradually increased. This pattern is then repeated; however, the arms are rotated in the opposite direction.
- Trunk circles—While standing with the feet shoulder-width apart and the hands on the hips, the trunk is moved in a circular manner. (Note: Avoid an excessive arch of the low-back by keeping the head in an upright position.)

Stretching

Stretching should be performed by slowly and gently extending each muscle group and joint to the point of slight discomfort. This position should be held for 6 to 30 seconds. The stretch should then be released and repeated in the same manner two or more times. Bouncing or fast, jerky movements are inappropriate in that they activate the muscles' stretch reflex mechanism and, therefore, limit rather than enhance flexibility.

Stretching exercises, used as part of a basketball conditioning program to maintain or increase flexibility, may reduce the occurrence of certain injuries, such as muscle strains and joint sprains, and may enhance performance of certain techniques. Because basketball involves virtually all major muscle groups and joints of the body, a variety of flexibility exercises, targeted at these regions, should be a part of each pre- and post-practice and game. The following flexibility exercises are some examples that are appropriate for basketball.

- Calf stretch—With the legs straddled in a forward-backward alignment, the knee of the back leg is bent while the entire sole of the back foot maintains contact with the ground. By switching the position of the feet, the other calf is stretched.
- Kneeling quad stretch—From a kneeling position, the hip is pressed forward. By switching the positions of the legs, the other quadriceps muscle and hip joint are stretched. Note that this exercise also stretches the trunk.
- Seated straddle (groin stretch)—From a seated position with the legs straddled, the trunk is moved forward. The head should be kept upright to reduce pressure on the lower back.
- Butterfly (groin stretch)—In a seated position, place the soles of the feet together with the knees bent no more than 90 degrees. Grasp the ankles with the hands and apply pressure with the elbows to the inside of the legs to rotate the legs outward. Keep the back straight with the head in an upright position.
- Trunk and hip stretch—From a supine position, both arms are placed 90 degrees from the trunk. The head is turned toward one of the outstretched arms while bringing the opposite leg (90 degrees from the trunk) over the midline of the body and toward the ground. This exercise should be performed on both sides.

- Shoulder stretch—Bend the elbow and position the arm behind the head. The hand of the opposite arm grasps the bent elbow and slowly pulls it toward the midline of the trunk. To stretch the other shoulder, the roles of the arms are switched.

Cool-Down

The importance of cooling down has not received sufficient emphasis among coaches of young athletes. Cool-down sessions are infrequently used to end a practice session and are rarely used following a game. A cool-down period helps to:

- clear out lactic acid accumulated in the muscles
- reduce the pooling of blood in the extremities
- prevent the loss of flexibility that may accompany intense muscular exercise

Like the warm-up, cool-down activities should include movements similar to those included in the practice or game. Thus, the warm-up and stretching activities, previously listed, are appropriate for the cool-down. Have your athletes perform the cool-down exercises first, then the stretching activities.

Supplement 20-2.
Year-Round Conditioning Program

Introduction

This supplement contains information on a year-round conditioning program. It is directed at conditioning the energy production system, through a program of interval training, and the muscular system, through a weight training program. This year-round program is appropriate for the highly motivated player who is 14 years of age or older. It is for players who have chosen to concentrate on basketball and wish to maximize their performance through enhanced conditioning on a year-round basis. This program is NOT for beginning players and/or players below the age of 14 years who would derive greater benefit by devoting their time to learning and perfecting the techniques of basketball.

Interval Training Program

Interval training is a method for developing the anaerobic energy-production system while maintaining and/or enhancing a previously established base of aerobic fitness. This type of training uses alternating periods of short-duration, high-intensity anaerobic ("sprint"

type) exercises with longer periods of moderate- to low-intensity aerobic exercises.

The training outlines provided in this supplement can be used with different modes of exercise, depending on individual preference and the availability of equipment and facilities. Dribbling, jogging and running, and/or bicycling are modes of exercise suggested for interval training in basketball. Specific distances are not indicated in this supplement because of the variety of exercises possible and because of variations in individual fitness. All players should, however, maintain a record of distances covered on individual forms provided in this supplement so their progress can be assessed. Distance records can be kept in yards, meters, miles, kilometers, blocks, or laps.

An important concept to keep in mind when planning an interval training program is that the program should progress to a point where it places a similar aerobic and anaerobic demand on the athlete as that of a hard-played game of basketball. This type of work load in an interval training program conditions the athletes to the demands they will be confronted with during competition. Regulation of the duration and intensity of exercise, as well as the rest intervals, are the components of an interval training program that can be manipulated to achieve the desired exercise levels.

The interval training program included in this supplement is divided into five phases. These phases are briefly described and followed by forms that can be used by athletes to keep records of their progress.

- Pre-season Aerobic/Anaerobic Transition Program—This four-week program is used to prepare athletes for high intensity anaerobic conditioning after they have developed a good aerobic fitness base (see Table 20-1s).
- Pre-season Anaerobic Developmental Interval-Training Program—This is an eight-week program to be started 10 weeks before the first game. The program should be preceded by anaerobic training and the four-week Aerobic/Anaerobic Transition Program (see Table 20-2s).
- In-Season Anaerobic Maintenance Program— This program should be completed once, a week starting two weeks before the first game and continuing through the end of the season (see Table 20-3s).
- Post-Season Aerobic Program—This program involves rhythmical, low intensity aerobic activities such as dribbling, jogging, running, and bicycling for three days per week to enhance aerobic fitness (see Table 20-4s).
- Post-Season Anaerobic Maintenance Program—This program should be done once a week to maintain anaerobic fitness levels during the aerobic phase of off-season conditioning (see Table 20-4s).

Weight Training Program

Weight training for basketball should focus on the development of muscular power, or the ability to quickly exert large muscular force. The load should be lifted explosively, then returned to the starting position slowly. Generally, the larger muscle groups should be exercised first. Also, the same muscle groups should not be exercised in succession. Table 20-5s contains weight-lifting exercises that can be used to meet the specific requirements of basketball. They are arranged in an appropriate order.

Since the weight training exercises listed can be done using a variety of equipment, details of technique and an explanation of procedures for each exercise will not be given here. Many good guides for weight training are available in local bookstores. A few examples of such guides that contain explanations of correct technique and details for each specific exercise are:

- *Sports Conditioning and Weight Training* by William J. Stone and William A. Kroll (Allyn & Bacon, 1978). This book is designed to offer sound, systematic training programs for those who wish to apply strength and conditioning techniques to specific sports.
- *Strength Training by the Experts* by Daniel P. Riley (2nd edition, Leisure Press, 1982). This book covers a variety of lifting equipment, including free weights, Universal equipment, and Nautilus equipment, and explains which muscle groups are used in each exercise.
- *Weightlifting for Beginners* by Bill Reynolds (Contemporary Books, 1982). This book is designed primarily for free weights and at-home weightlifting.

Year-round conditioning for muscular power can be divided into three parts: pre-season (developmental), in-season (maintenance), and post-season (developmental). Pre-season and post-season workouts have improvement in muscular power as their goals. In-season workouts are done less frequently and should be used to maintain the muscular fitness developed during the off-season.

Pre-season Weight Training

Athletes new to weight training should start a developmental program at least three months before the first competition. Overloaded muscles require about 48 hours to repair and recover sufficiently, so a lifting schedule of three days per week with a minimum of one day off between workouts will give best results.

For the first one to two weeks, the athlete should do one exercise eight to 12 times (repetitions), then move on to the next exercise until each exercise in the weight training program has been covered. This series of repetitions of each exercise is called a set.

Table 20-1s. Pre-Season Aerobic/Anaerobic Transition Program

(To be started 14 weeks before the first game)

Name_____

The information at the top of each week's schedule specifies a suggested duration and intensity of the workout for that week. Space is provided for a coach or player to write an alternate workout for each week. The frequency of workouts is three per week, on an every-other-day basis. Each workout should be preceded and followed by stretching exercises. Work intensity is specified in terms of percentage of effort as follows:

LM	= Light to Moderate	**50% of maximum effort***
H	= Hard	**80% of maximum** effort
S	= Sprint	**100% of maximum** effort

For example, **3x(2:H,2:LM)** means do three sets of (two minutes at 80% of effort followed by two minutes at 50% of effort). For each workout completed, record the **date** and the **total distance covered.**

Pre-season Aerobic/Anaerobic Transition Program				
WEEK		**Day 1**	**Day 2**	**Day 3**
1	**[9:LM,3x(2:H,2:LM),9:LM]** alternate workout: [			]
	Date:			
	Distance:			
2	**[7:LM,4x(2:H,2:LM),7:LM]** alternate workout: [			]
	Date:			
	Distance:			
3	**[5:LM,5x(2:H,2:LM),5:LM]** alternate workout: [			]
	Date:			
	Distance:			
4	**[3:LM,6x(2:H,2:LM),3:LM]** alternate workout: [			]
	Date:			
	Distance:			
TOTAL TIME FOR EACH WORKOUT = 30 MINUTES				

*If the intensity of the hard and sprint portions of the exercise intervals cannot be maintained, the athlete should reduce the intensity of the light to moderate intervals.

Table 20-2s. Pre-Season Anaerobic Developmental Interval Training Program

(To be started 10 weeks before the first game)

Name_____

The information at the top of each week's schedule specifies a suggested duration and intensity of the workout for that week. Space is provided for a coach or player to write an alternate workout for each week. The frequency of workouts is three per week, on an every-other-day basis. Each workout should be preceded and followed by stretching exercises. Work intensity is specified in terms of percentage of effort as follows:

LM	= Light to Moderate	50% of maximum effort*	
H	= Hard	80% of maximum effort	
S	= Sprint	100% of maximum effort	

For example, 4x(:20S,2:LM) means do four sets of (20 seconds at maximum effort followed by two minutes at 50% of effort). For each workout completed, record the **date** and the **total distance covered.**

	Pre-season Anaerobic Developmental Interval Training Program			
WEEK		**Day 1**	**Day 2**	**Day 3**
1	[4:LM,2x(1:H,2:LM),4x(:20S,:40LM),4:LM]			
	alternate workout: [		]	
	Date/Distance			
2	[4:LM,2x(1:H,2:LM),5x(:20S,:40LM),4:LM]			
	alternate workout: [		]	
	Date/Distance			
3	[4:LM,2x(1:H,2:LM),6x(:20S,:40LM),4:LM]			
	alternate workout: [		]	
	Date/Distance			
4	[4:LM,2x(1:H,2:LM),7x(:20S,:40LM),4:LM]			
	alternate workout: [		]	
	Date/Distance			
5	[4:LM,3x(1:H,2:LM),8x(:20S,:40LM),4:LM]			
	alternate workout: [		]	
	Date/Distance			
6	[4:LM,3x(1:H,2:LM),9x(:20S,:40LM),4:LM]			
	alternate workout: [		]	
	Date/Distance			
7	[4:LM,3x(1:H,2:LM),6x(:10S,:20LM),2:LM,6x(:10S,:20LM),4:LM]			
	alternate workout: [		]	
	Date/Distance			
8	[4:LM,3x(1:H,2:LM),8x(:10S,:20LM),2:LM,8x(:10S,:20LM),4:LM]			
	alternate workout: [		]	
	Date/Distance			

*If the intensity of the hard and sprint portions of the exercise intervals cannot be maintained, the athlete should reduce the intensity of the light to moderate intervals.

Table 20-3s. In-Season Anaerobic Maintenance Program

(To be started two weeks before the first game)

Name_____

A suggested workout is provided at the top of the In-Season Aerobic Maintenance Program form. Space is provided for the coach or player to write an alternate workout. The frequency of workouts is one per week. Workouts should be completed at the end of a practice but not on a day before a game. Each workout should be preceded and followed by stretching exercises. Intensity is specified in terms of percentage of effort as follows:

LM	= Light to Moderate	50% of maximum effort*
H	= Hard	80% of maximum effort
S	= Sprint	100% of maximum effort

For example, **3x(2:H,2:LM)** means do three sets of (two minutes at 80% of effort followed by two minutes at 50% of effort). For each workout completed, record the **date** and the **total distance covered.**

In-Season Anaerobic Maintenance Program					
[2:LM,2x(1:H,2:LM),2x(:20S,:40LM),8x(:10S,:20LM),4:LM]					
alternate workout: [				]	
MONTH		WEEK				

MONTH		1	2	3	4	5
1	Date:					
	Distance:					
2	Date:					
	Distance:					
3	Date:					
	Distance:					
4	Date:					
	Distance:					
5	Date:					
	Distance:					

*If the intensity of the hard and sprint portions of the exercise intervals cannot be maintained, the athlete should reduce the intensity of the light to moderate intervals.

Table 20-4s. Post-Season Aerobic and Anaerobic Maintenance Program

(To be started two to four weeks after the last game)

AEROBIC PROGRAM

Aerobic capabilities should be developed during the post-season to provide the base for building the more intense anaerobic work capacity required for top performance during the season. Aerobic work combined with muscular strength/power work on alternate days is a good variation from the typical season routine. In the post-season time period, the development of aerobic capacity and muscular strength/power become primary, rather than secondary, objectives.

Begin three days of aerobic activity (dribbling, jogging and running, bicycling, or other rhythmical, low intensity, long duration activities) alternated with three days of weight training. Progress up to 40 minutes of continuous aerobic activity and then work on increasing the speed or intensity at which the 40 minutes of work is done. Each workout should be preceded and followed by stretching exercises. Record the date and workout time on the "Year-Round Conditioning Checklist" in the portion of the checklist devoted to post-season.

ANAEROBIC MAINTENANCE PROGRAM

A suggested workout is provided at the top of the Post-Season Anaerobic Maintenance Program form. Space is also provided for the coach or player to write an alternate workout. The post-season anaerobic maintenance program should be done once a week. It should not be completed on the same day as an aerobic workout. Each workout should be preceded and followed by stretching exercises. Intensity is specified in terms of percentage of effort as follows:

LM	= Light to Moderate	50% of maximum effort*
H	= Hard	80% of maximum effort
S	= Sprint	100% of maximum effort

For example, **4x(:20S,:40LM)** means do four sets of (20 seconds at maximum effort followed by 40 seconds at 50% of effort). For each workout completed, record the **date** and the **total distance covered.**

<table>
<tr><td colspan="7">Post-Season Anaerobic Maintenance Program</td></tr>
<tr><td colspan="7">[4:LM,2x(1:H,2:LM),4x(:20S,:40LM),4x(:20S,:40LM),4:LM]</td></tr>
<tr><td colspan="7">alternate workout: [   ]</td></tr>
<tr><td colspan="2" rowspan="2">MONTH</td><td colspan="5">WEEK</td></tr>
<tr><td>1</td><td>2</td><td>3</td><td>4</td><td>5</td></tr>
<tr><td rowspan="2">1</td><td>Date:</td><td></td><td></td><td></td><td></td><td></td></tr>
<tr><td>Distance:</td><td></td><td></td><td></td><td></td><td></td></tr>
<tr><td rowspan="2">2</td><td>Date:</td><td></td><td></td><td></td><td></td><td></td></tr>
<tr><td>Distance:</td><td></td><td></td><td></td><td></td><td></td></tr>
<tr><td rowspan="2">3</td><td>Date:</td><td></td><td></td><td></td><td></td><td></td></tr>
<tr><td>Distance:</td><td></td><td></td><td></td><td></td><td></td></tr>
<tr><td rowspan="2">4</td><td>Date:</td><td></td><td></td><td></td><td></td><td></td></tr>
<tr><td>Distance:</td><td></td><td></td><td></td><td></td><td></td></tr>
</table>

*If the intensity of the hard and sprint portions of the exercise intervals cannot be maintained, the athlete should reduce the intensity of the light to moderate intervals.

Table 20-5s. Conditioning activities for basketball players.

Order	Exercise	Comment
1	Neck flexion	This exercise can be done on specially designed weight machines or can be accomplished by wrapping a towel around the forehead and having a partner provide resistance.
2	Squat lift	The angle at the back of the knee should not be allowed to become less than 90 degrees. An upright position of the head should be maintained, and the back should be kept as close to vertical as possible throughout the lift. Trained spotters must be used. If using free weights, wrap a towel or foam pad around the center of the bar to lessen the discomfort of the bar across the back of the neck.
3	Bench press	Trained spotters must be used.
4	Bent knee sit-ups	A weight can be held high on the chest and/or the sit-up can be done on an incline to increase resistance. The feet should be held down by a partner or restraining structure.
5	Finger flexion	Grip strength exercises can be done with a spring hand gripper
6	Hip abduction	This exercise can be done on a specially designed weight machine or by having a partner provide resistance. Both legs should be exercised.
7	Bent over row	The head should be supported, and the back should be in a horizontal position.
8	Neck extension	This exercise can be done on specially designed weight machines or can be accomplished by wrapping a towel around the head and having a partner provide resistance.
9	Hip abduction	This exercise can be done on a specially designed weight machine or by having a partner provide resistance. Both legs should be exercised.
10	Toe rise	If using free weights, wrap a towel or foam pad around the bar to lessen the discomfort of the bar across the back of the neck. Trained spotters must be used. A block of wood can be used under the toes to increase the range through which the muscles must exert force in lifting the body.
11	Arm curl	A rocking motion of the body should not be used to aid the arms in lifting the resistance.
12	Knee flexion	
13	Lat pull-down	Keep the hips extended and do not use hip flexion to aid in the pull-down motion.
14	Back hyperextension	A partner or restraining structure is needed to hold the legs down.
15	Knee extension	
16	Reverse forearm curl	

The appropriate weight load or resistance is a load the athlete can lift properly a minimum of eight times, but is not so light that it can be lifted more than 12 times. Some experimenting with weight loads will be necessary to determine correct starting weights for each exercise. Once these weight loads are determined, they should be recorded on the Weight Training Program Checklist included in this supplement (see Table 20-6s).

During this first phase of the weight training program (two weeks), the athlete should master the proper lifting technique and work through the initial muscle soreness that accompanies learning the correct weight loads. After this initial phase, the work can be increased to two sets while maintaining the initial weight levels for eight to 12 repetitions per exercise. Two sets of the same exercise are completed before the next exercise is done. This second phase also lasts two weeks.

In the third phase, three full sets are done during each workout. Three full sets of eight to 12 repetitions on an exercise are completed, then the next exercise is done. This phase should last for eight or more weeks and should end about two weeks before the first competition. It is during this third phase that weight levels are adjusted upward as strength increases. This information is summarized in Table 20-7s.

When 12 repetitions of a given exercise have been completed for each of the three sets for two successive workouts, the weight load for that exercise can be increased to the next level for the following workout. The athlete should be able to do a minimum of eight repetitions for each of the three sets at the new weight level. If this is not possible, a smaller weight increase is indicated.

In-Season Weight Training

Strength improvement is the goal of the preseason weight training developmental program. Maintenance of the increased strength is accomplished by a scaled-down in-season weight training program that should begin about two weeks before the first game. If weight training is done only during the preseason period, the strength gains will gradually be lost as the season progresses. Research has shown that a weight training maintenance program of one to two workouts per week will prevent the reversal of strength gains. Performance will not be hampered by in-season weight training if three general rules are followed:

- Lifting should be limited to once or twice a week, with two to three days between weight training workouts.
- Do not schedule weight training workouts for the day before or the day of a game.
- Maintain the resistance at the last load level

where 12 repetitions for all three sets could be done. Do not increase weight loads during in-season workouts. Use pre- and post-season periods for strength improvement with strength maintenance as the goal of the in-season workouts.

The workout program itself remains the same as in Phase 3 of the developmental program. The same series of exercises is followed, with eight to 12 repetitions per exercise, for a total of three sets. As long as the athlete lifts at least once every four days and does not increase the weight load, there should be no muscle soreness or undue fatigue that will interfere with performance during games.

Post-Season Weight Training

Once the competitive season is over, players can again focus on achievement of higher strength levels. A post-season break from training of at least two weeks can be followed by a return to the program outlined in Phase 3 of the preseason developmental program (see Table 20-2s). Three-set workouts, three times per week, can be continued throughout the off-season months. The Weight Training Program Checklist can be used to determine when weight loads should be increased. After the first year in which players build up gradually through the one-set and two-set phases during the preseason developmental program, Phase 1 and 2 should not be needed.

Year-Round Conditioning Program

The year-round conditioning program contains two components. They are: (a) an interval training program for conditioning the aerobic and anaerobic energy-production systems, and (b) a weight training program for conditioning the muscular system (see Tables 20-8s through 20-10s). These components are integrated into a year-round conditioning program (see Table 20-11s).

Table 20-6s. Weight Training Program Checklist

Name _____

INSTRUCTIONS:
* Record the weight load only when there is a change in load.
* Record the number of repetitions for each set (example: 12/10/10)
* Increase the weight load when you have done 12 repetitions for each of three sets for two consecutive workouts.
* Use a smaller load increase if you cannot do a minimum of eight repetitions per set at a new load.

Date		Neck flexion	Squat lift	Bench press	Bent knee sit-up	Finger flexion	Hip abduction	Bent over row	Neck extension	Hip adduction	Toe rise	Arm curl	Knee flexion	Lat pull-down	Back hyperextension	Knee extension	Reverse forearm curl
	WT.																
	REPS.	/ /	/ /	/ /	/ /	/ /	/ /	/ /	/ /	/ /	/ /	/ /	/ /	/ /	/ /	/ /	/ /
	WT.																
	REPS.	/ /	/ /	/ /	/ /	/ /	/ /	/ /	/ /	/ /	/ /	/ /	/ /	/ /	/ /	/ /	/ /
	WT.																
	REPS.	/ /	/ /	/ /	/ /	/ /	/ /	/ /	/ /	/ /	/ /	/ /	/ /	/ /	/ /	/ /	/ /
	WT.																
	REPS.	/ /	/ /	/ /	/ /	/ /	/ /	/ /	/ /	/ /	/ /	/ /	/ /	/ /	/ /	/ /	/ /
	WT.																
	REPS.	/ /	/ /	/ /	/ /	/ /	/ /	/ /	/ /	/ /	/ /	/ /	/ /	/ /	/ /	/ /	/ /
	WT.																
	REPS.	/ /	/ /	/ /	/ /	/ /	/ /	/ /	/ /	/ /	/ /	/ /	/ /	/ /	/ /	/ /	/ /
	WT.																
	REPS.	/ /	/ /	/ /	/ /	/ /	/ /	/ /	/ /	/ /	/ /	/ /	/ /	/ /	/ /	/ /	/ /
	WT.																
	REPS.	/ /	/ /	/ /	/ /	/ /	/ /	/ /	/ /	/ /	/ /	/ /	/ /	/ /	/ /	/ /	/ /
	WT.																
	REPS.	/ /	/ /	/ /	/ /	/ /	/ /	/ /	/ /	/ /	/ /	/ /	/ /	/ /	/ /	/ /	/ /
	WT.																
	REPS.	/ /	/ /	/ /	/ /	/ /	/ /	/ /	/ /	/ /	/ /	/ /	/ /	/ /	/ /	/ /	/ /
	WT.																
	REPS.	/ /	/ /	/ /	/ /	/ /	/ /	/ /	/ /	/ /	/ /	/ /	/ /	/ /	/ /	/ /	/ /
	WT.																
	REPS.	/ /	/ /	/ /	/ /	/ /	/ /	/ /	/ /	/ /	/ /	/ /	/ /	/ /	/ /	/ /	/ /
	WT.																
	REPS.	/ /	/ /	/ /	/ /	/ /	/ /	/ /	/ /	/ /	/ /	/ /	/ /	/ /	/ /	/ /	/ /
	WT.																
	REPS.	/ /	/ /	/ /	/ /	/ /	/ /	/ /	/ /	/ /	/ /	/ /	/ /	/ /	/ /	/ /	/ /
	WT.																
	REPS.	/ /	/ /	/ /	/ /	/ /	/ /	/ /	/ /	/ /	/ /	/ /	/ /	/ /	/ /	/ /	/ /
	WT.																
	REPS.	/ /	/ /	/ /	/ /	/ /	/ /	/ /	/ /	/ /	/ /	/ /	/ /	/ /	/ /	/ /	/ /
	WT.																
	REPS.	/ /	/ /	/ /	/ /	/ /	/ /	/ /	/ /	/ /	/ /	/ /	/ /	/ /	/ /	/ /	/ /
	WT.																
	REPS.	/ /	/ /	/ /	/ /	/ /	/ /	/ /	/ /	/ /	/ /	/ /	/ /	/ /	/ /	/ /	/ /

Table 20-7s. Pre-season developmental weight training program.

Phase	Duration	Reps	Sets	Days/Week	Comments
1	2 weeks	8-12	1	3	Maintain starting resistance level.
2	2 weeks	8-12	2	3	Maintain starting resistance level.
3	8 or more weeks	8-12	3	3	Increase resistance levels as strength gains are made.

Table 20-8s. Year-Round Conditioning Checklist.

Name _____

(Mark the date of each completed workout in the box.)

PRE-SEASON

WEEK	AEROBIC/ANAEROBIC TRANSITION PROGRAM AND WEIGHT TRAINING PROGRAM (Phases 1 and 2 or 3)					
	TRANSITION WORKOUT	WEIGHT TRAINING	TRANSITION WORKOUT	WEIGHT TRAINING	TRANSITION WORKOUT	WEIGHT TRAINING
1						
2						
3						
4						

Table 20-8s (continued)

Name_____
(Mark the date of each completed workout in the box.)

PRE-SEASON

	DEVELOPMENTAL INTERVAL TRAINING PROGRAM AND WEIGHT TRAINING PROGRAM (Phase 3)					
WEEK	INTERVAL TRAINING	WEIGHT TRAINING	INTERVAL TRAINING	WEIGHT TRAINING	INTERVAL TRAINING	WEIGHT TRAINING
5						
6						
7						
8						
9						
10						
11						
12						

(After 12th week, begin **in-season maintenance programs** (intervals once per week, weights one to two times per week)

Table 20-9s. Year-Round Conditioning Checklist

Name _____

IN-SEASON MAINTENANCE PROGRAMS

Place a check in the box corresponding to the month and week for each time you complete the interval and weight workout.

WEEK

MONTH	1		2		3		4		5	
	Wts.	Interval	Wts.	Interval	Wts.	Interval	Wts.	Interval	Wts.	Interval
1										
2										
3										
4										
5										
6										

Table 20-10s. Post-Season Conditioning Checklist

Name _____

Mark the date of each workout in the corresponding box. For aerobic workouts, record the distance covered and the total time of the workout.

WEEK	Aerobic	Weights	Aerobic	Weights	Aerobic	Weights	Anaerobic Maintenance
1							
2							
3							
4							
5							
6							

Table 20-10s (continued)

POST-SEASON CONDITIONING CHECKLIST

WEEK	Aerobic	Weights	Aerobic	Weights	Aerobic	Weights	Anaerobic Maintenance
7							
8							
9							
10							
11							
12							
13							
14							
15							
16							
17							
18							
19							
20							
21							
22							
23							
24							
25							
26							
27							
28							
29							
30							

Table 20-11s. Overview of year-round conditioning program.

Time	Interval Training Activity for Conditioning the Energy Production System*	Weight Training Activity for Conditioning the Muscular System**
Pre-season (start 14 weeks prior to first game)	Complete the Pre-season Aerobic/Anaerobic Transition program (four weeks).	New lifters complete the Pre-season Weight Training Program by beginning with four weeks of introductory weight training (Phase 1 and 2) and then starting the Post-Season Weight Training Program (Phase 3).
	Complete the Pre-season Anaerobic Developmental Interval Training Program (eight weeks).	Continuing lifters complete the Post-Season Weight Training Program.
In-Season (two weeks prior to first game until last game)	Participate in interval training as part of regularly scheduled practices. Complete the In-Season Anaerobic Maintenance Program.	Complete the In-Season Weight Training Maintenance Program.
Post-Season (two to four weeks after last game until 14 weeks before first game of next season)	Complete three days/week of aerobic activity (dribbling, jogging and running, or bicycling). Complete the Post-Season Anaerobic Maintenance Program.	Complete the Post-Season Weight Training Program.

*Note that all conditioning sessions should be preceded by warm-up and stretching and followed by cool-down and stretching (see Supplement 20-1).

**Descriptions of these activities are included in this supplement.

Supplement 20-3.
Circuit Training Program

Introduction

This supplement contains an example of a basketball training circuit and recording form (see Table 20-12s). These forms can be photocopied and duplicated on the front and back of a 5 x 8" card. Also included in this supplement is a blank form (see Table 20-13s) upon which you can write your own training circuit to meet the specific needs of your players.

Using A Training Circuit

A training circuit can be implemented one to three times per week during the season. The number of times per week you have your players engage in a training circuit should vary according to the number of games scheduled for a given week, the physical demands of an in-season interval training and weight training program, and other activities included in your practice. You should not have your players perform a circuit the day before or the day of a game.

The requirements for performance and scoring each station need to be thoroughly explained to the players. Players need to be informed that the correct performance of each station is as important as the number of repetitions. After all the players understand each of the items in the complete circuit, you may have them perform a partial circuit of four or five stations and then increase the number of stations by one on subsequent days until all stations of the training circuit are performed.

The prescribed time for exercise and for the rest interval, during which the players write their scores on their recording forms and rotate from one station to the next, should be controlled to create an exercise overload. The first day the team performs the entire circuit, 30 seconds of exercise and 20 seconds rest between each station might be appropriate. This results in an eight-station circuit that can be completed in 6 minutes and 20 seconds. Gradually the exercise interval should increase and the rest interval should decrease. You will need to judge what is the appropriate exercise/rest interval ratio for your players.

Table 20-12s. Example of a ten-station basketball training circuit and recording form on two sides of a 5 x 8″ card.

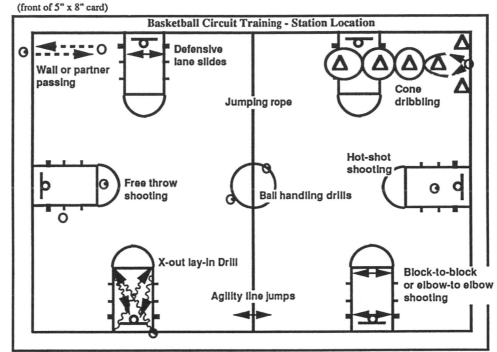

(front of 5″ x 8″ card)

Basketball Circuit Training - Station Location

10 Stations-
(30 sec./1 minute)
Rotate counter-clockwise

1. Free throw shooting
2. X-out lay-in drill
3. Ball handling drills
4. Line jumps
5. Shooting from block-to-block or elbow-to-elbow
6. Hot-shot shooting
7. Cone dribbling
8. Jumping rope
9. Lane defensive slides
10. Wall or partner passing

(back of 5″ x 8″ card)

Basketball Circuit Training - Recording Form

Name:														
Date (mo./day)														
Exercise/Rest interval (seconds)														
STATIONS	**Performance Scores**													
Free throw shooting														
X-out lay-in drill														
Figure 8 ball handling														
Agility line jumps														
Shooting from the block or elbow														
Hot-shot shooting														
Cone dribbling														
Jumping rope														
Defensive lane slides														
Wall or partner passing														

Table 20-12s (continued)

Station	Description	Equipment
Free throw shooting	Player 1 stands behind the free throw line and attempts to make as many free throws as possible in the allotted time. Player 2 rebounds the ball and passes the ball back to the shooter. The number of made baskets during the exercise interval is the score. Switch positions and repeat. Stress *concentration* and *proper shooting form.* *Variation:* To decrease difficulty, move the shooter closer to the basket using modified free throw line distances or lower the basket height.	2 basketballs
X-out lay-in drill	Player 1 begins under the left side of the backboard with a basketball in hand. The player dribbles out with the right hand to the right elbow, pivots to the outside, and dribbles in for a right-hand lay-up. The player then rebounds the ball and dribbles with the left-hand to the left elbow, pivots to the outside, and dribbles in for a left-hand lay-up. The shooter travels in an "X" pattern across the key, alternating right-hand and left-hand lay-ups. Continue the drill for 30 seconds, counting the number of lay-ups made. Stress proper lay-up technique using *both* the right and left hands.	1 basketball
Ball-handling drills	The player moves the ball around and through the legs in a "Figure 8" path. Count the number of completed Figure 8s in 30 sec./1 minute. If the ball is dropped, pick it up and continue. Stress *eyes up* and *ball control.* *Variation:* Practice other ball-handling skills (i.e., Figure 8 with a dribble, Around the World, Clap and Catch, Skip Dribble, etc.)	1 basketball per player
Line jumps	The player begins with both feet positioned on one side of the half-court line. The player jumps rapidly and continuously from one side of the line to the other. Count the number of jumps completed in 30 sec./1 minute. Stress *quick footwork.* *Variation:* square jumps, jump boxes	a line on the court
Shooting from block-to-block or elbow-to-elbow	The player begins at the right block or elbow and shoots a power lay-up or jump-shot, rebounds the ball, and then moves laterally to shoot from the left block or elbow. Count the number of made baskets. Stress *no dribbles* before the shot and following each shot attempt.	1 basketball
Hot-shot shooting	The player shoots from anywhere within the lane area, rebounds the shot, moves to a new spot, and quickly shoots again. Count the number of made baskets. Stress *squaring up* to the basket and proper shooting technique.	1 basketball

Table 20-12s (continued)

Station	Description	Equipment
	Variation: Partner may rebound ball for shooter.	
Cone dribbling	The player zig-zag dribbles in and out of the cones placed approximately 5 yards apart. Stress keeping *eyes up* and *changing hands* to keep body between the cone and the ball. Place arrows on the floor with tape to show proper direction. May not hit or miss any cone. Count the number of completed cones in 30 sec./1 minute.	5 cones, 1 basketball
	Variation: To increase difficulty, move cones closer together or use a pair of dribbling blinders.	
Jumping rope	The player jumps rope on both feet, counting the number of completed repetitions. Stress that if a mistake is made, keep going and continue to count.	1 jump rope per player
	Variation: Jump rope while alternating feet, turn rope backwards, crosscross rope, etc.	
Defensive lane slides	The player begins in the key facing the free throw line with the left foot on the lane line. Using quick slide steps, the player moves across the key to touch the opposite lane line with the right foot. Continue moving back and forth across the key as quickly as possible, counting the number of lines touched in 30 sec./1 minute. Stress *proper defense stance* and *footwork.* Do not allow the feet to cross or come closer than shoulder-width apart.	lane lines
	Variation: Substitute lane defensive attack and retreat drill.	
Wall or partner passing	Position players approximately 10 feet from each other with one ball. Players chest, bounce or overhead pass back and forth as quickly as possible. Count the number of successful passes in 30 sec./1 minute. Stress *proper passing and receiving form.* This station can also be performed at the ball with each player counting the number of passes successfully hitting the target.	tape for targets on wall, 1 basketball per player or for each set of two
	Variation: Alternate chest, bounce, and overhead passes, increase or decrease size of wall targets, increase or decrease distance from passer to receiver, shuffle and pass to a moving target.	

Table 20-13s. Recording form to photocopy and complete.

(front of 5" x 8" card)

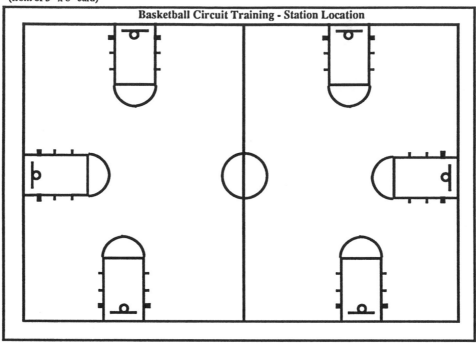

Basketball Circuit Training - Station Location

(back of 5" x 8" card)

Basketball Circuit Training - Recording Form														
Name:														
Date (mo./day)														
Exercise/Rest interval (seconds)														
STATIONS	**Performance Scores**													
Free throw shooting														
X-out lay-in drill														
Figure 8 ball handling														
Agility line jumps														
Shooting from the block or elbow														
Hot-shot shooting														
Cone dribbling														
Jumping rope														
Defensive lane slides														
Wall or partner passing														

21
Nutrition for Successful Performance

Elaina Jurecki, R.D.; M.S.
Glenna DeJong, M.S.; M.A.

QUESTIONS TO CONSIDER

- What is a proper diet for young basketball players?
- Do young athletes need protein, vitamin, and mineral supplements?
- Should there by any restriction on the amount of water consumed before, during, and after games and practices?
- Should salt tablets be provided for the players during practices and games?
- Are ergogenic aids important in improving basketball performance?
- When should a pre-game meal be eaten and what should it contain?

INTRODUCTION

All children have the same nutritional needs, but young athletes use more energy and, therefore, usually need to consume more calories. Good performance does not just happen; it requires training sessions to improve techniques, increase endurance, and develop game strategies. Good nutrition is another important factor that affects an athlete's performance, but it is less frequently understood and practiced. Studies have shown that good overall eating habits are more beneficial to the athlete than taking vitamin or protein supplements or eating special foods at a pre-competition meal.

Food consists of all the solid or liquid materials we ingest by mouth, except drugs. Breads, meats, vegetables, and fruits, as well as beverages—even water—are considered food, because they contain essential nutrients for the body. These nutrients include energy (calories from fat, protein, and carbohydrates), carbohydrates, protein (amino acids), fat, vitamins, salts (electrolytes), minerals, trace elements, and water. Water constitutes more than half the body's weight and provides the medium within which other nutrients are delivered to different body parts to perform their important functions.

What impact could you have on your athletes' diets? How can you influence what your athletes eat when you do not cook their meals? When you meet with the team's parents during an orientation meeting, explain to them how good nutrition can aid their children's performance. This information can be reinforced by giving your athletes similar nutritional advice.

Frequently, your athletes will listen more closely to your advice than that of their parents and use the tips you suggest on improving their diets because they believe these tips will also improve their performance.

PROPER DIET

A good diet is one that provides adequate energy (calories), proteins, carbohydrates, fats, vitamins, minerals, and water in the amounts needed by the body in order to perform its normal daily functions. A variety of foods needs to be eaten to provide the 40 plus nutrients essential for good health. This can be achieved by eating the specified number of servings from each of the four food groups (see Table 21-1).

Calories

Calories are the energy content of food used to satisfy the needs of the energy body so it can properly function. Energy obtained from food is temporarily stored as glycogen in the liver and muscle, as fat in various deposit sites, and as protein in muscle and other places although protein is used as an energy source only during extreme situations. Foods vary in calorie and nutrient content. Foods to avoid are those that are high in calories and low in nutrient content. Foods that are high in sugar (candy, cakes, soda pop, cookies) or fat (fried foods, chips, salad dressings, pastries, butter) supply "empty calories," meaning they do not contribute to the essential nutrients discussed earlier

but do contribute many calories. These foods should be used with discretion.

The energy cost of physical activity, or amount of calories burned, depends upon (a) the intensity of the physical activity, and (b) the length of time of exertion. A young basketball player, about 120 pounds in body weight, burns approximately 375 calories per hour of practice. During a game or training session, ranging from 45 to 90 minutes, your players burn up to 25 percent more energy than they do on a day in which they don't practice. Hence, heavy training may require an additional 280 to 560 calories per day intake to compensate for the calories burned during the activity.

An average adolescent burns differing amounts of calories during the various activities listed in Table 21-2.

When your players reach exhaustion, most of their bodies' energy stores are depleted and

Table 21-2. Caloric expenditure during various activities.

Activity	Calories/minute*	Activity	Calories/minute
Sleeping	0.9	Basketball	5-7
Sitting, normally	1.0	Calisthenics	4
Standing, normally	1.2	Skipping rope	8-12
Class work, lecture (listen to)	1.4	Running (10 mph)	16
Walking indoors	2.5	Soccer (game)	6-8

*Based on an average adolescent, 120 lbs. Add 10 percent for each 15 lbs. over 120, subtract 10 percent for each 15 lbs. under 120.

Table 21-1. Recommended daily intake of each of the four food groups.

Dairy Products	3-4 servings (milk, cheese, yogurt) to provide calcium, phosphorus, vitamin D, protein, and energy.	1 serving = 1 cup of milk or 2 oz. of cheese
Protein Products	2 servings (meat, fish, poultry, or vegetable protein foods such as beans and whole grains) to provide amino acids, B vitamins, iron, essential fatty acids, energy, and more.	1 serving = 2 to 3 oz. of meat
Fruits and Vegetables	4 servings (oranges, apples, pears, broccoli, carrots, green beans) to provide vitamin A and C, and electrolytes.	1 serving = 1/2 cup of vegetables or fruit
Grain Products	4 servings (bread, cereal, pasta, rice) to provide B vitamins and protein.	1 serving = 1 slice bread or 1 cup of cereal, pasta, or rice.

their blood sugar decreases, causing fatigue. This situation is remedied with appropriate rest and calorie ingestion—preferably from carbohydrate sources since these foods can replenish energy stores more efficiently.

Carbohydrates

Carbohydrates are a group of chemical substances which include sugars and starches. They are widely distributed in many foods. As stated previously, carbohydrates can be stored as liver and muscle glycogen or can be found in the blood as glucose. During moderate to high intensity exercise, carbohydrates supply the majority of the energy needed in the body (see "Energy Production Systems" in Chapter 20). However, the carbohydrate storage capacity of the body is limited and can be greatly decreased by skipping meals or with exercise. Since carbohydrates can be digested easily and quickly, they are the most readily available sources of food energy for storage energy replacement.

A diet high in carbohydrate (55-60 percent of total caloric intake) helps maintain adequate stores in the body. Most of the dietary carbohydrates should come from complex carbohydrate sources such as pasta, rice, fruits, and kidney beans. Refined sugars found in candy, cookies, and syrup should be avoided.

Carbohydrates are easily digested and are the most readily available source of food energy.

Fat

Fat is the most concentrated source of energy. It contains twice as much energy (calories) per unit weight as either carbohydrate or protein. Fats have many important functions in the body including carrying vitamins A, D, E, and K to perform their necessary functions, building blood vessels and body linings, and providing a concentrated store of energy (calories).

During mild to moderate exercise, fats are an important energy source along with carbohydrates (see "Energy Production Systems" in Chapter 20). The storage capacity for fat is much greater than that for carbohydrate and only in extreme cases are fat stores depleted. Therefore, dietary intake of fat should be 30%

or less of total caloric intake since replenishment isn't normally necessary. In fact, high levels of fat in the diet have been implicated in diseases such as coronary artery disease and cancer.

Foods high in fat content are digested at a slower rate than foods high in carbohydrates or protein. If players have high fat meals (hamburger, fries, pizza, etc.) before their game, chances are good that such meals will not empty completely from their stomachs for three to five hours, and this may adversely affect their play. Foods having a high concentration of fat include butter, margarine, vegetable oils, peanut butter, mayonnaise, nuts, chocolate, fried foods, chips, and cream products.

Figure 21-1 lists the percent of fat from a variety of food sources.

Protein

Proteins are important as structural components of all body tissues (e.g. muscle, skin, brain, etc.), regulators of metabolism (e.g. hormones and enzymes), and as an energy source during starvation and exercise although its contribution is minor as compared to fats and carbohydrates (see "Energy Production Systems" in Chapter 20). Amino acids are the "building blocks" which comprise all proteins. Of the twenty amino acids necessary for protein synthesis in the body, eleven can be manufactured in the body and are considered nonessential amino acids. The other nine are considered essential amino acids as they must be supplied in the diet. In a balanced diet, 12-15 percent of the total caloric intake should come from protein.

Foods from animal sources (e.g., meat, fish, poultry, eggs, milk, and cheese) provide the body with all of the essential amino acids. Vegetable foods (dried peas, beans, nuts, cereals, breads, and pastas) are also important sources of protein, but most vegetables are lacking in certain essential amino acids. Therefore, a combination of foods from animal and vegetable sources assures meeting the body's requirement for essential amino acids, as well as other nutrients.

Because of an increased rate of muscular growth, athletes have a *slightly* larger protein requirement than non-athletes. Studies on the dietary habits of athletes show that this increas-

Food Items

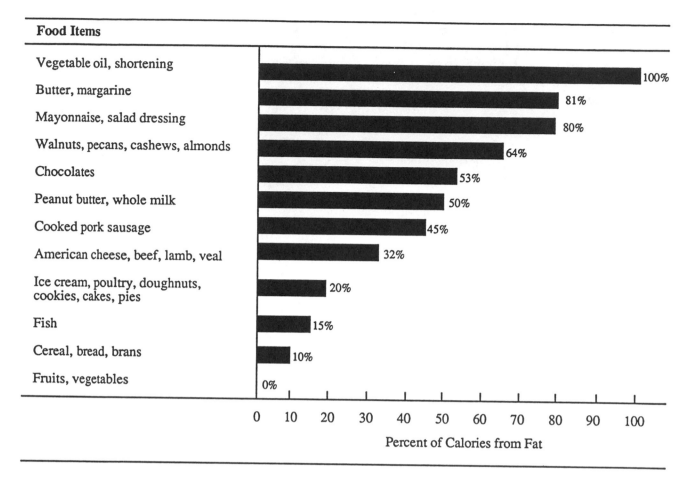

	Percent of Calories from Fat
Vegetable oil, shortening	100%
Butter, margarine	81%
Mayonnaise, salad dressing	80%
Walnuts, pecans, cashews, almonds	64%
Chocolates	53%
Peanut butter, whole milk	50%
Cooked pork sausage	45%
American cheese, beef, lamb, veal	32%
Ice cream, poultry, doughnuts, cookies, cakes, pies	20%
Fish	15%
Cereal, bread, brans	10%
Fruits, vegetables	0%

Figure 21-1. Percentage of calories from fat when ingested from specified food items.

ed requirement can be easily met by the athlete's normal diet; no protein supplement is necessary. During training, at most, an additional nine grams of protein (which can be provided by one cup of milk or two ounces of meat or cheese) is sufficient to meet increased demands. In fact, too much protein can place undo stress on the body.

Eating a high-protein diet could lead to dehydration of the body, which could actually decrease athletic performance.

Excessive amounts of ingested protein—greater than the body's needs—are converted into body fat. The waste products from this conversion must be excreted by the kidneys, placing a greater strain on these organs. Water also is excreted with the protein-waste products in the urine. Thus, eating a high-protein diet could lead to dehydration of the body, which could actually decrease athletic performance.

It is a myth that building muscle requires a high-protein diet featuring large quantities of meat. Another myth is that a steak dinner eaten before an athletic event will help team members improve their performance. This type of meal may actually work against them if consumed less than three or four hours before playing time. These meals, as well as any high protein meal, are also usually high in fat. Players cannot digest this type of meal as easily as a high-carbohydrate meal and may suffer from cramps and/or feel weighted down and sluggish.

Vitamins and Minerals

Vitamins and minerals are found in varying quantities in many different kinds of foods, from a slice of bread to a piece of liver. Vitamins and minerals are nutrients required by the body in very small amounts for a larger number of body functions. They do not contain calories or give the body energy. When an athlete feels "run down," *this is usually not caused by a vitamin deficiency.*

We need vitamins and minerals in only minute quantities. Requirements of most vitamins and minerals are in milligram (1/1000 gram) amounts. These substances taken in excess of the body's need will either be stored in the body or excreted in the urine. The extra amounts will not provide more energy or enhance performance; however, they can be toxic or interfere with normal metabolism.

Vitamin and mineral supplementation is not necessary for the athlete who consumes a balanced diet. However, in certain sports such as wrestling, bodybuilding, and ballet, where weight loss through starvation is achieved, the athlete may not be obtaining adequate amounts solely due to the diminished caloric intake. Therefore, in situations where the athlete's diet is not balanced or caloric intake is low, supplementation may be advised. A much better approach, however, would be to encourage proper eating habits.

Vitamins and minerals do not supply energy; high levels of vitamins and minerals can hinder the athlete's performance.

Some vitamin and mineral supplements contain 10 or more times the Recommended Daily Allowance (RDA), which is sometimes just below the level of toxicity. If vitamin and mineral supplements are used, a single daily multi-vitamin/mineral tablet, that provides 100 percent of the RDA or less for each nutrient is preferable to therapeutic level supplements providing greater than 100 percent of the RDA. The RDAs of vitamins and minerals are listed in Table 21-3.

Water

Water plays a vital role in the health and performance of an athlete. Your basketball players may lose more than two percent of their body weight due to dehydration from playing a fast-moving game or during a long workout. A player's performance significantly deteriorates after dehydration of more than two percent of his/her body weight. Drinking plenty of water is necessary for basketball players who are physically active in hot, humid weather (see Figure 21-2).

Physical exercise increases the amount of heat produced in the body. If sufficient water is not available for cooling of the body through perspiration, the body temperature may exceed safe limits. The individual will become tired more rapidly and in severe cases, heat exhaustion and heat stroke may result (see Chapter 24). A temperature/humidity guide for fluid and practice time is included in Table 21-4.

Maintenance of adequate body water levels is necessary to help prevent heat illness.

Feeling thirsty is not an adequate indication that the body needs water. In fact, by the time athletes feel thirsty, they already may have reached a dangerous level of body water depletion. It takes several hours to regain water balance once water loss has occurred. There is no

Table 21-3. Recommended daily dietary allowances.*

Age (Years)	Children 7-10	Males 11-14	Females 11-14
Weight (pounds)	62	99	101
Height (inches)	52	62	62
Energy (calories)	2,400	2,700	2,200
range of calories	1,650-3,300	2,000-3,700	1,500-3,000
Protein (grams)	34	45	46
Vitamin A (mg RE)	700	1,000	1,000
Vitamin C (mg)	45	50	50
Calcium (mg)	800	1,200	1,200
Iron (mg)	10	18	18

*Adapted from Food and Nutrition Board, National Academy of Sciences—National Research Council, Revised, 1980.

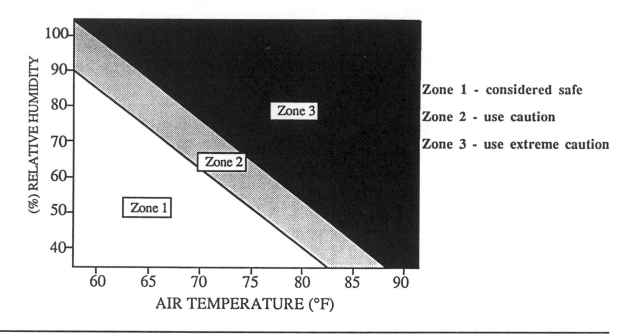

Figure 21-2. Guide for preventing heat illnesses associated with participation in physical activities under various conditions of temperatures and humidity.

Table 21-4. Temperature/humidity guide for taking precautionary action during basketball practices and games.

Temperature	Precautions to Take
Under 60° (F)	No precaution is necessary.
61-65° (F)	Encourage all players to take fluids. Make sure water is available at all times.
66-70° (F)	Take water breaks every 30-45 minutes of playing or practice time.
71-75° (F)	Provide rest periods with water breaks every 30-45 minutes of playing time—depending on the intensity of exercise. Substitute players during the game, so all may receive appropriate rest and fluids.
76° (F) and up	Practice during coolest part of the day. Schedule frequent rest breaks. Force water intake.
	Tell players to wear light, loose clothing that allows free circulation of air. Remove outer clothing when it gets wet because wet clothing reduces evaporation, thus hindering one of the body's cooling mechanisms.
	Move to the shade if possible.
	Drink water before, during, and after practice sessions and competition.
Relative humidity greater than 90%	Similar precautions should be taken as those listed for 76° (F) and up.

physiological reason for restricting water intake before, during, or after athletic contests and practices. Players should drink eight to 16 ounces of water 30 minutes before the game and eight ounces every 20 minutes during the game.

Athletes should be encouraged to drink water before, during, and after each game and practice session.

Salts and Electrolytes

Another common myth is that salt (sodium) tablets and electrolyte solutions (solutions containing the elements sodium, potassium, and chloride are needed by the athlete. These are not only unnecessary but can be harmful.

Salt tablets are irritating to the stomach and intestine and can increase the danger of dehydration by causing diarrhea when taken before a practice or game. Although the body needs to replace both water and sodium, the need for water is more critical.

Some coaches provide 0.2 percent salt solutions (drinking water containing small amounts of salt) during an athletic event, but research has shown that plain water is just as effective. The body needs water immediately to replace the water lost during a game or practice, but any sodium lost can easily be replaced by eating salted foods after the event. Most Americans get more sodium than they need from salt already in their diet; therefore, excessive salting of food is unnecessary and not recommended.

The best replacement fluid is water.

ERGOGENIC AIDS

Ergogenic is derived from the Greek words ergon meaning work and gennan meaning to produce. In sports, ergogenic aids are agents thought to increase potential for work output. Various mechanical, psychological, physiological, nutritional, and pharmacological aids exist which purportedly improve performance. This discussion will focus on nutritional and pharmacological aids.

Nutritional Aids

Ergogenic foods are those substances that claim to "give you more energy," "improve your performance," and/or "enhance your endurance." There is no scientific evidence supporting any of these claims. Most of these foods and dietary practices are harmless to the athlete. The only danger these foods pose occurs when they replace necessary foods that the athlete needs for normal bodily functions. Some examples of these foods are bee pollen, pangamic acid, honey, lecithin, wheat germ oil, phosphates, alkaline salts (e.g., sodium bicarbonate, tomato juice, or organic juice), and gelatin.

Inform your athletes that these substances do not improve performance contrary to advertiser's claims. Encourage them to eat healthy diets and explain that this is the key to improving their performance.

Pharmacological Aids

• Steroids

Anabolic steroids (Dianabol, Anavar, Winstrol, etc.) have structures similar to the male sex hormone, testosterone. They are referred to as anabolic because, under certain circumstances, they promote tissue-building via increases in muscle mass and decreases in muscle breakdown. This effect is most evident in males when great increases in muscle mass and strength are seen at puberty. A 20-fold magnification in circulating testosterone levels accompanies these increases at this time. However, muscle mass and/or strength gains following steroid administration on already sexually mature subjects are questionable or at best show only moderate improvements.

In addition to their anabolic effects, steroids used in athletics also have androgenic or masculinizing effects. Males and females both may experience increased facial and body hair, baldness, voice deepening, and aggressiveness while using these drugs. Anabolic steroids also produce many reversible and irreversible side effects that are of great concern to the medical community as described in Table 21-5.

Steroid abuse is a major problem in athletics today even at the junior high and high school levels despite cases of well-known athletes who have been negatively affected by such abuse. In the 1983 Pan American games, seven of the 19 athletes tested were disqualified for steroid use and many more withdrew from competition to prevent detection. Ben Johnson, the great Canadian sprinter, had his gold medal rescinded at the 1988 Olympic games following discovery of steroid abuse. Not only is steroid use unethical, it is dangerous. Your athletes should be informed of the dangerous and potentially fatal effects of steroid usage. The risk of infertility, liver damage, immune dysfunction, and aggressive behavior far outweighs any possible advantages of taking steroids.

• Amphetamines

The use of pep pills or amphetamines is on the rise in athletics. These drug compounds cause reactions similar to adrenaline in that they increase heart rate, blood pressure, metabolism, breathing rate, and blood sugar levels. They may also cause headaches, dizziness, confusion, and sometimes insomnia, all of which could actually be detrimental to good physical performance. In fact, research suggests that amphetamines have little or no positive effect on exercise performance. Urge your athletes to stay clear of amphetamines as evidence for their potential detriment far exceeds any known benefits.

Table 21-5. Harmful effects of anabolic steroids.*

Body System	Reversible Effects	Irreversible Effects
Cardiovascular (heart/blood vessels)	High blood pressure, changes in blood fats, predisposing to heart disease, sticky platelets	Abnormal heart muscle, heart disease, stroke, heart attack
Skeletal	Minor changes in height	Early closure of the growth plates, making you shorter than you would be otherwise
Muscular	Increased water in muscle	Abnormal muscle cells, tendon rupture
Reproductive—male	Shrunken testicles, decreased sperm production, breast development, increased size of the prostate gland	Cancer of the prostate, increased breast development, abnormal testicles
Reproductive—female	Decreased breast size, increased body hair (facial also), menstrual problems	Increased size of clitoris, deepening voice, baldness, use during pregnancy may cause fetal deformity or death
Liver	Increased leakage of liver enzymes, abnormal growth of liver cells, turning "yellow" from backup of bile in liver	Cancer of liver, blood-filled sacs in liver
Endocrine (hormones)	Too much insulin secreted, decreased thyroxine, decreases hormone secretion from pituitary gland in brain	Do not know which effects are permanent
Skin	Acne, increased facial hair	Severe acne, baldness
Mental Attitude	Irritability, aggressiveness, mood swings, problems getting along with people, change in sex drive	Relationships with people damaged, possible personality changes
Immune	Decreased functioning of the immune cells and antibody formation	Serious infections, cancer

*This table comes from a paper entitled "What the High School Athletes, Coaches and Parents Should Know About Anabolic-Androgenic Steroids." This paper is available upon request from the Michigan State University Sports Medicine Clinic, Clinical Center, East Lansing, MI 48824.

The best prescription for increased strength and improved performance is hard practice, plenty of rest, a good diet, healthy eating habits, and plenty of fluids.

• **Caffeine**

A stimulant commonly found in coffee, tea, cola, and chocolate is caffeine. Its ingestion has been found to improve physical performance in such long duration events as cycling and running. Therefore, its use may be warranted in endurance events and if used should be consumed one hour prior to the event. However, caffeine may cause headache, insomnia, and/or irritability in persons who normally avoid this drug. These people should avoid caffeine as these symptoms may be detrimental to performance. Don't rely on caffeine as a miracle performance drug, as it is not! Sensible training and proper diet are the best prescriptions that can't be beat for improving performance.

MEAL PATTERNS

Preadolescents and adolescents should eat at least three meals daily. Nutritional snacks may be added to the regular breakfast-lunch-dinner pattern if extra calories are needed. Most active athletes tend to skip meals, grab quick-fix meals, or depend on fast food restaurants and vending machines for meals on the run. This practice could lead to diets low in vitamins and minerals and high in fat and sodium. For example, a meal consisting of a hamburger, fries, and soda would provide 571 calories or approximately one-fourth of the energy requirement of a 15 to 18-year-old athlete, but less than one-tenth of the other nutritional requirements. Nutritional foods with good ratios of nutrients to calories are listed in Table 21-6. To maximize performance during periods of intense daily training, an athlete should consume approximately 500 grams (2000 Kcal) of carbohydrates per day.

Table 21-6. Contributions of nutritional snacks.

| Food | Amount | Calories | % Recommended Daily Allowance | | | |
			Vit A	Vit C	Calcium	Iron
Fresh orange	1 med. size	65	8	150	7	5
Orange juice	1 cup	110	14	200	3	5
Peanut butter	1 tablespoon	95	—	—	0.5	3
2% Milk	1 cup	120	14	4	37	1
Cheese and crackers	1 oz. cheese, 4 crackers	175	9	—	27	7
Carrot sticks	8 or 1 carrot	30	70	13	3	5
Ice cream	1 cup	270	15	2	22	1
Fruit-flavored yogurt	1 cup	230	14	2	43	2
Raisins	1/4 cup pressed	120	—	—	56	15
Applesauce	1/2 cup	115	1	3	—	7
Banana	1 med.	100	6	27	—	7
Ready-to-eat cereal	1 ounce	110	29	27	—	36

Pre-Game Meal

One of the biggest concerns of athletes and coaches is what the team members should eat for the pre-game meal. Unfortunately, there are no foods that contain any special, magical properties that can improve your basketball players' performances if eaten before the game. Performance during an event or workout is dependent more on food consumed hours, days, or even weeks before the event. The most important consideration should be to select foods that can be digested easily, tolerated well, and liked by the players.

Pre-game stress causes an athlete's stomach and intestine to be less active. Minor food intake is recommended before vigorous exercise to delay exhaustion, but should be eaten two or three hours before the competition to give the stomach and intestines sufficient time to empty. Meals eaten before a practice session should be given the same general consideration as the pre-game meal, except there is no need to compensate for nervous stress.

Carbohydrates leave the stomach earlier and are digested more readily than either fats or protein. Foods that are easily digested include cereals, bread, spaghetti, macaroni, rice, potatoes (baked, not fried), and fruits. Examples of high-fat foods which should be avoided include cake, peanut butter, nuts, luncheon-type meats, gravy, yellow cheese, butter, and ice cream. Gas-forming foods (e.g., cabbage, cucumbers, cauliflower, and beans) and foods high in fiber and roughage (e.g., whole wheat bread, bran cereal, and raw vegetables) may cause discomfort to the player if eaten the day of competition.

Those athletes who have difficulty digesting solid foods before competition may prefer a liquid meal. These products should not be confused with instant powdered meals or "instant breakfasts," which have too much fat, protein, and electrolytes to be eaten before athletic contests. Liquid meals have the following advantages: (a) they leave the intestine rapidly, (b) they provide substantial calories, and (c) they are more convenient than preparing a solid meal. However, liquid meals do not provide any greater benefits for improving performances than do easily digested, well-tolerated meals.

Lunch should be eaten about three hours prior to afternoon practices or games. Possible choices for lunch include: spaghetti with tomato sauce; sandwich of white bread with a thin spread; chicken noodle or vegetable soup; low-fat yogurt or cottage cheese; fresh or canned fruits and fruit juices; crackers with white cheese or cheese spread; low-fat milk; baked potato sprinkled with white cheese and bacon bits (not real bacon but the soybean-flavored brand); or pizza—heavy on the tomato sauce and light on the cheese. If the team has an early morning practice or game, (8:00 a.m.) athletes should eat breakfast about 5:00 a.m. to ensure plenty of time to digest their meal before playing time. If they do not wish to eat breakfast that early, they could eat a lighter meal (e.g., liquid meals or juice and a piece of white toast with jelly—no butter or margarine) an hour before playing time. However, eating the larger meal two or three hours before playing time would delay feelings of fatigue and hunger and would be recommended when the team has to play a basketball tournament lasting more than four hours. Possible selections for breakfast would include: cereal with low fat milk, pancakes, French toast, fruit juice, oatmeal or cream of wheat, white toast with jelly or cinnamon sugar, soft- or hard-boiled eggs, and fresh or canned fruit.

Pre-game meal:
- *Eat carbohydrate-rich foods*
- *Avoid fatty foods*
- *Avoid gas-forming and high-fiber foods*
- *Eat three or four hours before the game*
- *Drink plenty of fluids hourly*
- *Avoid concentrated sweets*

Candy bars are not a good source of quick energy and will not help your players perform better. A candy bar eaten right before the game may give your athletes a sudden burst of energy, but this energy boost is only temporary. The body over-compensates for the increase in blood sugar that results from eating a simple sugar (such as candy), causing feelings of tiredness and hunger. Your athletes will be full of energy for only a short time, then they will become sluggish and weak. Therefore, candies and anything high in sugar should be avoided especially just prior to activity.

Nutritional Support During Competition

Intense prolonged activities such as basketball and distance running require significant fluid and energy replacement during the event. Water is the most important replacement, but performance and endurance may be enhanced with proper carbohydrate replacement.

In a study of elite soccer players (Williams 1983), muscle glycogen (carbohydrate) stores were assessed after a 90-minute soccer match. The groups of players that drank one liter of a 7 percent sugar solution during the game had 63 percent more glycogen in their muscles than the group that drank plain water. In other words, the group that drank the sugar solution had much more "reserve" energy stores.

A 7 percent carbohydrate solution easily can be made by dissolving 70 grams (4.5 tablespoons) of glucose (sugar) in one quart (32 ounces) of water. Athletes should drink about 8 ounces of this mixture every 20 minutes during a match to maintain normal blood glucose levels. Many commercial carbohydrate replacement "sport drinks" are available with similar concentrations.

WEIGHT CONTROL

Each of your basketball players is different in height and build and, therefore, they have different ideal body weights. Rather than suggesting that your players weigh a specific number of pounds, you should work at improving their skill and physical fitness.

Weight Loss

Athletes who have too much fat will tend to be slower and tire more easily. For those individuals, some weight loss could improve their performance. In order to lose weight, energy output must exceed energy intake. Because of this, the more active athletes have an easier time losing weight than their less active peers.

One pound of fat has the energy equivalent of approximately 3,500 calories. Reducing food intake by 500 calories per day will result in a loss of about 1 pound per week. Increasing the athlete's activity or training may also result in extra weight loss. Because fat cannot be lost at a rate faster than one or two pounds per week, weight loss greater than this amount could result in loss of body protein and not body fat. Hence, crash diets are not recommended because loss of valuable body protein (muscle mass) can occur.

Sauna baths, cathartics, and diuretics are methods used to lose weight by dehydration. These methods are not recommended because body fluids, not body fat are lost which reduces strength and endurance. The key to losing weight is to begin months before the season starts, follow a healthy diet, avoid high-calorie foods, eat three balanced meals, and increase activity level.

Important points to consider when attempting to lose weight:

- *Start early*
- *Lose at a slow pace*
- *Lose fat, not fluid or muscle*
- *Avoid excessive weight loss, especially during growing periods*
- *Avoid use of saunas, diuretics, or cathartics*

Weight Gain

The goal for athletes trying to gain weight is to add more muscle, rather than fat. Eating an extra 500 calories per day should result in gaining one pound of muscle per week. This increase in caloric intake must be accompanied with intensive exercise, at a level that is slightly less than full exertion. A good way to add those extra calories is by adding a daily snack such as dried fruit, nuts, peanut butter sandwich, juice, milk shake, or oatmeal-raisin cookies. Trying to gain weight at a faster rate will result only in more body fat in the wrong places, rather than muscle in the right places.

Important points to consider when attempting to gain weight:

- *Start early*
- *Gain at a slow pace*
- *Eat nutritious foods, and not foods high in fat content*

As a coach, you can give your players some tips on how to gain or lose weight properly—eating the right foods and gaining/losing weight at the proper pace. Encourage your players to eat a healthy diet because they should naturally achieve their ideal body weight by eating balanced meals and snacks and exercising. Most of your athletes will still be growing and will require additional calories to meet the demands of their growing bodies.

If you have athletes who are excessively over- or underweight, you may tactfully approach their parents and suggest that they seek medical attention for their child.

At the ideal body weight, the athlete performs best.

Many teenagers eat a lot of junk foods—high in calories and low in nutrients—but the motivated athletes would prefer foods high in nutrients if they realize that these foods could help them in performing their best.

SUMMARY

Your group of basketball players is a motivated group of individuals who want to improve their performances to become a successful team. As their coach, you can provide them with the necessary information on how they can play their best. Providing your team with the nutritional advice presented in this chapter will assist them in obtaining maximum performance through eating a healthy diet and avoiding unsafe habits.

REFERENCES

Ivy, J.L. (1988). Muscle glycogen storage after different amounts of carbohydrate ingestion. *Journal of Applied Physiology*, 65, 2018-2023.

Ivy, J.L. (1988). Muscle glycogen synthesis after exercise: Effect of time on carbohydrate ingestion. *Journal of Applied Physiology*, 64, 1480-1485.

Mathews, D., & Fox, E. (1976). The physiological bases of physical education and athletics. Philadelphia: W.B. Saunders.

Williams, M.H. (1983). *Ergogenic aids in sports*. Champaign, IL: Human Kinetics.

SUGGESTED READINGS

American College of Sports Medicine. (1987). Position stand on the use of anabolic-androgenic steroids in sports. *Medicine and Science in Sports and Exercise*, 19(5), 534-539.

Clark, N. (1981). *The athlete's kitchen: A nutrition guide and cookbook*. Boston: CBI Publishing.

Darden, E. (1976) *Nutrition and athletic performance*. Pasadena, CA: The Athletic Press.

Food and Nutrition Board: Recommended dietary allowances. Rev. Ed., 1980. Washington, D.C.: National Academy of Sciences.

Higdon, H. (1978). *The complete diet guide for runners and other athletes*. Mountain View, CA: World Publications.

Katch, F.I., & McArdle, W.D. (1977). *Nutrition, weight control, and exercise*. Boston: Houghton Mifflin.

National Association for Sport and Physical Education. (1984). *Nutrition for sport success*. Reston, VA: American Alliance for Health, Physical Education, Recreation and Dance.

Smith, N.J. (1976) *Food for sport*. Palo Alto, CA: Bull Publishing.

Williams, E.R., & Caliendo, M.A. (1984) *Nutrition, principle issues, and application*. New York, NY: McGraw-Hill.

Williams, M.H. (1983) *Nutrition for fitness and sport*. Dubuque, Iowa: Wm. C. Brown.

22
Prevention of Common Basketball Injuries

Rich Kimball, M.A.
Eugene W. Brown, Ph.D.
Wade Lillegard, M.D.
Cathy Lirgg, A.T.C.

QUESTIONS TO CONSIDER

- What role does equipment and apparel play in the prevention of basketball related injuries?
- How can the facilities be made safer for basketball?
- What effect can warm-ups, cool-downs, and conditioning have on preventing injuries?
- What role does teaching players safety, appropriate basketball techniques, and proper drills have in injury prevention?
- What injury prevention techniques can be implemented over the course of a season?

INTRODUCTION

Basketball involves the application of large muscular forces and physical contact at all levels of the game. In spite of rules designed to decrease body contact, collisions between walls, bleachers, the floor, and other players are inevitable. Each collision presents an opportunity for an injury to occur. All of the muscular force and physical contact cannot be eliminated from basketball. However, if you follow several steps aimed at preventing injuries, you can make basketball a safer game.

As a youth basketball coach, you are responsible for doing everything reasonable to provide participants *the opportunity to compete in an environment that is healthy and safe.*

INJURY PREVENTION TECHNIQUES

Equipment and Apparel

Although little equipment is necessary to protect against injury, a properly equipped and attired basketball player is less likely to be injured. Because most basketball injuries are those occurring to the ankles, well-fitted, rubber soled shoes (especially 3/4-top or high-top shoes) should be required to lessen the severity and number of injuries. Shoes should be chosen from those designated as "basketball shoes" because shoes for running or tennis are not built to withstand the unique stresses to the feet and ankles encountered during a basketball game. Garments should be loose enough to allow freedom of movement. If a player must wear glasses, safety lenses or glass guards should also be required. In addition, a properly fitting mouth guard is recommended.

Parents should be informed during a preseason parents' orientation meeting about appropriate equipment and apparel for their children. They should be made aware that: (a) if eyeglasses are essential for their child to play, they should be safety glasses worn with a safety strap; (b) their child's shoes should fit properly and have the appropriate non-skid sole; (c) jewelry is not appropriate at practices or games; and (d) gum chewing is prohibited.

At the start of the first practice, you should reinforce what you told the parents about appropriate equipment and apparel and determine if:

- all players are properly attired
- optional equipment (e.g., eyeglasses, mouth guards) fits properly

This type of inspection should be carried out regularly.

Facilities

Inspection of a practice or game facility for safety hazards is the responsibility of the adults in charge. For practices, the coach is responsible for the safety of all facilities. For games, both the officials and coaches are responsible. Therefore, you or your assistant must inspect the facilities before permitting your players to participate in practices and games. Whoever is responsible for inspecting the facilities should arrive approximately 10 minutes before the players to carry out the inspection.

If a safety hazard is present, it must be avoided by either relocating, rescheduling, restricting the activity, or removing the hazard.

There are three categories of safety hazards associated with facilities. These are floor conditions, structural hazards, and environmental

hazards. Safety hazards that are not easily rectified must be reported to the league and/or program administrators. If corrections are not made quickly, you should resubmit your concerns in writing. Do not play in facilities that you consider hazardous to your athletes!

- **Floor Conditions**

Some gymnasia and outdoor courts are improper for basketball. Outdoor courts may have cracks in the concrete, rocks, and holes, which are dangers as well as detracting from the skill of playing the game. Other courts that have playable conditions can quickly change from one that is safe to one that is dangerous. These changing conditions are usually associated with an excessive buildup of water and mud from rain, loose boards or tiles, baskets that are too close to walls, bleachers that are too near the court, or floors that are too slippery for good traction.

- **Structural Hazards**

The basketball court should be free of obstacles near boundary lines (e.g., bleachers, water fountains, volleyball standards) and free of extraneous objects or debris on the court that might threaten the safety of the participants. In cases where boundary lines are very close to the walls, the walls should be well-padded. The playing area itself should be a smooth, nonslippery surface. If the backboard is portable, the support should be padded. The bottom of the backboard should also be padded, especially for older athletes. In addition, nets should be securely fastened.

- **Environmental Hazards**

When playing on outdoor courts lightning is an environmental condition that can be extremely hazardous. No matter how important a practice or game may seem to be, it is not worth the risk of an injury or a fatality due to environmental hazards. Other extreme weather conditions, such as high winds, hail, high temperatures, humidity, cold, snow, and rain need to be cautiously evaluated as potential safety hazards. Insufficient light is another environmental condition that could be hazardous.

Activity should not be permitted to continue under the threat of lightning or any other environmental hazard.

Management of Practices and Games

Every physical activity that occurs during practices and games has some potential to result in an injury. Fortunately, in basketball, most practice and game activities have only a rare chance in resulting in an injury. Injuries that do occur are the result of interactions between the situation in which the activity occurs and the physical status of the player. In addition to having an influence over the equipment, apparel, and facilities in reducing the risk of injuries, you have a major influence over the physical activities of your players during practices and games. There are several steps you can take to properly manage the physical activities to reduce the rate and severity of injuries. These steps include:

• Teaching Safety to Players

Whenever appropriate, inform your players about the potential risks of injury associated with performing certain basketball activities, and methods for avoiding injury. For example, teach correct passing and catching techniques so that injuries are not sustained by hard passes that are made when players are close together, or by incorrectly placing the hands when receiving the ball.

The key to teaching safety to your players is to prudently interject safety tips in your instruction whenever appropriate.

• Warming Up

A warm-up at the beginning of your team's practices and before games provides several important benefits. If the court is not immediately available for your team's use, warm-ups (i.e., stretching exercises) can start in the locker room. Specific warm-up suggestions are included in Chapter 20 under "Warm-Up, Cool-Down," and "Stretching Activities for Basketball." When warm-ups and stretching are completed, the skill-oriented drills on your practice plan or the formal drills before the game may begin. A warm-up period:

- increases the breathing rate, heart rate, and muscle temperature to exercise levels
- reduces the risks of muscle pulls and strains
- increases the shock-absorbing capabilities of the joints
- prepares players mentally for practices and games

• Teaching Appropriate Techniques

The instructions you provide during practices on how to execute the skills of basketball have an influence on the risks of injuries to your players as well as to their opponents. Teach your players the proper ways to perform basketball techniques, and avoid any temptation to teach how to intentionally foul opponents.

First, an improper technique often results in a greater chance of injury to the performer than does the correct execution. Acceptable techniques in sports usually evolve with safety as a concern.

Second, techniques involving intentional fouls should never be taught or condoned. Coaches who promote an atmosphere in which intentional violent fouls are acceptable should be eliminated from the youth basketball program. You should promote fair and safe play in practices and games with strict enforcement of the rules. Encourage skill as the primary factor in determining the outcome of the game.

• Selecting Proper Drills

Drills that you select or design for your practices and the ways in which they are carried out have an influence on the risks of injuries for your players. Drills should be selected and designed with safety as a primary feature. Before implementing a new drill into your practice, several safety questions should be considered.

- Is the drill appropriate for the level of maturation of the players?
- Are the players sufficiently skilled to comply with the requirements of the drill?
- Are the players sufficiently conditioned to handle the stress of participation in the drill?
- Are other, less risky drills available to achieve the same practice results?
- Can the drill be modified to make it less risky and yet achieve the desired training result?

- **Conditioning**

High intensity work is part of the game of basketball. How well your players can handle fatigue determines how well they perform during the latter part of a contest. Is there, however, any relationship between fatigue and injury? The following sequence of events draws an association linking fatigue with an increased potential for injury (see Figure 22-1).

In addition to improving performance, every conditioning program should be designed to minimize fatigue and the potential for injury. Being "in shape" can postpone fatigue and its detrimental effects. By progressively intensifying your practices throughout the season, you can produce a conditioning effect that can be an important deterrent to injury (see Chapter 20.)

Coaches must also be aware that older players who engage in intense, frequent practices and games may need time off as the season wears on. It is possible to overtrain, and predispose to, rather than prevent, injuries. Injuries caused by overtraining have grown to represent an increased portion of reported sports injuries. Some telltale signs of overtraining include:

- elevated resting heart rate
- poor performance
- loss of enthusiasm
- depression
- higher incidence of injury
- longer time to recover from injury

Antidotes to overtraining include time off from practice, shorter practices, alternating intense practices with lighter workouts, or any combination of these suggestions. Overtraining is not usually a problem when players are practicing two or three times a week, unless they are also: (a) playing two or more games per week, (b) playing on more than one basketball team, or (c) playing on a different sport team during the same season.

- **Avoiding Contraindicated Exercises**

Over the past several years, researchers and physicians have identified a list of exercises that are commonly used by coaches but are potentially harmful to the body. These are called contraindicated exercises. This information has

Figure 22-1. How fatigue is linked to an increased potential for injuries.

been slow in reaching coaches and their players. Table 22-1 contains a list of these exercises and how contraindicated exercises can be modified to eliminate their undesirable characteristics. Also included in Table 22-1 are substitute basketball exercises that accomplish the same purpose in a safer manner.

- **Cooling Down**

There are few feelings more uncomfortable than finishing a vigorous workout, sitting down for a while, then trying to walk. Muscles in the body tighten during periods of inactivity following hard work.

To minimize the stiffness that usually follows a workout, and the soreness the following day, take time to adequately cool down at the end of practice. A gradual reduction of activity (the reverse of the warm-up procedure) facilitates the dissipation of waste products associated with muscular activity. Letting the body cool off gradually may not prevent injuries, but the players may experience less discomfort and be better able to function at high levels during the next workout (see Chapter 20, "Warm-up, Cool Down," and "Stretching Activities for Basketball.")

Table 22-1. Contraindicated exercises and alternatives.
This table contains an outline of information on contraindicated exercises associated with the knee and spine. Safer alternative exercises that achieve the same objectives as the sample contraindicated exercises are provided.

I. PROBLEM AREA: KNEE JOINT

A. Problem Activity—Hyperflexion (over flexion)

Contraindicated Activities	Intended Purposes of Activities	Safer Alternatives
1. Hurdler's stretch 	Stretch the hamstring (back of thigh)	Seated straight leg stretch  Standing bent knee thigh pull  Lying hamstring stretch 
2. Deep knee bend 	To develop quadriceps (front of thigh), hamstrings, gluteal (buttocks), and back muscles	Half squat or half knee bend 

I. PROBLEM AREA: KNEE JOINT (continued)

A. Problem Activity—Hyperflexion (over flexion)

Contraindicated Activities	Intended Purposes of Activities	Safer Alternatives

3. Lunge

Wall sit

4. Landing from jumps

5. Deep squat lift

6. Squat thrust

A. Problem Activity—Hyperflexion (over flexion)

Contraindicated Activities	Intended Purposes of Activities	Safer Alternatives
7. Lying quad stretch (back lying position from hurdler's stretch)	Stretch quadricep muscles	Kneeling thigh stretch

8. Double leg lying quad stretch

9. Standing one leg quad stretch

B. Problem Activity—Hyperextension (over extension)

Contraindicated Activities	Intended Purposes of Activities	Safer Alternatives
10. Standing toe touch	Stretch the hamstring muscles	Seated straight leg stretch

I. PROBLEM AREA: KNEE JOINT (continued)

B. Problem Activity—Hyperextension (over extension)

Contraindicated Activities	Intended Purposes of Activities	Safer Alternatives
11. One leg standing hamstring stretch 		Standing bent knee thigh pull  Lying hamstring stretch 

C. Problem Activity—Twisting or forcing knee joint into unnatural position

Contraindicated Activities	Intended Purposes of Activities	Safer Alternatives
12. Hurdler's stretch—see Contraindicated Activity 1.		
13. Standing one leg quad stretch 	Stretch quadricep muscles	Seated straight leg stretch 

C. Problem Activity—Twisting or forcing knee joint into unnatural position

Contraindicated Activities	Intended Purposes of Activities	Safer Alternatives

14. Hero

Standing bent knee thigh pull

Lying hamstring stretch

15. Standing straddle groin stretch

Stretch inner thigh (groin) muscles

Seated straddle groin stretch

Butterfly

Lying groin stretch

Elevated legs straddle groin stretch

II. PROBLEM AREA: SPINE

A. Problem Activity—Forceful hyperflexion of cervical (neck) region

Contraindicated Activities	Intended Purposes of Activities	Safer Alternatives
16. Yoga plough 	Stretch back and neck muscles	Standing bent knee thigh pull 
17. Shoulder stand 		Alternate yoga plough (Note that when lifting legs from the floor to assume this position, the knees should initially be bent.) 

Supine tuck

Half neck circle

II. PROBLEM AREA: SPINE (continued)

B. Problem Activity—Hyperextension of the spine

Contraindicated Activities	Intended Purposes of Activities	Safer Alternatives
18. Wrestler's bridge	Stretch neck muscles	Half neck circle

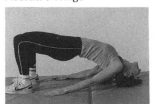

19. Full neck circle

20. Partner neck stretch

21. Donkey kick	Stretch abdominal muscles	Kneeling thigh stretch

22. Full waist circle — Reduced waist circle

II. PROBLEM AREA: SPINE (continued)

B. Problem Activity—Hyperextension of the spine

Contraindicated Activities	Intended Purposes of Activities	Safer Alternatives
23. Back bend 		
24. Back arching abdominal stretch 		
25. Donkey kick (see Contraindicated Activity 21)	Strengthen gluteal muscles	Half squat or half knee bend 

C. Problem Activity—Excessive lumbar curve or hyperextension of the low back

Contraindicated Activities	Intended Purposes of Activities	Safer Alternatives
26. Straight leg sit-ups 	Strengthen abdominal muscles	Bent knee sit-up 
27. Double leg lifts 		Reversed sit-up 

SUMMARY

This chapter has focused on three areas in which you can exert an influence to reduce the potential number and severity of injuries in basketball. The first area involves your insistence that your players wear appropriate apparel and, when necessary, protective equipment. Avoiding safety hazards associated with the facilities (court conditions, structural hazards, and environmental hazards) is the second area. Management of practices and games is the third area. Proper management includes teaching your players safety, appropriate basketball techniques, and proper drills; and conducting practices that include warming up, conditioning, and cooling down exercises but exclude known contraindicated exercises. Safety and injury prevention should be a primary factor to consider in whatever plans you make for your basketball team. You will be more than compensated for the extra time and effort required to implement the suggestions found in this chapter by the comfort of knowing that you have done as much as you can to assure that your players will have a safe season.

REFERENCES

Rutherford, G., et. al. (1981). *Overview of sports related injuries to persons 5-14 years of age.* Washington, DC: U.S.Consumer Product Safety Commission.
Seidel, B.L.et al. (1980). *Sport skills.* Dubuque, IA: W.C. Brown.

SUGGESTED READINGS

American College of Sports Medicine, American Orthopaedic Society for Sports Medicine & Sports Medicine Committee of the United States Tennis Association (1982). *Sports injuries—an aid to prevention and treatment.* Coventry, CT: Bristol-Myers Co.
DeBenedette, V. (1991). Bad breaks in basketball: Unforgettable injuries. *The Physician and Sportsmedicine, 19,* 135-139.
Jackson, D., & Pescar, S. (1981). *The young athletes health handbook.* Everest House.
Lane, S. (1990). Severe ankle sprains. *The Physician and Sportsmedicine, 18,* 43-51.
Micheli, L.J. (1985). Preventing youth sports injuries. *Journal of Health, Physical Education, Recreation and Dance, 76(6),* 52-54.
Mirkin, G., & Marshall, H. (1978). *The sportsmedicine book.* Little, Brown, & Co.
Ross Laboratories. (1987). *Nutrition and hydration in basketball: how they affect your performance.* Columbus, OH: Ross Laboratories.
Thomas, R., & Cantwell, J. (1990). Sudden death in basketball games. *The Physician and Sportsmedicine, 18,* 75-78.
Weil, L. et al. (1979). A biomechanical study of lateral ankle sprains in basketball. *Journal of the American Podiatry Association, 69,* 687-690.

23
Care of Common Basketball Injuries

Eugene W. Brown, Ph.D.
Rich Kimball, M.A.
Wade Lillegard, M.D.

QUESTIONS TO CONSIDER

- What are the steps to take in an emergency medical situation?
- What items belong in a well-stocked first aid kit?
- What procedures should you follow when a minor injury occurs?
- What information should you have about your players in case they become injured?

INTRODUCTION

Chris has the ball and is driving in for a lay-up. An opponent rushes in and attempts to block the shot. Both players are going full speed and a violent collision occurs. Chris lies motionless on the court. The referee, sensing the likelihood of an injury, immediately signals Chris's coach onto the court to tend to the injured player.

Watching from the bench, the first, and normal, reaction of a coach is to be frightened by the possible outcome of this violent collision. The sinking feeling in the stomach and the "Oh, no!" message sent out by the brain when Chris went down have been felt by most coaches at some point in their careers.

If this, or some similar situation confronted you, what would you do? Are you prepared to act appropriately? As a coach of a youth basketball team, it is your obligation to be able to deal with such an emergency. Before your first practice, you should:

- obtain medical information on your players

- establish emergency procedures
- prepare to provide first aid

You must not rely on the likelihood that a serious injury will not occur to the players on your team as an excuse for not being prepared to handle an emergency situation!

ESSENTIAL MEDICAL FORMS

Prior to the first practice, completed Athlete's Medical Information forms (see Supplement 23-1) and Medical Release forms (see Supplement 23-2) for all athletes must be in the possession of the coach. The Athlete's Medical Information form provides essential information about whom to contact during the emergency as well as a comprehensive overview of past and current medical conditions that may have implications for coaching and/or emergency care. The Medical Release form is a mechanism by which parents and guardians can give permission to the coach and/or someone else to seek medical attention for their child. If the parents or guardians of an injured athlete cannot be contacted, this signed and notarized form is an essential element in the process of providing emergency medical attention.

Note that for most athletes their responses will be negative to a high proportion of the questions on their medical information forms. Therefore, an Athlete's Medical Information Summary form (see Supplement 23-3) that parallels the Athlete's Medical Information form has been developed for transcribing any essential information. This summary, as well as the Medical Release, can be printed on the front and back sides of a 5 x 8-in. card. One completed card for each athlete must be present at all team events.

Another essential medical form is the On-Site Injury Report form (see Supplement 23-4). This information may be helpful to provide some guidance for medical care and may be very important if any legal problems develop in connection with the injury.

The final form that the coach must have is the Emergency Plan form (see Supplement 23-5). This form provides guidance for handling an emergency and is discussed in the next section.

EMERGENCY PLAN FORM

The Emergency Plan form provides directions to a number of people in helping them to carry out their assigned responsibilities in an emergency. One completed form is needed for each of these individuals. The form also contains space for inserting site-specific emergency information. The following paragraphs describe the procedures associated with the Emergency Plan form.

Before the first practice, a number of responsible individuals must be assigned roles to carry out in an emergency. These roles are: coach, attending to an injured athlete, attending to the uninjured athletes, calling for emergency medical assistance, and flagging down the emergency vehicle. Note that when a medical emergency occurs, all assignments must be simultaneously activated.

For most agency sponsored and for many school sponsored sports, a physician or athletic trainer are not present to assist the coach in handling the medical aspects of an emergency.

Thus, after taking charge of the situation and alerting individuals with assigned tasks, the coach is likely to be the person to attend to the injured athlete. The steps in attending to the injured athlete are presented in Supplement 23-5 under section B. In order to provide emergency care, knowledge and skill in cardiopulmonary resuscitation (CPR), controlling bleeding, attending to heat stroke, attending to shock, and use of an allergic reaction kit are essential. This knowledge and skill should be obtained through Red Cross courses offered in most communities. When emergency medical personnel arrive, responsibility for the injured athlete should be transferred to these professionals. The 5 x 8-in. card that includes the Medical Release should be presented to the emergency medical personnel. If the parents or guardians are not available, the person designated on the Medical Release form (usually the coach) must accompany the injured athlete to the medical center.

If the coach is attending the injured athlete, the uninjured athletes should be directed to a safe area within voice and vision of the coach. The responsibilities assigned to the person in charge of the uninjured athletes is presented in Supplement 23-5 under section C. A "rainy day" practice plan could have been prepared and available for an emergency or an accepted procedure for dismissing the uninjured athletes could be used.

Under section D of Supplement 23-5 the responsibilities of the individual assigned to call for emergency medical assistance are presented. This section also includes space for entering site-specific information for the location of the nearest telephone, emergency telephone number, directions to the injured athlete, and the location of the flag person. If known, the person calling for assistance should report the nature of the injury to the receptionist. After completing the call for assistance, this individual should privately report the status of emergency medical assistance to the person attending the injured athlete.

Whether or not someone is needed to flag down and direct the emergency vehicle will depend on the site of the team's activities. The procedures for the flag person are described in Supplement 23-5 under section E. In rare situations, where there is no telephone near the site of the injury, the flag person will be responsible for securing emergency medical assistance.

After the injured player is released to emergency medical personnel, the coach should complete the On-Site Injury Report form. Also, if the injured athlete's parents or guardians are unaware of the emergency situation, information on either the Athlete's Medical Information form or its Summary should be used to contact them.

PROVIDE FIRST AID

Aids for Proper Care

If the injury is less serious and does not require assistance from trained medical personnel, you may be able to move the player from the court to the bench area and begin appropriate care. Two important aids to properly care for an injured player include a first aid kit and ice.

• First Aid Kit

A well-stocked first aid kit does not have to be large but it should contain the basic items that may be needed for appropriate care. This checklist provides a guide for including commonly used supplies. You may wish to add and subtract from the kit on the basis of your experience and/or local policies or guidelines.

_____ white athletic tape	_____ plastic bags for ice
_____ sterile gauze pads	_____ coins for pay telephone
_____ Telfa no-stick pads	_____ emergency care phone numbers
_____ elastic bandages	
_____ Band-aids, assorted sizes	_____ persons to contact in an emergency
_____ foam rubber/moleskin	_____ scissors/knife
_____ tweezers	_____ safety pins
_____ disinfectant	_____ soap

A good rule of thumb for coaches is, "If you can't treat the problems by using the supplies in a well-stocked first aid kit, then it is too big a problem for you to handle." You should be able to handle bruises, small cuts, strains, and

sprains. When fractures, dislocations, back, or neck injuries occur, call for professional medical assistance.

• Ice

Having access to ice is unique to every local setting. Thus, every coach may have to arrange for its provision in a different way. Ice, however, is very important to proper, immediate care of many minor injuries and should, therefore, be readily available.

Care of Minor Injuries

• R.I.C.E.

Unless you are also a physician, you should not attempt to care for anything except minor injuries (e.g., bruises, bumps, sprains). Many minor injuries can be cared for by using the R.I.C.E. formula.

R = Rest: Keep the player out of action.

I = Ice: Apply ice to the injured area.

C = Compression: Wrap an elastic bandage around the injured area and the ice bag to hold the bag in place. The bandage should not be so tight as to cut off blood flow to the injured area.

E = Elevation: Let gravity drain the excess fluid.

Most minor injuries can benefit from using the R.I.C.E. formula for care.

When following the R.I.C.E. formula, ice should be kept on the injured area for 15 minutes and taken off for 20 minutes. Repeat this procedure three to four times. Icing should continue three times per day for the first 72 hours following the injury. After three days, extended care is necessary if the injury has not healed. At this time, options for care include:

- stretching and strengthening exercises
- contrast treatments
- visiting a doctor for further diagnosis

• Contrast Treatments

If the injured area is much less swollen after 72 hours, but the pain is subsiding, contrast treatments will help. Use the following procedure:

1. Place the injured area in an ice bath or cover with an ice bag for one minute.
2. After using the ice, place the injured area in warm water (100° - 110°) for three minutes.
3. Continue this rotation for five to seven bouts of ice and four to six bouts of heat.
4. Always end with the ice treatment.

Contrast treatments should be followed for the next three to five days. If swelling or pain still persists after several days of contrast treatments, the player should be sent to a physician for further tests. Chapter 24 deals with the rehabilitation of injuries. Read it carefully, because proper care is actually a form of rehabilitation.

COMMON MEDICAL PROBLEMS IN BASKETBALL

Information about 24 common medical conditions that may occur in basketball is presented in this section. The information about each condition includes: (1) a definition, (2) common symptoms, (3) immediate on-court treatment, and (4) guidelines for returning the player to action.

Abrasion

Definition:
- superficial skin wound caused by scraping

Symptoms:
- minor bleeding
- redness
- burning sensation

Care:
- Cleanse the area with soap and water.
- Control the bleeding.
- Cover the area with sterile dressing.
- Monitor over several days for signs of infection.

Return to Action:
- after providing immediate care

Back or Neck Injury

Definition:
- any injury to the back or neck area that causes the player to become immobile or unconscious

Symptoms:
- pain and tenderness over the spine
- numbness
- weakness or heaviness in limbs
- tingling feeling in extremities

Care:
- Make sure the player is breathing.
- Call for medical assistance.
- Do not move the neck or back.

Return to Action:
- with permission of a physician

Blisters

Definition:
- localized collection of fluid in the outer portion of the skin

Symptoms:
- redness
- inflammation
- oozing of fluid
- discomfort

Care:
- Put disinfectant on the area.
- Cut a hole in a stack of several gauze pads to be used as a doughnut surrounding the blister.
- Cover the area with a Band-aid.
- Alter the cause of the problem when possible (e.g., proper size and/or shape of the basketball shoes).

Return to Action:
- immediately, unless pain is severe

Contusion

Definition:
- a bruise; an injury in which the skin is not broken

Symptoms:

- tenderness around the injury
- swelling
- localized pain

Care:

- Apply the R.I.C.E. formula for first 3 days.
- Use contrast treatments for days 4-8.
- Restrict activity.
- Provide padding when returning the player to activity.

Return to Action:

- when there is complete absence of pain and full range of motion is restored

Cramps

Definition:

- involuntary and forceful contraction of a muscle; muscle spasm

Symptoms:

- localized pain in contracting muscle

Care:

- Slowly stretch the muscle.
- Massage the muscle.

Return to Action:

- when pain is gone and full range of motion is restored

Dental Injury

Definition:

- any injury to mouth or teeth

Symptoms:

- pain
- bleeding
- loss of tooth (partial or total)

Care:

- Clear the airway where necessary.
- Stop the bleeding with direct pressure.
- Make sure excess blood does not clog the airway.
- Save any teeth that were knocked free; store them in the player's own mouth or a moist, sterile cloth.

- Do not rub or clean tooth that has been knocked out.
- Transport player to a hospital or dentist.

Return to Action:

- when the pain is gone (usually within two to three days)
- with permission of a dentist or physician

Dislocation

Definition:

- loss of normal anatomical alignment of a joint

Symptoms:

- complaints of joint slipping in and out (subluxation)
- joint out of line
- pain at the joint

Care:

- mild
  —Treat as a sprain (i.e., R.I.C.E.).
  —Obtain medical care.
- severe
  —Immobilize before moving.
  —Must be treated by a physician.
  —Obtain medical care. Do not attempt to put joint back into place.
  —R.I.C.E.

Return to Action:

- with permission of a physician

Eye Injury—Contusion

Definition:

- direct blow to the eye and region surrounding the eye by a blunt object

Symptoms:

- pain
- redness of eye
- watery eye

Care:

- Have the player lie down with his/her eyes closed.
- Place a folded cloth, soaked in cold water, gently on the eye.

- Seek medical attention if injury is assessed as severe.

Return to Action:

- for minor injury, player may return to action after symptoms clear
- for severe injury, with permission of a physician

Eye Injury—Foreign Object

Definition:

- object between eyelid and eyeball

Symptoms:

- pain
- redness of eye
- watery eye
- inability to keep eye open

Care:

- Do not rub the eye.
- Allow tears to form in eye.
- Carefully try to remove loose object with sterile cotton swab.
- If object is embedded in the eye, have the player close both eyes, loosely cover both eyes with sterile dressing, and bring the player to an emergency room or ophthalmologist.

Return to Action:

- with permission from a physician

Fainting

Definition:

- dizziness and loss of consciousness that may be caused by an injury, exhaustion, heat illness, emotional stress, or lack of oxygen

Symptoms:

- dizziness
- cold, clammy skin
- pale
- seeing "spots" before one's eyes
- weak, rapid pulse

Care:

- Have the player lie down and elevate his/her feet or have the player sit with his/her head between the knees.

Return to Action:

- with permission of a physician

Fracture

Definition:

- a crack or complete break in a bone [A simple fracture is a broken bone, but with unbroken skin. An open fracture is a broken bone that also breaks the skin.]

Symptoms:

- pain at fracture site
- tenderness, swelling
- deformity or unnatural position
- loss of function in injured area
- open wound, bleeding (open fracture)

[Note that a simple fracture may not be evident immediately. If localized pain persists, obtain medical assistance.]

Care:

- Stabilize injured bone by using splints, slings, or bandages.
- Do not attempt to straighten an injured part when immobilizing it.
- If skin is broken (open fracture), keep the open wound clean by covering it with the cleanest available cloth.
- Check for shock and treat if necessary.

Return to Action:

- with permission of a physician

Head Injury—Conscious

Definition:

- any injury that causes the player to be unable to respond in a coherent fashion to known facts (name, date, etc.)

Symptoms:

- dizziness
- pupils unequal in size and/or non-responsive to light and dark
- disoriented
- unsure of name, date, or activity
- unsteady movement of eyeballs when trying to follow a finger moving in front of eyes
- same symptoms as noted for back or neck injury may be present

Care:

- If above symptoms are present, player may be moved carefully when dizziness disappears. Players with head injuries should be removed from further practice or competition that day and should be carefully observed for a minimum of 24 hours.
- Obtain medical assistance.

Return to Action:

- with permission of a physician

Head Injury—Unconscious

Definition:

- any injury in which the player is unable to respond to external stimuli by verbal or visual means

Symptoms:

- player is unconscious
- cuts or bruises around the head may be evident

Care:

- ANY TIME A PLAYER IS UNCONSCIOUS, ASSUME AN INJURY TO THE SPINAL CORD OR BRAIN.
- If necessary, clear the airway keeping the player's neck straight.
- Do not move the player.
- Call for medical assistance.

Return to Action:

- with permission of a physician

Heat Exhaustion

Definition:

- heat disorder that may lead to heat stroke

Symptoms:

- fatigue
- profuse sweating
- chills
- throbbing pressure in the head
- nausea
- normal body temperature
- pale and clammy skin
- muscle cramps

Care:

- Remove the player from heat and sun.
- Provide plenty of water.
- Rest the player in a supine position with feet elevated about 12 inches.
- Loosen or remove the player's clothing.
- Fan athlete.
- Drape wet towels over athlete.

Return to Action:

- next day if symptoms are no longer present

Heat Stroke

Definition:

- heat disorder that is life-threatening

Symptoms:

- extremely high body temperature
- hot, red, and dry skin
- rapid and strong pulse
- confusion
- fainting
- convulsions

Care:

- Immediately call for medical assistance.
- Immediately cool body by cold sponging, immersion in cool water, and cold packs.

Return to Action:

- with permission of a physician

Lacerations

Definition:

- a tearing or cutting of the skin

Symptoms:

- bleeding
- swelling

Care:

- Elevate area.
- Direct pressure with gauze (if available) to the wound for four or five minutes usually will stop bleeding.
- Continue to add gauze if blood soaks through.
- Clean the wound with disinfectant.
- Use the R.I.C.E. formula.
- If stitches are required, send to a doctor within six hours.

Return to Action:

- as soon as pain is gone, if the wound can be protected from further injury
- with permission of a physician, if stitches are required

Loss of Wind

Definition:

- a forceful blow to mid-abdomen area that causes inability to breathe

Symptoms:

- rapid, shallow breathing
- gasping for breath

Care:

- Check player to determine if other injuries exist.
- Place player in a supine position.
- Calm the player in order to foster slower breathing.

Return to Action:

- after five minutes of rest to regain composure and breathing has returned to normal rate

Nose Bleed

Definition:

- bleeding from the nose

Symptoms:

- bleeding
- swelling
- pain
- deformity of nose

Care:

- Calm the athlete.
- Get the athlete into a sitting position.
- Pinch the nostrils together with fingers while the athlete breathes through the mouth.
- If bleeding cannot be controlled, call for medical assistance.

Return to Action:

- minor nosebleed—if no deformity and no impairment to breathing, pack nose with gauze before athlete continues competition—when bleeding has stopped for several minutes
- serious nosebleed—no more competition that day; doctor's permission if a fracture has occurred

Plantar Fasciitis

Definition:

- inflammation of the connective tissue (fascia) that runs from the heel to the toes

Symptoms:

- arch and heel pain
- sharp pain ("stone bruise") near heel
- gradual onset of pain, that may be tolerated for weeks
- morning pain may be more severe
- pain may decrease throughout day

Care:

- Rest the foot.
- Stretch the Achilles tendon before exercise.
- Use shoes with firm heel counter, good heel cushion, and arch support.
- Use of a heel lift may reduce shock to the foot and decrease the pain.
- Use adhesive strapping to support the arch.

Return to Action:

- when pain is gone

Puncture Wound

Definition:

- any hole made by the piercing of a pointed instrument

Symptoms:

- breakage of the skin
- minor bleeding, possibly none
- tender around wound

Care:

- Cleanse the area with soap and water.
- Control the bleeding.
- Cover the area with sterile dressing.
- Consult physician about the need for a tetanus shot.
- Monitor over several days for signs of infection.

Return to Action:

- with permission of a physician

Shin Splints

Definition:

- pain in the anterior-lateral (front-side) region of the shin associated with running activities that may be caused by a tearing of the muscle (tibialis anterior) away from the tibia (shin), overuse of the muscle, fallen arches or excessive and repeated pronation (turning inward) of the ankle

Symptoms:

- generalized pain in the anterior-lateral region of the shin
- usually night and morning pain
- pain may subside with activity

Care:

- R.I.C.E.
- Have athlete engage in ankle flexibility exercises if pain free.
- If severe pain, see physician.

Return to Action:

- when athlete no longer experiences pain
- when running no longer produces post activity pain

[Note that mild pain may be tolerated. However, if post activity pain is pronounced, the athlete should continue the R.I.C.E. process and refrain from running types of activity.]

Shock

Definition:

- adverse reaction of the body to physical or psychological trauma

Symptoms:

- pale
- cold, clammy skin
- dizziness
- nausea
- faint feeling

Care:

- Have the athlete lie down.
- Calm the athlete.
- Elevate the feet, unless it is a head injury.
- Send for emergency help.
- Control the player's temperature.

- Loosen tight-fitting clothing.
- Control the pain or bleeding if necessary.

Return to Action:

- with permission of a physician

Sprain

Definition:

- a stretching or a partial or complete tear of the ligaments surrounding a joint

Symptoms:

- pain at the joint
- pain aggravated by motion at the joint
- tenderness and swelling
- looseness at the joint

Care:

- Immobilize at time of injury if pain is severe.
- Use the R.I.C.E. formula.
- Send the player to a physician.

Return to Action:

- when pain and swelling are gone
- when full range of motion is reestablished
- when strength and stability are within 95 percent of the non-injured limb throughout range of motion
- when light formal activity is possible with no favoring of the injury
- when formal activity can be resumed with moderate to full intensity with no favoring of the injury

Strain

Definition:

- stretching or tearing of the muscle or tendons that attach the muscle to the bone (commonly referred to as a "muscle pull")

Symptoms:

- localized pain brought on by stretching or contracting the muscle in question
- unequal strength between limbs

Care:

- Use the R.I.C.E. formula.
- Use contrast treatments for days 4-8.

Return to Action:

- when the player can stretch the injured segment as far as the non-injured segment
- when strength is equal to opposite segment
- when the athlete can perform basic basketball tasks without favoring the injury

[*Note that, depending on the severity of the strain, it may take from one day to more than two weeks for an athlete to return to action.*]

MAINTAINING APPROPRIATE RECORDS

The immediate care you provide to an injured player is important to limit the extent of the injury and to set the stage for appropriate rehabilitation. However, immediate care is not the end of prudent action when an injury occurs. Two additional brief but valuable tasks should be completed. The first of these is to fill out an On-Site Injury Report form (see Supplement 23-6) and the second is to log the injury on the Summary of Season Injuries form (see Supplement 23-7).

On-Site Injury Report Form

It is important for you to maintain a record of the injuries that occur to your players. This information may be helpful to guide delayed care or medical treatment and may be very important if any legal problems develop in connection with the injury. Supplement 23-6 includes a standard form that will help guide the recording of pertinent information relative to each injury. These records should be kept for several years following an injury. You should check on legal requirements in your state to determine how long these records should be kept.

Summary of Season Injuries Form

Supplement 23-7 lists each of the common medical conditions that occur in basketball and also provides a space for you to record when each type of injury occurred. At the end of the season, you should total the incidences of each injury type to see if there is any trend to the kind of injuries your team has suffered. If a trend exists, evaluate your training methods in all areas of practices and games. Try to alter drills or circumstances that may be causing injuries. Review Chapter 22 for techniques that may help you prevent injuries. Perhaps your practice routine ignores or overemphasizes some area of stretching or conditioning. Decide on a course of action that may be implemented for next season, and write your thoughts in the space provided or note the appropriate changes you wish to make on your season or practice plans.

SUMMARY

This chapter attempts to acquaint you with various injuries associated with basketball and how you should be prepared to deal with these injuries. If you have prepared your first aid kit, brought along the medical records, and familiarized yourself with the different types of injuries, you should be able to handle whatever situation arises. Follow the steps that are outlined for you, and remember—you are not a doctor. If you are in doubt about how to proceed, use the coins in your first aid kit and call for professional medical help. Do not make decisions about treatments if you are not qualified to make them.

Remember, react quickly and with confidence. Most injuries will be minor and the injured players will need only a little reassurance before they can be moved to the bench area. Injuries cannot be completely avoided in basketball. Therefore, you must prepare yourself to deal with whatever happens in a calm, responsible manner.

REFERENCES

American Red Cross. (1981). *Cardiopulmonary resuscitation.* Washington, D.C.: American Red Cross.

Tanner, S.M., & Harvey, J.S. (1988). How we manage plantar fasciitis. *The Physician and Sportsmedicine, 16*(8), 39-40, 42, 44, 47.

Whitesel, J., & Newell, S.G. (1980). Modified low-dye strapping. *The Physician and Sportsmedicine, 8*(9), 129-131.

SUGGESTED READINGS

American College of Sports Medicine, American Orthopaedic Society for Sports Medicine & Sports Medicine Committee of the United States Tennis Association. (1982). *Sports injuries—An aid to prevention and treatment.* Coventry, CT: Bristol-Myers Co.

Hackworth, C. et al. (1982). *Prevention, recognition, and care of common sports injuries.* Kalamazoo, MI: SWM Systems, Inc.

Jackson, D., & Pescar, S. (1981). *The young athlete's health handbook.* New York, NY: Everest House.

Rosenberg, S.N. (1985). *The Johnson & Johnson first aid book.* New York: Warner Books, Inc.

Athlete's Medical Information

(to be completed by parents/guardians and athlete)

Athlete's Name: _____ Athlete's Birthdate: _____

Parents' Names: _____ Date: _____

Address: _____

Phone No's.: (____)_____   (____)_____   (____)_____
     (Home)   (Work)   (Other)

Who to contact in case of emergency (if parents cannot be immediately contacted):

Name: _____ Relationship: _____

Home Phone No.: (____)_____ Work Phone No.: (____)_____

Name: _____ Relationship: _____

Home Phone No.: (____)_____ Work Phone No.: (____)_____

Hospital preference: _____ Emergency Phone No.: (____)_____

Doctor preference: _____ Office Phone No.: (____)_____

MEDICAL HISTORY

Part I. Complete the following:

	Date	Doctor	Doctor's Phone No.
1. Last tetanus shot?	_____		
2. Last dental examination?	_____	_____	_____
3. Last eye examination?	_____	_____	_____

Part II. Has your child or did your child have any of the following?

General Conditions:	Circle one		Circle one or both		Injuries:	Circle one		Circle one or both	
1. Fainting spells/dizziness	Yes	No	Past	Present	1. Toes	Yes	No	Past	Present
2. Headaches	Yes	No	Past	Present	2. Feet	Yes	No	Past	Present
3. Convulsions/epilepsy	Yes	No	Past	Present	3. Ankles	Yes	No	Past	Present
4. Asthma	Yes	No	Past	Present	4. Lower legs	Yes	No	Past	Present
5. High blood pressure	Yes	No	Past	Present	5. Knees	Yes	No	Past	Present
6. Kidney problems	Yes	No	Past	Present	6. Thighs	Yes	No	Past	Present
7. Intestinal disorder	Yes	No	Past	Present	7. Hips	Yes	No	Past	Present
8. Hernia	Yes	No	Past	Present	8. Lower back	Yes	No	Past	Present
9. Diabetes	Yes	No	Past	Present	9. Upper back	Yes	No	Past	Present
10. Heart disease/disorder	Yes	No	Past	Present	10. Ribs	Yes	No	Past	Present
11. Dental plate	Yes	No	Past	Present	11. Abdomen	Yes	No	Past	Present
12. Poor vision	Yes	No	Past	Present	12. Chest	Yes	No	Past	Present
13. Poor hearing	Yes	No	Past	Present	13. Neck	Yes	No	Past	Present
14. Skin disorder	Yes	No	Past	Present	14. Fingers	Yes	No	Past	Present
15. Allergies	Yes	No			15. Hands	Yes	No	Past	Present
Specify:_____			Past	Present	16. Wrists	Yes	No	Past	Present
_____			Past	Present	17. Forearms	Yes	No	Past	Present
16. Joint dislocation or					18. Elbows	Yes	No	Past	Present
separations	Yes	No			19. Upper arms	Yes	No	Past	Present
Specify:_____			Past	Present	20. Shoulders	Yes	No	Past	Present
_____			Past	Present	21. Head	Yes	No	Past	Present
17. Serious or significant ill-nesses not included above	Yes	No			22. Serious or significant in-juries not included above	Yes	No		
Specify:_____			Past	Present	Specify: _____			Past	Present
_____			Past	Present	_____			Past	Present
18. Others:_____			Past	Present	23. Others: _____			Past	Present
_____			Past	Present	_____			Past	Present

Part III. Circle appropriate response to each question. For each "Yes" response, provide additional information.

	Circle one	Additional information

1. Is you child currently taking any medication? If yes, describe medication, amount, and reason for taking.   Yes   No   _____

2. Does your child have any allergic reactions to medication, bee stings, food, etc.? If yes, describe agents that cause adverse reactions and describe these reactions.   Yes   No   _____

3. Does your child wear any appliances (e.g., glasses, contact lenses, hearing aid, false teeth, braces, etc.)? If yes, describe appliances.   Yes   No   _____

4. Has your child had any surgical operations? If yes, indicate site, explain the reason for the surgery, and describe the level of success.   Yes   No   _____

5. Has a physician placed any restrictions on your child's present activities? If yes, describe restrictions.   Yes   No   _____

6. Does your child have any existing and/or past medical or emotional conditions that require special concern and attention by a sports coach? If yes, explain.   Yes   No   _____

7. Does your child have any deformities (e.g., abnormal curvature of the spine, heart problems, one kidney, blindness in one eye, one testicle, etc.)? If yes, describe.   Yes   No   _____

8. Is there a history of serious family illnesses (e.g., diabetes, bleeding disorders, heart attack before age 50, etc.)? If yes, describe illnesses.   Yes   No   _____

9. Has your child lost consciousness or sustained a concussion?   Yes   No   _____

10. Has your child experienced fainting spells or dizziness while exercising?   Yes   No   _____

Part IV. Has your child or did your child have any of the following personal habits?

Personal Habit	Circle one		Circle one or both		Indicate extent or amount
1. Smoking	Yes	No	Past	Present	_____
2. Smokeless tobacco	Yes	No	Past	Present	_____
3. Alcohol	Yes	No	Past	Present	_____
4. Recreational drugs (e.g., marijuana, cocain, etc.)	Yes	No	Past	Present	_____
5. Steroids	Yes	No	Past	Present	_____
6. Others					
Specify: _____	Yes	No	Past	Present	_____
_____	Yes	No	Past	Present	_____
_____	Yes	No	Past	Present	_____

Part V. Please explain, below, any "Yes" responses in Parts II, III, and IV or any other concerns that have present implications for my coaching your child. Also, describe special first aid requirements, if appropriate. An additional sheet may be attached if necessary.

_____

_____

_____

_____

_____

_____

Medical Release Form

I hereby give permission for any and all medical attention necessary to be administered to my child in the event of an accident, injury, sickness, etc., under the direction of the people listed below until such time as I may be contacted. My child's name is _____.
This release is effective for the time during which my child is participating in the _____
_____ basketball program and any tournaments for the 19___/19___
season, including traveling to or from such tournaments. I also hereby assume the responsibility
for payment of any such treatment.

PARENTS' OR GUARDIANS' NAMES: _____

HOME ADDRESS: _____

	Street	City	State	Zip

HOME PHONE: (____)_____ (____)_____(W)

(____)_____(W)

INSURANCE COMPANY: _____

POLICY NUMBER: _____

FAMILY PHYSICIAN: _____

PHYSICIAN'S ADDRESS: _____ PHONE NO. (____)_____

In case I cannot be reached, either of the following people is designated:

COACH'S NAME: _____ PHONE NO. (____)_____

ASS'T. COACH OR OTHER: _____ PHONE NO. (____)_____

SIGNATURE OF PARENT OR GUARDIAN _____

SUBSCRIBED AND SWORN BEFORE ME THIS _____ OF _____, 19 ____

SIGNATURE OF NOTARY PUBLIC _____

Athlete's Medical Information Summary

(important medical information to be transcribed by the coach or designee
from the Athlete's Medical Information form)

Athlete's Name: _____ Athlete's Birthdate: _____

Parents' Names: _____ Date: _____

Address: _____

Phone No's.: (____)_____ (____)_____ (____)_____

          (Home)   (Work)   (Other)

Who to contact in case of emergency (if parents cannot be immediately contacted):

Name: _____ Relationship: _____

Home Phone No.: (____)_____ Work Phone No.: (____)_____

Name: _____ Relationship: _____

Home Phone No.: (____)_____ Work Phone No.: (____)_____

Hospital preference: _____ Emergency Phone No.: (____)_____

Doctor preference: _____ Office Phone No.: (____)_____

MEDICAL HISTORY

Part I. Transcribe Part I.

	Date	Doctor	Doctor's phone no.
1. Last tetanus shot?	_____		
2. Last dental examination?	_____	_____	_____
3. Last eye examination?	_____	_____	_____

Part II. This athlete has or has had the following:

A. __General Conditions:__	Circle one or both	B. __Injuries:__	Circle one or both
_____	Past Present	_____	Past Present
_____	Past Present	_____	Past Present
_____	Past Present	_____	Past Present
_____	Past Present	_____	Past Present
_____	Past Present	_____	Past Present
_____	Past Present	_____	Past Present

Part III. Summary of Part III responses that have present implications: _____

_____

_____

_____

_____

Part IV. This athlete has or has had the following personal habits:

__Personal Habit__	Circle one or both	Indicate extent or amount
_____	Past Present	_____
_____	Past Present	_____
_____	Past Present	_____

Part V. Responses in Parts II, III, and IV or any other concerns that have present implications for my coaching. Also describe special first aid requirements, if appropriate. _____

_____

_____

_____

_____

_____

_____

_____

On-Site Injury Report Form

Name _____ Date of injury ____/____/____
        (Injured Player)   mo   day   yr

Address _____
       (Street)   (City, State)   (Zip)

Telephone _____
        (Home)   (Other)

Nature and extent of injury: _____

_____

How did the injury occur? _____

_____

Describe first aid given, including name(s) of attendee(s): _____

_____

Disposition: to hospital   to home   to physician

Other _____

_____

Was protective equipment worn?   _____ Yes   _____ No

Explanation: _____

_____

Condition of the playing surface _____

_____

Names and addresses of witnesses:

Name	Street	City	State	Tel.
Name	Street	City	State	Tel.
Name	Street	City	State	Tel.

Other comments: _____

_____

Signed	Date	Title-Position

Supplement 23-5.

Emergency Plan Form*

Essential Items:

1. Well-stocked first aid kit
2. Medical forms for each athlete (Athlete's Medical Information, Athlete's Medical Information Summary, and Medical Release)
3. On-Site Injury Report form

PROCEDURES

A. COACH

1. Take charge of situation
2. Alert previously assigned people to their tasks

B. ___ / ___

(Name and alternate person in charge of injured athlete; likely the coach or assistant coach.)

1. Calm and assure athlete.
2. If possible, determine nature and extent of injury.
3. If possible, privately report nature and extent of injury to person calling for emergency medical assistance.
4. If athlete is unconscious or a spinal injury is suspected, do not move the athlete.
5. Provide appropriate emergency care if warranted.
   a. ABC's (open Airways, restore Breathing, and restore Circulation)
   b. Control bleeding by direct pressure.
   c. For heat stroke, immediately cool body by cold sponging, immersion in

C. ___ / ___

(Name and alternate person in charge of uninjured athletes.)

1. Direct uninjured athletes to safe area within voice and vision of coach.
2. Have a plan in place to divert the attention of uninjured athletes from the emergency situation.
3. Use accepted procedure to dismiss athletes from practice/competition.

D. ___ / ___

(Name and alternate person responsible for phoning for emergency medical assistance.)

1. Get coins from first aid kit if needed for phone call.
2. Location of nearest phone by site of activity:

   Site   Location
   _____   _____
   _____   _____
   _____   _____

3. Emergency phone number by site of activity:

   Site   Phone No.
   _____   _____
   _____   _____
   _____   _____

4. Report the nature of the injury and calmly respond to questions.

E. ___ / ___

(Name and alternate person responsible for flagging down emergency vehicle.)

1. Go to designated location to flag down emergency vehicle.

   Site   Location
   _____   _____
   _____   _____
   _____   _____

   Note that the site and location information corresponds to D.6. If no phone is within reasonable distance from the activity site, flag person should go to location where a vehicle can be flagged down.

2. Direct emergency medical personnel to injured athlete.

cold water, and cold packs.
d. For shock, have athlete lie down, calm athlete, elevate feet unless head injury, control athlete's temperature, loosen tight fitting clothing, and control pain or bleeding if necessary.
e. For allergic reaction, use ana-kit if available.
6. Transfer care to emergency medical personnel. (Note that the Medical Release Form and one individual whose name appears on the form must accompany athletes to medical center unless parents or guardians are available.)
7. Provide Athlete's Medical Information Summary to emergency medical personnel.

5. Directions to sites:
Site   Directions
_____   _____
_____   _____
_____   _____
_____   _____

6. Location of flag person by site:
Site   Location
_____   _____
_____   _____
_____   _____

7. Remain on the phone until the other person hangs up.
8. Return to person attending to injured athlete and privately report status of emergency medical assistance.

A. COACH, cont.

3. Use the information on the Roster Summary of Contacts in an Emergency to phone the injured athlete's parents (guardians) or their designees.
4. Complete the On-Site Injury Report form.

*A minimum of 4 completed copies of this form is needed; one for each of the individuals with assigned tasks. Make sure that information is included on all practice and competition sites.

On-Site Injury Report Form

Name _____ Date of injury ___/___/___
        (Injured Player)   mo   day   yr

Address _____
        (Street)   (City, State)   (Zip)

Telephone _____
        (Home)   (Other)

Nature and extent of injury: _____

_____

How did the injury occur? _____

_____

Describe first aid given, including name(s) of attendee(s): _____

_____

Disposition: to hospital   to home   to physician

Other _____

_____

Was protective equipment worn?   _____ Yes   _____ No

Explanation: _____

_____

Condition of the playing surface _____

_____

Names and addresses of witnesses:

Name	Street	City	State	Tel.
Name	Street	City	State	Tel.
Name	Street	City	State	Tel.

Other comments: _____

_____

Signed	Date	Title-Position

Supplement 23-7.

Summary of Season Injuries Form

Injury Type	First 4 Weeks	Middle Weeks	Last 4 Weeks	Total
1. Abrasion				
2. Back or Neck Injury				
3. Blisters				
4. Contusion				
5. Cramps				
6. Dental Injury				
7. Dislocation				
8. Eye Injury—Cintusion				
9. Eye Injury—Foreign Object				
10. Fainting				
11. Fracture				
12. Head Injury Conscious				
13. Head Injury Unconscious				
14. Heat Exhaustion				
15. Heat Stroke				
16. Lacerations				
17. Loss of Wind				
18. Nose Bleed				
19. Plantar Fascitis				
20. Puncture Wound				
21. Shin Splints				
22. Shock				
23. Sprain				
24. Strain				
25. Others:				

Do you see a trend?   YES   NO

Steps to take to reduce injuries next season:

(1) _____

(2) _____

(3) _____

SUMMARY OF SEASON INJURIES

(4) _____

(5) _____

(6) _____

(7) _____

(8) _____

(9) _____

(10) _____

(11) _____

(12) _____

(13) _____

(14) _____

(15) _____

(16) _____

(17) _____

(18) _____

(19) _____

(20) _____

(21) _____

(22) _____

(23) _____

(24) _____

(25) _____

(26) _____

(27) _____

(28) _____

(29) _____

(30) _____

(31) _____

(32) _____

(33) _____

(34) _____

24
Rehabilitation of Common Basketball Injuries

Rich Kimball, M.A.
Eugene W. Brown, Ph.D.
Wade Lillegard, M.D.

QUESTIONS TO CONSIDER

- What are the important components of a rehabilitation program?
- How can a coach tell when athletes are trying to "come back" too fast?
- Is it necessary to obtain permission from parents and a physician before returning an injured athlete to competition?
- Following an injury, what determines if an activity is too stressful?

INTRODUCTION

Decisions about the rehabilitation of injuries and reentry into competition must be made according to a flexible set of guidelines; not hard and fast rules. Every individual on your team and each injury is unique. Therefore, rehabilitation techniques and reentry criteria will differ for each injured player.

GENERAL PROCEDURES

Most injuries suffered by your athletes will not be treated by a physician. Therefore, you, the athlete, and the athlete's parents will determine when the athlete returns to action.

Athletes, coaches, and parents realize that missing practices will reduce the athlete's ability to help the team. Pressure is often exerted on the coach to return injured athletes to action before they are fully recovered, especially if they are the stars of the team. If an athlete has been treated by a physician for an injury, written clearance by both the physician and the parents should be obtained before permitting the athlete to return to practices and games. Also, clarification as to any limitations on participation should be obtained from the physician.

Chances of an injury recurring are greatly increased if an athlete returns too soon. The following five criteria should be met, in order, before allowing an injured athlete back into full physical activity:

1. absence of pain
2. full range of motion at the injured area
3. normal strength and size at the injured area

4. normal speed and agility
5. normal level of fitness

If a physician is not overseeing an injured athlete's rehabilitation, the task of rehabilitation will probably fall upon the coach. Stretching activities, calisthenics and possibly weight training exercises should form the basis of a rehabilitation program. Start with simple stretches. Presence of pain during movement is the key to determining if the activity is too stressful. The onset of pain means too much is being attempted too soon. When athletes can handle the stretching, then calisthenics and possibly weight training can be added to the program. The principles of training included in Chapter 20 should guide all phases of the rehabilitation program.

Absence of Pain

Most injuries are accompanied by pain, although the pain is not always evident immediately when the injury occurs. Usually, the pain disappears quickly if the injury is a bruise, a strain, or a minor sprain. For more serious injuries such as dislocations or fractures, the pain may remain for days or weeks. Once the pain is gone, the athlete can start the stretching portion of a rehabilitation program.

The main goal of a rehabilitation program is to reestablish range of motion, strength, power, and muscular endurance at the site of the injury. As long as athletes remain free of pain, they should proceed with their program. If pain recurs, they should eliminate pain-producing movements until they are pain-free again. The athletes should be in close contact with their physicians during any rehabilitations from injury.

The chance of an injury recurring is greatly increased if an athlete returns to action too soon.

Full Range of Motion

Injuries generally reduce the range of motion around a joint. The more severe the injury, the greater the reduction in range of motion, particularly when the injured area has been immobilized. As soon as they are able to move an injured area without pain, athletes should be encouraged to progressively increase the range of movement until a normal range is achievable. For example, if the athlete has strained a groin muscle, a fairly common injury early in the season, the muscle should be stretched as much as possible without causing pain. Initially, the movement may be slight if the injury was severe. With stretching, the full range of motion will eventually return. The athlete's physicians must be involved at this stage of rehabilitation. Physicians often prescribe specific exercises to safely increase range of motion. When the athlete can move the injured joint through its normal range, strengthening exercises should begin.

Normal Strength and Size

After a body part has been immobilized (by cast, splint wrap, or disuse), muscles become smaller and weaker than they were before the injury. Just because a cast is removed and the injuries have "healed" does not mean that athletes are ready to practice or play at full speed. Loss of muscle mass means a loss of strength. Letting athletes resume a normal practice schedule before their strength has returned to pre-injury levels could lead to re-injury. Strengthening the injured area should be done conservatively and under a physician's direction. If weights are used, start with light weights and perform the exercise through the entire range of motion. If the exercise causes pain, then lighter weights should be used. To determine when full strength and size has been regained, compare the injured area to the non-injured area on the opposite side of the body. When both areas are of equal size and strength, then the athletes may progress to the next phase of recovery.

Your goal is to have the athletes regain full strength through the entire range of motion before allowing them to return to competition.

Normal Speed and Agility

When a physician gives written clearance for an athlete to return to practice, incorporate progressively greater levels of intensity of activity. You should be careful to gradually challenge the previously injured body part. In your observation of injured athletes, try to detect any favoring of an injured part or inability to smoothly perform a skill at increasing intensities. When athletes can move at pre-injury speed and agility, they are almost ready to play. However, they must still establish their pre-injury level of fitness.

The main goal of a rehabilitation program is to reestablish range of motion, strength, power, and muscular endurance to the injured area.

Normal Level of Fitness

Every extended layoff reduces the level of muscular fitness. While recovering, the athlete may be able to exercise other body parts without affecting the injured area. For example, someone with a sprained ankle may not be able to run and dribble the ball, but he/she may be able to swim. Someone with a broken wrist may be able to do a variety of lower body activities such as jog, play defense, or walk through plays. Cautiously encourage this type of activity, because it helps to maintain portions of the athlete's pre-injury levels of fitness. Athletes who have missed long periods of time due to an injury should practice for several days after meeting the previous criteria before being allowed to play in a game. Their cardiovascular system and the endurance of the injured musculature need time to adjust to the demands of the game. The longer the layoff, the more conditioning work the athlete will need.

SUMMARY

When the pain is gone, and the range of motion, strength, agility, and conditioning are back to normal, your athlete is ready to reenter practice and competition. The entire process may have taken two days for a bruise to 12 or more weeks and assistance from physicians for a fracture. In either case, if you have followed the general guidelines of this chapter, you know you have acted in the best long-term interest of the athlete. Participation is important, but only if participation is achieved with a healthy body. Resist the pressure and the temptation to rush athletes into a game before they are ready. Your patience will be rewarded in the games to come.

Index